DISCOVERING OUR[...]
A HISTORY OF THE WO[...]

READING ESSENTIALS & STUDY GUIDE

Mc Graw Hill Education

networks

mheducation.com/prek-12

Send all inquiries to:
McGraw-Hill Education
8787 Orion Place
Columbus, OH 43240

ISBN: 978-0-07-676733-5
MHID: 0-07-676733-7

Printed in the United States of America.

5 6 7 8 9 QVS 23 22 21 20

Table of Contents

Medieval Europe

Renaissance and Reformation

Age of Exploration and Trade

The Scientific Revolution and the Enlightenment

Political and Industrial Revolutions

Imperialism and World War I

World War II and the Cold War

Building Today's World

To the Student

Dear Student,

We know that taking notes, using graphic organizers, and developing critical-thinking skills are vital to achieve academic success. Organizing solid study materials can be an overwhelming task. McGraw-Hill Education has developed this workbook to help you master content and develop those skills necessary for academic success.

This workbook includes all core content found in the *Discovering Our Past: A History of the World* program. The note-taking, graphic organizer, and Foldables® activities will help you learn to organize content for improved comprehension and testing.

Note-Taking System

You will notice that the pages in the *Reading Essentials and Study Guide* are arranged in two columns. The large column on the page contains running text and graphics that summarize each lesson of the chapter. The smaller column will help you use information in various ways and develop note-taking skills.

Graphic Organizers

Many graphic organizers appear in this workbook. Graphic organizers allow you to see the lesson's important information in a visual format. In addition, they help you summarize information and remember the content.

Notebook FOLDABLES®

Notebook Foldables®, invented by Dinah Zike, M.Ed., show you how to make interactive graphic organizers based upon skills. Foldables® are easy to create. Every Notebook Foldable® is placed directly within the content pages, helping you with your note-taking skills. Making a Foldable® gives you a fast way to organize and retain information. Each Notebook Foldable® is designed as a study guide for the main ideas and key points presented in lessons of the chapter.

The *Reading Essentials and Study Guide* is a thoroughly interactive workbook that will help you learn social studies content. You will master the content while learning important critical-thinking and note-taking skills that you will use throughout your life.

Notebook Foldable® Basics

Notebook Foldables® are an easy-to-use, unique way to enhance learning. Instructions are located where the Foldable® is used and every template is provided at the back of this workbook. You will cut out the appropriate Foldable® template and place it into the workbook as instructed. This quickly turns a workbook into a study guide.

Using Notebook Foldables®

You will write information such as titles, vocabulary words, concepts, questions, main ideas, summaries, definitions, and dates on the tabs of the Foldables®. This will help you easily recognize main ideas and important concepts as you read the content.

In the back of this workbook are several pages with four different Foldable®-style templates—one-tab, two-tab, three-tab, and Venn diagram. Each style has an instruction page followed by the templates. Cutting and using the different templates is very simple to master.

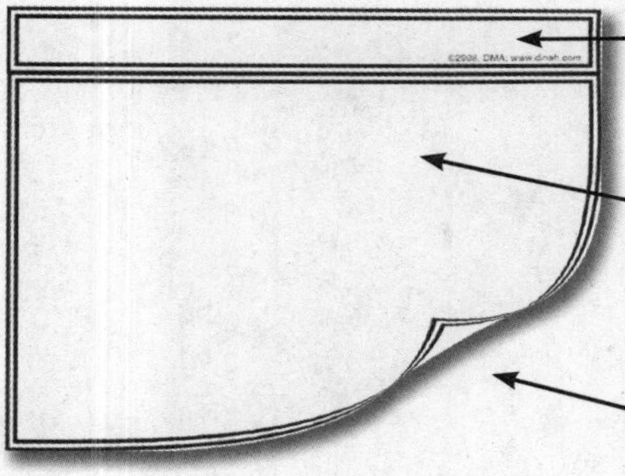

Anchor Tab—Glue the back of the Foldable® to the workbook with the anchor tab. A dotted line is provided on the workbook page to guide you to proper placement.

Information Tab—Write information on the front and reverse of the information tab. This tab may be cut again after gluing if it is a two-tab, three-tab, or Venn diagram style.

Reverse Tab

Folding Instructions

1. **Cut** out the appropriate Foldable® template.
2. **Fold** the anchor tab over the information tab.
3. **Glue** the anchor tab to the workbook page according to the instructions. *(Just a dab is needed!)*

Multiple Foldables® can be glued on top of each other by gluing anchor tabs on top of anchor tabs. This would make a small book on the page.

Supplies

The only supplies needed to utilize Notebook Foldables® are scissors and glue. All paper templates are in the back of the workbook. Consider using crayons and colored pencils, a stapler, clear tape, and anything else you think might make your Foldables® more interesting.

Who is Dinah Zike?

Dinah Zike, M.Ed., is an award-winning author, educator, and inventor recognized for designing three-dimensional, hands-on manipulatives and graphic organizers known as Foldables®. Foldables are used nationally and internationally by parents, teachers, and other professionals in the education field. Zike has developed more than 180 supplemental educational books and materials. Two of her books, *Envelope Graphic Organizers™* and *Foldables® and VKVs® for Phonics, Spelling, and Vocabulary PreK-3rd*, were each awarded *Learning* Magazine's Teachers' Choice Award for Professional Development in 2014. Two other books, *Notebook Foldables®* and *Foldables®, Notebook Foldables®, and VKVs® for Spelling and Vocabulary 4th-12th*, were each awarded *Learning* Magazine's Teachers' Choice Award in 2011. In 2004, Zike was honored with the CESI Science Advocacy Award. She received her M.Ed. from Texas A&M University in College Station, Texas.

NAME______________________________ DATE ____________ CLASS ________

networks

What Does a Historian Do?

Lesson 1 What Is History?

ESSENTIAL QUESTION

Why is history important?

GUIDING QUESTIONS

1. ***What types of things can history reveal about the past?***
2. ***What are historical periods?***
3. ***What do students of prehistory look for?***

Terms to Know

era a large division of time

archaeology the study of objects to learn about past human life

artifact an object made by people

paleontology the study of fossils

fossil plant or animal remains that have been preserved from an earlier time

anthropology the study of human culture and how it develops over time

species a class of individuals with similar physical characteristics

Where in the world?

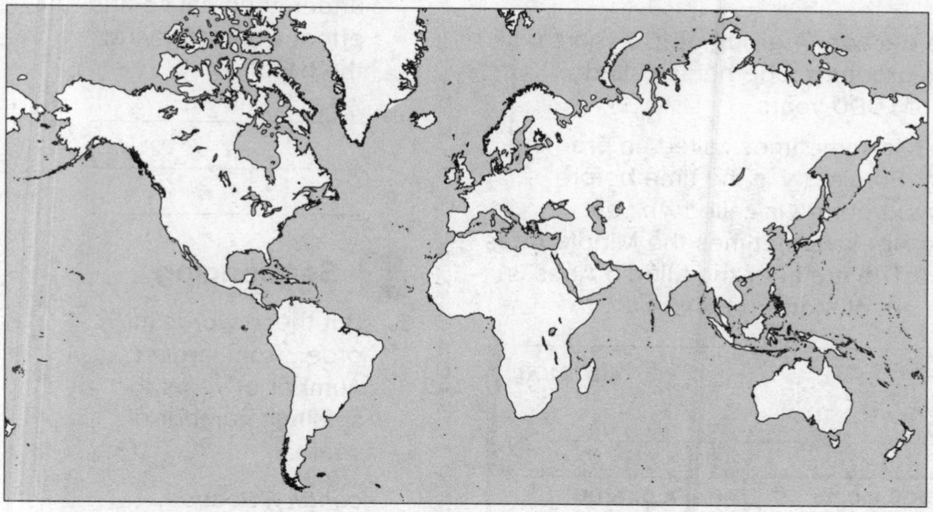

What do you know?

In the first column, answer the questions based on what you know before you study. After this lesson, complete the last column.

Now...		Later...
	Why do people want to learn about the past?	
	What is a period of 10 years called?	
	How many days are in a calendar year?	
	What is a leap year?	

Why Study History?

People who study history are called historians. Historians study causes and effects of historical events. A cause is a reason that something happened. An effect is what happened because of an event. Historians try to figure out why things happened. They use their understanding to think about how those things make a difference today.

Learning about the past helps us understand the present. It helps us decide what to do in the future. Knowing what went wrong in the past can help us make better decisions today when we face similar choices.

Measuring Time

A group of 10 years is called a decade. A group of 100 years is called a century. Ten centuries grouped together is called a millennium, which is a period of 1,000 years.

A period of several centuries is sometimes called an **era**. The earliest era is called *prehistory*. Prehistory is the time before people invented writing. The next period is called *Ancient History*. Then come the *Middle Ages*. Sometimes the Middle Ages are called the medieval period. The era after the Middle Ages is *Modern History*. We live in the era of Modern History.

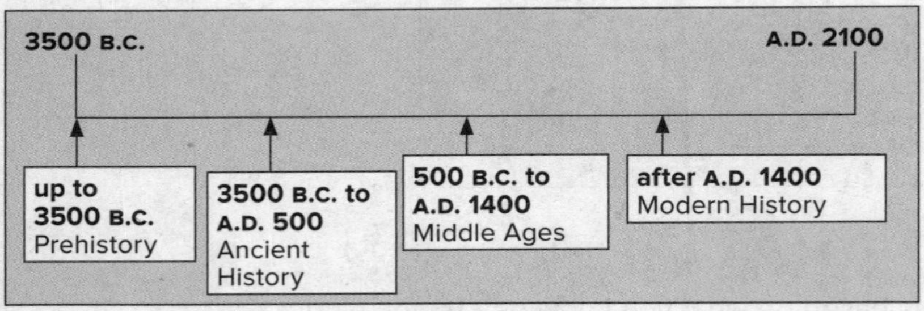

To keep track of days and months, we use a calendar. Some cultures use calendars that are different from ours. Some calendars are arranged according to nature or the position of the moon.

Our modern calendar is based on one that started in ancient Rome. Julius Caesar invented it. We call it the Julian calendar. It started counting years from the time that Rome began. It was created with 365 days each year and one extra day every fourth year, called a leap year. However, there was a problem with the Julian calendar. It lost several minutes each year. That meant there was one day lost every 128 years. It needed to be fixed.

Marking the Text

1. Underline the sentence explaining what historians look for when they study history.

Reading Check

2. Why is it important to understand cause and effect when studying the past?

____

____

____

Sequencing

3. Put these words in order, from largest number of years to smallest number of years.

century, decade, millennium

____

____

____

Marking the Text

4. On the time line, circle the earliest era that historians study. Draw a box around the era in which we live.

NAME______________________________ DATE ______________ CLASS __________

networks

What Does a Historian Do?

Lesson 1 What Is History?, *Continued*

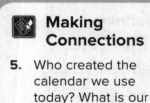

Making Connections

5. Who created the calendar we use today? What is our calendar called?

____

____

____

Defining

6. What do the letters B.C. and A.D. mean?

____

____

____

Reading Check

7. When would a historian use a calendar? When would a historian use a time line?

____

____

____

____

Pope Gregory XIII decided to create a new calendar. Pope Gregory changed the starting date of his calendar. He began counting years on his calendar from what he thought was the birth of Jesus. He also fixed the mistake from the Julian calendar. Pope Gregory included leap years in his calendar, too. We call Pope Gregory's calendar the Gregorian calendar. Although there are other calendars, most of the world uses the Gregorian calendar today.

The Gregorian calendar has a special way to mark the years. Years that happened after the birth of Jesus are marked A.D. The letters stand for the words *anno domini*. Those are the Latin words for "in the year of the Lord." The years before the birth of Jesus have different letters. They are marked as B.C., which means "before Christ."

To date events before the birth of Jesus, or B.C., historians count backwards from A.D. 1. There is no year 0. The year before A.D. 1 is 1 B.C.

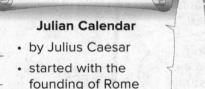

Julian Calendar

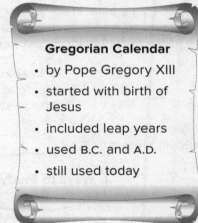

- by Julius Caesar
- started with the founding of Rome
- included leap years
- lost several minutes each year

Gregorian Calendar

- by Pope Gregory XIII
- started with birth of Jesus
- included leap years
- used B.C. and A.D.
- still used today

Sometimes historians avoid the religious reference when they write. They use a different way to explain the years. Instead of B.C., they use B.C.E., which means "before the common era." Instead of A.D., they use C.E., which means "common era." The years are still numbered the same way.

A time line shows the order of events in a period of time. Most time lines are divided into even sections of time. They have labels that tell when something happened. Sometimes a time line cannot show all the events in a long period. In this case, a time line might have a slanted or jagged line in the middle. That means that some years are left out of the time line. A multilevel time line is one that has two or more lines stacked on top of each other.

Digging Up the Past

Archaeology is the study of the past by looking at what people left behind. An archaeologist digs in the earth for artifacts. An **artifact** is an object made by people. Tools, pottery, weapons, and jewelry are artifacts. They help archaeologists learn what life was like in the past.

Paleontology studies prehistoric times. Paleontologists study fossils. **Fossils** are the remains of plant and animal life that have been preserved from an earlier time.

Anthropology is the study of human culture. Anthropologists study artifacts and fossils, too. They look for clues about what people valued and believed.

A paleontologist named Donald Johanson made an important discovery in Africa in 1974. He found the skeleton of an early human who lived more than 3.2 million years ago. He called the skeleton Lucy. Lucy belonged to a different species of early human. A **species** is a group of animals or humans. The members of a species are alike in some way. Lucy is the oldest human species that scientists have ever found. Lucy can help us learn more about how humans developed.

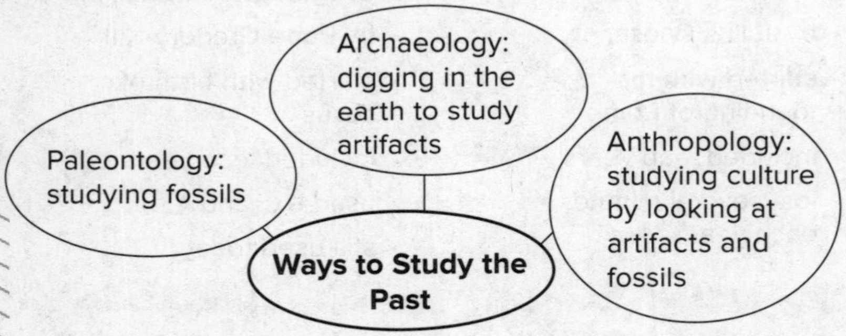
Archaeology: digging in the earth to study artifacts
Paleontology: studying fossils
Anthropology: studying culture by looking at artifacts and fossils
Ways to Study the Past

Check for Understanding

What is the difference between a time line and a calendar?

1. ____________________

____

What is the difference between an artifact and a fossil?

2. ____________________

____

Glue Foldable here

Defining

8. What is a *species*?

____

____

Reading Check

9. How are archaeologists, paleontologists, and anthropologists like detectives?

____

____

____

FOLDABLES®

10. Place a two-tab Foldable along the dotted line to cover the Check for Understanding. Label the anchor tab *Learning about the Past*. Label the two tabs *Measuring Time* and *Digging Up the Past*.

On the front and back of the tabs, write three words or phrases that you remember about each. Use your notes to help you answer the questions under the tabs.

NAME ______________________ DATE ____________ CLASS ________

networks

What Does a Historian Do?

Lesson 2 How Does a Historian Work?

ESSENTIAL QUESTION

How do we learn about the past?

GUIDING QUESTIONS

1. ***What types of evidence do historians use to understand the past?***
2. ***How do we write about history?***

Terms to Know

evidence something that shows proof or an indication that something is true

primary source firsthand evidence of an event in history

secondary source a document or written work created after an event

point of view a personal attitude about people or life

bias an unreasoned, emotional judgment about people and events

scholarly concerned with academic learning or research

conclusion a decision reached after examining evidence

Where in the world?

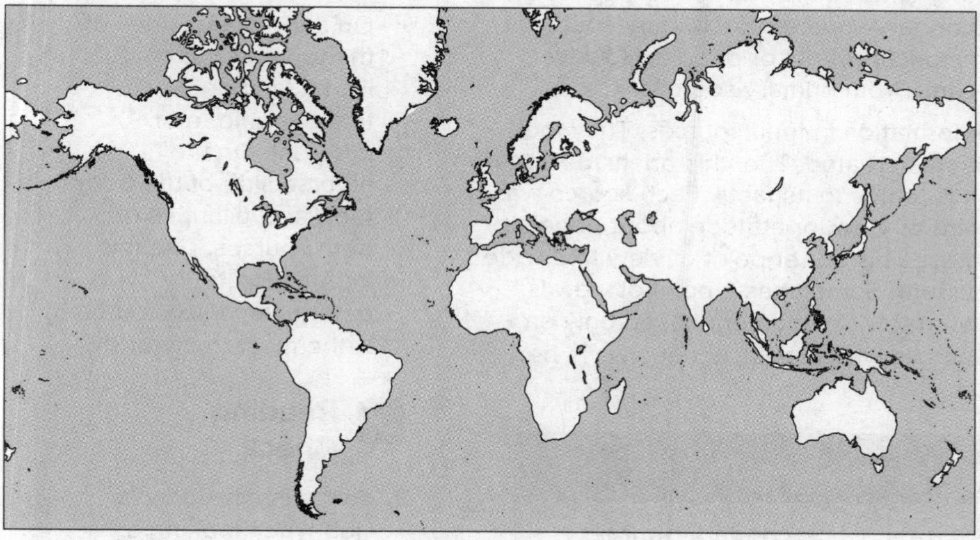

What do you know?

In the K column, list what you already know about how a historian works. In the W column, list what you want to know. After reading the lesson, fill in the L column with the information that you learned.

K	W	L

Lesson 2 How Does a Historian Work?, *Continued*

What Is the Evidence?

Historians look at **evidence** to find out about the past. Evidence is proof that something is true. Evidence might be an object, such as a soldier's uniform or a scrap of pottery. Evidence might also be a document or book that was written during a historical event.

A **primary source** is a kind of evidence. Primary sources are created by people who saw or were part of an event. Letters and diaries are primary sources. Tools and clothing are also primary sources. Historians use primary sources to learn what people were thinking at the time of the event. Primary sources can help historians explain events that happened long ago.

A **secondary source** is also evidence. Secondary sources are created after an event. They are created by people who were not part of the event. Your history textbook is a secondary source. Encyclopedias are also secondary sources. Secondary sources can give a broad view of historical events or people. However, new information can only come from primary sources.

Historians analyze the information in their sources. They look for reasons that the source was created. Then historians decide if the source is reliable when it comes to its facts. Each source was written with a particular **point of view**, or attitude about people or life. The author of a source uses his or her point of view to decide what to include in the document. Sometimes a point of view is based on feelings and not on facts. A judgment based only on feelings is called a **bias.** Sources with a bias cannot always be trusted to be factual or true.

Sources That Historians Use

Primary Sources	Secondary Sources
• Written at the time of the event • Eyewitness to history • Reliable source for historians • Includes letters, diaries, tools, clothing	• Written after an event • Author did not witness the event • Contains facts about an event • Includes textbooks and encyclopedias

Glue Foldable here

FOLDABLES®

Comparing and Contrasting

1. Place a three-tab Venn diagram Foldable along the dotted line. Label the top tab *Primary Source*, the middle tab *Both*, and the bottom tab *Secondary Source*.

On the reverse sides of the top and bottom tab, list facts about each that are unique or different. On the reverse side of the *Both* tab, list similarities of both sources. Use this information to determine which source is the most trustworthy.

Reading Check

2. What is a historian's job when looking at primary sources?

____

____

____

Lesson 2 How Does a Historian Work?, *Continued*

Paraphrasing

3. In your own words, explain how to make an inference.

____

____

____

Marking the Text

4. Underline the text that explains what a scholarly journal is.

Explaining

5. Explain why it is important for historians to read articles in scholarly journals.

____

____

____

Writing About History

Historians interpret information from primary sources to make inferences. Making an inference means choosing the most likely explanation for the facts. Sometimes the inference is simple. When you see someone with a wet umbrella, you can make the inference that it is raining. Making inferences about historical events is not so easy.

To make an inference, historians start with primary sources. They use sources they already know are trustworthy. Next, they read secondary sources. They think about the different points of view. Finally, they make an inference to explain what happened.

Many historians write articles about their inferences. Most articles are published in **scholarly** journals, or magazines. Scholarly magazines are concerned with learning. Usually, other historians read the articles to make sure the facts are correct. They decide whether they agree with the inferences in the article. Historians must be careful to make inferences based on facts. They do not want to show a bias in their writing.

How Historians Make Inferences

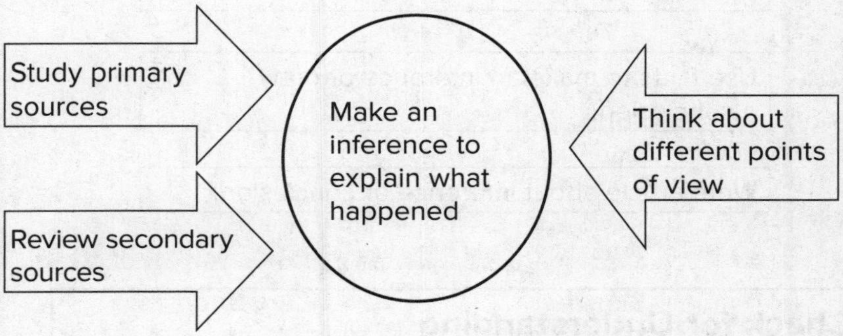
Study primary sources
Review secondary sources
Make an inference to explain what happened
Think about different points of view

Historians can write and review scholarly articles because they become experts on a historical subject. They focus their research. Some historians focus on a very narrow area of study. Someone might study a particular historical person, such as Queen Elizabeth I of England. Someone else studying the past might focus on the events of a single place and time.

Other historians may have a very broad focus. For example, they may study the economic history of many places in a certain period of time. Others may study the history of an idea, such as medicine or technology.

Lesson 2 How Does a Historian Work?, *Continued*

A **conclusion** is a final decision that is reached by reasoning. It is like an inference. Historians draw conclusions about events of the past. They look for facts and evidence in their sources. Then, they use reasoning to draw a conclusion.

Sometimes historians disagree in their conclusions. For example, some historians say that Genghis Khan was a brutal warrior. They tell how he would destroy cities and kill people when he came to a new land. Other historians disagree. They say that Genghis Khan was a good ruler. His empire had a time of peace. Traders were safe to trade goods. People were protected by good laws.

Which conclusion is correct? Was Genghis Khan a cruel warrior or a good leader? A historian may use evidence to explain his or her conclusions. If both conclusions are supported by evidence, they both can be correct.

Examine primary sources.
↓
Use already-known facts.
↓
Read secondary sources.
↓
Use facts to make an inference or draw a conclusion.
↓
Write article about inference or conclusion.

/ / / / / / / / / / / / / / Glue Foldable here / / / / / / / / / / / / / /

Check for Understanding

Explain how historians use different sources to draw conclusions.

1. ____________

____

How are a person's point of view and bias related?

2. ____________

____

Marking the Text

6. Underline the definition of *conclusion*.

Reading Check

7. Why do historians draw different conclusions about events of the past?

____

____

____

FOLDABLES®

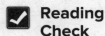

8. Place a one-tab Foldable along the dotted line. Label the anchor tab *Historians*. Label the Foldable *Evidence*, *Inferences*, *and Conclusions*.

Make a memory map by drawing three arrows below the title and writing three words or phrases that you remember about historians and their work. Use your memory notes to help you complete the activity under the tab.

NAME ______________________ DATE ____________ CLASS ________

networks

What Does a Historian Do?

Lesson 3 Researching History

ESSENTIAL QUESTION

How do you research history?

GUIDING QUESTIONS

1. *How do you begin a research project?*
2. *How do you safely research on the Internet?*
3. *How do you interpret historical events accurately?*

Terms to Know

credentials evidence that a person is qualified for a task

URL abbreviation for *uniform resource locator*; the address of an online resource

.gov the ending of a URL for a government Web site

.edu the ending of a URL for a Web site of an educational institution

.org the ending of a URL for a Web site of an organization

plagiarize to present someone's work as your own without giving that person credit

Where in the world?

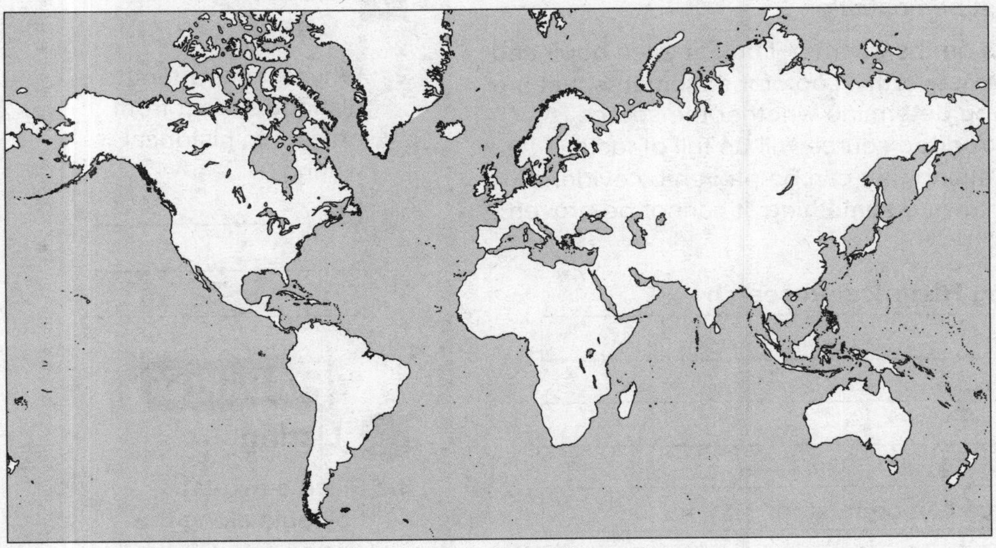

What do you know?

Read the list of words that relate to the Internet. Circle the words you know. Write something you know about each circled word.

browse ______________________

URL ______________________

Web site ______________________

home page ______________________

blog *or* blogger ______________________

search engine ______________________

Planning Your Project

The first step in researching a history topic is to choose a topic. Your topic should not be too broad or too narrow. To test your topic, look it up in an encyclopedia. If there is no entry for your topic, it may be too small. If there are many entries, or a very long entry, the topic may be too large.

After you choose a topic, decide what you want to learn about. Create six questions to help you find out who, what, when, where, why, and how. Write each question on a separate note card. As you find the information that answers each question, write it on the card.

The next step is to collect your research materials. Start with an encyclopedia. Then visit the library to find a book about your subject. The sources must be nonfiction.

Finally, look for articles on the Internet. Look at each book and article to make sure it is trustworthy. Look for statements that are opinions. This can help you determine whether the source is biased or untrustworthy. A good source will be full of facts. Remember, a fact is something that can be proven by evidence. An opinion is an attitude toward something. It cannot be proven true or false.

Starting Historical Research

Choose a topic.
↓
Collect sources.
↓
Decide if each source can be trusted.

As you collect information about your topic, write a short phrase on your notecard to help you remember the facts. On the back of each card, make notes about the books where you found the information.

Researching on the Internet

Looking for information on the Internet is quick. However, finding sources you can trust can be tricky. Many articles on Web sites do not name the author. The reader cannot tell whether the person who wrote it is an expert on the subject. A trustworthy article will include the author's name and **credentials.** Credentials are evidence that someone is an expert.

Glue Foldable here

Identifying

1. Circle the research topics that are too broad for a short research paper.

World War II

Swimming the backstroke

Trees

Vampire bats

Reading Check

2. Why is it important to distinguish fact from opinion in historical writing?

______

______

______

FOLDABLES®

Listing

3. Place a two-tab Foldable along the dotted line. On the anchor tab, write *Using the Internet as a Source*. Label the first tab *Advantages* and the second tab *Disadvantages*.

On both sides of the tabs, list advantages and disadvantages of using the Internet for historical research.

Lesson 3 Researching History, *Continued*

Listing

4. What are two examples of URLs that come at the end of trustworthy Web sites?

____

____

Reading Check

5. What are the consequences of using an Internet resource with biased information?

____

____

____

Explaining

6. Explain why plagiarism is a problem.

____

____

____

The homepage of the Web site can give more clues about the trustworthiness of the article. If the article is on the Web site of a university, government office, or museum, it is probably reliable.

A good clue to find out about a Web site is its online address, or **URL.** Look at the end of the URL. A URL that ends in **.gov** is a government site. This site probably has reliable information that is usually up to date. A URL that ends in **.edu** is the site of a school or college. Most .edu sites pride themselves on accuracy. However, some documents may contain opinions as well as facts.

Nonprofit organizations usually end their URLs in **.org.** These sites may be very accurate. However, they often contain opinions.

You have now collected information about your topic. You have answered the questions on your cards. Now you must sort your information into categories.

Use these categories to help you create an outline for your project. Follow your outline to make sure that your project makes logical sense.

Internet Tips

If you answer NO to any of the questions below, the Web site is probably not a good source.

- Can you tell who wrote the article?
- Can you easily find out who is responsible for the Web site?
- Has the page been updated recently?
- Does the writing show a bias toward one point of view?

Writing Without Bias

Putting all the facts of your research together can be hard work. You should keep in mind some important guidelines for writing about history.

One problem to watch out for when you are writing a research paper is **plagiarism.** Plagiarism happens when a writer uses the exact words or ideas from another person without giving credit. Readers are wrongly led to believe that those words or ideas were the writer's. Copying someone else's work is wrong, and it is against the law. Some authors and researchers have ruined their careers because of plagiarism. Students who plagiarize are likely to get a failing grade.

NAME_______________ DATE __________ CLASS ______

networks

Lesson 3 Researching History, *Continued*

> To avoid plagiarism, follow these rules:
> - Put the ideas you read in your own words.
> - When you restate an opinion from something you read, include a reference to the author: "According to Smith and Jones, ..."
> - Always include a footnote when you use a direct quotation from one of your sources.

Here is another important problem to avoid. When you write about history, be careful that you do not use values from today to make a judgment about what happened in the past. Ideas and values have changed over time. For example, long ago, women lived differently than they do today. A historian should use evidence to draw conclusions. They should not use modern ideas about how women work and live in today's society.

Check for Understanding

List three rules for doing historical research.

1. ______________________

2. ______________________

3. ______________________

What are the four steps for researching history?

4. ______________________

5. ______________________

6. ______________________

7. ______________________

Glue Foldable here

Explaining

7. Why is it important to not use values from today to judge what happened in the past?

____

____

____

Reading Check

8. What is one way to avoid plagiarism when writing about history?

____

____

FOLDABLES®

9. Place a two-tab Foldable along the dotted line to cover the Check for Understanding. Label the anchor tab *Research*. Label the two tabs *Before the Internet* and *Using the Internet.*

List the ways you think people conducted research before the Internet was available and list important things you remember about using the Internet for research.

Lesson 1 Studying Geography

ESSENTIAL QUESTION

How does geography influence the way people live?

GUIDING QUESTIONS

1. ***What methods do geographers use to show the Earth's surface?***
2. ***How do geographers use the five themes and six essential elements of geography?***
3. ***What are some of the key ways that maps are used?***
4. ***What are the uses of charts, graphs, and diagrams?***
5. ***How do geographers study population and culture?***

Terms to Know

projection a way of showing the Earth on a flat sheet of paper

hemisphere a "half sphere," used to refer to one-half of the globe

latitude imaginary lines that circle the Earth parallel to the Equator

longitude imaginary lines that circle the Earth from pole to pole

physical map a map that shows land and water features

political map a map that shows the names and borders of countries

special-purpose map a map that shows themes or patterns such as climate, natural resources, or population

scale a measuring line that shows the distances on a map

cardinal directions north, south, east, and west

choropleth a special-purpose map that uses colors to show population density

migration the movement of people from one place to settle in another place

culture the set of beliefs, behaviors, and traits shared by a group of people

What do you know?

Read the list of Six Essential Elements of Geography. Draw a line to match the element on the left with the description on the right of what a geographer in that field might study.

The World in Spatial Terms	How people change their environment
Places and Regions	Earthquakes and volcanoes
Physical Systems	Where things are located
Human Systems	The relationships among people, places, and environments
Environment and Society	How people have shaped the world
The Uses of Geography	Land, weather, and the plants and animals of an area

Lesson 1 Studying Geography, *Continued*

Displaying the Earth's Surface

Geographers use globes and maps to show where things are on the Earth. Globes are round models of the Earth. Maps are flat drawings of the Earth. They can show very detailed areas and are easy to carry. On a globe, the land and water look the same as on the Earth. A map stretches out the Earth, changing the size and shape of land and water. Mapmakers choose different ways of showing the Earth on a flat map. Each way is called a **projection**.

Globe
A round, 3-D model that shows the surface of the Earth as it is

Map Projection
A flat drawing that stretches the Earth's surface out of proper size and shape

Globes and maps have some features in common. Both use imaginary lines to locate places on Earth. One key line is the Equator. It circles the Earth from east to west and divides Earth into northern and southern hemispheres. A **hemisphere** is half of a globe. Another key line is the Prime Meridian. It circles the Earth from north to south. It divides Earth into the eastern and western hemispheres.

Lines of **latitude** circle the Earth from east to west. Lines of **longitude** circle the Earth from north to south. The two sets of lines cross each other. Each point where they cross has a latitude measurement and a longitude measurement. These are shown in units called degrees. If you know the latitude and longitude of a spot, you know its exact location on the Earth.

Five Themes and Six Essential Elements of Geography

For many years, geographers have used the Five Themes of Geography to study the world. The Five Themes of Geography are (1) location, (2) place, (3) human-environment interaction, (4) movement, and (5) regions.

Geographers now divide their field into Six Essential Elements. Each element looks at a different set of facts about our world and the people in it.

? Finding the Main Idea

1. Why do maps and globes show the Earth in different ways?

____

____

____

? Analyzing

2. How are the Equator and Prime Meridian related to latitude and longitude?

____

____

____

✓ Reading Check

3. What are an advantage and a disadvantage to using a map rather than a globe to study the Earth's geography?

____

____

____

Reading Check

4. Which Essential Elements of Geography might be involved in the study of an area's landforms and how they affect people living there?

____

____

Reading Check

5. Why is reading the map key important when looking at a special-purpose map?

____

____

FOLDABLES®

Describing

6. Cut a two-tab Foldable to make four tabs. Place it along the dotted line. Write *Geography uses* ... on the anchor tab. Label the four tabs *Maps*, *Charts*, *Graphs*, and *Diagrams*. On the back, describe how each item is used in geography.

Geographers who study *The World in Spatial Terms* want to know where things are located. People interested in *Places and Regions* study the land, the weather, and the plants and animals of an area. Geographers analyze how *Physical Systems,* such as earthquakes and volcanoes, shape the Earth's surface. They also learn how living things depend on one another and their surroundings. *Human Systems* deals with how people have shaped the world. Those who study *Environment and Society* want to know how people change their environment and are changed by it. *The Uses of Geography* helps us understand the relationships among people, places, and environments.

Types of Maps

Geographers use different types of maps to show different information. **Physical maps** show land and water on the surface of Earth. **Political maps** show the borders and names of countries. **Special-purpose maps** show specific kinds of information. They could show the number of people who live in a state or where resources are located.

Most maps have a map key. This tells you what the lines and colors used on a map represent. It also explains any symbols, or signs and pictures. A map **scale** helps you measure distances on a map. Many maps also show the **cardinal directions**—north, south, east, and west.

Using Charts, Graphs, and Diagrams

/ / / / / / / / / / / / / / Glue Foldable here / / / / / / / / / / / / / /

Charts, graphs, and diagrams are tools for showing information. Charts arrange numbers and other data in rows and columns. To read a chart, look at the labels at the top of each column and on the left side. They explain what the chart is showing.

There are different types of graphs. Bar graphs use wide lines to show data. They are useful for comparing amounts. Line graphs work well for showing changes over time. The amounts being measured are shown on a grid above each year. To read line and bar graphs, first look at the labels along the side and bottom of the graph. Circle graphs show how the whole of something is divided into parts.

NAME ______________________ DATE ____________ CLASS ________

networks

Diagrams are special drawings. They show steps in a process, point out the parts of an object, or explain how something works.

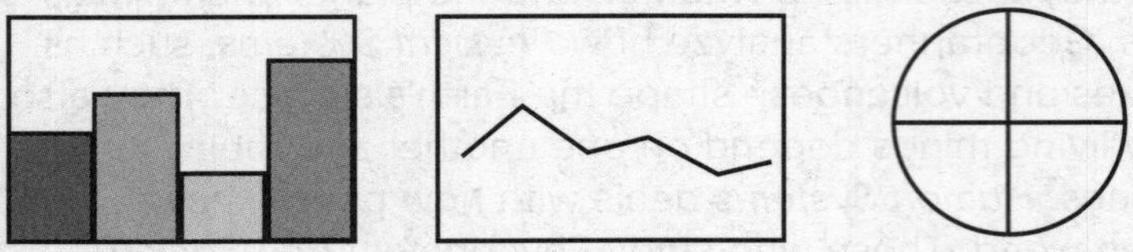

Bar Graph Line Graph Circle Graph

Population and Culture

Population is the number of people who live in a specific place. Geographers study this in great detail. A **choropleth** map uses colors to show population density. This is the average number of people living in a square mile or square kilometer. Geographers also study the movement of people from one place to settle in another place. This movement is called **migration.**

Geographers are interested in how people think and act. They study this by looking at **culture,** the set of beliefs, behaviors, and traits shared by members of a group. Language, religion, and government are part of culture.

Throughout history, different peoples have met through exploration, migration, and trade. Change often happens as a result of such meetings. Strong groups may conquer weaker ones. Different groups may share part of their culture with others. In this way, ideas are spread from one group to another. Sometimes the mixing of two or more groups forms a new culture. Such meetings between different peoples are a key part of world history.

Check for Understanding

Why do geographers use different types of maps and map projections?

1. ______________________________________

____

List two things that geographers study other than the location of places on Earth.

2. ______________________________________

3. ______________________________________

Glue Foldable here

Reading Check

7. What type of graph shows changes over time?

____

____

____

Reading Check

8. Why are geographers interested in contact between cultures?

____

____

____

FOLDABLES®

9. Place a two-tab Foldable to cover the Check for Understanding. Label the anchor tab *Geographers Study* .... Label the two tabs *Physical Systems* and *Human Systems*. Make a memory map by drawing arrows below each title. List words or phrases that you remember about each. Use your notes to help you answer the questions under the tabs.

NAME ______________________ DATE ____________ CLASS ________

networks

Studying Geography, Economics, and Citizenship

Lesson 2 Exploring Economics

ESSENTIAL QUESTION

Why do people trade?

GUIDING QUESTIONS

1. *What are the basic ideas of economics?*
2. *What are the different types of economic systems?*
3. *What are the benefits and disadvantages of trade?*

Terms to Know

capital money and goods used to help people make or do things

entrepreneurship the act of running a business and taking on the risks of that business

supply the amount of a good or service that a producer wants to sell

demand the amount of a good or service that a consumer wants to buy

scarcity lack of a resource

opportunity cost what a person gives up when they choose to make or buy a product

traditional economy an economic system in which custom decides what people do, make, buy, and sell

command economy an economic system in which a central government decides what goods will be made

recession a period of slow economic growth or decline

inflation a rise in prices and a drop in the value of money

exports goods sent from one country to another in trade

imports goods brought into one country from another in trade

barter to trade by exchanging one good or service for another

globalization the growth in free trade between countries

What do you know?

Read each statement. Circle T if you think the statement is true. Circle F if you think the statement is false.

1. Economics is the study of how and why people make, sell, and buy things. T F
2. People generally want to sell things at lower prices. T F
3. Opportunity cost means how much you have to spend to do something. T F
4. Rare things are worth more than things that are easy to get. T F
5. Once money was invented, trade became simpler. T F

Lesson 2 Exploring Economics, *Continued*

What Is Economics?

Economics is the study of how and why people make, buy, and sell things. Economists ask three questions: *What* goods and services should people offer? *How* should they make and sell them? *Who* will use them?

Land	Labor	
the surface of the Earth and the resources found in and on it	the ability of people to do work	
Capital		**Entrepreneurship**
the money and goods used to help people make or do things	←	the act of running a business and taking risks to succeed

Resources are the factors that people need to make goods and offer services. In economics, there are four key resources. Land includes the surface of the Earth and its natural resources, such as minerals and water. Labor is the ability of people to do work. **Capital** is the money and goods used to help people make or do things. **Entrepreneurship** is the act of running a business. It also means taking on risks.

Having the right resources is just the first step in making something. How much should you make? What price should you charge for it? These choices are shaped by the law of supply and demand.

Supply is how much of something people want to sell. It is also how much of a good or service is available. **Demand** is how much of something people want to buy. It can also show how strongly someone wants to buy something. In general, people want to sell goods at high prices and buy goods at low prices.

Other things affect supply and demand, such as **scarcity,** or lack of availability. If something is very rare, it is usually worth more than something that is easy to find. This means that buyers have to choose between paying a high price or not buying the good.

Identifying

1. What are the three main questions that economists ask?

____

____

____

Marking the Text

2. Circle the word *resources* and each of the four key resources.

Defining

3. What is *supply*? What is *demand*?

____

____

____

Explaining

4. Why do buyers pay a high price for something that is *scarce*?

____

____

____

Lesson 2 Exploring Economics, *Continued*

Reading Check

5. How will the people who make goods and those who buy the goods react if the price goes down?

____

____

____

Making Connections

6. Think of something you chose to buy or do recently. Write down its opportunity cost, or what you gave up when you made your choice.

____

____

____

Contrasting

7. How are traditional and command economies different from each other?

____

____

____

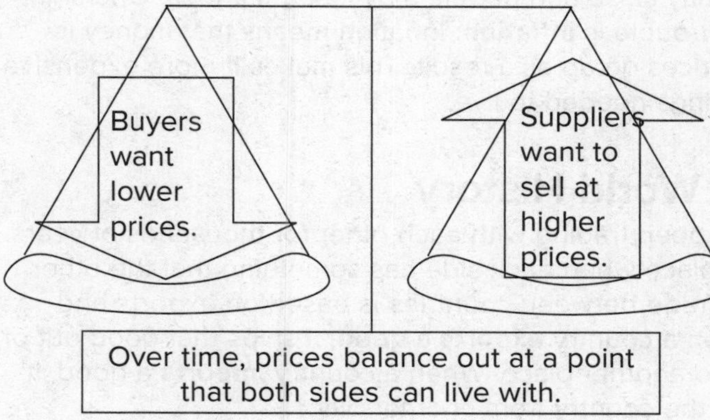
Buyers want lower prices.
Suppliers want to sell at higher prices.
Over time, prices balance out at a point that both sides can live with.

Such choices happen all the time when people buy and sell. One name for these kinds of choices is opportunity cost. The **opportunity cost** of something is based on what you gave up to make or buy it. For example, you are a farmer. You must choose what to grow. If you grow wheat, you cannot use the land to grow beans. You gave up that chance, or opportunity, when you chose to grow wheat.

Managing and Measuring Economies

There are four major kinds of economic systems. These systems are ways of deciding who should make goods and who should use them.

The oldest system is a **traditional economy**. In a traditional economy, people live in small groups. They make what their family or others in their group need. Children often do the same kind of work as their parents.

The early civilizations of Egypt and Mesopotamia began as command economies. In a **command economy**, a central government decides what goods will be made in a society and who will get them. A command economy can bring together many resources. People, however, have limited choices in this economic system.

In a *market economy*, each person makes their own choices about what to make, sell, or buy. The United States has a market economy. In a *mixed economy*, the government has some control over what is made and how much. Individuals make the rest of the economic choices.

When an economy grows, more goods are made. When an economy shrinks, fewer goods are made. When an economy grows slowly or shrinks, it is called a **recession**.

Companies may close and people may lose their jobs. One sign of economic trouble is **inflation.** Inflation means that money is worth less. Prices go up as a result. This makes it more expensive to buy the things needed to live.

Trade in World History

People have been trading with each other for thousands of years. Trade takes place when each side has something that the other side wants. Trade between countries is based on exports and imports. When a country **exports** a good, it ships that good out of the country to another place. When a country **imports** a good, it brings it into the country from another place.

Early civilizations first traded with each other by bartering. When people **barter**, goods are traded for other goods. However, barter only works if you have what the other person wants. Once money was invented, trade became simpler. Money has an agreed-upon value. This means it can be traded for almost anything.

Trade is not always possible. Sometimes geography makes it hard to travel between places. Fighting or other kinds of conflict can also make travel too dangerous. Sometimes one group does not want to trade with other groups. This might happen because the two groups disagree about politics or other issues. Or a country may want to limit trade if it hurts its own producers.

Today most countries trade with each other. This is called **globalization.** Globalization has increased the ties between the world's economies. When a large economy like that of the United States struggles, it affects the world.

/ / / / / / / / / / / / / / Glue Foldable here / / / / / / / / / / / / / /

Check for Understanding

List two factors that affect the price of a good or service.

1. ____________________

2. ____________________

List two methods of trade between countries.

3. ____________________

4. ____________________

Reading Check

8. In which type of economic system are all decisions made by a central government?

____

Reading Check

9. Why do countries agree to trade with one another?

____

FOLDABLES®

10. Glue two one-tab Foldables together along the anchor tabs. Glue the anchor tabs along the dotted line. Label the top anchor tab *The Importance of . . .* . Write *Supply and Demand* on the top Foldable and *Imports and Exports* on the bottom Foldable. Draw arrows below the titles and write as many words and phrases as you can remember about each topic.

NAME _______________ DATE _________ CLASS _______

networks

Studying Geography, Economics, and Citizenship

Lesson 3 Practicing Citizenship

ESSENTIAL QUESTION

Why do people form governments?

GUIDING QUESTIONS

1. ***What are the key principles of the U.S. government?***
2. ***What are the civic rights, duties, and responsibilities of U.S. citizens?***
3. ***What does it mean to be a global citizen?***

Terms to Know

representative government government in which citizens elect officials who govern

federal system government which divides power between a central government and state governments

separation of powers the division of power between the branches of government

legislative branch the part of government that passes laws

executive branch the part of government that enforces laws

judicial branch the part of government that interprets laws

checks and balances system in which each branch of government limits the power of another branch

What do you know?

In the first column, answer the questions based on what you know before you study. After this lesson, complete the last column.

Now...		Later...
	What is a representative democracy?	
	What are checks and balances?	
	How is voting both a right and a responsibility of citizenship?	
	Why should citizens stay informed about important issues?	
	What does it mean to be a global citizen?	

Principles of Government

The government of the United States is based on the rules in the U.S. Constitution. The United States has a **representative government.** This means that citizens elect, or choose, people who will serve in government. These people must act in the interests of the citizens who voted for them.

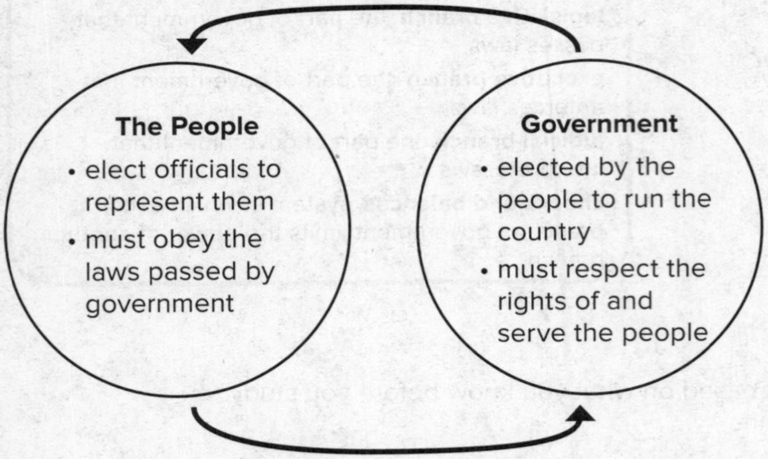
The People
• elect officials to represent them
• must obey the laws passed by government
Government
• elected by the people to run the country
• must respect the rights of and serve the people

The Constitution also limits the powers of government. The United States has a **federal system.** The federal, or central, government is the highest authority. It shares some power with the state governments. The Constitution also divides the federal government into three equal branches, or parts. Each branch has its own set of powers. This idea is called **separation of powers.** This idea was adopted so that no single branch would become too powerful.

The **legislative branch** makes laws. The U.S. Congress is the legislative branch. It is made up of the House of Representatives and the Senate. The **executive branch** carries out the laws. The president is the leader of the executive branch. The **judicial branch** reviews and interprets the laws. The Supreme Court is the leading court of the judicial branch.

The Constitution creates a system of **checks and balances** among the branches. This means that each branch can limit the power of another branch. For example, the president can veto, or reject, a law proposed by Congress. Congress, however, can overturn a veto with enough votes. The system of checks and balances keeps any one part of government from becoming too powerful.

Marking the Text

1. In the text, underline the definition of a federal system.

Identifying

2. List each branch of the federal government and one of its key powers.

____

____

____

____

Drawing Conclusions

3. How do separation of powers and checks and balances limit the power of government?

____

____

____

____

Reading Check

4. What type of government does the United States have?

____

FOLDABLES®

Defining

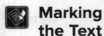

5. Place a three-tab Foldable along the dotted line. Write *Citizens have* ... on the anchor tab. Label the first tab *rights*, the middle tab *duties*, and the bottom tab *responsibilities*. On the front of the tabs, write definitions for the rights, duties, and responsibilities of citizens. On the back, give examples of each.

Marking the Text

6. In the text, underline three duties of citizenship.

Finding the Main Idea

7. Why is being a responsible citizen important?

____

____

____

What is Citizenship?

American citizens have rights, duties, and responsibilities. Rights are freedoms protected by law. All Americans have the right to seek, or look for, life, liberty, and happiness. All Americans may speak their minds and write what they think. Together these rights are called freedom of expression. Americans have the right to go to meetings and other gatherings that are peaceful. If they have a problem, they can write to government officials and ask them to help. This is called the right to petition.

The Constitution also protects freedom of religion. This means that people can worship as they choose. If someone is accused of a serious crime, they have a right to a fair trial by jury. A **jury** is a group of people who listen to both sides in a court case. Citizens also have the right to vote. This allows them to choose their leaders. These and other rights are discussed in the Bill of Rights and other amendments to the Constitution.

Glue Foldable here

Duties are things that all citizens must do. All citizens must obey the law and pay taxes. This applies to federal, state, and local governments. Citizens must serve on a jury if asked. They must also be ready to defend the United States and the Constitution.

Responsibilities are actions that are not required by law. Citizens should stay informed about important issues. Issues are topics that affect many people, such as crime or education. Learning about issues helps citizens make wise choices when they vote. Voting is a key responsibility of citizenship. Citizens should vote so they can choose representation in government.

Responsibilities of Citizenship

- respecting the rights of others
- staying informed on issues
- voting
- volunteering in the community

Citizens should also respect the rights and views of other people. The United States welcomes people of many different backgrounds. All these people share the same freedoms in America. Before you deny a right to someone else, put yourself in his or her place. Think about how you would feel if someone tried to take away your rights.

Finally, by working with each other, citizens help make neighborhoods and towns better places to live. There are different ways to keep our communities strong. We can volunteer our time. We can join neighborhood groups, and we can serve in public office.

Being a Global Citizen

Today the world faces many problems. Often these problems are too big for any one country to handle alone. Pollution is one example. It can spread from one country to another. Trade is a world issue. Most countries trade with at least one other country, so the laws about trade are important to many countries.

Another global issue is human rights. Around the world, many people do not have the same basic rights as Americans. However, the idea is growing that all people should have these rights.

Being a global citizen means learning about these and other issues that affect the world as a whole. It also means understanding how people live in other countries. That helps us work together more easily to solve big problems, such as drought or hunger.

Being a global citizen does not mean giving up your duties and responsibilities as a U.S. citizen. It means thinking about how you can make the world a better place by your actions.

/ / / / / / / / / / / / / / / / / Glue Foldable here / / / / / / / / / / / / / / / / /

Check for Understanding

List two facts about the structure of the government of the United States.

1. ______________________________

2. ______________________________

List one right, one duty, and one responsibility of U.S. citizenship.

3. Right: ______________________________

4. Duty: ______________________________

5. Responsibility: ______________________________

Reading Check

8. What duties do citizens have?

____

Reading Check

9. What are some ways in which you could become a better global citizen?

____

FOLDABLES®

10. Glue a one-tab Foldable along the dotted line. Label the anchor tab *Citizens and Government*. Write *Representative Government* in the middle of the one-tab Foldable. Make a memory map by drawing five arrows pointing away from the title. Write five words or phrases that you remember about representative government.

NAME________________________ DATE ____________ CLASS ________

networks

Early Humans and the Agricultural Revolution

Lesson 1 Hunter-Gatherers

ESSENTIAL QUESTION

How do people adapt to their environment?

GUIDING QUESTIONS

1. ***What was life like during the Paleolithic Age?***
2. ***How did people adapt to survive during the ice ages?***

Terms to Know

Paleolithic the early part of human history, also known as the Old Stone Age

nomads people who move from place to place to survive

technology the use of new ideas and tools to do work

ice ages long periods of extreme cold on Earth

Where in the world?

Paleolithic Sites in Europe and Southwest Asia

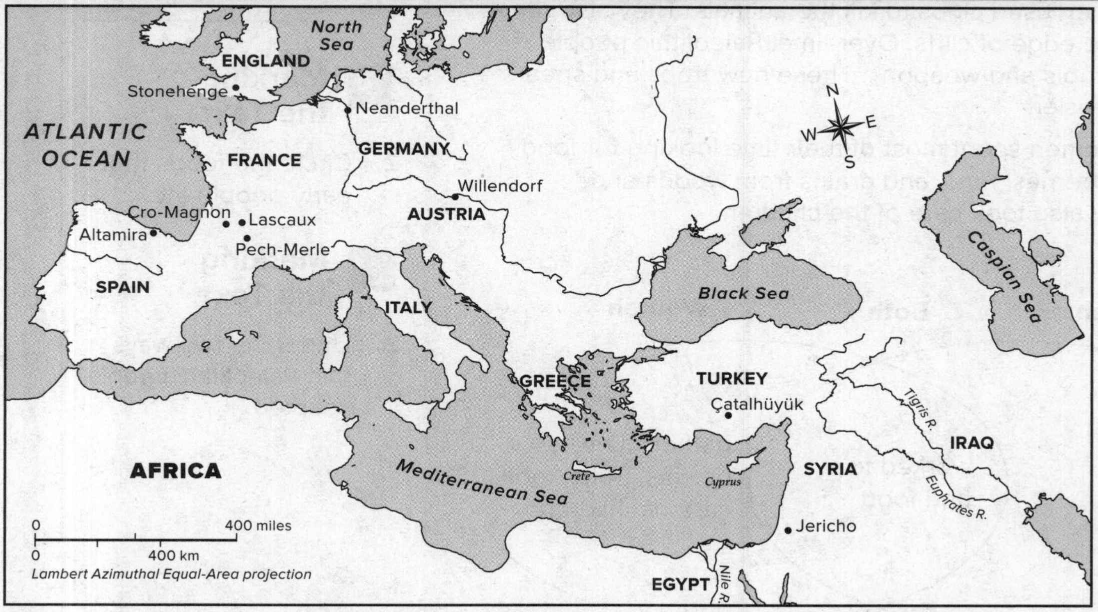

Historians have found evidence of human activity dating from Paleolithic times at each of these sites.

When did it happen?

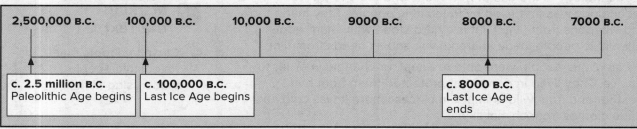

2,500,000 B.C. — **100,000 B.C.** — **10,000 B.C.** — **9000 B.C.** — **8000 B.C.** — **7000 B.C.**

- **c. 2.5 million B.C.** Paleolithic Age begins
- **c. 100,000 B.C.** Last Ice Age begins
- **c. 8000 B.C.** Last Ice Age ends

The Paleolithic Age

The early period of human history is called the Stone Age. That's when people made tools and weapons from stone. The earliest part of the Stone Age is the **Paleolithic** Age. The Paleolithic Age began about 2.5 million years ago. It lasted until about 8000 B.C.

The first humans spent most of their time looking for food. They hunted animals and gathered, or collected, plants, nuts, and berries. For this reason, early people are known as "hunter-gatherers." Early people moved from place to place looking for food. People who move from place to place in order to survive are called **nomads.**

In the Paleolithic Age, men hunted the large animals. They learned how animals behaved. They learned the best way to hunt them. At first, men used clubs to kill the animals. They also drove animals over the edge of cliffs. Over time, Paleolithic people created better tools and weapons. These new traps and spears made hunting easier.

Paleolithic women spent most of their time looking for food. They gathered berries, nuts, and grains from woods and meadows. They also took care of the children.

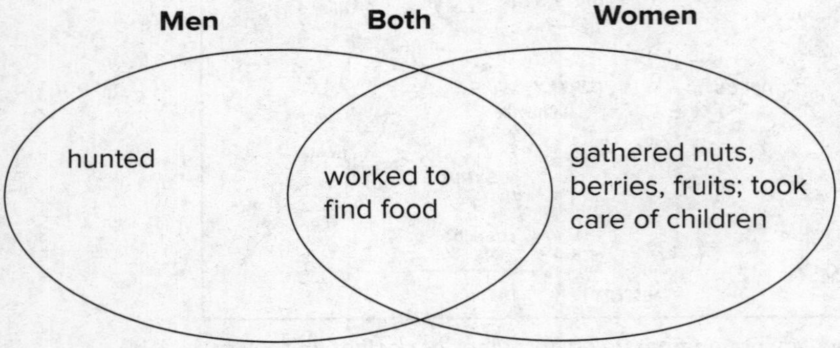

Technology is the use of new ideas and tools to do work. Technology was first used by Paleolithic people. They made tools and weapons from flint. Flint is a hard stone with sharp edges. Paleolithic people made sharp knives and ax heads from flint.

Paleolithic people were able to adapt, or change, in order to survive. They lived in caves that protected them from bad weather and from wild animals. In places where it was cold, they made clothes from animal skins.

Connecting to Today

1. The Stone Age gets its name from the type of tools people used. What do you think people in the future will call our time period?

____

____

____

Marking the Text

2. Circle the foods that early people ate.

Marking the Text

3. Underline two ways that Paleolithic people adapted.

Marking the Text

4. Circle two tools that Paleolithic people made using flint.

Reading Check

5. Why was fire important for Paleolithic people?

____

____

____

Marking the Text

6. Underline the sentence that tells why the development of spoken language was so important.

Connecting to Today

7. The ice ages are an example of climate change. Where else have you heard about climate change?

____

____

____

During the Paleolithic Age, people learned how to make fire. Can you imagine how hard life was before that? Once people had fire, they could eat cooked food. They had light at night. Fire also provided warmth and scared away wild animals.

Early people probably made fire by creating friction. They rubbed two pieces of wood together until the wood became so hot it caught on fire. They also started fires by hitting one stone against another. This would create a spark that could set dry grass or leaves on fire.

Other advancements took place during the Paleolithic Age. During this time, people developed spoken language. Before this, humans communicated through sounds and hand motions. Spoken language made it easier for people to work together. Just like language today, the language of early people was constantly growing and changing. Just like today, new ideas and new technology required new words.

Early people expressed their ideas through language. They also expressed themselves through art. Early artists painted the walls of their caves with paints made from crushed rock mixed with animal fat. Early cave paintings show animals in bright colors.

Paleolithic Age Achievements

- Improved technology
- Flint tools and weapons
- Animal skin clothes
- Ability to make fire
- Spoken language
- Cave art

The Ice Ages

About 100,000 B.C. Earth began to get very cold. Thick sheets of ice moved across much of the land. Early people had to adapt, or change, if they were to survive. This was the beginning of Earth's most recent Ice Age. **Ice ages** are long periods of extreme cold on Earth.

During the ice ages, more and more ice formed on the Earth. The levels of the oceans dropped because so much water was taken from the oceans to form the ice. Land that was once covered by water was now above it. One place this happened was between Asia and North America.

Lesson 1 Hunter-Gatherers, *Continued*

During the ice ages, a land bridge connected the two land masses. A land bridge is a strip of dry land that was once covered by water. People could now walk from Asia into the Americas.

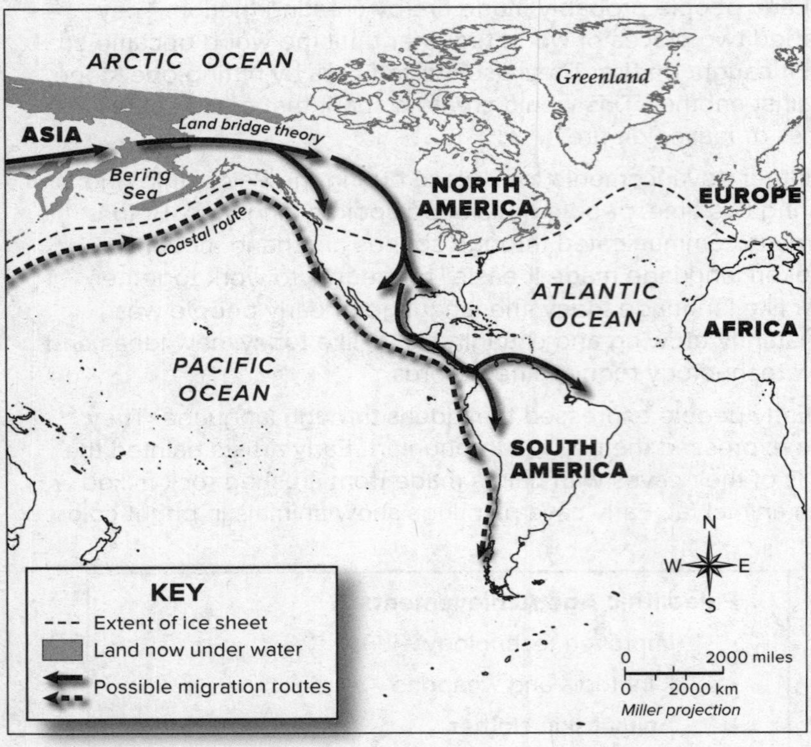

Check for Understanding

Why were the first people nomads?

1. ______________________________

____

List two advancements of the Paleolithic Age, and tell how each one made life easier for early humans.

2. ______________________________

3. ______________________________

Glue Foldable here

Reading Check

8. How were land bridges formed?

____

____

____

____

____

____

____

____

FOLDABLES®

9. Place a two-tab Foldable along the dotted line to cover the Check for Understanding. Label the anchor tab *Stone Age*. Label the two tabs—*Food* and *Shelter*. On both sides of the Foldable tabs, write words and phrases that you remember about each title. Use your notes to help you answer the questions under the tabs.

NAME______________________________ DATE ____________ CLASS ________

networks

Early Humans and the Agricultural Revolution

Lesson 2 The Agricultural Revolution

ESSENTIAL QUESTION

How do people adapt to their environment?

GUIDING QUESTIONS

1. *How did farming change people's lives?*
2. *What was life like during the Neolithic Age?*
3. *What characteristics did early civilizations share?*

Terms to Know

domesticate to tame
systematic agriculture farming
Neolithic Age the period of time from 8000 to 4000 B.C.
shrine a place where people worship
specialization training for a particular job
Bronze Age the period of time from 3000 to 1200
monarchy a government led by a king or a queen

Where in the world?

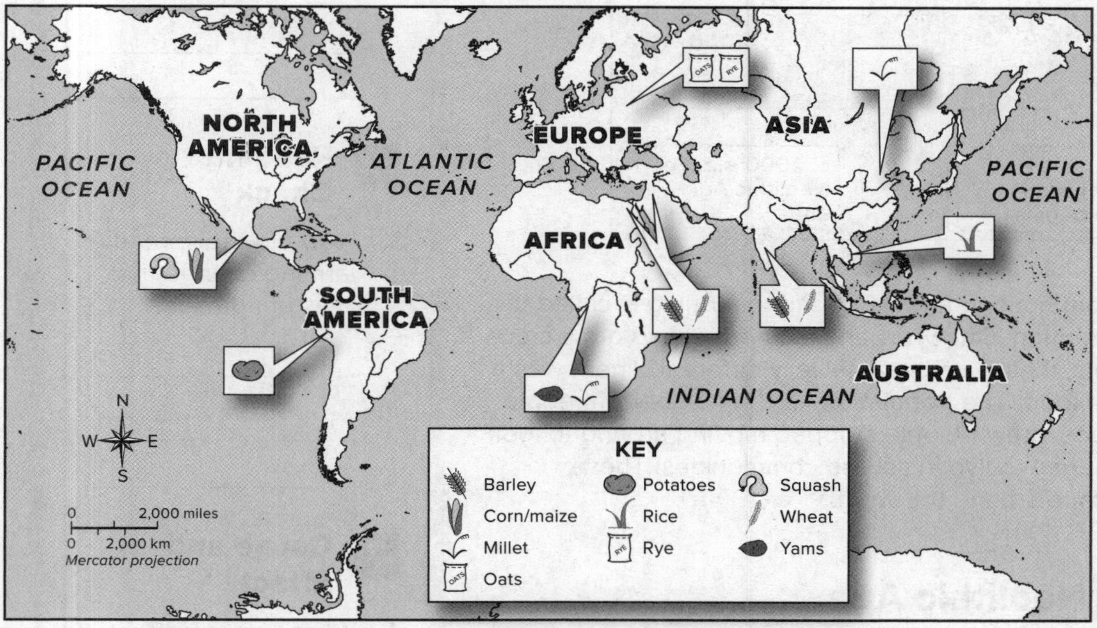

When did it happen?

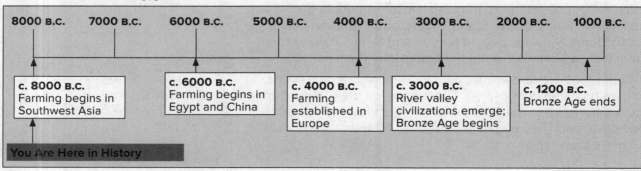

8000 B.C. | 7000 B.C. | 6000 B.C. | 5000 B.C. | 4000 B.C. | 3000 B.C. | 2000 B.C. | 1000 B.C.

c. 8000 B.C. Farming begins in Southwest Asia

c. 6000 B.C. Farming begins in Egypt and China

c. 4000 B.C. Farming established in Europe

c. 3000 B.C. River valley civilizations emerge; Bronze Age begins

c. 1200 B.C. Bronze Age ends

You Are Here in History

Lesson 2 The Agricultural Revolution, *Continued*

Neolithic Times

The last Ice Age ended about 10,000 years ago. The climate on Earth became warmer and the ice melted. People began to stay in one place. They started to grow grains and vegetables. People also began to **domesticate,** or tame, animals. This was the beginning of **systematic agriculture,** or farming. Farming slowly replaced hunting and gathering as the main source of food for people.

This change in the way people lived marked the start of the **Neolithic Age.** The Neolithic Age began about 8000 B.C. and ended about 4,000 years later. Agriculture was the biggest change that took place during the Neolithic Age. This change happened very slowly.

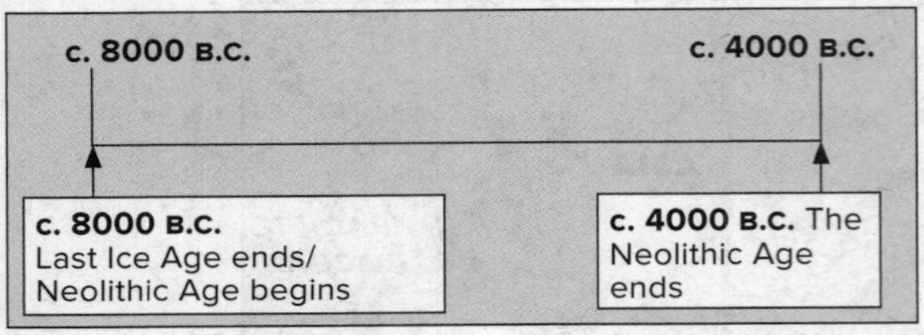

The switch from hunting and gathering to farming is called the Agricultural Revolution. Once humans learned how to grow crops and tame animals, their lives became very different. There was a steady supply of food. The population, or the number of people who live in a place, grew. People stopped moving around to look for food. They began to live in settled communities. These changes took place around the world.

Life in the Neolithic Age

Neolithic people settled in villages made up of permanent homes. Villages and homes had **shrines**, or holy places where gods and goddesses were honored. Neolithic people grew fruits, nuts, and different grains. Sheep, goats, and cattle were also raised. Some Neolithic people hunted and fished. Early settled communities often had more and better food than nomads.

Better food led to healthier people. Healthier people lived longer and had more children. The population grew. More people could grow more crops. Eventually, farmers grew more food than they could eat. They began to trade food for things they could not make themselves.

Marking the Text

1. Circle the word that means the same as *tame*. Circle the word that means the same as *farming*.

Defining

2. What is the Agricultural Revolution?

____

____

____

Reading Check

3. How did the spread of farming change the lives of nomads?

____

____

____

Cause and Effect

4. What was the effect of having a better supply of food?

____

____

____

NAME_______________________ DATE ___________ CLASS ________

Lesson 2 The Agricultural Revolution, *Continued*

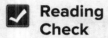

Marking the Text

5. Underline the work done by men. Circle the work done by women.

Reading Check

6. How did the spread of agriculture affect trade?

____

____

____

Comparing

7. What were two things that early civilizations had in common?

____

____

____

People began to do work other than farming. They could do tasks that matched their talents. This is called **specialization.** Some people made jewelry or weapons. Others made pottery or wove cloth. These people also traded their products for goods they did not have.

In Neolithic communities, most men were farmers. They grew the food and protected the village. Women took care of the children and wove cloth for clothing.

People continued to make advancements. In western Asia, people discovered that mixing tin and copper created bronze. Bronze was stronger than copper. Bronze tools and weapons were better than those made of stone. Bronze became widely used between 3000 and 1200 B.C. This period is known as the **Bronze Age.**

Civilizations Emerge

By the beginning of the Bronze Age, four great civilizations had appeared in river valleys. These civilizations were Mesopotamia, Egypt, India, and China.

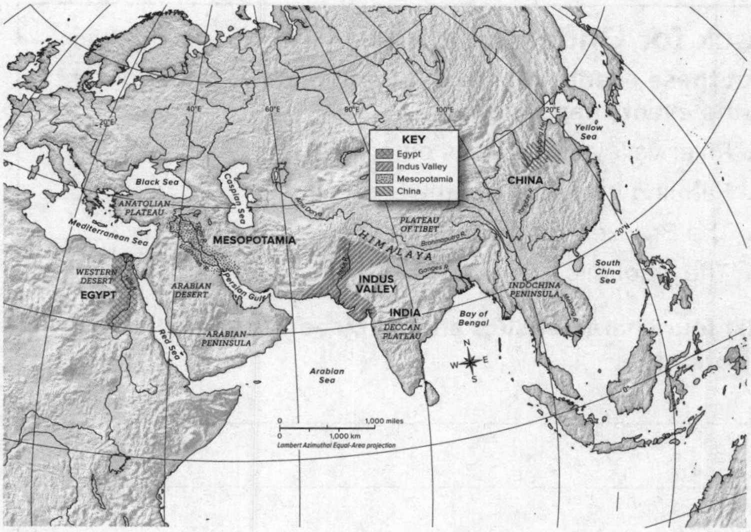

These civilizations were far apart. But they had things in common.

- They developed in river valleys. The rich soil in river valleys made it easier to grow crops. Rivers provided fish. Rivers also encouraged trade.
- Increased trade led to the development of cities. Cities became the centers of civilization.

Lesson 2 The Agricultural Revolution, *Continued*

- People formed governments. Governments protected their people and food supplies. The first governments were monarchies. A **monarchy** is a government led by a king or a queen. Monarchs made laws to keep order.
- Religion became more complex. Priests performed ceremonies to win the approval of gods and goddesses. Rulers claimed that their own power rested on the support of these powerful beings. Rulers claimed that their own power rested on the support of these powerful beings.
- People were organized into social classes. The classes were based on the type of work people did and the amount of wealth or power they had. Rulers and priests belonged to the highest class. Below this class were farmers and craftspeople. Enslaved people formed the lowest class.

During this time, written language developed. Early writing used symbols. People in early civilizations also produced art. They created paintings and sculptures. They built huge buildings, such as places of worship or burial tombs for rulers.

Glue Foldable here

Check for Understanding

Put these events in order. Write the letters in the order that the events happened.

a. River valley civilizations emerge. **1.** ________

b. Farming begins in Southwest Asia. **2.** ________

c. The Bronze Age begins. **3.** ________

d. The Neolithic Age ends. **4.** ________

List four characteristics shared by early river valley civilizations.

5. ____________________

6. ____________________

7. ____________________

8. ____________________

Reading Check

8. Why did early peoples form governments?

____

____

FOLDABLES®

9. Place a two-tab Foldable along the dotted line to cover the Check for Understanding. Label the anchor tab *Warmer Climate Brings Change.* Label one of the two tabs *Neolithic Age* and the other *Bronze Age.* On the front of the tabs, list three words or phrases that you remember about each title. Use your notes to help you complete the activity under the tabs.

NAME_______________________________ DATE ____________ CLASS ________

networks

Mesopotamia

Lesson 1 The Sumerians

ESSENTIAL QUESTION

How does geography influence the way people live?

GUIDING QUESTIONS

1. ***Why did people settle in Mesopotamia?***
2. ***What was life like in Sumer?***
3. ***What ideas and inventions did Sumerians pass on to other civilizations?***

Terms to Know

silt small particles of fertile soil

irrigation a way to supply dry land with water through ditches, pipes, or streams

surplus an amount that is left over after a need has been met

city-state an independent nation made up of a city and the land around it

polytheism a belief in more than one god

ziggurat a pyramid-shaped tower with a temple at the top

cuneiform a Sumerian writing system that used wedge-shaped marks made in soft clay

scribe a person who copies or writes out documents; often a record keeper

epic a long poem that tells the story of a hero

Where in the world?

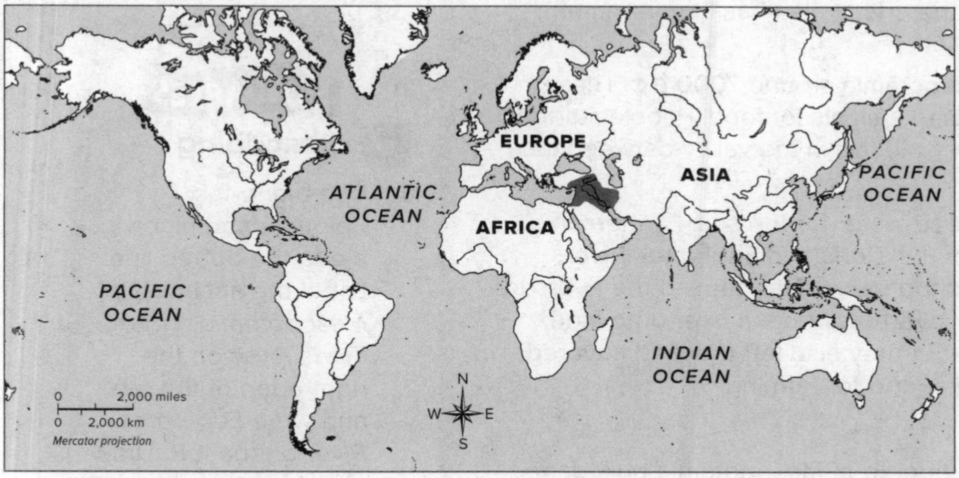

When did it happen?

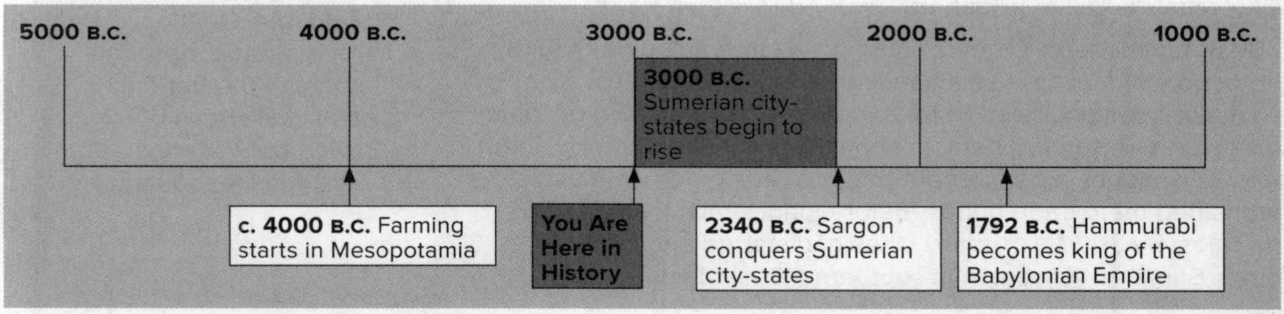

The First Civilizations in Mesopotamia

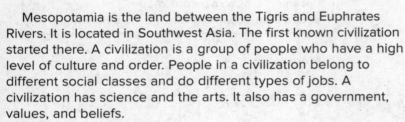

Characteristics of Civilization

- high level of culture and order
- social classes
- different types of jobs
- science and the arts
- government
- values and beliefs

Mesopotamia is the land between the Tigris and Euphrates Rivers. It is located in Southwest Asia. The first known civilization started there. A civilization is a group of people who have a high level of culture and order. People in a civilization belong to different social classes and do different types of jobs. A civilization has science and the arts. It also has a government, values, and beliefs.

People first stayed in Mesopotamia around 7000 B.C. These people hunted. They also raised animals for food. People started to farm around 4000 B.C. They did this in the valley between the two rivers.

To grow crops, farmers need water for the soil. Farmers in Mesopotamia got water from the Tigris and Euphrates Rivers. Sometimes, though, it rained too much. This caused the rivers to flood. A flood is when water overflows from a river onto land. Floods could destroy crops, but they also left the land covered with **silt.** Silt is a rich soil. It is good for farming.

/ / / / / / / / / / / / / Glue Foldable here / / / / / / / / / / / / /

To control the floods, the people of Mesopotamia built dams. A dam is a wall that stops the flow of water. They also dug canals. A canal is a ditch that lets water flow to the fields. Watering crops using canals is called **irrigation.**

By using irrigation, farmers could grow large amounts of food. The people of Mesopotamia had extra food, or a **surplus.** As a result, not everyone needed to farm. Some people could become artisans. An artisan is a person who makes a good, such as cloth, tools, or weapons. Soon people began to live together in places that helped them trade goods. Before long, small villages grew into cities. By 3000 B.C., many cities had started and grown in Sumer. Sumer is the region in southern Mesopotamia.

Identifying

1. Why is 4000 B.C. an important date?

____

____

____

Reading Check

2. How did floods sometimes help farmers?

____

____

____

FOLDABLES®

Describing

3. Use a one-tab Foldable and place it along the dotted line. Label the anchor tab *Mesopotamia.* Write *Tigris River* on the right edge of the tab and write *Euphrates River* on the left. Draw or color the surface of the land across the bottom of the Foldable. On the reverse side, describe some of the benefits and challenges of living between the rivers in Mesopotamia.

NAME____________________ DATE __________ CLASS ______

networks

Making Connections

4. Are cities in the United States considered city-states? Why or why not?

____

____

____

Defining

5. What is *polytheism*?

____

____

____

Marking the Text

6. Using a different colored marker for each social class, highlight the people who belonged to the upper class, the middle class, and the lowest class.

Reading Check

7. Why did the Sumerians build cities with walls around them?

____

____

____

Sumer's Civilization

The people of Sumer were called Sumerians. They built many cities. The cities of Sumer had deserts around them. Deserts were hard to travel across. As a result, each city stood alone.

As cities grew, they gained control of the land around them. In this way, they formed city-states. Each **city-state** had its own government. It was not part of a larger nation. Historians believe that each city-state was surrounded by a large wall. Sometimes Sumerian city-states fought each other. During times of peace, they traded with each other.

The Sumerian people worshiped many gods. This type of belief is called **polytheism**. Each city-state, though, claimed one god as its own. To honor this god, the city-state built a large temple called a **ziggurat**. A temple is a building used to worship a god or many gods.

People in Sumer were divided into social classes. The upper class included kings, priests, warriors, and government workers. People in this class were powerful and wealthy. The middle class had farmers, fishers, and artisans. It was the largest group. Enslaved people made up the lowest class. They had no money and no power.

The basic unit of Sumerian life was the family. Men were the head of the family. Women ran the home and cared for the children.

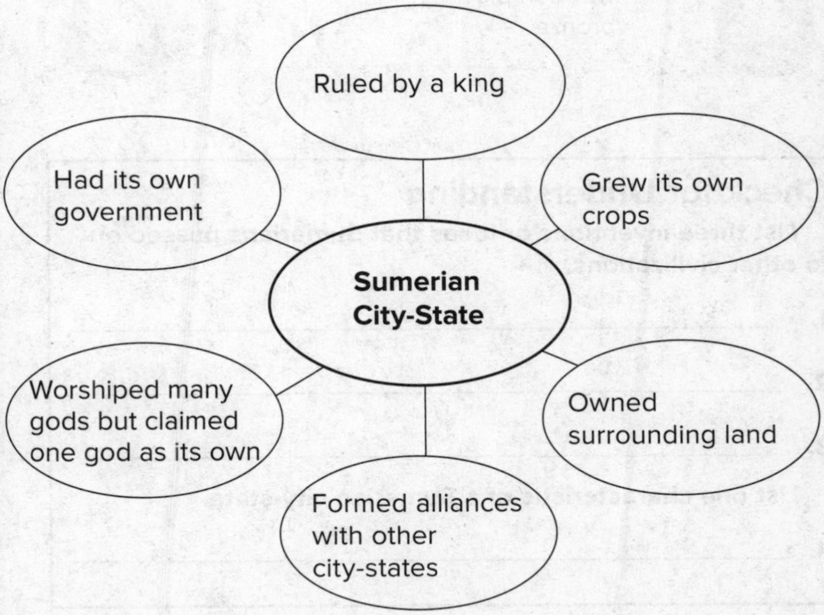

NAME ____________________ DATE __________ CLASS ________

networks

Sumerian Contributions

Sumerians created a way of writing called **cuneiform**. Cuneiform was written by using wedge-shaped marks cut into damp clay. Only a few people learned to read and write cuneiform. Some of these people became **scribes**. A scribe is a person who records business dealings and important events.

The oldest known story in the world comes from Sumer. This story is called the *Epic of Gilgamesh*. An **epic** is a long poem that tells the story of a hero.

The Sumerians made many useful inventions. An invention is something new that is made. The Sumerians were the first people to use the wheel. They were also the first to use sailboats and wooden plows. In addition, they were the first to make bronze out of copper and tin.

The Sumerians studied mathematics and astronomy. Astronomy is the study of planets, stars, and other objects in space. By watching the position of the stars they learned the best times to plant crops.

Sumerian Inventions

- cuneiform
- wheel
- sailboats
- wooden plows
- bronze

/ / / / / / / / / / / / / / Glue Foldable here / / / / / / / / / / / / / /

Check for Understanding

List three inventions or ideas that Sumerians passed on to other civilizations.

1. ____________________

2. ____________________

3. ____________________

List one characteristic of a Sumerian city-state.

4. ____________________

Analyzing

8. Do you think people had to go to school to become scribes? Explain.

____

____

Reading Check

9. Why did the Sumerians invent a writing system?

____

____

____

FOLDABLES®

10. Place a one-tab Foldable along the dotted line to cover the Check for Understanding. Label the anchor tab *Sumer's Civilization*. In the middle of the tab write *Sumerian Life*.

Make a memory map by drawing five arrows around the title and writing words or phrases that you remember about life in Sumer. Use your notes to help you complete the lists.

NAME _______________ DATE _______ CLASS _______

networks

Mesopotamia

Lesson 2 Mesopotamian Empires

ESSENTIAL QUESTION

Why does conflict develop?

GUIDING QUESTIONS

1. *How did Mesopotamia's first empires develop?*
2. *How did the Assyrians influence Southwest Asia?*
3. *Why was Babylon an important city in the ancient world?*

Terms to Know

empire a group of many different lands under one ruler

tribute a payment made to a ruler or state as a sign of surrender

province a district within a larger country or empire

caravan a group of merchants traveling together for safety, usually with a large number of camels

astronomer a person who studies stars, planets, and the moon

Where in the world?

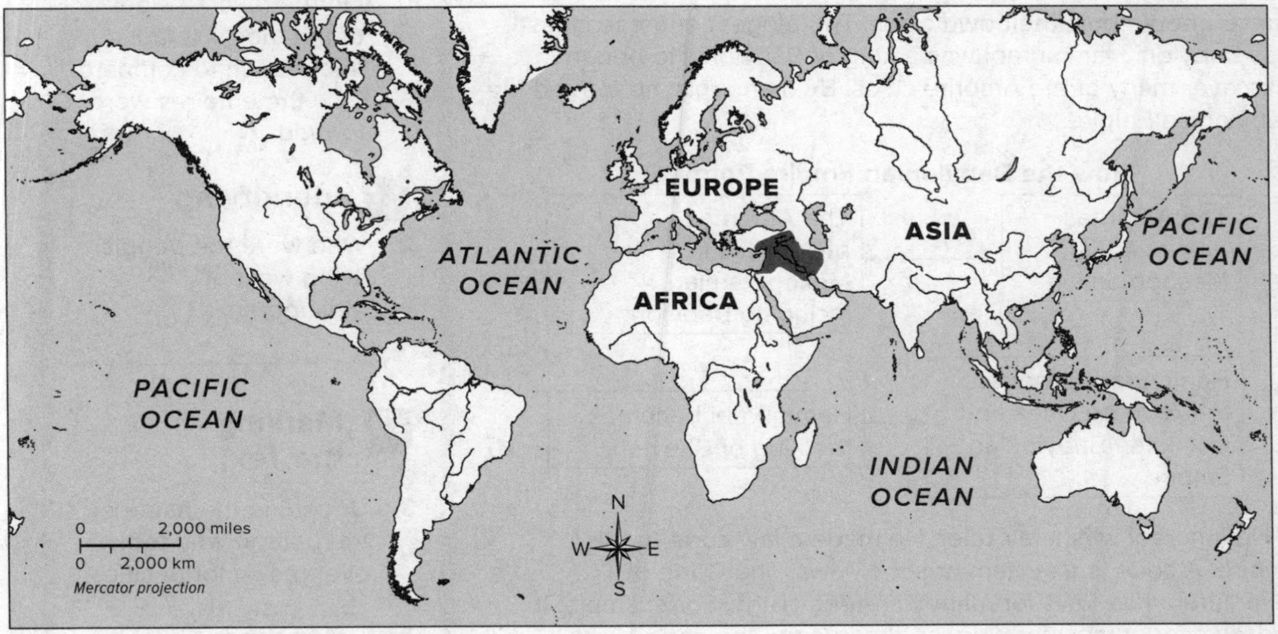

When did it happen?

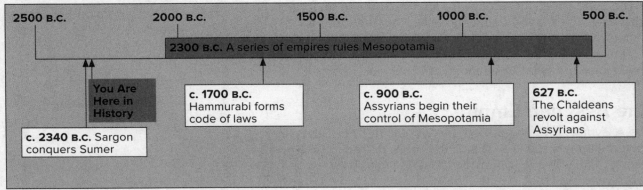

2500 B.C. | 2000 B.C. | 1500 B.C. | 1000 B.C. | 500 B.C.

2300 B.C. A series of empires rules Mesopotamia

c. 2340 B.C. Sargon conquers Sumer

You Are Here in History

c. 1700 B.C. Hammurabi forms code of laws

c. 900 B.C. Assyrians begin their control of Mesopotamia

627 B.C. The Chaldeans revolt against Assyrians

NAME ______________________ DATE ____________ CLASS ________

networks

Lesson 2 Mesopotamian Empires, *Continued*

The First Empires

The city-states of Sumer often fought each other. By 2400 B.C., the fighting weakened these city-states. The kingdom of Akkad was in northern Mesopotamia. Akkad's leader, Sargon, and his armies fought the city-states of Sumer. One at a time, Sargon defeated them all. He then united Akkad and Sumer to form an **empire.** An empire is a group of different lands under one ruler. The empire of Sargon was the first known empire ever formed. In time, the empire grew to include all of Mesopotamia. It lasted for more than 200 years.

A people called the Amorites lived in a region west of Mesopotamia. They took over Mesopotamia in the 1800s B.C. These people built their own cities. The biggest of these cities was Babylon. Hammurabi was a king of Babylon. He began to take over many of the Amorite cities. By doing this, he formed the Babylonian Empire.

How the Babylonian Empire Formed

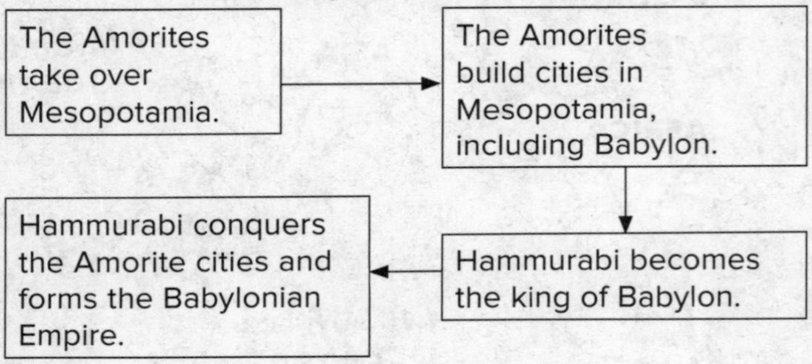

Hammurabi was a fair ruler. He made a law code for his empire. A code is a system or set of laws. The Code of Hammurabi had laws for many different things. For example, it had laws for crimes, farming, and marriage. The code had a punishment for each crime.

The code called for "an eye for an eye, and a tooth for a tooth." What does this mean? If a man knocked out the teeth of someone, then the man would have his own teeth knocked out as punishment. The Code of Hammurabi shaped later law codes. These later codes included those of Greece and Rome.

The Assyrian Empire

The Assyrians lived in northern Mesopotamia. They built a large, powerful army. Around 900 B.C., this army started to take over Mesopotamia. The Assyrians destroyed towns. They robbed people and set crops on fire. The Assyrians forced the people

Glue Foldable here

FOLDABLES®

Listing

1. Place a three-tab Venn diagram Foldable along the dotted line. Label the top tab *Akkad*, the middle tab *Empire of Sargon*, and the bottom tab *Sumer*. On the reverse sides of the tabs, list facts about each to compare how the empires were formed.

Identifying

2. Who were the people living west of Mesopotamia?

____

Marking the Text

3. Underline the name of the person who took over the Amorite cities.

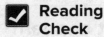

Reading Check

4. Why was Hammurabi's Code important?

____

____

____

Lesson 2 Mesopotamian Empires, *Continued*

Defining

5. What is *tribute*?

Identifying

6. Who ruled the Assyrian empire?

Reading Check

7. Why was Assyria's army so strong?

Comparing

8. How were the Assyrians similar to the Babylonians?

Marking the Text

9. Circle the length of time that the Assyrian Empire lasted.

they defeated to pay them money. This forced payment is called a **tribute.**

Why was the Assyrian army so strong? One reason was their weapons. They made their weapons out of iron. Before this, people made weapons out of tin or copper. Iron is much stronger than tin or copper.

Nineveh was the major city of the Assyrian Empire. This city was located along the Tigris River. The empire was ruled by a king. It was divided into regions called **provinces.** Roads connected the provinces. The king chose a person to rule each province. These people were under the control of the king.

The Assyrians used law codes. These codes had harsh punishments. The Assyrians worshiped the same gods as the Babylonians. The Assyrians built large temples and palaces. They also wrote stories. They put these works in a large library in Nineveh. It was one of the first libraries in the world.

The Assyrians did a large amount of trading. They brought in wood and metal from far away. They used these materials to make buildings, tools, and weapons.

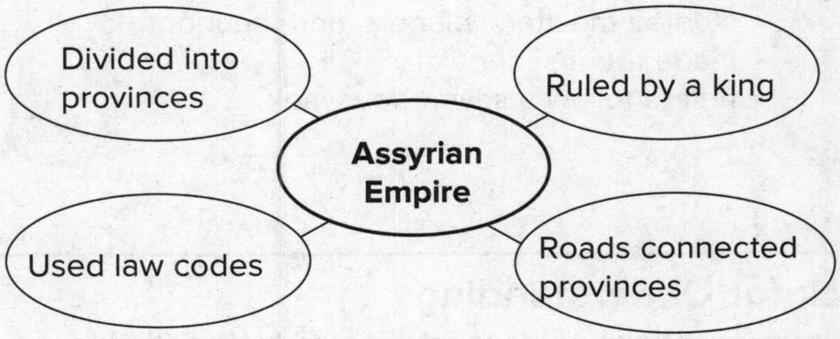

The Chaldean Empire

The Assyrian Empire lasted for about 300 years. Around 650 B.C., the Assyrians began to argue about who would be the next ruler. Their arguments turned into fights. This weakened the empire. While the Assyrians were divided, a group of people called the Chaldeans fought the Assyrians and defeated them.

The Chaldeans took over the lands held by the Assyrians. They moved the capital to Babylon. The empire of the Chaldeans is sometimes called the New Babylonian Empire. King Nabopolassar was the first ruler. After he died, his son took control. His son was named Nebuchadnezzar.

Lesson 2 Mesopotamian Empires, *Continued*

King Nebuchadnezzar rebuilt Babylon. He made it the largest and richest city in the world. Large walls surrounded the city. The city had many temples and palaces. The king also built the Hanging Gardens of Babylon. These gardens had many levels. The plants were watered by an irrigation system.

A major trade route went through Babylon. As a result, many caravans passed through the city. A **caravan** is a group of traveling merchants. The merchants bought goods in Babylon. These goods included cloth, baskets, and jewelry. Babylon grew rich from this trade.

The people of Babylon also made advances in science. Chaldean **astronomers** studied the stars, planets, and the moon. The Chaldeans made the first sundial to measure time. They also were the first to use a seven-day week.

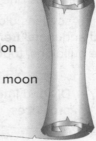

Contributions of the New Babylonian Empire

- built the Hanging Gardens of Babylon
- promoted trade
- studied the stars, planets, and the moon
- made the first sundial
- first to follow a seven-day week

Glue Foldable here

Check for Understanding

List two inventions or ideas introduced by the Chaldeans.

1. ______________________

2. ______________________

Who was Nebuchadnezzar? What contributions did he make to the city of Babylon?

3. ______________________

____

Explaining

10. What effect did caravans have on Babylon? Explain.

____

____

____

Reading Check

11. Which wonder of the ancient world was located in Babylon?

____

____

FOLDABLES®

12. Place a one-tab Foldable along the dotted line to cover the Check for Understanding. Label the anchor tab *The First Empires*. Draw a large circle and write *Chaldean Empire* along the edge of the circle. Draw a smaller circle inside the large circle and label it *Babylon*. Inside each circle, write two or more words and phrases that you remember about each title.

NAME________________________ DATE ______________ CLASS ________

networks

Ancient Egypt and Kush

Lesson 1 The Nile River

ESSENTIAL QUESTION

How does geography influence the way people live?

GUIDING QUESTIONS

1. ***Why was the Nile River important to the ancient Egyptians?***
2. ***How did the ancient Egyptians depend on the Nile River to grow their crops?***
3. ***How did Egypt become united?***

Terms to Know

cataracts dangerous, fast-moving waters

delta a fan-shaped area of marshy land near where a river flows into the sea

shadoof a bucket attached to a long pole, used to move water for irrigation

papyrus a reed plant that grows along the Nile River

hieroglyphics a writing system made up of picture and sound symbols

dynasty a line of rulers from one family

Where in the world?

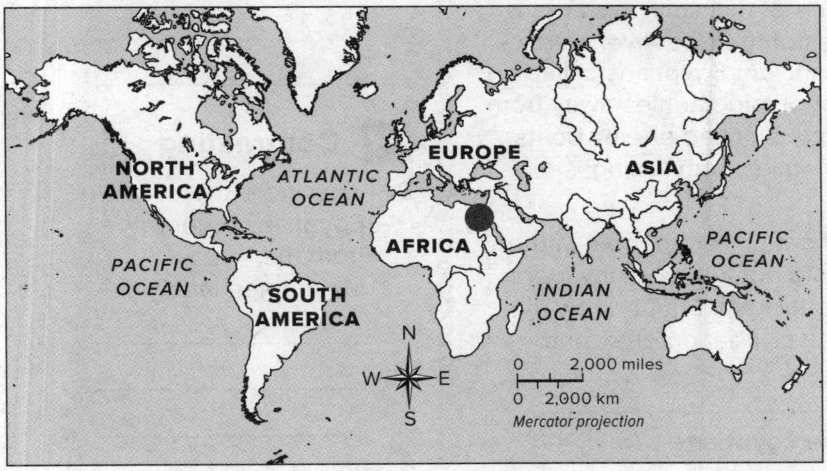

When did it happen?

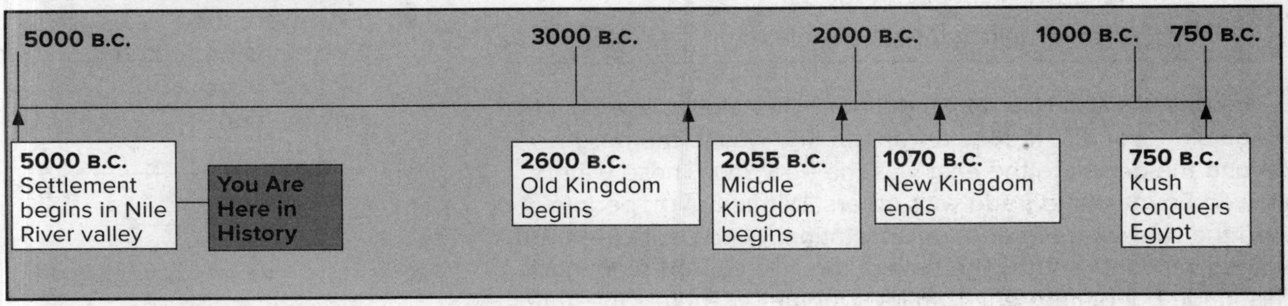

The Nile River Valley

By 5000 B.C., hunters and gatherers had moved into the Nile River valley. They settled there, farmed the land, and built villages. These people became the earliest Egyptians.

Because Egypt gets little rainfall, Egyptians relied on the Nile River for water. They used its water for fishing, farming, cooking, and cleaning. The Nile River flows north from the heart of Africa to the Mediterranean Sea, about 4,000 miles. Two rivers meet to form the Nile. They are the Blue Nile in eastern Africa and the White Nile in central Africa. The water forms rapids where the rivers meet. These are called **cataracts.** Large ships cannot sail through the cataracts.

In Egypt, the Nile runs through a narrow valley. Just before it reaches the Mediterranean Sea, it divides into many branches. These branches spread out over an area of rich soil. This area is called a **delta.** Deserts lie on both sides of the Nile River valley. Because the deserts were so hot, the ancient Egyptians called them "the Red Land." These areas kept outside armies away from Egypt. To the south, dangerous cataracts blocked enemy boats. In the north, the delta marshes kept enemies from sailing into Egypt.

The geography of Mesopotamia did not protect people in the same way. The deserts and the rivers did not keep out invaders. Mesopotamians constantly fought off attackers. Egypt rarely faced such threats. As a result, Egyptian civilization grew and prospered.

How the Nile River Helped the Egyptians

- River provided water for drinking and growing crops
- Cataracts kept out invaders
- Marshy delta kept out enemies

The deserts and Nile rapids did not completely close Egypt to the outside world. The Mediterranean Sea was to the north. Beyond the desert to the east was the Red Sea. These waters allowed Egyptians to trade with others. Within Egypt, people used the Nile for trade and transportation. Winds from the north pushed sailboats south. The flow of the Nile carried them north. This made Egypt different from Mesopotamia. There, city-states constantly fought each other. Egyptian villages, however, had friendly contact.

Marking the Text

1. Underline the reason the Egyptians had to rely on the Nile River for water.

Defining

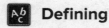

2. What are *cataracts*? What is a *delta*?

____

____

____

Contrasting

3. How were the Egyptians different from the Mesopotamians?

____

____

____

Reading Check

4. How were the Egyptians protected by their physical environment?

____

____

____

Contrasting

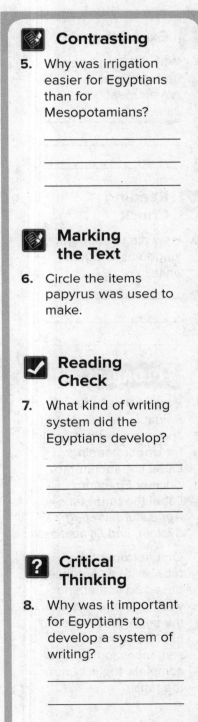

5. Why was irrigation easier for Egyptians than for Mesopotamians?

____

____

____

Marking the Text

6. Circle the items papyrus was used to make.

Reading Check

7. What kind of writing system did the Egyptians develop?

____

____

____

Critical Thinking

8. Why was it important for Egyptians to develop a system of writing?

____

____

____

People of the River

Farmers in Mesopotamia never knew when the nearby rivers would overflow or if flooding would be bad. This made it difficult to farm there. In Egypt, the Nile River also flooded, but its floods were regular. Farmers did not have to worry that floods would destroy crops or farms. Water came to the Nile from rain and melted snow. Then, during the summer, the Nile spilled over its banks. When the waters went down, they left a layer of dark, rich mud.

The Egyptians became successful farmers. They planted wheat, barley, and flax seeds. They grew enough food to feed themselves and their animals. They used irrigation when the weather was dry. To trap floodwaters, Egyptian farmers first dug basins, or bowl-shaped holes, in the earth. Then they dug canals to carry water from the basins to the fields. They used a **shadoof,** a bucket on a long pole. It could lift water from the river into the basins.

How Egyptians Farmed

- Used rich soil brought by floods
- Planted wheat, barley, and flax in wet soil
- Irrigated during dry seasons
- Dug basins and canals to catch water
- Used shadoof to move water

Egyptians also developed ways to use **papyrus.** This was a reed plant that grew along the shores of the Nile. They harvested papyrus to make baskets, sandals, and river rafts. The Egyptians also used papyrus for making writing paper. Like the Mesopotamians, Egyptians developed their own system of writing called **hieroglyphics.** It was made up of thousands of picture and sound symbols. Some symbols stood for objects and ideas. For example, to communicate the idea of a boat, a scribe would draw a tiny boat. Other symbols stood for sounds, like the letters of our own alphabet.

In ancient Egypt, few people could read and write. Some Egyptian men went to special schools to study reading and writing. They learned to become scribes, or record keepers for the rulers, priests, and traders. Some hieroglyphics conveyed public messages. Scribes carved these into stone walls and monuments. For everyday use, scribes invented a simpler script and wrote on papyrus.

Uniting Egypt

Skillful farming led to more food than was needed, or a surplus. This freed some people to work as artisans instead of farmers. Artisans wove cloth, made pottery, and carved statues. They also shaped copper into weapons and tools. Now Egyptians had goods to trade. First, they traded with each other. Then they traveled to Mesopotamia to trade. There they may have learned new ideas about writing and government.

Irrigation systems needed to be built and maintained. Grain had to be stored. Disputes over land needed to be settled. Over time, a government formed in Egypt. By 4000 B.C., Egypt was made up of two large kingdoms. Lower Egypt was in the north in the Nile delta. Upper Egypt was in the south along the Nile River.

About 3100 B.C., Narmer was king of Upper Egypt. He led his armies north and took control of Lower Egypt. Narmer's kingdom stayed together long after his death. His family passed power from father to son to grandson. This is called a **dynasty.** Over time, ancient Egypt would be ruled by 30 dynasties over a period of about 2,800 years. Historians group Egypt's dynasties into three main eras—the Old Kingdom, the Middle Kingdom, and the New Kingdom. Each kingdom had a long period of strong leadership and safety.

Check for Understanding

List three ways that the Egyptians used the Nile River.

1. _______________

2. _______________

3. _______________

List two ways Narmer changed Egypt.

4. _______________

5. _______________

Glue Foldable here

Explaining

9. Why did Egypt need an organized government?

____

____

____

Reading Check

10. How did the separate kingdoms of Egypt unite?

____

____

____

FOLDABLES®

11. Place a three-tab Foldable on the dotted line to cover the Check for Understanding. Label the anchor tab *Ancient Egyptians*. Label the three tabs—*Agriculture*, *Writing System*, and *Dynasties*.

On the front of the tabs, write a sentence based on something you remember about the importance of each title. Use your sentences to help you complete the list under the tabs.

NAME________________________ DATE ____________ CLASS ________

networks

Ancient Egypt and Kush

Lesson 2 Life in Ancient Egypt

ESSENTIAL QUESTION

What makes a culture unique?

GUIDING QUESTIONS

1. ***How was ancient Egypt governed?***
2. ***What kind of religion did the ancient Egyptians practice?***
3. ***Why and how were pyramids built?***
4. ***How was Egyptian society organized?***

Terms to Know

theocracy a government in which the same person is the political and religious leader

pharaoh ruler of ancient Egypt

bureaucrat government official

embalming the process of preserving dead bodies

pyramid a great stone tomb built for an Egyptian pharaoh

When did it happen?

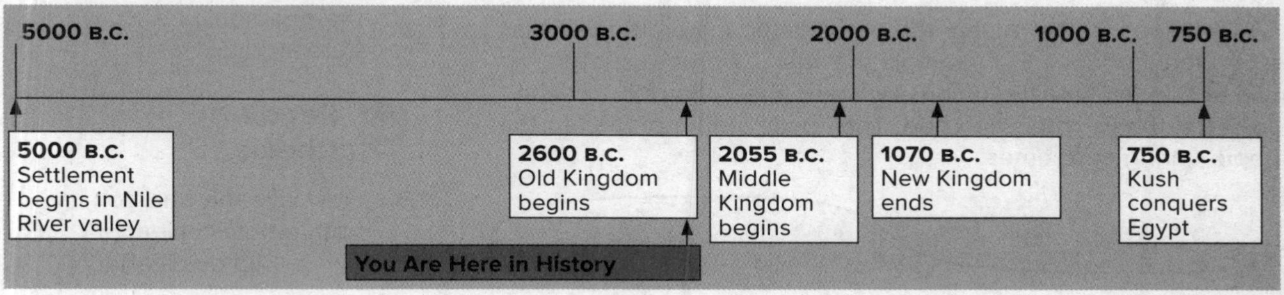

What do you know?

In the K column, list what you already know about life in ancient Egypt. In the W column, list what you want to know. After reading the lesson, fill in the L column with the information that you learned.

K	W	L

Egypt's Early Rulers

The Old Kingdom began in Egypt around 2600 B.C. It lasted about 400 years. During this time, the Egyptians built cities and expanded trade. Their kings, or **pharaohs,** set up a government. Egypt was a **theocracy.** That means that the pharaoh was both the political and religious leader.

The pharaoh had total power. He could use all the land in Egypt any way he wanted. His orders were obeyed without question. Pharaohs appointed officials called **bureaucrats.** They were in charge of irrigation canals and crop planting. They made sure grain was saved to help people get through hard times. Bureaucrats also controlled trade and collected tax payments from farmers.

As religious leader, a pharaoh participated in ceremonies that helped the kingdom. For example, he was the first to cut the grain at harvest time. Egyptians believed their pharaoh was the son of Re, the Egyptian sun god. They believed he protected the people during hard times.

Pharaoh's Duties

- to unify Egypt
- to lead during good and bad times
- to hire officials
- to give orders
- to participate in religious ceremonies

Religion in Egypt

Religion affected every part of Egyptian life. Egyptians worshiped many gods and goddesses. They believed that the gods controlled nature. The sun god, Re, was important because the sun was necessary for good crops.

Egyptians believed that life after death was better than the present life. They thought that the dead made a long journey. At the end, they reached a place of peace.

The Book of the Dead was a collection of prayers and magic spells. Egyptians studied it, learned the spells, and tried to lead good lives. They believed that if they did these things, the god Osiris would grant them life after death.

Defining

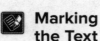

1. Define the term *theocracy.*

____

____

____

Marking the Text

2. Underline the duties of the pharaoh's bureaucrats.

Reading Check

3. How was the pharaoh both a political leader and a religious leader?

____

____

____

Examining Details

4. List three ways that religion affected life in ancient Egypt.

____

____

____

FOLDABLES®

Describing

5. Place a two-tab Foldable along the dotted line. Write *Describe* ... on the anchor tab. Label the top tab *Embalming* and the bottom tab *Pyramid Building*. Use both sides of the tabs to describe each.

Reading Check

6. Why did Egyptians protect a person's body after death?

____

____

Explaining

7. How were the pyramids built?

____

____

____

Reading Check

8. Why did the Egyptians build the pyramids?

____

____

____

Glue Foldable here

For centuries, Egyptians believed that if the pharaoh's soul reached the afterlife, he would continue to protect Egypt. To live in the afterlife, the pharaoh's soul needed a body. Eventually, Egyptians believed all people could reach the afterlife. They developed a process called **embalming** to protect the body. It involved removing organs from the dead body and then drying and wrapping the body in cloth. Embalming taught the Egyptians about the human body. They learned how to treat illnesses. They wrote down what they learned in the world's first medical books.

Pyramid Tombs

Egyptians built **pyramids,** or large triangle-shaped tombs, to hold the bodies of the pharaohs. Pyramids protected the bodies from floods, wild animals, and grave robbers. They also held the things the pharaoh might need in the afterlife, such as clothing, furniture, and jewelry.

Thousands of people worked for many years to build a pyramid. Farmers, surveyors, engineers, carpenters, stonecutters, and enslaved people all worked on pyramids.

Workers found the stone. Artisans cut it into blocks. Others tied the blocks to wooden sleds and pulled them to barges, or boats. The barges floated to the building site. There workers unloaded the blocks, pushed them up ramps, and set them in place. Each pyramid sat on a square base with a north entrance. To find true north, the Egyptians studied the sky.

Egyptians had to figure out the amount of stone and the angles for the walls. They developed and used mathematics and geometry to do this.

Egyptian Achievements

- astronomy
- a 365-day calendar
- geometry/mathematics
- a system of written numbers
- fractions

About 2540 B.C., the Egyptians built the Great Pyramid. It is located about 10 miles south of the modern city of Cairo. It is one of three pyramids still standing in Giza. The Great Pyramid is about the height of a 48-story building and is made of more than 2 million stone blocks.

Daily Life

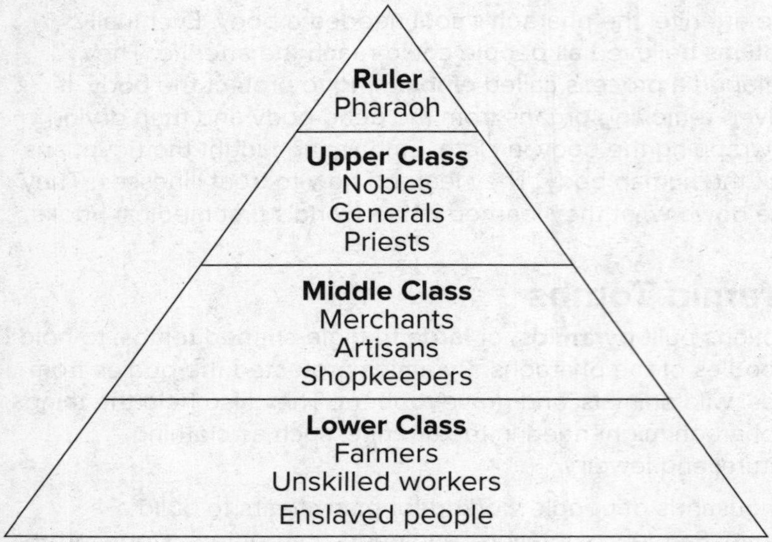

Every Egyptian had a place in society. The pharaoh and his family were at the very top. The upper class lived in cities and on large estates along the Nile. Servants waited on them. The middle class ran businesses or made goods. They lived in smaller homes. Egypt's lower class was its largest class. Most farmers lived in one-room mud homes. Unskilled workers lived in small homes with dirt floors.

In ancient Egypt, the father headed the family. Women had the right to own property, buy and sell goods, and get divorced. Few Egyptians sent their children to school. Mothers taught their daughters to run a household. Boys learned job skills from their fathers.

/ / / / / / / / / / / / / / / / Glue Foldable here / / / / / / / / / / / / / / / /

Check for Understanding

Name four duties of the pharaoh.

1. ____________________ **3.** ____________________

2. ____________________ **4.** ____________________

List two inventions by the Egyptians.

5. ____

6. ____

Reading Check

9. What types of people made up Egypt's upper class?

____

____

____

Marking the Text

10. Underline the rights of ancient Egyptian women.

FOLDABLES®

11. Place a one-tab Foldable along the dotted line to cover the Check for Understanding chart. Label the anchor tab *What made Egypt* … and write … *unique* in the middle of the tab. Make a memory map by drawing five arrows around the word and writing five things that were unique to ancient Egypt. Use your notes to help you complete the lists under the tab.

NAME _______________ DATE _______________ CLASS _______________

networks

Ancient Egypt and Kush

Lesson 3 Egypt's Empire

ESSENTIAL QUESTION

Why do civilizations rise and fall?

GUIDING QUESTIONS

1. ***Why was the Middle Kingdom a "golden age" for Egypt?***
2. ***Why was the New Kingdom a unique period in ancient Egypt's history?***
3. ***How did two unusual pharaohs change ancient Egypt?***
4. ***Why did the Egyptian empire decline in the late 1200s B.C.?***

Terms to Know

incense a material burned for its pleasant smell

envoy a person who represents his country in a foreign place

When did it happen?

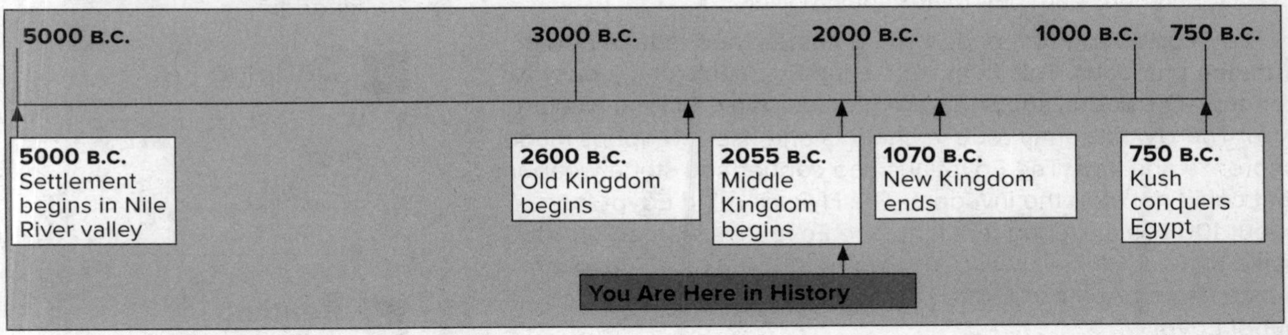

What do you know?

Read the list of pharaohs. Circle the names that you know or have heard before. For each circled name, write one fact that you know about that pharaoh.

Ahmose _______________

Hatshepsut _______________

Thutmose III _______________

Akhenaton _______________

King Tut _______________

Ramses II _______________

Glue Foldable here

A Golden Age

The Middle Kingdom lasted from about 2055 B.C. to 1650 B.C. It was a time of power, wealth, and achievement for Egypt. During the Middle Kingdom, Egypt took control of new lands. The pharaoh required tribute, or payments from the conquered peoples. The pharaoh used this wealth to build dams and improve farmlands. The pharaoh also built a canal between the Nile River and the Red Sea.

During the Middle Kingdom:

- Arts and architecture grew more popular.
- Painters covered tombs and temples with colorful scenes.
- Sculptors created large carvings of the pharaohs, which showed the pharaohs as ordinary people.
- Pharaohs had their tombs cut into cliffs.

The Middle Kingdom ended when nobles tried to take power from the pharaohs. This fight weakened Egypt, making it easy to conquer. Outsiders, known as the Hyksos, invaded from western Asia. The Hyksos army rode in chariots and used weapons made of bronze and iron. The Egyptians had copper and stone weapons that could not stop the invaders. The Hyksos ruled Egypt for about 100 years. During that time, the Egyptians learned how to make and use Hyksos weapons. Around 1550 B.C., an Egyptian prince named Ahmose formed an army and drove the Hyksos out of Egypt.

Building an Empire

Ahmose's rule began an era known as the New Kingdom. From 1550 B.C. to 1070 B.C., Egypt grew richer and more powerful. Most pharaohs focused on bringing other lands under their control.

About 1473 B.C., a queen named Hatshepsut came to power. First she ruled with her husband. After he died, she made herself pharaoh and ruled for her young nephew. She became the first woman to rule Egypt by herself.

Hatshepsut used trade to expand the empire. During her rule, Egyptians traded beads, metal tools, and weapons for gold, ivory, and ebony wood. Traders also brought **incense,** a material burned for its pleasant smell. One important trading partner was Phoenicia. The Phoenicians lived on the Mediterranean. They had their own alphabet and system of writing. The Phoenicians traded goods all over the ancient world.

FOLDABLES®

Categorizing

1. Place a two-tab Foldable along the dotted line to cover the text. Label the anchor tab *Kingdoms*. Label the two tabs in order—*Middle* and *New*. Use both sides to describe what was important about each kingdom.

Defining

2. Who pays tributes and why?

____

____

Reading Check

3. How were the Egyptians able to defeat the Hyksos?

____

____

____

Identifying

4. What was unusual or special about Queen Hatshepsut?

____

____

____

Lesson 3 Egypt's Empire, *Continued*

New Kingdom rulers also sent **envoys,** or representatives, to other rulers. This was the first time in history that a group of nations worked together in this way.

When Hatshepsut died, her nephew, Thutmose III, became pharaoh. Thutmose expanded the empire through war. His armies extended the northern border of Egypt. His troops also took back control of Nubia, which had broken free from Egypt. The empire grew rich. It took gold, copper, ivory, and other goods from conquered peoples. Egypt also enslaved prisoners of war. However, it did let enslaved people own land, marry, and gain their freedom.

Hatshepsut	Thutmose III
• Expanded Egypt through trade • Was the first woman to rule Egypt	• Expanded Egypt through war • Made Egypt rich with gold and valuables from other kingdoms

Two Unusual Pharaohs

About 1370 B.C., Amenhotep IV came to the throne. He and his wife, Nefertiti, tried to lead Egypt in a new direction. The pharaohs were losing power to the priests, so Amenhotep IV started a new religion. People could worship only one god, called Aton. When the priests protested, Amenhotep IV removed many from their positions. He seized their lands and closed their temples. He changed his name to Akhenaton, or "Spirit of Aton." He began ruling Egypt from a new city.

Most Egyptians refused to accept Aton as the only god. They still worshiped many gods. The priests of the old religion were unhappy about losing their power. Army leaders believed Akhenaton was so devoted to his new religion that he did not do his job as pharaoh. Outside invaders took most of Egypt's lands in western Asia.

When Akhenaton died, his son-in-law took the throne. The new pharaoh, Tutankhamen, was only 10 years old. With help from officials and priests, he quickly restored the old religion. After nine years, Tutankhamen suddenly died. In 1922 Howard Carter, a British archaeologist, unearthed Tutankhamen's tomb and all its treasures. The boy king and his riches fascinated people living in the modern world. He became known around the world as "King Tut."

Reading Check

5. Why did the Egyptians want to trade with the Phoenicians?

____

____

____

Explaining

6. What made Hatshepsut's rule different from that of Thutmose III?

____

____

____

Paraphrasing

7. How did ancient Egypt change under Amenhotep IV?

____

____

____

Reading Check

8. Why are Akhenaton and Tutankhamen considered unusual pharaohs?

____

____

____

Recovery and Decline

The most successful leader during the New Kingdom was Ramses II. Ramses II came to power in 1279 B.C. He took back much of the territory lost by earlier pharaohs. He fought the Hittites in what is now Turkey and signed peace treaties. The Hittites and the Egyptians agreed to keep peace between them. They agreed to fight together if an enemy attacked one of them.

Under Ramses II and other New Kingdom leaders, many temples were built. The most magnificent temple was Karnak at Thebes. Karnak still impresses visitors today.

Ramses II's Accomplishments

- Regained lost lands for Egypt
- Signed peace treaties
- Built temples

The Egyptians believed that their gods and goddesses lived in the temples. Priests and priestesses served the gods by leaving food for them and by washing their statues. Temples also served as banks. Egyptians stored valuable items, such as gold jewelry, in them.

After Ramses II, Egypt's power faded. Egypt was attacked by groups with more and better weapons. By 1150 B.C., Egypt ruled only the Nile delta, a small area. Starting in 900 B.C., one outside group after another took over Egypt. These outside groups included the Libyans, the people of Kush, and the Assyrians from Mesopotamia.

/ / / / / / / / / / / / / / Glue Foldable here / / / / / / / / / / / / / /

Check for Understanding

List one accomplishment for each pharaoh.

1. Ahmose ____________________

2. Hatshepsut ____________________

3. Thutmose III ____________________

4. Amenhotep IV ____________________

5. Tutankhamen ____________________

6. Ramses II ____________________

Reading Check

9. What were the accomplishments of Ramses II?

____

____

____

Marking the Text

10. Circle the groups that took over Egypt after its decline.

FOLDABLES®

11. Place a one-tab Foldable along the dotted line to cover the Check for Understanding. Label the anchor tab *Powers and Responsibilities*. Write *Egyptian Pharaohs* in the middle of the tab. Make a memory map by drawing five arrows around the title. Write five words or phrases that you remember about the pharaohs. Use your notes to help you with the list under the tabs.

NAME ______________________ DATE ____________ CLASS ________

networks

Ancient Egypt and Kush

Lesson 4 The Kingdom of Kush

ESSENTIAL QUESTION

Why do civilizations rise and fall?

GUIDING QUESTIONS

1. ***How did Nubia and Egypt influence each other?***
2. ***Why did the kingdom of Kush prosper?***

Terms to Know

savanna a flat grassland, sometimes with scattered trees, in a tropical or subtropical region

textile woven cloth

When did it happen?

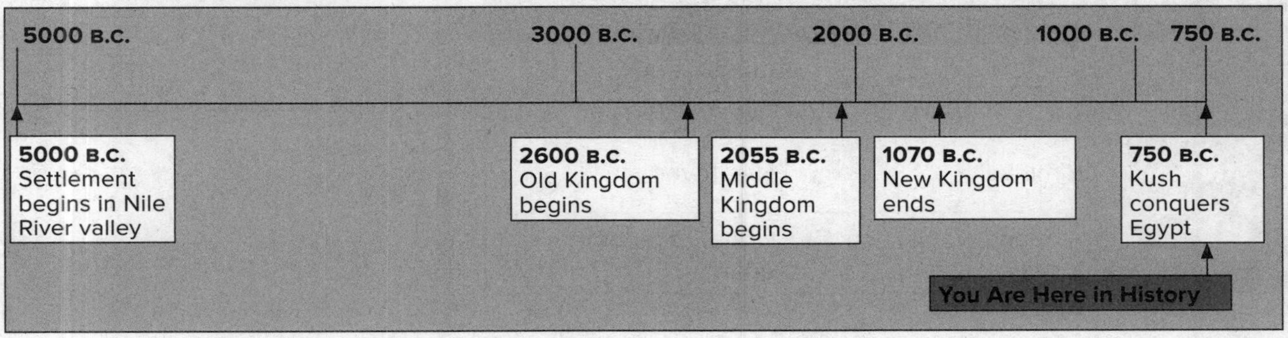

What do you know?

Read each statement. Circle T if you think the statement is true. Circle F if you think the statement is false.

1. All civilizations that lived by the Nile River were the same.	T	F
2. The Egyptians were the only civilization to build pyramids.	T	F
3. The kingdom of Kush became famous for making iron.	T	F
4. The first people to settle in Nubia were farmers.	T	F
5. Egypt ruled Nubia for 700 years.	T	F
6. The capitals of Kush were near the Nile River.	T	F

The Nubians

Egypt was not the only civilization along the Nile River. The Nubians lived along the Nile River south of Egypt. Nubia later became known as Kush. Today this area is the country of Sudan.

The first Nubians were cattle herders. Their cattle grazed on **savannas,** or grassy plains. These savannas still stretch across Africa south of the Sahara. Nubia got plenty of rainfall throughout the year. As a result, farmers did not need water from the Nile River. They settled in villages and grew crops such as beans, yams, and rice. The Nubians also hunted for food. They were very skilled at using bows and arrows.

	Nubia	Egypt
Land	savannas	desert lands river valley
Water Source	rainfall	Nile River
Crops	beans, yams, rice, grains	wheat, rice, other grains

Over time, stronger Nubian villages conquered weaker ones. In this way, the kingdom of Kerma was formed. Farming and gold mining made Kerma wealthy.

The location of the kingdom in the Nile valley helped Kerma become an important trade center. It connected Egypt with the tropical areas of southern Africa. From Kerma, the Egyptians acquired cattle, gold, incense, ivory, giraffes, and leopards. They also obtained enslaved people. Egyptians also hired Nubians to fight in their armies because of their skills in battle.

Kerma's craft-makers made fine pottery, jewelry, and metal goods. As in Egypt, Kerma's kings were buried in tombs with their personal belongings. These belongings often included gold, jewelry, and pottery.

In the 1400s B.C., the armies of Egyptian pharaoh Thutmose III invaded Nubia. After a 50-year war, Kerma collapsed. The Egyptians ruled it for the next 700 years.

During this time, the people of Nubia adopted many Egyptian beliefs and ways of doing things. For example, they worshipped Egyptian gods and goddesses along with their own. They worked with copper and bronze to make tools. They also adapted

Defining

1. What are *savannas*?

____

____

____

Explaining

2. How was Nubia's land different from Egypt's?

____

____

____

Marking the Text

3. Underline the items that Egypt received in trade from Kerma.

Reading Check

4. Why did Kerma become an important center for trade?

____

____

____

Lesson 4 The Kingdom of Kush, *Continued*

Marking the Text

5. Circle the names of the first two Kush rulers of Egypt.

Critical Thinking

6. How did learning to make iron help the Kushites?

____

____

____

Identifying

7. Name two items that helped Meroë become an iron-making center.

____

____

____

Egyptian hieroglyphics to their own language and created an alphabet.

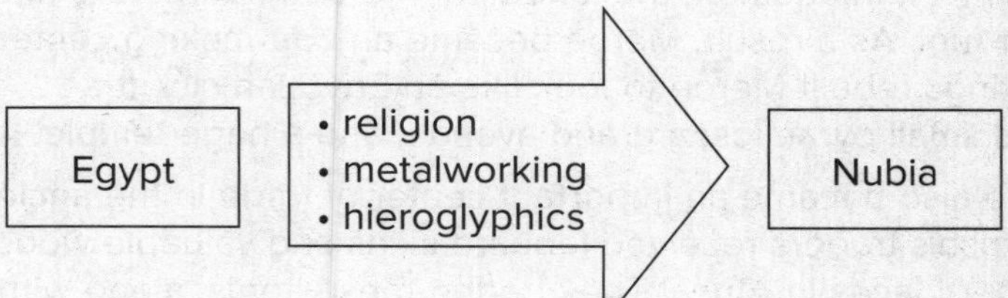

The Kushite Kingdom

By 850 B.C., the Nubians had formed the kingdom of Kush. Powerful Kushite kings ruled for the next few centuries. Their capital was the city of Napata. It was located along the upper part of the Nile River. Trade caravans carried gold, ivory, valuable woods, and other goods from central Africa to Kush and then on to Egypt.

In time, Kush became strong enough to stand up to Egypt. About 750 B.C., a Kushite king named Kashta headed north. He began the conquest of Egypt. After Kashta died, his son Piye completed the conquest in 728 B.C. He ruled both Egypt and Kush from the city of Napata. Even though the Kushites had become the rulers, the people continued to have a high opinion of Egyptian culture. The kings of Kush built temples and monuments similar to those built by the Egyptians. The people of Kush built small pyramids in which to bury their kings. They also continued to believe in Egyptian gods.

Kushite Kings	
Kashta	**Piye**
• Led Kushites north • Began to conquer Egypt	• Completed conquest • Ruled Egypt and Kush from Napata

Kush's rule over Egypt was short. In 671 B.C., the Assyrians invaded Egypt. They drove the Kushites back to their homeland. The Kushites, however, gained something from the Assyrians—the secret to making iron. The Kushites became the first Africans to make iron. Soon, farmers in Kush could use iron to make stronger plows. With better tools, they could grow more crops. Kush's warriors also began using iron spears and swords.

Lesson 4 The Kingdom of Kush, *Continued*

In about 540 B.C., Kush's rulers moved to the city of Meroë. It became the capital city. Like Napata, the new capital was near the Nile River. In addition, the land near Meroë had iron ore and trees for fuel. As a result, Meroë became an iron-making center. Kush's kings rebuilt Meroë to look like an Egyptian city. It included small pyramids, a grand avenue, and a huge temple.

Meroë also became an important center of trade in the ancient world. Kush's traders received leopard skins and valuable woods from other places in Africa. They traded these items, along with their own iron products, to places as far away as Arabia, India, China, and Rome. Enslaved people were also traded. In return they brought back cotton **textiles**, or woven cloth, and other goods.

Kush stayed a powerful trading kingdom for nearly 600 years. By the A.D. 200s, the kingdom began to weaken. Then another kingdom called Axum came to power. Axum started near the Red Sea in eastern Africa. It was located in the present-day country of Ethiopia. Around A.D. 350, the armies of Axum invaded Kush and destroyed Meroë.

Check for Understanding

Name three ways that Egypt influenced Nubia.

1. ______________________

2. ______________________

3. ______________________

List two tools the Kushites made out of iron.

4. ______________________

5. ______________________

Glue Foldable here

Defining

8. What are *textiles*?

____

____

Identifying

9. Circle the name of the kingdom that conquered Kush.

FOLDABLES®

10. Place a three-tab Venn diagram Foldable along the dotted line to cover the Check for Understanding. Label the top tab *Egypt*, the middle tab *Both*, and the bottom tab *Nubia*. On both sides of the tabs, list facts about Egypt and Nubia to compare and contrast the kingdoms. Use your notes to help you with the lists under the tabs.

NAME______________________ DATE ____________ CLASS ________

networks

The Israelites

Lesson 1 Beginnings

ESSENTIAL QUESTION

How do religions develop?

GUIDING QUESTIONS

1. ***What did the ancient Israelites believe?***
2. ***How did the Israelites settle Canaan?***

Terms to Know

prophet a messenger sent by God to share God's word with people

monotheism the belief in only one God

tribe a group of people who share a family member in the past

Exodus the journey of the Israelites out of slavery in Egypt

covenant an agreement with God

Torah the teachings that Moses received from God on Mount Sinai; later they became a part of the Hebrew Bible

commandment a rule that God wanted the Israelites to follow

alphabet a group of letters that stand for the sounds made when talking

Where in the world?

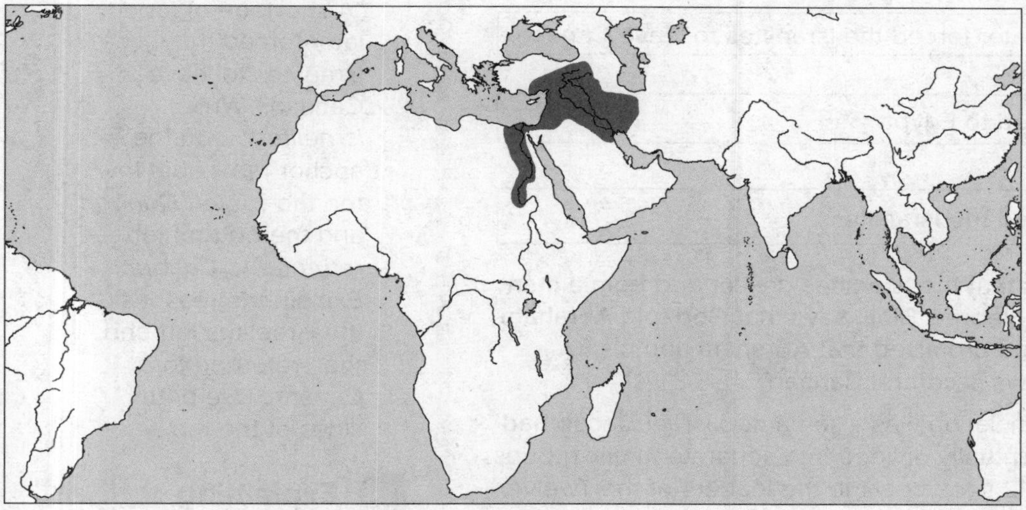

When did it happen?

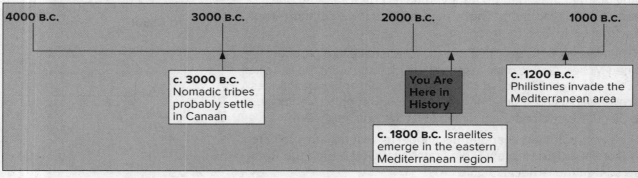

4000 B.C. — 3000 B.C. — 2000 B.C. — 1000 B.C.

c. 3000 B.C. Nomadic tribes probably settle in Canaan

You Are Here in History

c. 1800 B.C. Israelites emerge in the eastern Mediterranean region

c. 1200 B.C. Philistines invade the Mediterranean area

Beginnings

Around 1800 B.C., a group called the Israelites appeared in southwest Asia. The Israelites were different from many other groups at the time. They practiced **monotheism.** This means they believed in one God. Other groups practiced polytheism, the worship of more than one god.

The Israelites also believed that God sent **prophets.** These prophets were messengers who shared God's words. The Israelites wrote about their religious beliefs and history. Some of these writings became the Hebrew Bible. These beliefs eventually became a religion called Judaism. Today, the followers of this religion are called Jews.

According to the Hebrew Bible, God told Abraham to settle in Canaan.

↓

A shortage of food later forced the Israelites to leave Canaan.

↓

Many Israelites moved to Egypt.

↓

The pharaoh enslaved the Israelites.

Jewish belief states that the Israelites descended from a man named Abraham. The Hebrew Bible says that God told Abraham to settle in Canaan. God promised that Abraham and his descendants would always control Canaan.

Abraham's grandson Jacob was also named Israel. Jacob had 12 sons. His family eventually divided into separate family groups, called **tribes.** Jacob's 12 sons became the leaders of the Twelve Tribes of Israel.

A shortage of food later forced the Israelites to leave Canaan. Many of them moved to Egypt. Eventually, Egypt's leader, the pharaoh, enslaved them. The Israelites had to work at hard labor. They prayed to God for freedom.

The Hebrew Bible says that one day God spoke to a prophet named Moses. God told Moses to tell the pharaoh to let the Israelites go. The pharaoh refused, so God sent 10 plagues to Egypt. Plagues are events that cause great problems for many people. Eventually, the plagues convinced the pharaoh to let the Israelites leave.

The pharaoh then changed his mind. He sent his army to catch the Israelites. The Hebrew Bible states that God parted the Red Sea so that the Israelites could cross.

Glue Foldable here

Defining

1. What is a *prophet*?

____

____

____

FOLDABLES®

Explaining

2. Place a two-tab Foldable along the dotted line to cover the text that begins "A shortage of food later forced the Israelites to leave Canaan." Write *Israelites* . . . on the anchor tab. Label the top tab . . . *left Canaan* and the bottom tab . . . *returned to Canaan.* Explain the reasons the Israelites left and then returned to Canaan. Use both sides of the tab.

Explaining

3. According to the Hebrew Bible, why did God send 10 plagues to Egypt?

____

____

____

Examining Details

4. List three details about the Ten Commandments.

____

____

____

Reading Check

5. How did the Israelites' beliefs differ from most other ancient peoples?

____

____

____

Explaining

6. What challenge did the Israelites face when they returned to Canaan?

____

____

Analyzing

7. How could an alphabet have helped the Phoenicians trade?

____

____

____

When the Egyptians followed, they drowned. The journey of the Israelites out of Egypt is called the **Exodus.** The Jewish holy festival of Passover celebrates their freedom from slavery.

During their journey, the Israelites received a **covenant,** or agreement, with God. The Hebrew Bible says God promised to guide the Israelites safely back to Canaan. The Israelites promised to follow his teachings. The teachings are known as the **Torah.** These teachings later became part of the Hebrew Bible.

The Ten Commandments are part of the Torah. A **commandment** was a rule that God wanted the Israelites to follow. The laws of many nations are also based on principles in the Ten Commandments.

Person	Role
Abraham	God promised that his descendants would always control Canaan.
Jacob	His 12 sons became leaders of the Twelve Tribes of Israel.
Moses	He led the Israelites out of slavery in Egypt; this event is known as the Exodus.

The Land of Canaan

The Hebrew Bible says that Moses died before reaching Canaan. A new leader named Joshua led the Israelites to Canaan. They found other groups already living there. Two of these groups were the Phoenicians and the Philistines. These groups had different beliefs and ways of life than the Israelites.

The Phoenicians lived in cities by the Mediterranean coast. They became skilled sailors and traders. Soon, the Phoenicians controlled Mediterranean shipping and trade. This helped spread Phoenician ideas. They developed an **alphabet** to help them trade. An alphabet is a group of letters that stands for sounds made when talking. Their alphabet influenced the Greek and Roman alphabets. We still use the Roman alphabet today.

The other group was the Philistines. They came from near present-day Greece. The Philistines made iron tools and weapons. They built walled towns and a put together a strong army.

Lesson 1 Beginnings, *Continued*

The Israelites believed that God wanted them to claim Canaan as their homeland. According to the Hebrew Bible, Joshua led them into battle to achieve this goal. At the city of Jericho, the Israelites marched around the city walls for six days. On the seventh day, the walls fell. The Israelites took control of Jericho.

Joshua led the Israelites into other battles. They divided the lands they captured between the 12 tribes. When Joshua died, leaders called judges ruled the tribes. The judges settled disputes and led troops into battle. A woman judge named Deborah became known for her bravery. She helped advise troops in battle.

After many battles, the Israelites won control of central Canaan. The Hebrew Bible states that they worshiped God in a tabernacle. This is a large tent-like building that could be taken along as they moved from place to place. The tabernacle housed the Ark of the Covenant, a wooden chest. The Israelites believed the Ten Commandments were written on tablets kept in the Ark. They carried the Ark into battle with them. The believed it would ensure a victory, or make certain they won.

Groups living in Canaan

Phoenicians	Philistines
• sailors and traders • settled throughout Mediterranean world • created an alphabet	• settled in southern Canaan • built walled cities along Mediterranean coast • made tools and weapons; built a strong army

Check for Understanding

List two features of Judaism.

1. ______________

2. ______________

Name one reason Canaan was important to the Israelites.

3. ______________

____

Identifying

8. Who was Deborah?

____

Reading Check

9. Who were the Phoenicians, and what was their major contribution to world civilization?

____

FOLDABLES®

10. Place a one-tab Foldable along the dotted line to cover the Check for Understanding. Label the anchor tab *Beliefs and God's Promises*. In the middle of the Foldable, write *The Hebrew Bible*. Draw five arrows around the title. List five words or phrases about the beliefs outlined in the Hebrew Bible.

Glue Foldable here

NAME ______________________ DATE ______________ CLASS ____________

networks

The Israelites

Lesson 2 The Israelite Kingdom

ESSENTIAL QUESTION

What are the characteristics of a leader?

GUIDING QUESTIONS

1. ***What was the role of kings in Israelite history?***
2. ***How did neighboring empires respond to the Israelites?***

Terms to Know

psalm a sacred song or poem used in worship

proverb a wise or familiar saying that shares lessons for living

exile a period of time when people are forced to live away from their homes

Where in the world?

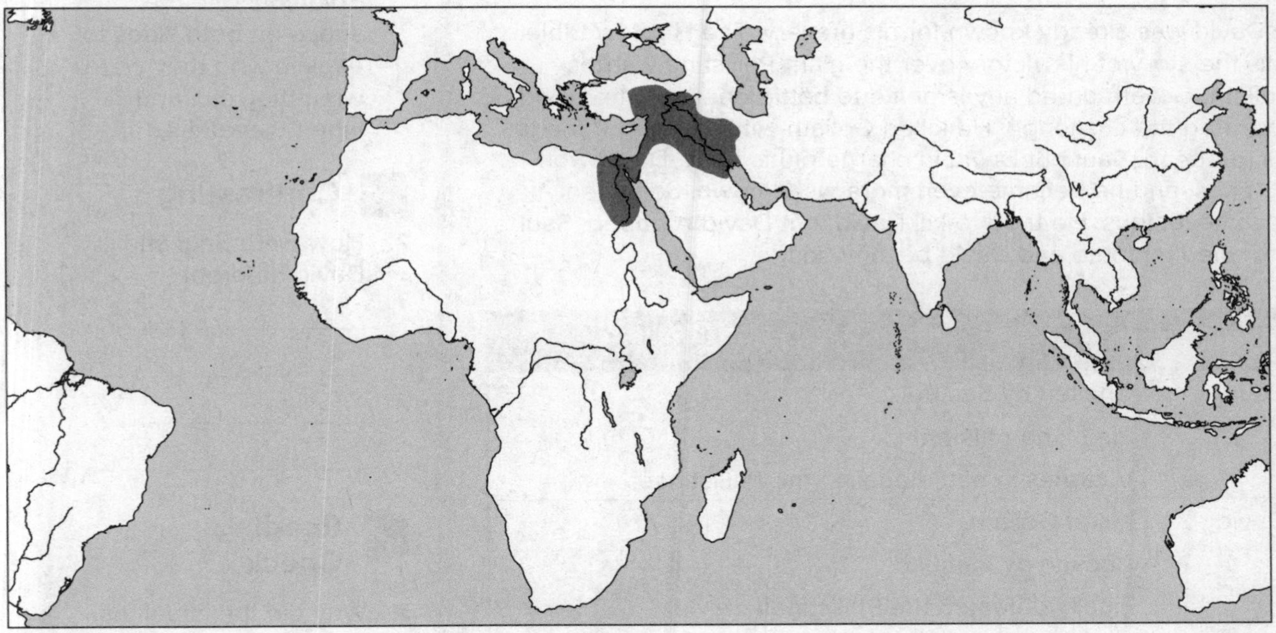

When did it happen?

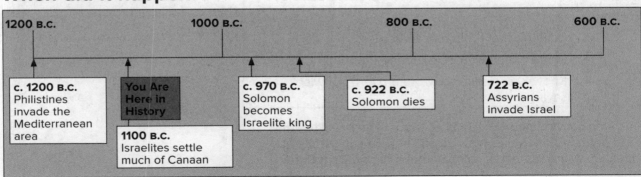

1200 B.C. — 1000 B.C. — 800 B.C. — 600 B.C.

- **c. 1200 B.C.** Philistines invade the Mediterranean area
- You Are Here in History
- **1100 B.C.** Israelites settle much of Canaan
- **c. 970 B.C.** Solomon becomes Israelite king
- **c. 922 B.C.** Solomon dies
- **722 B.C.** Assyrians invade Israel

Glue Foldable here

Early Kings

The Israelites had settled much of Canaan by 1100 B.C. However, they feared the powerful Philistines. The Israelites called for a king to unite them against this enemy. They asked the judge Samuel to choose a king. He warned that a king would tax or enslave them. Still, the Israelites demanded a king. Samuel chose Saul to become the first Israelite king.

Saul helped the Israelites win many battles against the Philistines. However, according to the Hebrew Bible, he disobeyed some of God's commands. God told Samuel to choose a new king. Samuel then chose a young shepherd named David to be king.

David was already known for his bravery. The Hebrew Bible tells the story of his victory over the giant Philistine warrior, Goliath. Goliath dared any Israelite to battle one-on-one. David accepted the challenge. He killed Goliath with a single stone to his forehead. Saul put David in charge of his army. David won victories, and he became even more well-known. Saul then became jealous. He tried to kill David, but David escaped. Saul later died in battle and David became king.

King	Known For
Saul	Chosen by Samuel First king of Israel Victories in battle against the Philistines
David	Killed Goliath Chosen by Samuel Finally defeated the Philistines Built the capital city of Jerusalem Wrote sacred poems and songs called psalms
Solomon	Son of David Built the first temple in Jerusalem Made peace with neighboring groups Known as wise, also wrote proverbs or wise sayings

As king, David united the Twelve Tribes. The Israelite army finally defeated the Philistines. David set up a capital city at Jerusalem. Many Israelites gained wealth during David's rule.

FOLDABLES®

Summarizing

1. Use a three-tab Foldable and place it along the dotted line to cover the text. Label the top tab *Saul*, the middle tab *David*, and the bottom tab *Solomon*. Use the space on both sides to explain who they were, what they did, and when they did it.

Contrasting

2. How were Saul and David different?

____

____

____

____

Reading Check

3. Why did the Israelites believe David was their greatest king?

____

____

____

Lesson 2 The Israelite Kingdom, *Continued*

Identifying

4. What two kingdoms were formed when the Israelite tribes divided?

____

____

____

Defining

5. What are *proverbs*?

____

____

____

Comparing

6. What feature did the kingdoms of Israel and Judah share in common?

____

____

____

Explaining

7. How did the Assyrians make conquered people afraid of them?

____

____

____

____

David is also believed to have written many **psalms,** sacred songs and poems. David is considered the greatest Israelite king.

After David died, his son Solomon became king. Solomon made peace with many nearby groups. He also built cities and Jerusalem's first temple. Solomon was known as a wise leader. His **proverbs** are found in the Hebrew Bible. Proverbs are familiar sayings that share lessons for living. Solomon did many good things as king. However, the Israelites eventually turned against him. They did not like working on his many building projects or paying his high taxes. After Solomon died around 922 B.C., the Israelites entered a difficult period. Their kingdom became divided and powerful neighbors threatened them.

Two Kingdoms

The 10 northern tribes rebelled against Jerusalem after Solomon died. These tribes started a new kingdom called Israel. Samaria was its capital. The two southern tribes formed Judah. The capital of this smaller kingdom was Jerusalem.

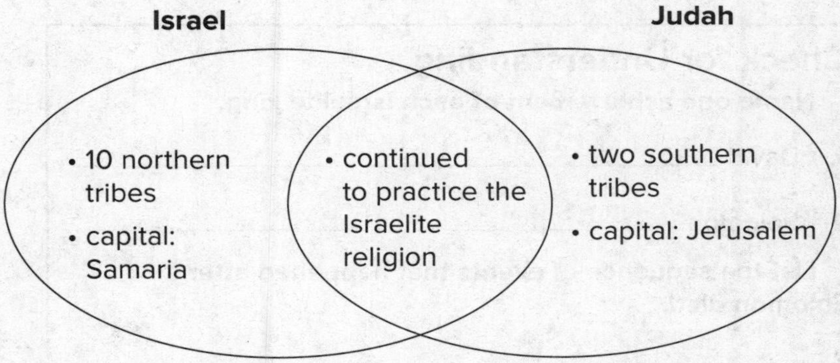

During this time, large empires grew around Israel and Judah. The Assyrians and Chaldeans became powerful. They wanted to control the trade routes that ran through the Israelite kingdoms.

The Assyrians spread fear across the region. They forced the people they conquered to pay tribute. This meant that people had to give the Assyrians money or enslaved people. If they did not receive tribute, the Assyrians would destroy buildings or entire towns. The kingdom of Israel refused to pay tribute to the Assyrians. As a result, the Assyrians invaded Israel in 722 B.C. They captured Samaria and other major cities. They wanted complete control. They brought people into Israel from other parts of the Assyrian Empire. These new settlers mixed with the Israelites. This produced a new culture, whose people were called Samaritans.

The Samaritans accepted many Israelite religious beliefs. They also adopted religious practices that the Israelites did not accept. Eventually, the two groups had little in common. Today's Judaism grew from the religious practices in the kingdom of Judah.

Later, the Chaldeans conquered Jerusalem and began making major changes. At first, the Chaldeans chose a Judean king to rule Judah. This king secretly planned to set Judah free. He did not listen to those people who warned against a revolt. After a long conflict, the Chaldeans retook the city. They then destroyed much of it, including the temple. The Chaldeans took the king and thousands of other people to live in Babylon. This time became known as the Babylonian Exile. To **exile** a people means to force them to leave their home or country.

During this difficult time, prophets played an important role in Jewish life. They provided encouragement and guidance for the Israelites. They tried to get people to change their ways. Their goal of making the world a better place influenced many people who came after them.

/ / / / / / / / / / / / / / Glue Foldable here / / / / / / / / / / / / / /

Check for Understanding

Name one achievement of each Israelite king.

1. David ______________________

2. Solomon ______________________

List the sequence of events that happened after Solomon died.

3. ______________________

4. ______________________

5. ______________________

Examining

8. Why might the Chaldeans have decided to send so many Israelites to live in Babylon?

____

____

____

Reading Check

9. What empires conquered Israel and Judah?

____

____

____

FOLDABLES®

10. Glue a one-tab Foldable along the dotted line. Label the anchor tab *Characteristics of …* and write … *early Hebrew kings* in the middle of the Foldable.

Draw five arrows pointing away from the title. Write words or phrases that you remember about early Hebrew kings.

NAME ______________________ DATE ____________ CLASS ________

networks

The Israelites

Lesson 3 The Development of Judaism

ESSENTIAL QUESTION

How does religion shape society?

GUIDING QUESTIONS

1. ***How did the people of Judah practice their religion while in exile and in their homeland?***
2. ***How did religion shape the Jewish way of life?***

Terms to Know

synagogue a Jewish house of worship
Sabbath a weekly day of worship and rest
scroll a long document made from pieces of rough paper, called parchment, and sewn together
kosher describes food that has been made according to Jewish dietary law

Where in the world?

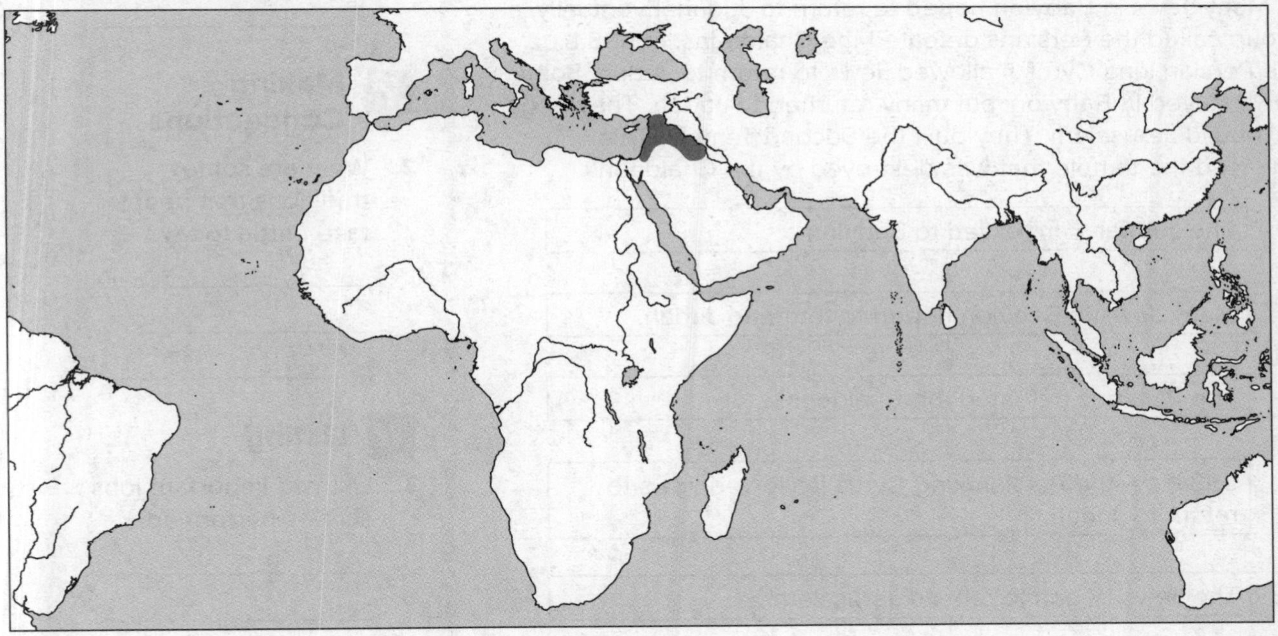

When did it happen?

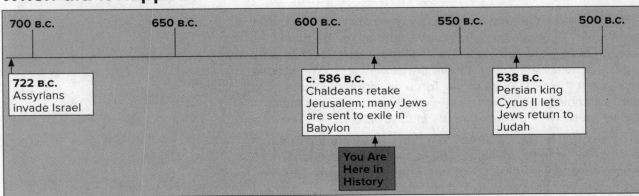

700 B.C. | 650 B.C. | 600 B.C. | 550 B.C. | 500 B.C.

722 B.C. Assyrians invade Israel

c. 586 B.C. Chaldeans retake Jerusalem; many Jews are sent to exile in Babylon

538 B.C. Persian king Cyrus II lets Jews return to Judah

You Are Here in History

Return to Judah

The Judeans' time in Babylon was called an exile. This is a period of time when people are forced to live away from their homes. During this time, they became known as the Jews. Their religion became known as Judaism.

In Babylon, the Jews did not have a large temple. Instead, they gathered in smaller houses of worship. These were called **synagogues.** The Jews came together on the **Sabbath.** This is a weekly day of rest and worship. According to tradition, it lasts from sundown Friday to nightfall Saturday. Jews still observe the Sabbath today.

Many Jews in Babylon hoped to return to Judah. Eventually, a group called the Persians defeated the Chaldeans. In 538 B.C., the Persian king Cyrus II allowed Jews to return to Judah. Some Jews stayed in Babylon, but many returned to Judah. They began to rebuild Jerusalem. They built the Second Temple. This replaced the temple that was destroyed by the Chaldeans.

The Judeans are exiled to Babylon.
↓
Many Jews in Babylon hoped to return to Judah.
↓
The Persians defeated the Chaldeans.
↓
538 B.C.—the Persian king Cyrus II allowed Jews to return to Judah.
↓
The Jews began to rebuild Jerusalem.
↓
The Jews built the Second Temple.

The Jews could not have their own government or king under Persian rule. They looked to religious leaders to guide their society. These leaders included priests and scribes. Priests were religious scholars who often taught the Jewish faith. The scribes wrote down the five books of the Torah on rough pieces of paper called parchment. They sewed these pieces together to make **scrolls.** These writings make up the Hebrew Bible.

The Hebrew Bible has three main parts. They are the Torah, the Prophets, and the Writings. The Hebrew Bible contains 24 books that were written over many centuries. It presents the laws and rules of the Israelites. It also tells about Jewish history,

Determining Cause and Effect

1. How did the exile of the Jews affect the way they practiced their religion?

____

____

____

Making Connections

2. What are some traditions that people take partin today?

____

____

____

Listing

3. List two important jobs scribes performed.

____

____

____

Marking the Text

4. Circle the parts of the text that describe the books of the Hebrew Bible.

Reading Check

5. Why did religious leaders guide Jewish society after the Jews returned from exile?

___

___

___

Contrasting

6. How did education for Jewish sons and daughters differ?

___

___

___

Identifying

7. What did Jewish women learn?

___

___

___

art, literature, poetry, and proverbs. The first book of the Hebrew Bible is Genesis. It gives the Israelite view of how humans began. Genesis also explains how God punished the world for wicked behavior. This is told through the story of Noah's ark. This book also describes why the world has many languages.

The book of Isaiah details God's plan for a peaceful world. The book of Daniel says that the Jews believed that goodness would eventually replace evil and suffering. Daniel was an adviser to a Babylonian king. He was a Jew and he refused to worship Babylonian gods. The Chaldeans threw him into a lion's den. God protected Daniel. This story reminds Jews that God will rescue them from evil. Christians and Muslims also share this hope for a better world.

The Hebrew Bible

- made up of three parts: the Torah, the Prophets, and the Writings
- includes a series of 24 books
- presents laws and rules of the Israelites
- reflects Jewish culture

Jewish Daily Life

The teachings of the Torah shaped daily life for the early Jews. These teachings affected family life, food, and clothing. The Torah required Jews to help others and treat them fairly. It also encouraged responsibility, self-control, and loyalty to God.

The Torah described roles for Jewish fathers and mothers. Jewish families valued education, especially for young men. Sons learned a trade. They also learned to read the Torah. Reading the Torah was the center of Jewish daily life. Everything the students learned, such as the alphabet or Jewish history, they learned from the Torah. This is why religious teachers became leaders in Jewish communities.

Daughters learned to be wives, mothers, and housekeepers. They studied Jewish rules about food, the Sabbath, and holidays. They also learned about women of ancient Israel, such as Ruth and her mother-in-law, Naomi.

NAME ________________________ DATE ____________ CLASS ____________

networks

Lesson 3 The Development of Judaism, *Continued*

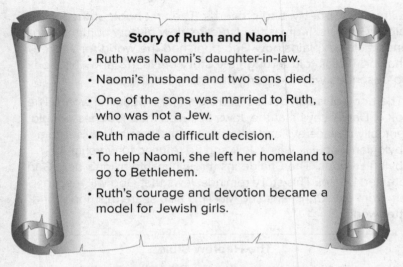

Story of Ruth and Naomi

- Ruth was Naomi's daughter-in-law.
- Naomi's husband and two sons died.
- One of the sons was married to Ruth, who was not a Jew.
- Ruth made a difficult decision.
- To help Naomi, she left her homeland to go to Bethlehem.
- Ruth's courage and devotion became a model for Jewish girls.

Jewish dietary laws tell what Jews can eat. Ancient Jews could eat only animals that were considered clean. These included cattle and sheep, but not swine (pigs). Food prepared according to Jewish dietary laws is called **kosher.** Animals used for kosher meat must be killed in a certain way. This meat is inspected, salted, and soaked in water. Jews cannot eat meat and dairy products together. They also cannot eat crab, shrimp, or other shellfish.

Check for Understanding

List five features of Judaism.

1. ____________________

2. ____________________

3. ____________________

4. ____________________

5. ____________________

Glue Foldable here

Drawing Conclusions

8. Why do you think Ruth became a model for Jewish girls?

____

____

____

Reading Check

9. Why did religious teachers become important leaders in Jewish communities?

____

____

____

FOLDABLES®

10. Place a two-tab Foldable along the dotted line to cover the Check for Understanding. Label the anchor tab *Laws of the Torah.* Label the two tabs *Family Life* and *Food.* List three words or phrases that you remember about each.

Lesson 4 The Jews in the Mediterranean World

ESSENTIAL QUESTION

Why does conflict develop?

GUIDING QUESTIONS

1. *What was life like for the Jews in Greek-ruled lands?*
2. *How did the Jews react to Roman rule of their homeland?*

Terms to Know

Diaspora the groups of Jewish people living outside of the Jewish homeland

rabbi the official leader of a Jewish congregation

Where in the world?

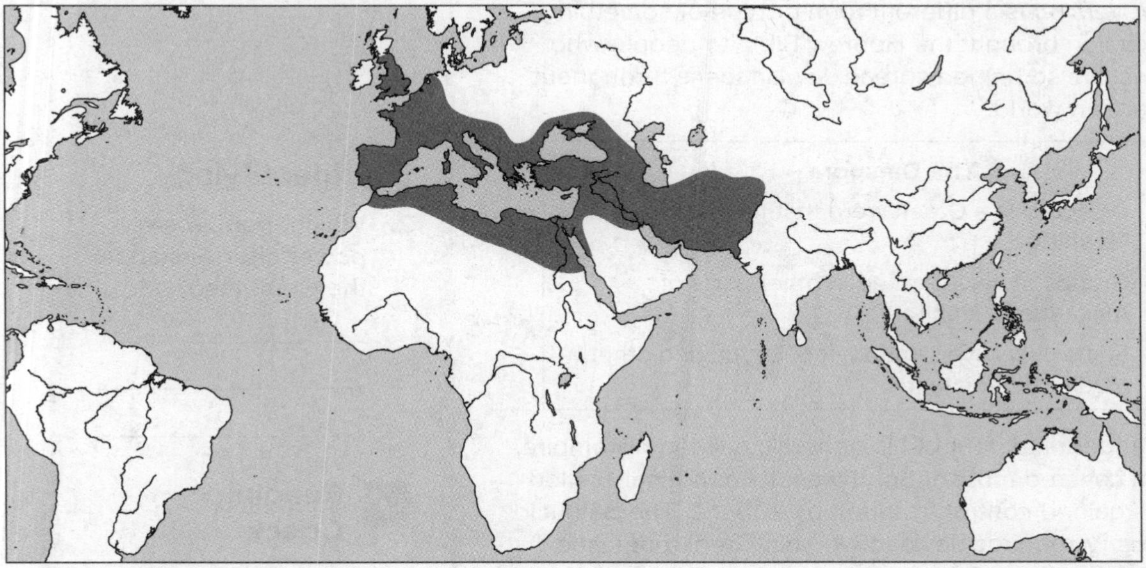

When did it happen?

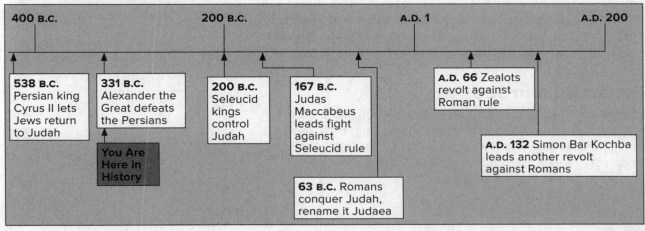

400 B.C. | 200 B.C. | A.D. 1 | A.D. 200

- **538 B.C.** Persian king Cyrus II lets Jews return to Judah
- **331 B.C.** Alexander the Great defeats the Persians
- You Are Here in History
- **200 B.C.** Seleucid kings control Judah
- **167 B.C.** Judas Maccabeus leads fight against Seleucid rule
- **63 B.C.** Romans conquer Judah, rename it Judaea
- **A.D. 66** Zealots revolt against Roman rule
- **A.D. 132** Simon Bar Kochba leads another revolt against Romans

The Arrival of Greek Rule

In 331 B.C., Alexander the Great defeated the Persians. Alexander brought Greek language and culture to Judah. He also allowed Jews to stay in Judah.

Judah remained the center of Judaism. Many Jews, however, had moved to other parts of Alexander's empire. Groups of Jews living outside Judah became known as the **Diaspora.** The members of the Diaspora remained loyal to Judaism. Many also spoke Greek and adopted parts of Greek culture. Some Jewish scholars in Egypt copied the Hebrew Bible into the Greek language. This Greek version of the Hebrew Bible is called the Septuagint. A *version* is a different form or type of something. This Greek version brought the Hebrew Bible to people who were not Jews. It also helped spread Jewish ideas throughout the Mediterranean world.

The Diaspora

- *Diaspora* is a Greek word that means "scattered."
- Groups of Jews settled in other parts of Alexander's empire.
- Some Jews lived in Babylon, Egypt, and other Mediterranean lands.

After Alexander died, four of his generals divided his empire. One kingdom covered most of Southwest Asia. A family called the Seleucids gained control of Judah by 200 B.C. The Seleucid king Antiochus IV required Jews to worship Greek gods and goddesses. Many Jews refused to give up their religion.

A priest named Judas Maccabeus led the fight against the Seleucids. His army was called the Maccabees. They drove the Seleucids out of Judah. They also removed all of the statues of Greek gods and goddesses from the temple. The annual festival of Hanukkah, an important Jewish holiday, celebrates this event.

Roman Rule in Judaea

In 63 B.C., Roman forces conquered the land of Judah and renamed it Judaea. The name *Roman* came from their capital, Rome. This city was located far away from Judaea in what is now the country of Italy. At first, the Romans chose a follower of Judaism to be the king of Judaea.

Summarizing

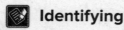

1. How did Jewish ideas spread throughout the Mediterranean world?

______

______

______

Identifying

2. Which group rose to power after Alexander the Great died?

______

______

______

Reading Check

3. How did Alexander and later the Seleucids affect the people of Judah?

______

______

______

The Israelites

Lesson 4 The Jews in the Mediterranean World, *Continued*

Marking the Text

4. Underline the accomplishments of the first king of Judaea.

Identifying

5. Which Jewish group had the support of the common people?

____

____

Contrasting

6. How did the Sadducees differ from the Essenes?

____

____

____

____

Explaining

7. What did the Zealots believe the Jews should do to gain their freedom?

____

____

____

This ruler, Herod, built forts and cities. The Second Temple in Jerusalem was also built during his reign. This temple was the center of Jewish worship.

After Herod died, Roman officials ruled Judaea. Jews began to disagree about how to practice Judaism. They also disagreed about how to interact with the Romans.

One group of Jews was called the Pharisees. They had the support of the common people. They taught in synagogues. The Pharisees worked to make Judaism a religion of the home and family. They focused on both written and oral law. Oral law is the unwritten understandings that are passed down by word of mouth.

Another group was the Sadducees, which included wealthy noble families. Many served as priests and scribes in the Temple. They focused on applying the Torah's laws to temple ceremonies. They disagreed with many of the Pharisees' teachings. For example, they rejected the idea of oral law.

A third group was called Essenes. These priests had broken away from the Temple in Jerusalem. They lived in the desert by the Dead Sea. They prayed and waited for God to deliver them from Roman rule. They also followed only the written law of the Torah. The Essenes may have written the Dead Sea Scrolls.

A fourth group, the Zealots, lived in Judaea. They believed that the Jews should fight the Romans for their freedom. In the A.D. 60s, many Jews were waiting for a deliverer. A deliverer is a person sent by God to rescue people from trouble. Anger at Roman rule reached its peak during this time. The Zealots got ready for battle.

Jewish Groups Respond to Roman Rule

Group	Response
Pharisees	• wanted Judaea free from Roman rule • urged resistance through greater devotion to the Torah
Sadducees	• favored cooperation with the Romans • wanted to keep peace and order in Judaea
Essenes	• prayed for God to deliver them from Roman rule
Zealots	• prepared to fight the Romans for their freedom

Lesson 4 The Jews in the Mediterranean World, *Continued*

In A.D. 66, the Zealots revolted. They drove the Romans from Jerusalem. However, the Romans reclaimed the city four years later. They killed thousands of Jews and forced many others to leave. The Romans also destroyed the Second Temple. Today, the Western Wall is all that remains of the Temple complex.

In A.D. 132, the Jews again revolted. The Romans also defeated this rebellion. The Jews were no longer allowed to live in or visit Jerusalem. The Romans renamed Judaea and called it Palestine.

The Jews regrouped with help from religious leaders called **rabbis.** The synagogues and rabbis became important because the Jews no longer had temples or priests. One famous rabbi was named Yohanan ben Zaccai. When the Romans captured Jerusalem in A.D. 70, he persuaded them to spare the city of Yavneh. There, he set up a school to keep teaching the Torah. His efforts helped the Jewish religion survive the destruction of the temple and the loss of Jerusalem.

The rabbis eventually put their teachings about Jewish laws in writing. These writings, along with other Jewish legal traditions, are called the Talmud. The Talmud discusses issues faced in daily life. It remains an important record of Jewish teachings.

/ / / / / / / / / / / / / / Glue Foldable here / / / / / / / / / / / / / /

Check for Understanding

For each cause, identify one effect.

Cause: Alexander the Great conquered Judah.

Effect: 1. ______________________________

Cause: The Seleucids took control of Judah.

Effect: 2. ______________________________

Cause: The Zealots rebelled against Roman rule.

Effect: 3. ______________________________

Analyzing

8. Why is the Talmud still a valuable record of Jewish law?

____

____

____

Reading Check

9. How did the rabbis help Judaism survive after the Roman conquest?

____

____

____

FOLDABLES®

10. Place a one-tab Foldable along the dotted line to cover the Check for Understanding. Write *Conflict in Judah* in the middle of the one-tab. Make a memory map by drawing five arrows around the title and writing five words or phrases that you remember about the conflict. Use your notes to help you complete the activity under the tab.

NAME_________________________ DATE ____________ CLASS ________

networks

The Ancient Greeks

Lesson 1 Rise of Greek Civilization

ESSENTIAL QUESTION

How does geography influence the way people live?

GUIDING QUESTIONS

1. ***How did physical geography influence the lives of the early Greeks?***
2. ***How did the civilization of the Minoans develop?***
3. ***How did the Mycenaeans gain power in the Mediterranean?***
4. ***How did early Greeks spread their culture?***
5. ***How did Greek city-states create the idea of citizenship?***

Where in the world?

Terms to Know

peninsula a piece of land nearly surrounded by water

bard someone who writes or performs epic poems or stories about heroes and their deeds

colony a group of people living in a new territory with close ties to their homeland; the new territory itself

polis a Greek city-state

agora a gathering place or marketplace in ancient Greece

phalanx a group of armed foot soldiers in ancient Greece arranged close together in rows

When did it happen?

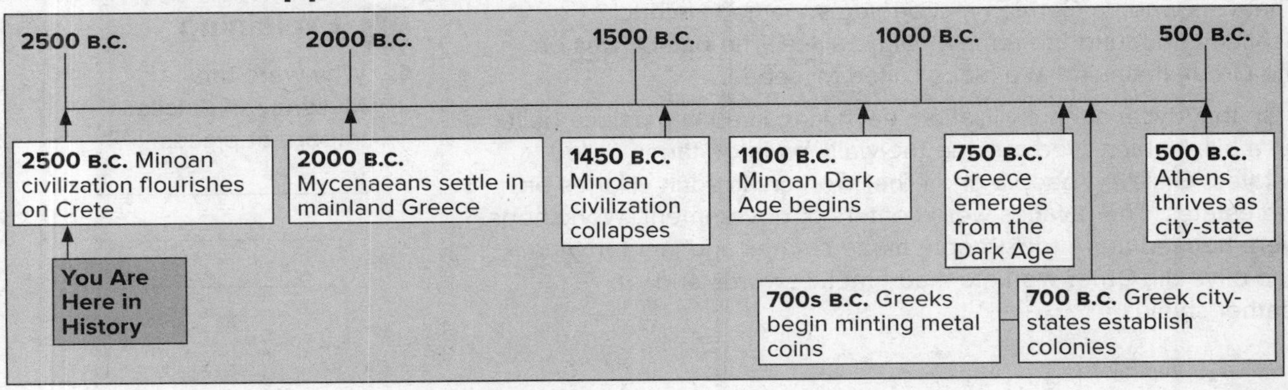

Mountains and Seas

Greece is a **peninsula.** This means that it is surrounded by water on three sides. There are also many islands that are part of Greece. Ancient people traded among the islands and along the coastline. Many fished for a living. The land on the Greek peninsula has many mountains. On the plains between the mountains, farmers raised crops and sheep and goats. The sea and mountains greatly influenced how ancient Greek culture developed.

An Island Civilization

Another civilization developed on one of the islands off the coast of southern Greece. That island is Crete. About 1900 a British archaeologist named Arthur Evans found items from this civilization.

The place he discovered on Crete is called Knossos.

- He dug up remains of an amazing palace.
- The palace had many rooms that stored food.
- Other rooms were workshops where people made jewelry and vases.
- An ancient people called the Minoans built the palace.

Trade was an important economic activity for the Minoans. They traded pottery and vases for ivory and metals in Egypt and Syria. Sometime around 1450 B.C. the Minoan civilization ended. Historians do not know why.

A Mainland Civilization

Another early civilization in the area was the Mycenaean civilization. They lived in Greece from about 2000 B.C. to 1100 B.C.

Little was known about the Mycenaeans until the late 1800s. That was when a German archaeologist named Heinrich Schliemann found the remains of a palace. The palace was on the Greek mainland in a place called Mycenae.

In the Mycenaean civilization, each king lived in a palace built on a hill. Nobles lived outside the walls on large farms called estates. Enslaved people and other workers lived in villages on the estates. The palaces were centers of government. Workshops were housed there too. People made clothes and jars for wine and olive oil. Other workers made metal swords and leather shields.

Reading Check

1. How did seas influence the way many ancient Greeks lived?

____

____

____

Marking the Text

2. Circle the word that means “the system in a country that includes making, buying and selling goods.”

Reading Check

3. What did the discovery at Knossos reveal about the Minoans?

____

____

____

Explaining

4. Why were the Mycenaean palaces important places?

____

____

____

Identifying

5. Name two things the Mycenaeans learned from the Minoans.

____

____

FOLDABLES®

Listing

6. Place a two-tab Foldable along the dotted line to cover the flow chart titled *What Mycenaeans Adopted from Minoans*. Write the question *What do excavations reveal?* on the anchor tab. Label the two tabs—*Mainland Civilization* and *Island Civilization*. Use both sides of the Foldable to list words and short phrases to answer the question for each.

Reading Check

7. How did the Dorian invasion help spread Greek culture?

____

____

____

By the mid-1400s B.C., the Mycenaeans grew wealthy. They built a strong military and fought in the Trojan War. The Mycenaeans conquered the Minoans and controlled the entire Agean Sea region. Later the many Mycenaean kings fought one another. Earthquakes destroyed their palaces. By 1100 B.C. the civilization had crumbled.

Glue Foldable here

What Mycenaeans Adopted from Minoans

- Built ships
- Used sun and stars to navigate seas
- Worked with bronze
- Worshipped Earth Mother as chief god

A group called the Dorians invaded the Greek mainland. Historians call the following 300 years a Dark Age. Trade slowed down. People made fewer things to sell. Farmers grew enough food only for their families. As the Dorians continued to push into Greece, people fled to other areas. They took Greek culture with them.

Finally, by 750 B.C., the difficult time started to end. Small communities formed on the Greek mainland. They were independent and ruled by kings. The people of these communities called themselves Greeks.

Greek farmers grew more food than they could use. Trade increased, so the Greeks needed a system of writing to record their trade. They adopted or used an alphabet from the Phoenicians.

The Greek alphabet made reading and writing easier for the Greeks. Soon **bards,** or storytellers, were writing down old stories. Until then, the stories had been told out loud.

Colonies and Trade

The population increased in Greece when the Dark Age ended. By 700 B.C. farmers could not grow enough food for all of the people. Greek communities started to send people outside the area to form **colonies.** A colony is a settlement in a new territory with close ties to its homeland. Greek people started colonies along the coasts of the Mediterranean Sea and the Black Sea.

The colonies shipped grains, metals, and timber to "parent" cities in Greece. They also sent enslaved people. In return, the cities shipped wine, olive oil, and pottery to the colonies.

Lesson 1 Rise of Greek Civilization, *Continued*

In the 700s B.C., the Greeks started to make coins from metals to make trading easier. A coin is small and can be traded for many different types of goods. This makes it convenient to carry and use. Trade increased and made the Greek colonies wealthier.

The Greek City-State

The **polis,** or city-state, was the basic political unit in early Greece. At the center of each polis was a fort built on a hilltop. This fort was called an acropolis. The open area outside the acropolis was called the **agora.** This space was used as a marketplace. People gathered in the agora and debated issues, passed laws, and chose officials.

Each polis was governed by its own citizens. The Greeks developed the modern idea of citizenship. In early Greece, only males who had been born in the polis and owned land were citizens. They had the right to vote, hold public office, and defend themselves in court. Their responsibilities included serving in government and fighting to defend their polis. Women and children, however, had no political rights.

Citizens fought to defend their city-state. These citizen soldiers were called hoplites. They fought on foot. Each was armed with a round shield, a short sword, and a spear. When fighting, the hoplites would march shoulder to shoulder into battle. This formation was called a **phalanx.**

The polis gave Greek citizens a sense of belonging. However, strong loyalty to their individual city-states also divided Greece. This lack of unity weakened Greece and made it easier for outsiders to conquer Greece.

Glue Foldable here

Check for Understanding

List three ways Greek city-states created the idea of citizenship.

1. ______________

2. ______________

3. ______________

How did loyalty to the city-states divide Greece?

4. ______________

Reading Check

8. How did the colonies affect trade and industry in the Greek world?

____

____

Explaining

9. Why were coins invented?

____

____

Reading Check

10. What were the rights and responsibilities of Greek citizens?

____

____

____

____

FOLDABLES®

11. Cover the Check for Understanding with a one-tab Foldable. Write *City-State* on the anchor tab. On the front, draw and label a diagram of a typical city-state. On the reverse side, describe a city-state.

NAME ______________________________ DATE ______________ CLASS ________

networks

The Ancient Greeks

Lesson 2 Sparta and Athens: City-State Rivals

ESSENTIAL QUESTION

Why do people form governments?

GUIDING QUESTIONS

1. ***Which types of government did the Greek city-states have?***
2. ***Why did the Spartans focus on military skills?***
3. ***How did the culture in Athens differ from other Greek city-states?***

Terms to Know

tyrant an absolute ruler unrestrained by law

oligarchy a government in which a small group has control

democracy a government by the people

helots enslaved people in ancient Sparta

ephor a high-ranking government official in Sparta who was elected by the council of elders

Where in the world?

When did it happen?

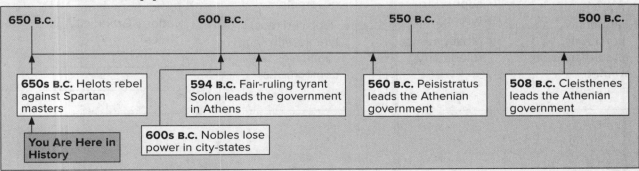

650 B.C. | 600 B.C. | 550 B.C. | 500 B.C.

You Are Here in History

650s B.C. Helots rebel against Spartan masters

600s B.C. Nobles lose power in city-states

594 B.C. Fair-ruling tyrant Solon leads the government in Athens

560 B.C. Peisistratus leads the Athenian government

508 B.C. Cleisthenes leads the Athenian government

Political Changes

As the Greek city-states grew, there were political changes. The wealthy nobles had seized power from the kings. Owners of small farms did not like the nobles ruling, however. Many of them had borrowed money from the nobles. When the farmers could not repay their loans, the nobles took their farms.

By 650 B.C. merchants and artisans also wanted change. They were not citizens because they did not own land. That meant they did not have a say in ruling the polis.

The growing political unrest led to the rise of **tyrants.** A tyrant is someone who seizes power and rules with total authority. Most of the tyrants who controlled city-states ruled fairly. It was the harshness of a few tyrants that gave the word *tyranny* its current meaning; rule by a cruel and unjust person.

The common people and the hoplites, or citizen soldiers, supported the tyrants overthrowing the nobles. Tyrants became more popular by building new marketplaces, temples, and fortresses. Most people in the Greek city-states objected to rule by one person, however. They wanted a government in which all citizens had a say.

Tyrants ruled many Greek city-states until about 500 B.C. Then most Greek city-states changed to either an **oligarchy** or a **democracy.** In an oligarchy, a few wealthy people hold power over the larger group of citizens. In a democracy, all citizens have a say in the government. Each polis chose its own type of government.

Sparta and Athens, two important Greek city-states, had different types of government. They also had very different societies.

Political Changes in Ancient Greece

• Nobles took control from kings. • Farmers, merchants, and artisans wanted changes.	→ • Common people supported tyrants. • Most tyrants ruled fairly.	→ • Greeks wanted more say in government. • Replaced most tyrants with oligarchies or democracies

Defining

1. What is a *tyrant?*

____

____

____

Listing

2. List two groups of people who lived in Greek city-states that did not want the nobles to rule.

____

____

____

Marking the Text

3. Underline the definitions of *oligarchy* and *democracy.*

Reading Check

4. Why were tyrants able to hold power in various Greek city-states?

____

____

____

Lesson 2 Sparta and Athens: City-State Rivals, *Continued*

Marking the Text

5. Circle the word that means "relating to soldiers and war."

Describing

6. What were Spartan women expected to do as adults?

____

____

____

FOLDABLES®

Outlining

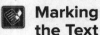

7. Place a one-tab Foldable along the dotted line to the right. On the anchor tab, write *Military Society.* Use both sides of the tab to outline events in the lives of Spartan boys and men.

Reading Check

8. Why did Sparta fall behind other Greek city-states in many areas?

____

____

____

Glue Foldable here

Sparta: A Military Society

Sparta was located on the Peloponnesus Peninsula in southern Greece. Sparta invaded nearby city-states and enslaved the people who lived there. The Spartans called these enslaved people **helots.**

In about 650 B.C. the helots rebelled. The Spartans crushed the uprising. The leaders decided to make Sparta a military society. The leaders thought this would make citizens more loyal and obedient.

All boys and men were prepared for a life of war. Boys left home at age seven. They lived in harsh military camps where they learned to read, write, and to use weapons. Spartan leaders believed harsh treatment would make boys into adults who could survive the pain of battle.

Life for Men in Sparta

Age 7: Left home for military camps

Age 20: Joined the regular army

Age 30: Could live at home while serving in the military

Age 60: Finally left military service

Spartan women enjoyed more freedom than women in other city-states because the men were often away from home. Girls were trained in sports such as wrestling. The main role of women was to raise sons for the military.

Sparta's government was an oligarchy. Two kings ruled together, but had little power. The council of elders acted as judges and the assembly made decisions about war and peace. The assembly elected five people each year to be **ephors.** The ephors enforced laws and collected taxes.

Sparta's leaders believed education could lead to unrest. For this reason, the government discouraged people from studying literature and the arts. Foreign visitors were not welcome. People could leave Sparta only for military purposes. Trade was limited. Sparta became isolated.

Athens: A Young Democracy

Athens was another important Greek city-state. It was located northeast of Sparta. The people who lived in Athens were descended from the Mycenaean people. The Athenian people had different ideas about government and society than the people of Sparta.

Lesson 2 Sparta and Athens: City-State Rivals, *Continued*

In Athens, boys studied arithmetic, geometry, drawing, music, and public speaking. They also practiced sports. Boys finished school at age 18. At that age, they were expected to be active in public affairs.

Girls in Athens were educated at home.

- They learned spinning, weaving, and other household duties.
- In some wealthy families they learned to read, write, and play music.
- Women were expected to marry and raise children.

About 600 B.C. most Athenian farmers owed money to the nobles. To avoid an uprising, the nobles turned to a respected merchant named Solon. Solon ended the farmers' debts and freed those who had been enslaved.

In 560 B.C. another tyrant took over the government. His name was Peisistratus. He gave citizenship to people who did not own land. He hired the poor to build temples.

After Peisistratus died, Cleisthenes took over. He gave the assembly even greater powers. Cleisthenes also created a new council of 500 citizens to help the assembly manage government business. Each year a lottery was held to choose the council members. Using a lottery meant that every citizen had a chance to be a council member.

Cleisthenes' changes made the Athenian government more democratic. However, people who were not citizens still could not participate in the government. This included all women, foreign-born men, and enslaved people.

/ / / / / / / / / / / / / / Glue Foldable here / / / / / / / / / / / / / /

Check for Understanding

Name one way Cleisthenes made the Athenian government more democratic.

1. ______________________

List the three groups who were not helped by his changes.

2. ______________________

3. ______________________

4. ______________________

Reading Check

9. What did Solon do to help farmers?

____

____

Explaining

10. What was the benefit of using the lottery system?

____

____

____

Reading Check

11. Why was Solon chosen to be leader of Athens?

____

____

FOLDABLES®

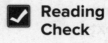

12. Place a one-tab Foldable to cover the Check for Understanding. Write *Cleisthenes* on the anchor tab. Use both sides to list what you remember about Cleisthenes. Use your notes to complete the lists under the tab.

NAME ______________________ DATE ____________ CLASS ________

networks

Lesson 3 Greece and Persia

ESSENTIAL QUESTION

Why does conflict develop?

GUIDING QUESTIONS

1. *How did the Persians rule a vast empire?*
2. *How did the Greeks defeat the Persians?*

Terms to Know

satrapy a province in ancient Persia

satrap the governor of a province in ancient Persia

Zoroastrianism a Persian religion based on the belief in one god and founded by the religious teacher Zoroaster

Where in the world?

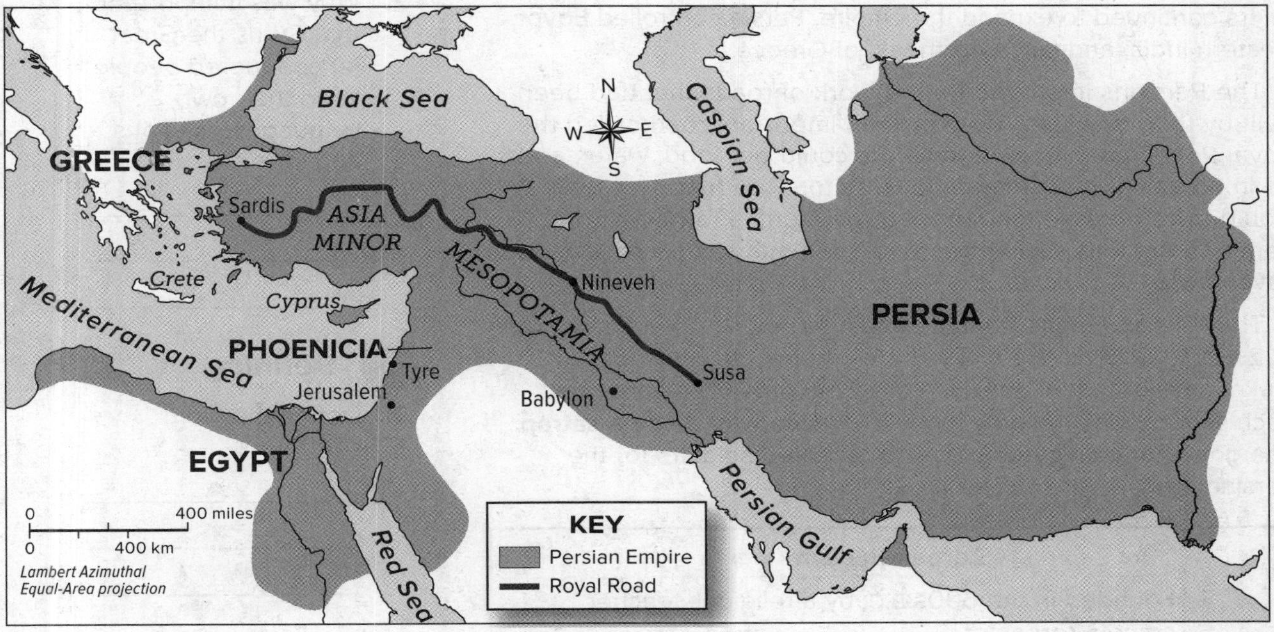

When did it happen?

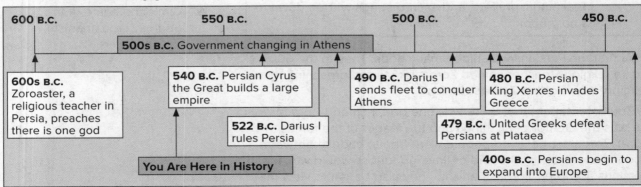

600 B.C. — 550 B.C. — 500 B.C. — 450 B.C.

- **500s B.C.** Government changing in Athens
- **600s B.C.** Zoroaster, a religious teacher in Persia, preaches there is one god
- **540 B.C.** Persian Cyrus the Great builds a large empire
- **522 B.C.** Darius I rules Persia
- **490 B.C.** Darius I sends fleet to conquer Athens
- **480 B.C.** Persian King Xerxes invades Greece
- **479 B.C.** United Greeks defeat Persians at Plataea
- **400s B.C.** Persians begin to expand into Europe

You Are Here in History

Lesson 3 Greece and Persia, *Continued*

Persia's Empire

While Greek city-states were going through changes in their governments, the Persians were building a large empire in southwest Asia. Persia was located in what is today called Iran.

In the 500s B.C., a Persian king named Cyrus the Great built a powerful army. Cyrus conquered Mesopotamia, Syria, and Judah. He also conquered Greek city-states that were in the area of Anatolia. Today Anatolia is called Turkey. The Persian empire became the largest in the ancient world.

Cyrus ruled fairly. He allowed the people he conquered to keep their own languages, religions, and laws. After Cyrus, new rulers continued to expand the empire. Persia controlled Egypt, western India, and lands northeast of Greece.

The Persians improved the network of roads that had been built by the Assyrians. They built an important road called the Royal Road. On this road, travelers could get food, water, and fresh horses at roadside stations. Before the road was built, it would take a messenger about three months to travel from Persia to Anatolia. Using the road, the time was cut to just seven days.

The Persian Empire kept expanding. Darius I ruled Persia from 522 B.C. to 486 B.C. He divided the empire into provinces to make it easier to manage. He called the provinces **satrapies.** Each satrapy was ruled by a governor who was called a **satrap.** The governor collected taxes and recruited soldiers for the Persian army.

Zoroastrianism

- Founded in the 600s B.C. by a religious teacher named Zoroaster
- Believed in one god named Ahura Mazda
- Believed people could choose good or evil
- Teachings, prayers, and sacred songs written down in a holy book

At first the Persians worshiped many gods. Then in the 600s B.C., a religious teacher named Zoroaster started preaching a new religion. It was called **Zoroastrianism.**

Zoroaster taught that there was one god, named Ahura Mazda. He was the creator of all things and the leader of the forces of good. Zoroaster believed people were free to choose between good and evil, but at the end of time, goodness would win. Most Persians accepted Zoroastrianism. They also began to view the

Marking the Text

1. Underline the names of the lands that Persia conquered and controlled.

Drawing Conclusions

2. Why was it important that Cyrus the Great let conquered people keep their own languages, religions, and laws?

____

____

____

Defining

3. Define the word *satrap*.

____

____

____

Marking the Text

4. Circle the name of the god of Zoroastrianism.

Lesson 3 Greece and Persia, *Continued*

Listing

5. In the graphic organizer, list facts about aspects of the Persian Empire.

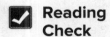

Reading Check

6. How did Persian rulers unite their vast empires?

Contrasting

7. How was Greek civilization different from Persian civilization?

Marking the Text

8. Circle the word that is the name of a long-distance race.

monarchy as sacred. Persian kings believed they ruled by the power of Ahura Mazda.

Persian Empire	Facts
Cyrus the Great	
Royal Road	
satrapy	
Zoroastrianism	

The Persian Wars

In the 400s B.C., the Persians wanted to expand their empire into Europe. They soon clashed with the Greeks who had a very different civilization. The Persians believed in an all-powerful king. Many Greeks believed that citizens should choose their own rulers.

The Persians already controlled Greek city-states in Anatolia. In 499 B.C. these city-states revolted. The Athenians sent warships to support the Greek rebels. The Persians crushed the revolt. The Persian king Darius I was angry at Athens for interfering.

In 490 B.C. Darius I sent a fleet of 600 ships to invade Greece. The Persians landed at Marathon. The Athenians knew they were outnumbered and would lose if they attacked. The Persians then decided to board their ships and attack Athens by sea. When the strongest Persian fighting units were on the ships, the Athenians attacked. The Persians suffered a terrible defeat.

According to Greek legend, a young runner raced to Athens with the news. He reached Athens and cried out "Victory." Then he fell and died from exhaustion. Today, marathon races are named for that famous run.

The Persians vowed revenge against the Athenians. In 480 B.C. a new Persian king named Xerxes invaded Greece with a large army and thousands of warships. His force even had its own supply ships.

The Greek city-states joined together to fight the Persians. Sparta's King Leonidas supplied the most soldiers. Themistocles of Athens directed the Greek navy. His plan was to attack the Persian supply ships. That would cut off the Persian army's supplies.

Lesson 3 Greece and Persia, *Continued*

For three days Spartan soldiers fought the Persians at Thermopylae. The Spartans fought bravely but could not stop the Persians. Many troops abandoned the battle. Only 300 Spartan soldiers remained and fought to the death.

The Spartans' heroic fight gave Themistocles and the Athenians time to carry out the plan. The Athenian fleet lured the Persian fleet into the strait of Salamis near Athens. A strait or channel is a narrow strip of water between two pieces of land. The large, heavy Persian ships crowded together in the channel. The Greek ships were smaller and could maneuver more easily. The Greek navy destroyed most of the Persian fleet.

The Persian army continued to attack. It marched to Athens and burned the city. Finally in 479 B.C. the last battle was fought. With improved fighting and better weapons, the Greek forces defeated the Persians at Plataea, northwest of Athens.

The Persian Empire now faced many challenges. Its army was no longer able to defend the whole empire. The people grew unhappy with their government and paying heavy taxes. The royal family disagreed over who should rule.

Persia weakened and became open to outside attacks. In the 300s B.C., Persia was invaded by a young and powerful Greek ruler named Alexander. The Persian Empire ended and a new Greek empire grew. It eventually became even larger than the Persian Empire.

Check for Understanding

List two advantages that should have helped the Persians defeat the Greeks at Marathon in 490 B.C.

1. ______________________

2. ______________________

How did the Greeks finally defeat the Persians?

3. ______________________

____

Glue Foldable here

Marking the Text

9. Underline the names of important battles in the text.

Reading Check

10. After the losses in Greece, why did the Persians grow unhappy with their government?

____

____

____

FOLDABLES®

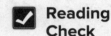

11. Place a two-tab Foldable along the dotted line to cover the Check for Understanding. Title the anchor tab *Soldiers and Sailors*. Label the top tab *Land* and the bottom tab *Sea*. Use both sides of the tabs to outline what you remember about important events occurring on land and sea.

NAME ______________________ DATE __________ CLASS ________

networks

The Ancient Greeks

Lesson 4 Glory, War, and Decline

ESSENTIAL QUESTION

How do governments change?

GUIDING QUESTIONS

1. ***How did Pericles influence government and culture in Athens?***
2. ***What was life like for Athenians under the rule of Pericles?***
3. ***How did the Peloponnesian War affect the Greek city-states?***

Terms to Know

direct democracy a form of democracy in which all citizens can participate firsthand in the decision-making process

representative democracy a form of democracy in which citizens elect officials to govern on their behalf

philosopher a person who searches for wisdom or enlightenment

Where in the world?

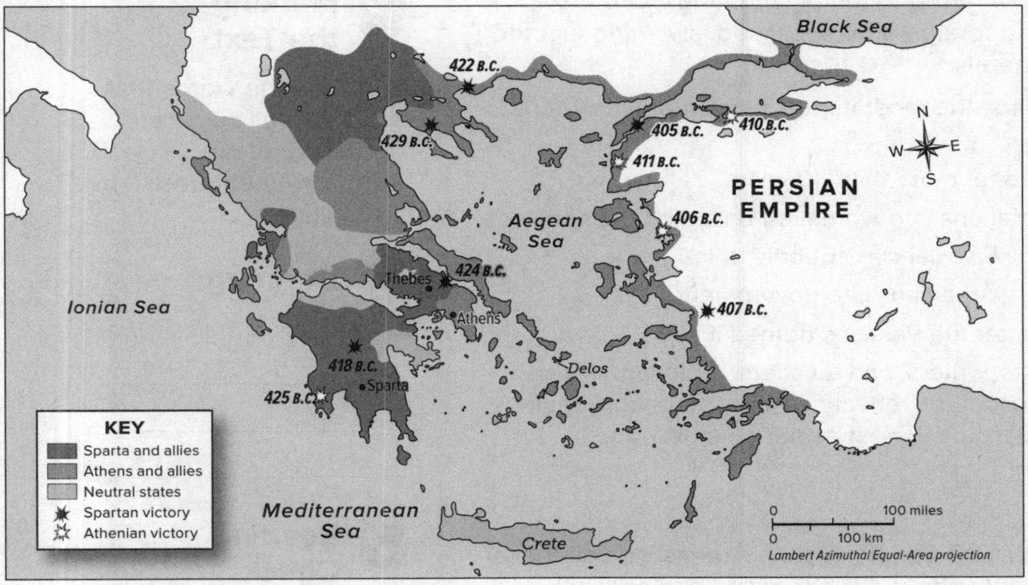

When did it happen?

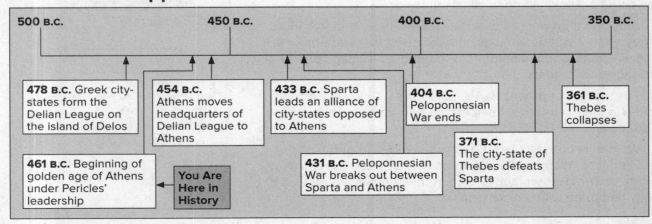

500 B.C. — 450 B.C. — 400 B.C. — 350 B.C.

- **478 B.C.** Greek city-states form the Delian League on the island of Delos
- **461 B.C.** Beginning of golden age of Athens under Pericles' leadership ← **You Are Here in History**
- **454 B.C.** Athens moves headquarters of Delian League to Athens
- **433 B.C.** Sparta leads an alliance of city-states opposed to Athens
- **431 B.C.** Peloponnesian War breaks out between Sparta and Athens
- **404 B.C.** Peloponnesian War ends
- **371 B.C.** The city-state of Thebes defeats Sparta
- **361 B.C.** Thebes collapses

Lesson 4 Glory, War, and Decline, *Continued*

The Rule of Pericles

When the Persian wars ended, Athens became a powerful city-state. From 461 B.C. to 429 B.C., Athens enjoyed a golden age as the economic and cultural center of Greece.

The government of Athens was a **direct democracy.** That means that all citizens of Athens met to debate and vote on government matters. In the United States, we have a **representative democracy.** Citizens elect a smaller group of people to represent the citizens. It makes laws and governs on behalf of the citizens.

In ancient Athens, direct democracy worked because of the small number of citizens. At the assembly meetings, citizens made policy on war and foreign affairs, passed laws, and elected officials, known as generals.

After the Persian Wars, the most important general in Athens was Pericles:

- led the city-state for more than 30 years
- gave people positions in government based on their abilities
- did not care which social class people belonged to
- brought ordinary Athenians into government
- rebuilt Athens after the Persians burned it.
- supported artists, writers, and teachers. **Philosophers** also flourished. Philosophers reflect or think about the meaning of life. Athens became a great center of knowledge.

Athenian Life

At its height, about 285,000 people lived in Athens. Not all these people were citizens. Only about 43,000 males had political rights. Women, foreign-born men, and enslaved people could not be citizens. They had no political rights.

Athenian men worked as farmers, artisans, and merchants. They often worked mornings and exercised in the afternoons. In the evenings, upper-class men discussed politics and philosophy during social dinners.

The women of Athens had different lives. Girls married early, often in their mid-teens. Their duties were to have children and take care of the households.

Women in poor families did farm work or sold goods at the marketplace. Women in upper-class homes spun, dyed, or wove cloth. Upper-class women rarely left their homes. When they did, they had to be with a male relative.

Identifying

1. What kind of democracy do we have in the United States?

____

____

____

Marking the Text

2. Circle the words that mean "all citizens participate in government decision-making."

Defining

3. What is a *philosopher*?

____

____

____

Reading Check

4. How was Athens able to become a direct democracy?

____

____

____

Lesson 4 Glory, War, and Decline, *Continued*

Analyzing

5. Why was slavery important in Athens?

____

____

____

Reading Check

6. How did the roles of Athenian men and women differ?

____

____

____

Explaining

7. Why was the Delian League created?

____

____

____

Making Inferences

8. Why was the Delian League able to drive the Persians out of Anatolia?

____

____

____

Athenian Citizenship

Citizens	Non-Citizens
Free native-born men	Women, foreign-born men, enslaved people

Athenian women could not attend school. Many, however, learned to read and to play music. Educated women in Athens were not considered equal to men. Women could not participate in politics or own property. Greek women were always under the care of males.

Foreign-born women were not treated the same way as Athenian women, however. One such woman was Aspasia. She was known for her intelligence and charm. She taught public speaking. Her ideas were popular among Athenians. Pericles was influenced by her.

Slavery was common in ancient civilizations. Most Athenian households had at least one enslaved person. Many enslaved people were prisoners of battles. They included both Greeks and non-Greeks.

Enslaved men worked on farms and in the shops of artisans. Some worked at hard labor. Enslaved women were cooks and servants in wealthy homes. Sometimes they were teachers to upper-class children. The treatment of enslaved people was different from place to place. Slavery helped Athens develop a thriving economy.

War Between Athens and Sparta

The Greek city-states learned over time that their survival depended on cooperation. Even after the Persian Wars, Persia remained a threat.

In 478 B.C. the Greek city-states joined together to form a defensive league. Its purpose was to defend its members against the Persians. Sparta did not join this league.

It was called the Delian League because its headquarters was on the island of Delos. The league drove the Persians out of Greek territories in Anatolia. As a result, trade increased and Greece became richer.

Lesson 4 Glory, War, and Decline, *Continued*

Over time, however, the Delian League failed. Athens began to control the other member city-states. In 433 B.C. Athens interfered with some of Sparta's allies. These allies pressured Sparta to attack Athens. The conflict is called the Peloponnesian War because Sparta was located in the Peloponnesus region of Greece.

At a funeral ceremony for soldiers and sailors killed in battle, Pericles made a famous speech called the Funeral Oration. In the speech, Pericles gave reasons why democracy is worth fighting for.

After about two years, a deadly disease broke out in Athens. One-third of the people died, including Pericles. During the next 25 years, each side won some victories. Neither side was able to defeat its opponent.

Finally, Sparta made a deal with the Persians. The Spartans agreed to give Persia some territory in Anatolia. In return, Persia gave Sparta money to build a navy. In 405 B.C. Sparta's new navy destroyed the Athenian fleet. Athens surrendered a year later.

- The Peloponnesian War brought disaster to the Greek city-states.
- Governments were left weak and divided.
- Many people had died in battle and from disease.
- After the war ended, Sparta ruled its new empire much like Athens had ruled.
- Sparta's allied city-states grew angry at the harsh treatment.

While the city-states fought each other, a kingdom grew to the north. The kingdom was Macedonia. Eventually the strength of Macedonia cost the Greek city-states their independence.

Check for Understanding

List three changes Pericles made to life in Athens.

1. ____________________

2. ____________________

3. ____________________

Glue Foldable here

Determining Cause and Effect

9. Name two things that helped cause the Peloponnesian War.

____

____

Reading Check

10. Why was Sparta's deal with Persia so important in the war against Athens?

____

____

____

FOLDABLES®

11. Place a three-tab Foldable along the dotted line to cover the Check for Understanding. Write *Athenian Life* on the anchor tab. Label the three tabs—*Men*, *Women* and *Enslaved People*. Use both sides of the Foldable to list what you remember about the life of each group in Athens.

NAME________________________________ DATE ______________ CLASS ________

networks

Greek Civilization

Lesson 1 Greek Culture

ESSENTIAL QUESTION

What makes a culture unique?

GUIDING QUESTIONS

1. ***How did the ancient Greeks honor their gods?***
2. ***Why were epics and fables important to the ancient Greeks?***
3. ***How did Greek dramas develop?***
4. ***What ideas did the Greeks express in their art and architecture?***

Terms to Know

myth a traditional story that explains a culture's beliefs or part of the natural world

ritual words or actions that are part of a religious ceremony

oracle a priestess who speaks for the gods and answers questions about what will happen in the future

fable a story that teaches a lesson

oral tradition the custom of passing stories from one generation to the next by telling the stories out loud

drama a story that is told by the actions and spoken words of actors

tragedy a drama in which characters struggle to overcome problems, but fail

comedy a drama that tells a humorous story

Where in the world?

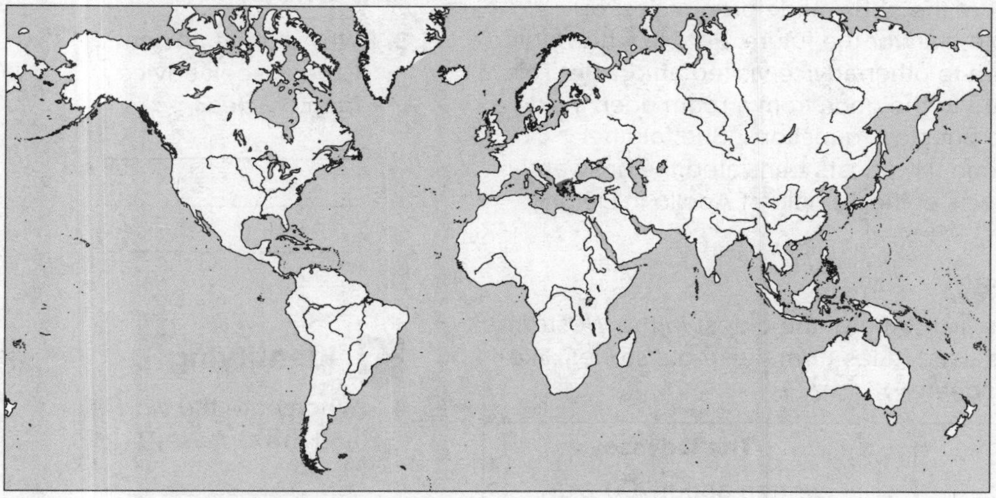

When did it happen?

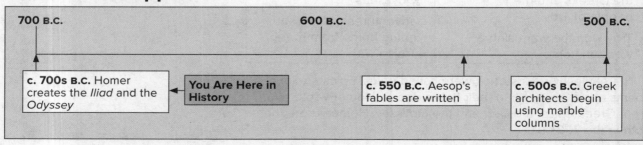

700 B.C. — 600 B.C. — 500 B.C.

- **c. 700s B.C.** Homer creates the *Iliad* and the *Odyssey*
- **You Are Here in History**
- **c. 550 B.C.** Aesop's fables are written
- **c. 500s B.C.** Greek architects begin using marble columns

Greek Beliefs

The Greeks believed in many gods and goddesses, and they told **myths** about them. Greek myths are traditional stories about gods and heroes. The Greeks believed these gods affected everyday life. Every city-state had a god or goddess who protected its people. The Greeks worshiped their gods in temples and at home.

The Greek gods and goddesses had great powers. However, the Greek people did not fear them because the gods acted like humans. Greeks believed the 12 most important gods and goddesses lived on Mount Olympus and were protected by a gate of clouds. Zeus was the king of the gods.

To please their gods, the people performed **rituals,** or religious ceremonies in honor of the gods. They had festivals, or celebrations, and feasts for the gods. They prayed and offered gifts to the gods. They believed that the gods were pleased when the people showed skill in the arts or athletics. Every four years they had athletic competitions, called the Olympic Games.

The Greeks believed that the gods made prophecies, or predictions, to help people plan for the future. People who wanted to know the future or listen to other advice visited an **oracle**. This was a priestess who talked to the gods from a room deep inside a temple. People asked the priestess questions. She told her answers to the priests. Then the priests translated the answers. The most famous oracle was at the Temple of Apollo in Delphi.

Epics and Fables

Greek poems and stories are some of the oldest in the Western world. Many writers have used ideas from these old stories, like England's William Shakespeare.

The Iliad	The Odyssey
• written about 700 B.C. • story of a war between the Greeks and the people of Troy • Troy won the war using a wooden horse	• written about 700 B.C. • story of the hero Odysseus • adventures of Odysseus going home from the Trojan war

The earliest Greek stories were called epics. Epics are long poems about heroes and their brave deeds. Homer wrote two great Greek epics: the *Iliad* and the *Odyssey*. Homer wrote them both in the 700s B.C.

Marking the Text

1. Underline what the Greek gods and goddesses were like.

Paraphrasing

2. Why did the Greeks have festivals and rituals for their gods?

____

____

____

Reading Check

3. Why did the ancient Greeks seek advice from oracles?

____

____

____

Identifying

4. Who wrote the *Iliad* and the *Odyssey*?

____

Lesson 1 Greek Culture, *Continued*

The *Iliad* tells of a war between the Greeks and the people of Troy. The story describes how this war was won with a wooden horse. The *Odyssey* tells about the hero, Odysseus, and his long journey home from the Trojan War.

The Greeks believed that the *Iliad* and the *Odyssey* were true stories. These epics gave them a history filled with heroes and brave deeds. Homer's stories taught important lessons, such as, friendship and marriage should be valued. Homer's heroes were role models for the Greeks.

Glue Foldable here

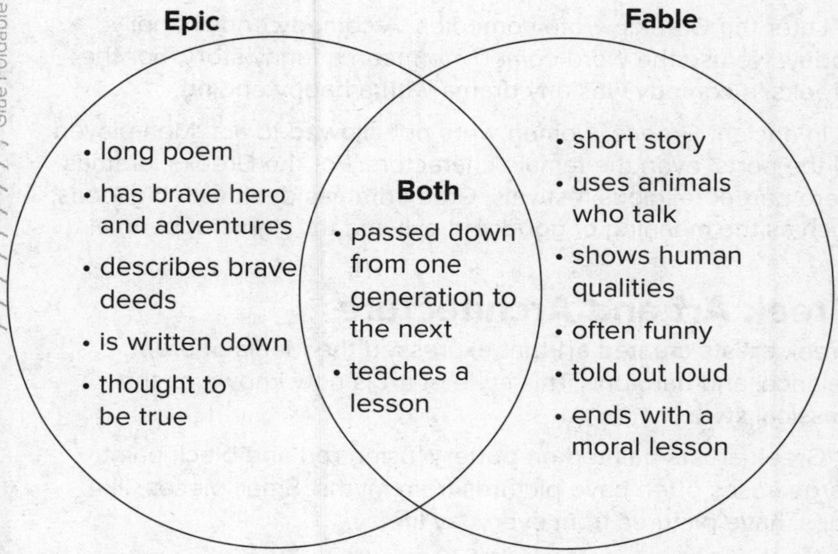

Have you heard the story of "The Boy Who Cried Wolf?" This story and others like it were said to have been written by a man named Aesop. He is supposed to have lived around 550 B.C. Historians now know that there was probably never anyone named Aesop who wrote these stories. However, the stories do exist. They are known as Aesop's **fables.**

Fables are short tales that teach a lesson. They always have a point, or moral. The moral is a truth that teaches a useful life lesson. Fables are often funny and show human weaknesses and strengths.

Aesop's fables were part of Greece's **oral tradition** for about 200 years. This means that people told the stories out loud to their children and grandchildren. Later, people wrote down the fables. Aesop's fables are read and told today by people all around the world.

FOLDABLES®

Listing

5. Place a three-tab Venn diagram Foldable along the dotted line next to *Epics and Fables*. Write *Epics* on the anchor tab. Label the top tab *Iliad*, the middle tab *Both*, and the bottom tab *Odyssey*. On the reverse sides, list facts about each to compare and contrast the stories.

Critical Thinking

6. Why do you think Aesop's fables are still told today?

____

____

____

Reading Check

7. How do fables usually end?

____

____

____

The Impact of Greek Drama

A **drama** is a story told by people who act out the events. They play the parts of the characters in the story, saying their words and acting out their feelings and actions. Movies, plays, and television shows are often dramas.

The Greeks developed two types of drama—**tragedy** and **comedy.** A tragedy has an unhappy ending. The characters in a tragedy cannot solve their problems no matter how hard they try. The first Greek plays were tragedies.

Later the Greeks wrote comedies. A comedy ends happily. Today, we use the word *comedy* to mean a funny story. For the Greeks, a comedy was any drama with a happy ending.

In ancient Greece, women were not allowed to act. Men played all the parts, even the female characters. For the Greeks, dramas were part of religious festivals. Greek dramas dealt with big ideas, such as the meaning of good and evil and the rights of people.

Greek Art and Architecture

Greek artists created art that expressed the ideals of order, balance, and harmony. This style of art is now known as the classical style.

Greek artists painted on pottery, using red and black paint. Large vases often have pictures from myths. Small pieces, like cups, have pictures from everyday life.

The Greeks built beautiful buildings. These buildings had large columns to support the roof. The most important buildings were the temples. Each temple was dedicated to a god or goddess. The Parthenon of Athens honored the goddess Athena.

Many Greek temples were decorated with sculpture. Sculpture, like all of Greek art, expressed artists' ideas of perfection and beauty.

Glue Foldable here

Check for Understanding

List three kinds of writing that were started by the ancient Greeks.

1. ______________________

2. ______________________

3. ______________________

Reading Check

8. How did Greek drama influence how people are entertained today?

____

____

Explaining

9. Why were temples built?

____

____

Reading Check

10. How did the Greeks design their buildings?

____

____

FOLDABLES®

11. Place a two-tab Foldable to cover the Check for Understanding. Write *Greek* on the anchor tab. Label the top tab *Writing* and the bottom tab *Art and Architecture*. Use both sides of the tabs to list what you remember about Greek writing, art, and architecture.

NAME________________________ DATE __________ CLASS ________

networks

Greek Civilization

Lesson 2 The Greek Mind

ESSENTIAL QUESTION

How do new ideas change the way people live?

GUIDING QUESTIONS

1. ***What ideas did the Greeks develop to explain the world around them?***
2. ***What did the Greeks believe about history and science?***

Terms to Know

Sophists Greek teachers of philosophy, reasoning, and public speaking

rhetoric the art of public speaking and debate

Socratic method philosophical method of questioning to gain truth; developed by Socrates

Hippocratic Oath a set of promises about patient care that new doctors make when they start practicing medicine

When did it happen?

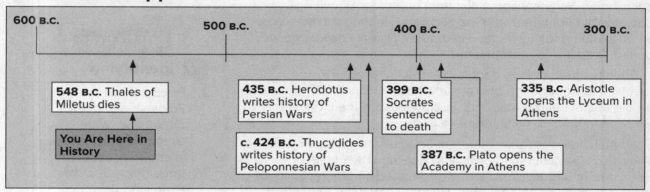

600 B.C. — 500 B.C. — 400 B.C. — 300 B.C.

- **548 B.C.** Thales of Miletus dies
- **You Are Here in History**
- **435 B.C.** Herodotus writes history of Persian Wars
- **c. 424 B.C.** Thucydides writes history of Peloponnesian Wars
- **399 B.C.** Socrates sentenced to death
- **387 B.C.** Plato opens the Academy in Athens
- **335 B.C.** Aristotle opens the Lyceum in Athens

What do you know?

In the K column, list what you already know about ancient Greek philosophers, historians, and scientists. In the W column, list what you want to know. After reading the lesson, fill in the L column with the information that you learned.

K	W	L

Lesson 2 The Greek Mind, *Continued*

Greek Thinkers

The word *philosophy* comes from the Greek word for "love of wisdom." Greek thinkers known an philosophers created a new body of knowledge that later shaped the Western world.

A group of Philosophers called the **Sophists** were teachers in ancient Greece. Sophists taught **rhetoric,** the art of public speaking and formal argument. Sophists did not believe that the gods influenced everyday life. They did not believe in absolute, or definite, right and wrong. They thought that something wrong for one person could be right for another.

Socrates was trained as a sculptor but became a teacher of philosophy. We know about him from his students' writings. Socrates did not agree with the Sophists. He thought there was an absolute right and wrong. He thought all real knowledge was buried deep inside each person.

Socrates tried to help people find the knowledge inside themselves through the **Socratic method** of teaching. This meant he did not lecture his students. Socrates asked them questions. He wanted them to think for themselves.

Some leaders in Athens thought Socrates was dangerous. They said he encouraged people to question their leaders' decisions. In 399 B.C., Socrates was arrested and found guilty of teaching young people to rebel. He was sentenced to death. Socrates could have left Athens, but he refused. He said that he lived in Athens, so he had to obey the city's laws. He drank poison to carry out his death sentence.

Plato was one of Socrates' students. He wrote a book called *The Republic*. In it, he described his plan for the ideal society. Plato did not like Athenian democracy. He did not believe that everyone in society could make good decisions. His ideal government divided people into three groups. The top group was philosopher kings. Plato felt they were wise enough to do what was best for everyone rather than only what was best for themselves.

Plato's Ideas About Government

- Wise philosopher kings should rule.
- Brave warriors should defend society.
- The common people should do all the work.

Glue Foldable here

Understanding Word Origins

1. Where does the word *philosophy* come from?

____

____

____

FOLDABLES®

Identifying

2. Place a three-tab Foldable along the dotted line. Write *Greek Thinkers* on the anchor tab. Label the three tabs—*Socrates*, *Plato,* and *Aristotle*.

Use both sides of the tabs to write about the beliefs of each philosopher.

Identifying

3. Who made up the top group of Plato's ideal government?

____

____

Explaining

4. In Plato's ideal society, who would do all the work to provide food, clothing and shelter? Why?

____

____

____

____

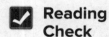

Reading Check

5. Why did Plato dislike Athenian democracy?

____

____

____

Marking the Text

6. Underline the way people explained the past before Herodotus.

Warriors were the second group in Plato's ideal society. Their job was to defend the society against attack. The third group was everyone else. They did all of the jobs in society that were necessary to provide food, clothing, and shelter. Plato believed that the common people were too easily influenced and would make foolish decisions.

Unlike most men at that time, Plato believed that women should have the same education and the same jobs as men. Plato started a school in Athens. It was called the Academy. His best student was Aristotle. Aristotle wrote more than 200 works on government, science, and the planets.

In 355 B.C., Aristotle opened his own school called the Lyceum. His teaching focused on the idea that people should live moderately. His belief in observation, or looking at the world around him, was an important step in the development of modern science.

Aristotle also wrote about government in his book *Politics*. He divided governments into three types. The first was monarchy, or rule by one person, such as a king. The second was oligarchy, or rule by just a few people. The third was democracy, or rule by the majority of the people.

Aristotle thought that the best government was a combination of all three types. Aristotle's ideas influenced the founders of the United States government.

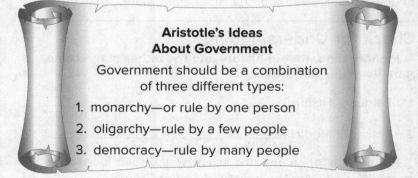

Aristotle's Ideas About Government

Government should be a combination of three different types:

1. monarchy—or rule by one person
2. oligarchy—rule by a few people
3. democracy—rule by many people

New History and Science Ideas

For thousands of years, people did not write history. They believed that the legends and myths passed from one generation to the next were true.

Then, in 435 B.C., Herodotus wrote the history of the Persian Wars. Though he believed that the gods affected historical events,

Lesson 2 The Greek Mind, *Continued*

he tried to separate fact from legend. He was the first to do careful research. Today, he is called the "father of history." Thucydides was another famous historian of the ancient world. He did not believe that the gods affected human history. Thucydides tried to write everything the way it actually happened.

In ancient times, most people thought that the gods controlled nature. However, the early Greek scientists thought that people could discover the causes of natural events by observing, investigating, and thinking.

The first important Greek scientist was Thales of Miletus. He made discoveries and developed theories by observing and thinking.

Another Greek scientist, Pythagoras, believed that all relationships in the world could be expressed in numbers. He is famous for developing the Pythagorean theorem. It is still used in geometry to figure out the length of the sides of a triangle.

Hippocrates was a physician who is called the "father of medicine." He believed that diseases came from natural causes. He made important discoveries about different kinds of diseases. He also developed his own treatments to cure sick people.

Hippocrates wrote a list of rules about how doctors should treat their patients. The rules are listed in the **Hippocratic Oath.** It says doctors should do their best to help the patient. It says they should protect the patient's privacy. Today, doctors around the world still promise to honor the Hippocratic Oath.

Check for Understanding

Identify the father of history and the father of medicine. Both were ancient Greeks.

1. Father of History ____________________

2. Father of Medicine ____________________

List one historian and one scientist and their ideas that were different from the beliefs of earlier Greeks.

3. ______________________________

4. ______________________________

Glue Foldable here

Contrasting

7. How were Herodotus and Thucydides different?

____

____

____

Reading Check

8. Why is Herodotus called "the father of history?"

____

____

____

FOLDABLES®

9. Glue a two-tab Foldable behind a one-tab Foldable along the anchor tabs. Glue the Foldable booklet along the dotted line to cover the Check for Understanding. On the anchor tab, write *New Ideas* …. Label the one-tab Foldable *Philosophy.* Label the two tabs—*History* and *Science.* Use both sides of the tabs to list what you remember about Greek ideas that are still used today.

NAME________________________ DATE ____________ CLASS ________

networks

Greek Civilization

Lesson 3 Alexander's Empire

ESSENTIAL QUESTION

What are the characteristics of a leader?

GUIDING QUESTIONS

1. ***Why did Macedonia become powerful?***
2. ***What were Alexander's goals as a ruler?***
3. ***How successful was Alexander in achieving his goals?***

Terms to Know

cavalry soldiers who fight while riding horses

Hellenistic Era the time period after Alexander died when Greek culture spread to all the lands in his empire

Where in the world?

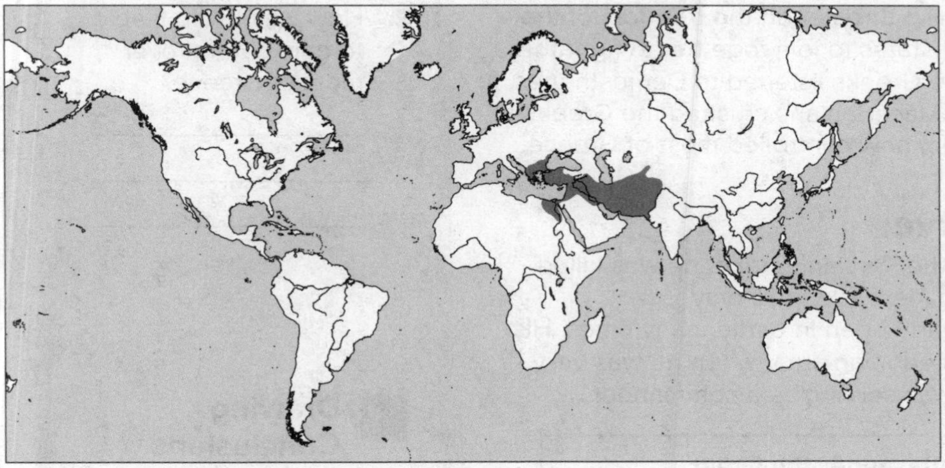

When did it happen?

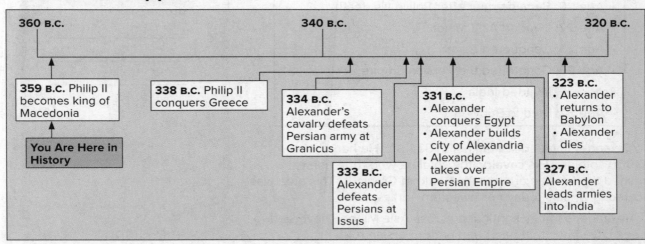

360 B.C. — **340 B.C.** — **320 B.C.**

- **359 B.C.** Philip II becomes king of Macedonia
  - You Are Here in History
- **338 B.C.** Philip II conquers Greece
- **334 B.C.** Alexander's cavalry defeats Persian army at Granicus
- **333 B.C.** Alexander defeats Persians at Issus
- **331 B.C.**
  - Alexander conquers Egypt
  - Alexander builds city of Alexandria
  - Alexander takes over Persian Empire
- **327 B.C.** Alexander leads armies into India
- **323 B.C.**
  - Alexander returns to Babylon
  - Alexander dies

Lesson 3 Alexander's Empire, *Continued*

Philip II of Macedonia

Macedonia was a kingdom north of Greece. The people raised sheep and horses, and they farmed. For much of its history, Macedonia had not been a powerful country.

In 359 B.C., Philip II became king of Macedonia. He wanted to defeat the Persian Empire. First he had to unite the Greek city-states and put them under his rule. Philip built a strong army and trained them to fight like the Greeks.

The Greek city-states were weak. They had been divided by the Peloponnesian War. Philip took control of the city-states one by one. He defeated some in battle. He bribed some to give up. Others joined him by their own choice.

Demosthenes was a lawyer and one of Athens's great public speakers. He warned that Philip threatened the freedom of the Greeks. He urged all the city-states to join together to fight the Macedonians. By the time the Greeks listened to Demosthenes, it was too late. In 338 B.C., the Macedonians crushed the Greeks at the Battle of Chaeronea. Philip now controlled most of Greece.

Alexander Takes Over

Before Philip could conquer the Persian Empire, he was killed. His son Alexander took over. Alexander was only 20 years old, but he had already been in battle many times. His father had put him in the Macedonian army when he was very young. By the age of 16, he was serving as a commander.

The Life of Alexander the Great

- Age 16: Commander in his father's army
- Age 20: Became ruler after Phillip II's death
- Age 22: Invaded Asia Minor
- Age 25: Conquered Egypt
- Age 26: Conquered the Persian Empire
- Age 29: Invaded India
- Age 32: Died in Babylon

Alexander invaded Asia Minor in 334 B.C. He had about 40,000 soldiers. His **cavalry**, the soldiers who rode horses, crushed the Persian army at the battle of Granicus. This area was located in what is today northwestern Turkey.

Alexander's forces continued across Asia Minor. They freed Greek city-states that had been under Persian rule.

Marking the Text

1. Circle the name of the person who warned the Greeks about Philip's army.

Reading Check

2. How was Philip II able to gain control over most of Greece?

____

____

____

Drawing Conclusions

3. How did Alexander fulfill his father's dream?

____

____

____

Analyzing

4. Why do you think Alexander and his armies were so successful in their battles against the Persians?

____

____

____

Marking the Text

5. Underline the kinds of hardships Alexander and his soldiers experienced when they crossed the desert.

Reading Check

6. Why was the Battle of Guagamela so important to Alexander?

____

____

____

In 333 B.C. Alexander defeated the Persian army at Issus, in Syria. The Persian king, Darius III, had to run away.

Then Alexander went south. In 331 B.C. he conquered Egypt. There he built the city of Alexandria, naming it after himself. It became one of the most important cities of the ancient world. Later that year, Alexander went northeast to Mesopotamia. He defeated Darius's forces at Guagamela, near the Tigris River. After this victory, Alexander's army took over the rest of the Persian Empire.

Defeating the Persian Empire

334 B.C. Alexander's cavalry crushes Persian Army at Granicus.

↓

334 B.C. Alexander's army frees Greek city-states in Asia Minor from Persian rule.

↓

333 B.C. Alexander defeats Persian Army at Issus and Darius flees.

↓

331 B.C. Alexander conquers Egypt.

↓

331 B.C. Alexander's army smashes Darius's forces at Gaugamela.

↓

331 B.C. Alexander takes over Persian Empire.

Alexander did not stop. In 327 B.C. he and his army marched into northwestern India. They fought a number of bloody battles. His soldiers grew tired of war, so Alexander agreed to lead them home.

On the way there, the army crossed a desert in what is modern Iran. There was very little water. Heat and thirst killed thousands of soldiers. When soldiers found some water, they gave it to Alexander in a helmet. Alexander poured the water on the ground. He showed his soldiers that he was willing to suffer the same thirst and pain that they did.

Alexander arrived back in Babylon in 323 B.C. The journey and all the battles had wrecked Alexander's health. He died in Babylon. He was only 32 years old.

Lesson 3 Alexander's Empire, *Continued*

Alexander's Legacy

Alexander was a great and brave military leader. Alexander is thought to have always tried to copy his hero, Achilles. Achilles was one of the warriors in the *Iliad* by Homer.

When he died, Alexander was the most powerful ruler in the ancient world. That is one reason we call him Alexander the Great.

A legacy is what a person leaves to other people when he or she dies. Alexander's legacy was a world that knew about Greek culture. Wherever Alexander's army went, they spread the Greek language, ideas, and art. This is another reason why he is called Alexander the Great.

Alexander's accomplishments were the beginnings of the **Hellenistic Era.** *Hellenistic* means "like the Greeks." The Hellenistic Era is the time when Greek ideas spread to non-Greek people in all the lands Alexander had conquered.

Alexander wanted the Macedonians, the Greeks, the Egyptians, and the Persians to unite under a single empire. It did not happen.

After Alexander died, his generals fought with each other. The empire fell apart. It became four separate Hellenistic kingdoms: Macedonia, Pergamum, Egypt, and the Seleucid Empire. The kings often gave jobs to Greeks or Macedonians. It was one way to control the government.

By 100 B.C., Alexandria was the largest city in the Mediterranean world. Its library had the largest number of writings in ancient times. The Hellenistic kings built many other cities, too. These cities needed many workers. The kings asked Greeks and Macedonians to move to these cities. These colonists helped spread the Greek culture into Egypt and as far east as India.

Check for Understanding

List two things Alexander did to try to unify the Greeks and Macedonians with the peoples they conquered.

1. ______________________________

2. ______________________________

Name two legacies that Alexander left behind.

3. ______________________________

4. ______________________________

Glue Foldable here

Explaining

7. Give two reasons why Alexander was called "Alexander the Great."

____

____

____

Reading Check

8. What happened to Alexander's empire after he died?

____

____

____

FOLDABLES®

9. Place a two-tab Foldable along the dotted line to cover the Check for Understanding. On the anchor tab, write *Alexander the Great.* Label the top tab *Military Leader* and the bottom tab *Hellenistic Era.*

Use both sides of the tabs to record what you remember about Alexander the Great.

NAME________________________________ DATE _______________ CLASS ___________

Lesson 4 Hellenistic Culture

ESSENTIAL QUESTION

How do new ideas change the way people live?

GUIDING QUESTIONS

1. ***How did Greek culture spread during the Hellenistic Era?***
2. ***What ideas and discoveries emerged during the Hellenistic Era?***
3. ***How did Greece fall under Roman rule?***

Terms to Know

Epicureanism the philosophy of Epicurus, which says that the purpose of life is to find happiness and peace

Stoicism the philosophy of the Stoics, which says that people should use reason and not emotion

circumference the outer border of a circle; the measurement of that border

plane geometry branch of mathematics that shows the relationships of points, lines, angles, and surfaces of figures that are flat or level

solid geometry branch of mathematics that shows the relationships of points, lines, angles, surfaces, and solids in three-dimensional space

When did it happen?

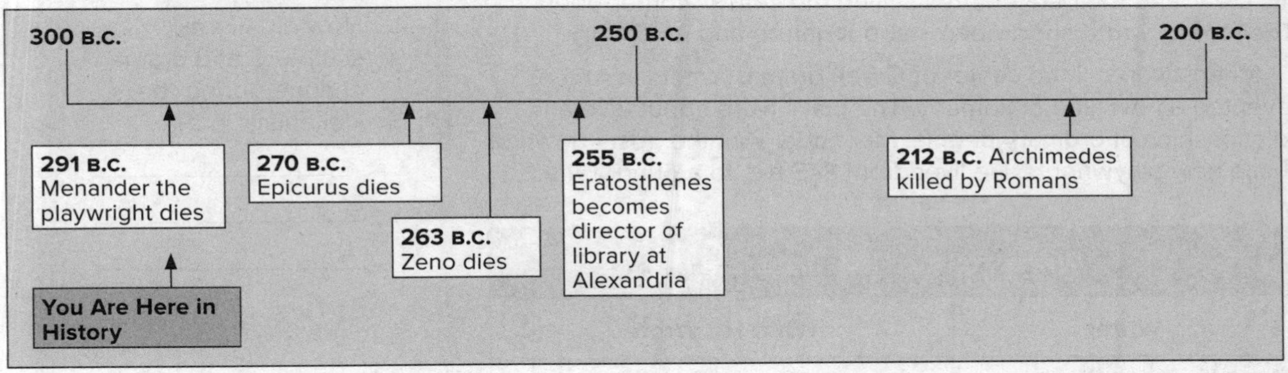
300 B.C.
250 B.C.
200 B.C.
291 B.C. Menander the playwright dies
270 B.C. Epicurus dies
263 B.C. Zeno dies
255 B.C. Eratosthenes becomes director of library at Alexandria
212 B.C. Archimedes killed by Romans
You Are Here in History

What do you know?

In the first column, answer the questions based on what you know before you study. After this lesson, complete the last column.

Now...		Later...
	What do you know about Greek culture?	
	Why did the Greeks fall to the Romans?	

Hellenistic Arts

During the Hellenistic Era, scientists, writers, philosophers, and poets moved to the new Greek cities in Egypt and Southwest Asia. Many came to use Alexandria's library. It had more than 500,000 scrolls. Alexandria also had a museum that brought people to study and do research.

The Hellenistic kings built new cities and rebuilt old ones. They brought in Greek architects to design the new baths, temples, and theaters in the Greek style. The kings and other rich citizens hired Greek sculptors to make statues. Hellenistic sculptors developed new styles. They did not carve ideal versions of the perfect human body. They showed people more realistically. They even showed people being angry or sad.

Writers wrote drama, poetry, and histories at this time, but most of this writing has been lost or destroyed. Appolonius of Rhodes wrote an epic poem called *Argonautica*. It is about Jason, his crew, and their adventures sailing the seas. Another poet, Theocritus, wrote short poems about nature and its beauty.

Athens was still the center of Greek drama. Writers in Athens invented a new kind of comedy. The plays were about love and relationships of ordinary people. Menander was the best-known of these new playwrights. He lived from 343 B.C. to around 291 B.C.

Writers of the Hellenistic Era

Writer	What He Wrote
Appolonius of Rhodes	epic poem *Argonautica*
Theocritus	short poems about nature and its beauty
Menander	plays about love and relationships of ordinary people

Thinkers and Scientists

During this time, the most famous philosophers still went to Athens. The two most important Hellenistic philosophers were Epicurus and Zeno.

Epicurus developed **Epicureanism.** This philosophy taught people that happiness should be the goal of life. Today, *epicurean* means a love of good food or comfortable things. To Epicurus, happiness meant spending time with friends and not worrying.

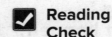

Examining Details

1. How did the Hellenistic kings spread Greek culture?

______

______

______

Reading Check

2. How did Greek sculpture and drama change during the Hellenistic Era?

______

______

______

Lesson 4 Hellenistic Culture, *Continued*

Defining

3. What is *Stoicism*?

____

____

____

Applying

4. If you wanted to figure out how much air is in a basketball, would you use plane geometry or solid geometry?

____

____

Drawing Conclusions

5. Why do you think the effects of Hellenistic culture were so long-lasting?

____

____

____

____

A thinker named Zeno developed **Stoicism.** Stoics believed that happiness came from following logic and reason. Emotions, like anger or sadness, caused problems. Today we call someone a stoic if they do not seem to be affected by joy or sadness. Stoics also believed that people were happy when they did their duty to the community.

Science flourished during the Hellenistic Era. Scientists of that time had only simple instruments, but they performed experiments and made discoveries. Aristarchus was an astronomer. Astronomers study stars, planets, and other objects outside the Earth's atmosphere. Aristarchus said that the sun was at the center of the universe and that Earth went around the sun. Other astronomers thought he was wrong.

Eratosthenes was a scientist in charge of Alexandria's library. He figured out that Earth was round. He also measured the **circumference** of Earth, or how big around it was. The estimate that Eratosthenes made was only 185 miles (298 kilometers) off the actual distance.

Euclid was a mathematician who wrote *Elements*. The book teaches **plane geometry**—a branch of mathematics concerned with how points, lines, angles, and surfaces work together.

Greek Scientist	Occupation	Discoveries
Aristarchus	Astronomer	sun was at the center of the universe; Earth went around the sun
Eratosthenes	Scientist; in charge of library at Alexandria	Earth was round; measured the circumference of Earth
Euclid	Mathematician	wrote the book, *Elements*, which teaches plane geometry
Archimedes	Mathematician; Inventor	worked on solid geometry; figured out the value of *pi*; invented the catapult

Archimedes was the most famous scientist of the Hellenistic Era. He worked on **solid geometry**—the branch of mathematics concerned with the study of spheres [ball-like shapes] and cylinders [tube-like shapes]. He figured out the value of *pi*, which is used to measure how much space a circle covers. Its symbol is π.

Lesson 4 Hellenistic Culture, *Continued*

Archimedes was also an inventor. He invented the catapult, a war machine that hurled rocks, arrows, and spears at the enemy. In 212 B.C. the Romans attacked Syracuse. The catapults worked so well that it took the Romans three years to capture Syracuse. Finally the Romans got inside the city walls. They massacred most of the people, including Archimedes.

Hellenistic thinking and culture had long-lasting effects. More than 700 years after the Hellenistic Era, the mathematician Hypatia lived in Alexandria. Like the earlier Greeks, she studied philosophy and mathematics. She believed in the use of reason instead of superstition.

Greece and Rome

The four kingdoms that formed from Alexander's empire often fought wars against each other. Some Greek city-states became independent, but they did not have strong armies. They were not free for very long.

Rome was a city-state in central Italy. In the late 200s B.C., Rome conquered all of Italy. The Greeks tried to stop Rome. They supported Rome's enemies in wars. The Romans won all those wars, though. Soon, Rome gained control of the Greek mainland.

Check for Understanding

List two discoveries made in math and astronomy during the Hellenistic Era that are still important to us today.

1. ______________________________

2. ______________________________

People from Greece moved to cities in the Hellenistic kingdoms. List two jobs they did there.

3. ______________________________

4. ______________________________

Glue Foldable here

Reading Check

6. How were Epicureanism and Stoicism similar? How were they different?

____

____

____

____

Reading Check

7. How did the Greek city-states react to Rome's growing power?

____

____

____

FOLDABLES®

8. Place a two-tab Foldable to cover the Check for Understanding. On the anchor tab, write *Hellenistic Era.* Label the top tab *Thinkers and Writers* and the bottom tab *Scientists and Mathematicians.* Use both sides of the tabs to list what you know about each.

Ancient India

Lesson 1 Early Civilizations

ESSENTIAL QUESTION

How does geography influence the way people live?

GUIDING QUESTIONS

1. ***How did physical geography and climate influence the development of civilization in India?***
2. ***How did the people of the Indus River valley build cities?***
3. ***How did the Aryans influence early India?***
4. ***How was society in ancient India organized?***

Terms to Know

subcontinent a large landmass that is smaller than a continent
monsoon seasonal wind, especially in the Indian Ocean and southern Asia
language family a group of similar languages
Sanskrit the first written language of India
Vedas ancient sacred writings of India
raja an Indian prince
guru a teacher

Where in the world?

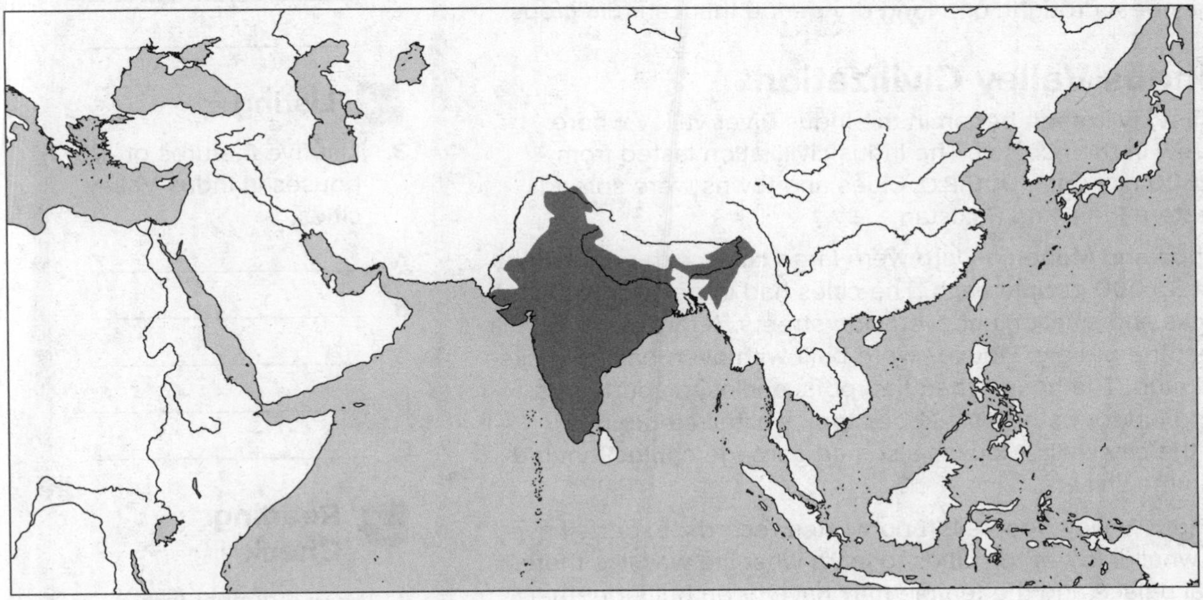

When did it happen?

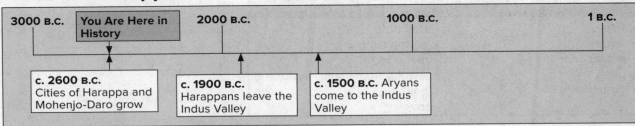

3000 B.C. — **You Are Here in History** — 2000 B.C. — 1000 B.C. — 1 B.C.

- **c. 2600 B.C.** Cities of Harappa and Mohenjo-Daro grow
- **c. 1900 B.C.** Harappans leave the Indus Valley
- **c. 1500 B.C.** Aryans come to the Indus Valley

The Geography of India

India's northern border starts on the southern edge of the continent of Asia. The Himalaya is a mountain system which blocks off India from the rest of Asia. This makes India a **subcontinent.**

The Ganges and Indus Rivers are in northern India. The Ganges runs southeast into the Indian Ocean. The Indus flows southwest into the Arabian Sea. Their water comes from melting snow in the Himalaya. The Deccan Plateau is south of the river valleys. It is dry and hilly. The coastal areas have plains, or flat land, that is good for farming.

India's climate, or usual weather, has **monsoons,** or strong winds. The winter monsoon blows in cold, dry air from the mountains. The summer monsoon brings warm, wet air from the Arabian Sea. Summer monsoons bring the rainy season. If the rain comes in time, the crops will be good. If the rains are late, then there may be a drought, or a long dry period that can ruin crops.

The Indus Valley Civilization

India's first civilization began in the Indus River valley where crops grew in the rich soil. The Indus civilization lasted from about 2600 B.C. until 1900 B.C. Cities and towns were spread over western India and Pakistan.

Harappa and Mohenjo-Daro were large cities with populations of about 35,000 people each. The cities had large streets paved with bricks and smaller, unpaved side streets. A fortress was built to protect the people. Houses were built with oven-baked bricks made of mud. The houses had flat roofs, enclosed courtyards, wells, and indoor bathrooms. Pipes took wastewater to pits outside the city walls. Houses also had garbage chutes that led to bins in the streets.

The Indus Valley people left no written records. Experts have studied what is left of the cities to learn what life was like there. The royal palace and the temple may have been built together inside a fortress.

Farmers Grew	City Dwellers Made
• rice • barley • wheat • peas • cotton	• clay pots • cotton cloth • metal tools • jewelry from shells, ivory, and gold • toys

Marking the Text

1. In the text, circle the landform that separates India from the rest of Asia.

Reading Check

2. How do monsoon winds affect life in India?

____

____

____

Listing

3. List five features of houses in Indus Valley cities.

A. _______________

B. _______________

C. _______________

D. _______________

E. _______________

Reading Check

4. How did most Indus Valley people earn a living?

____

____

____

Most people were farmers. City dwellers made goods that could be traded. Indus Valley merchants traded with the Mesopotamians. Some traders sailed across the Arabian Sea. Others made the difficult trip through the mountains.

Aryan Migrations and Settlements

Around 1900 B.C., the people of the Indus Valley began to leave their cities. Soon, people called the Aryans began settling the river valley.

The Aryans came from central Asia. They were nomads, so they traveled around to find food for their herds of cattle. The Aryans were not a single race or a tribe. They were a group of people who spoke similar languages. This **language family** was called Indo-European. The Aryans were good warriors, and expert horse riders and hunters.

Aryan Civilization

- nomads became farmers
- made up of groups who spoke similar languages
- made iron tools
- developed language of Sanskrit
- lived in groups ruled by rajas

After awhile, the Aryans stopped living as nomads and became farmers. Over time, they decided that cattle were sacred, so people in India stopped eating meat from cattle. The Aryans began to make iron tools. With these, they cleared India's forests and dug canals to bring water from the river to the fields. This made the Ganges River valley good for growing crops. Farmers in north India grew wheat, barley, and other grains. In the river valleys, farmers grew rice. In the south, they grew spices like pepper, ginger, and cinnamon.

The early Aryans did not write things down when they were nomads. When they became farmers, they developed a written language called **Sanskrit.** Using Sanskrit, they wrote down sales and trade information. They also wrote down songs, stories, poems, and prayers in sacred books called the **Vedas.**

The Aryans lived in groups, each ruled by a **raja,** or prince. Rajas often fought with each other over treasure and cattle.

Identifying

5. The Aryans were different groups of people. In what way were they alike?

____

____

____

Listing

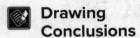

6. What two activities did the Aryans stop after moving into the Indus River valley?

____

____

____

Drawing Conclusions

7. Why did the Aryans develop written language?

____

____

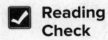

Reading Check

8. How did the Aryans change their way of life after they settled in India?

____

____

____

Ancient India Society

Ancient Indian society was grouped into four classes called *varnas*. The top *varna* was the Brahmins, who were priests. The next *varna* was the Kshatriyas, the warriors. They ran the government and the army. After the Kshatriyas came the Vaisyas, or "common" people." They were farmers, craftspeople, and merchants. Then came the Sudras. They were lower-class workers and servants who had few rights. Most Indians were Sudras.

The four *varnas* gradually divided into thousands of smaller groups known as ***jati***. A person was born into one *jati* and could never move into another. The *jati* system had rules for almost every part of life, including marriage, work, and friendships.

One group was too low to be part of the *jati* system—the Untouchables. Untouchables did work considered too dirty for *jati* members, such as collecting trash. Most Indians thought Untouchables were unclean. As a result, Untouchables were made to live apart from everyone else.

Grandparents, parents, and children all lived together with the oldest man in charge. This is called an extended, or enlarged, family.

Men had many more rights than women. Only men went to school or could become priests. When they were young, some boys studied with a **guru,** or teacher. Older boys went to schools in the cities. Parents chose marriage partners for their children. Divorce was not allowed.

Check for Understanding

Write whether each feature was from the Indus Valley civilization, Aryan civilization, or both.

________ **1.** developed the *varna* system

________ **2.** used mud bricks to make buildings

________ **3.** grew rice, wheat, and barley

________ **4.** used the Sanskrit language

________ **5.** built large cities with paved streets

Marking the Text

9. In the text, circle the names of the four *varnas* and the group that was not part of the *jati* system. Underline the types of people who belonged to each.

Reading Check

10. What was family life like in ancient India?

____

____

____

FOLDABLES®

11. Place a three-tab Venn diagram to cover the Check for Understanding. Label the top tab *Indus Valley Civilization* and the bottom tab *Aryan Civilization*. Label the center tab *Both*.

List what you remember about each civilization. On the center tab, list similarities between the two civilizations.

Glue Foldable here

Ancient India

Lesson 2 Religions of Ancient India

ESSENTIAL QUESTION

How do religions develop?

GUIDING QUESTIONS

1. ***What are the basic beliefs of Hinduism? How did Hinduism develop?***
2. ***Why did Buddhism appeal to many people in various parts of Asia?***
3. ***What are the teachings of Jainism?***

Terms to Know

Hinduism major religion that developed in ancient India; main belief: all souls are part of one universal spirit

Brahman the universal spirit worshipped by Hindus

reincarnation the idea that the soul is reborn into many different lives

dharma a person's personal duty, based on the individual's place in society

karma a good or bad force created by a person's actions; it determines whether a person's soul will be reborn into a higher or lower form of life

Buddhism religion founded by Siddhartha Gautama; main belief: inner peace comes from ending desire

nirvana a state of perfect happiness that is achieved after giving up all desires

Jainism religion that does not believe in a supreme being; it emphasizes nonviolence and respect for all living things

When did it happen?

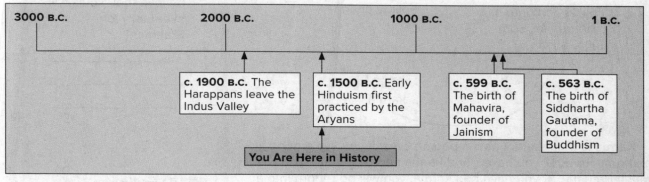

3000 B.C. — 2000 B.C. — 1000 B.C. — 1 B.C.

c. 1900 B.C. The Harappans leave the Indus Valley

c. 1500 B.C. Early Hinduism first practiced by the Aryans

You Are Here in History

c. 599 B.C. The birth of Mahavira, founder of Jainism

c. 563 B.C. The birth of Siddhartha Gautama, founder of Buddhism

What do you know?

Put a check mark (✓) next to each term that you know. For every word that you check, write a short description or definition.

_______ Sanskrit ______________________________

_______ the Vedas ______________________________

_______ varnas ______________________________

_______ guru ______________________________

_______ Untouchables ______________________________

Lesson 2 Religions of Ancient India, *Continued*

Origins of Hinduism

Hinduism is one of the oldest religions in the world. It grew from the faith of the Aryans. Hinduism has no one founder and no one holy book.

Hindus believe in one great spirit called **Brahman.** They also believe that all living things and even the gods are part of Brahman.

Hindus believe that a person's soul will eventually join Brahman. Before that can happen, however, a soul must live many lives—even some as an animal. The idea of living many lives in different forms, one after another, is called **reincarnation.** According to Hinduism, if people do the duties of their jati, they will get a better next life. They must follow **dharma,** or their personal duty. If a person follows dharma, then they have good karma.

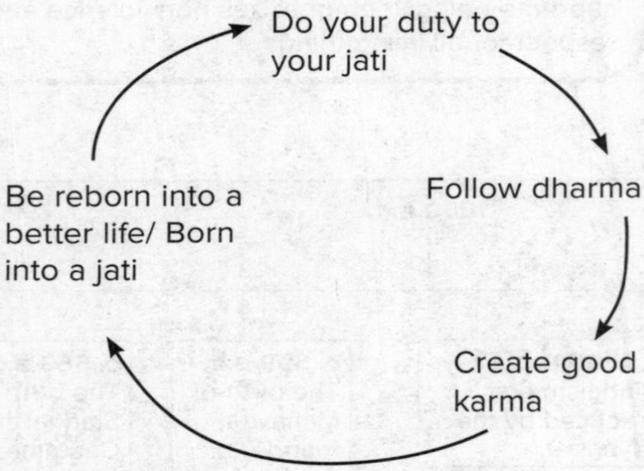
Do your duty to your jati
Follow dharma
Create good karma
Be reborn into a better life/ Born into a jati

Karma is the result of how a person lives. If you live a good life and do your duty, you have good karma and eventually, you will reach Brahman. If you have bad karma, you will be reborn into a lower jati or as an animal and will remain in the cycle of reincarnation.

This belief in dharma and karma mean that people have to obey the rules of their jati because that is where they have to stay until their next lifetime. The idea of reincarnation gives them their only hope.

Rise of Buddhism

Prince Siddhartha Gautama was born about 563 B.C. Siddhartha was wealthy, married, and had a son. One day he left the palace and was shocked to see that most people were poor. He asked himself why people suffered.

Sequencing

1. Fill in the blanks with words from this section.

   Hindus believe that the soul goes through ________. A person is born into a ________. If they follow the ________ of their jati, they make good ________ and the cycle starts again.

Describing

2. How do Hindus believe their souls will eventually join Brahman?

   ____
   ____
   ____

Reading Check

3. How did Hinduism affect the way ancient Indians lived day to day?

   ____
   ____
   ____

Lesson 2 Religions of Ancient India, *Continued*

Identifying

4. Who was the founder of Buddhism?

____

____

Explaining

5. How does a Buddhist get to nirvana?

____

____

____

Defining

6. What is the Eightfold Path?

____

____

____

Contrasting

7. What is the difference between Theravada Buddhism and Mahayana Buddhism?

____

____

____

To search for answers, he left his family and lived alone. Legend says that Siddhartha meditated under a tree. Finally, he came to understand the meaning of life. This is called "Enlightenment."

Siddhartha spent the rest of his life teaching people about his discovery. People called him the Buddha, which means "Enlightened One." His lessons about life and suffering are called **Buddhism**.

The Buddha taught that everyone should stop wanting fame, money, and worldly things. Then they would reach **nirvana**, a feeling of perfect peace and happiness. The Buddha said that the only way to stop desiring things was to follow the Eightfold Path—the Buddhist rules for right living.

The Buddha did not agree with the jati system. He taught that all people could reach nirvana. This made Buddhism very popular among the lower jati and the Untouchables.

The Eightfold Path

1. Know and understand the Four Noble Truths.
2. Give up worldly things and do not harm others.
3. Tell the truth, do not gossip, and do not speak badly of others.
4. Do not **commit** evil acts, such as killing, stealing, or living an unclean life.
5. Do rewarding work.
6. Work for good and oppose evil.
7. Make sure your mind keeps your senses under control.
8. Practice meditation to see the world in a new way.

The Buddha taught his ideas for more than 40 years. When he died, his disciples could not agree about what his message really meant. They split into two groups. One was Theravada Buddhism. *Theravada* means "teachings of the wise men." It says that the Buddha was a great teacher, but not a god. Theravada Buddhism spread south and east. It also became popular in Indochina.

The other kind of Buddhism is Mahayana Buddhism. It says that the Buddha is a god. Mahayana Buddhists also honor *bodhisattvas*. Bodhisattvas are enlightened people who choose not to go to heaven even though they could. Instead, they stay on Earth to help others reach nirvana.

Lesson 2 Religions of Ancient India, *Continued*

In Tibet, Mahayana Buddhism mixed with Hinduism and Tibet's own religions. Buddhist leaders called *lamas* led the government. Tibetans believed lamas were reincarnations of the Buddha.

Today, very few Buddhists live in India. Buddhism is widely practiced in Southeast Asia and East Asia. There are about 376 million Buddhists in the world today.

BUDDHISM	
Theravada Buddhism	**Mahayana Buddhism**
• Buddha was a great teacher. • Buddha was not a god.	• Buddha was a god. • People who worship Buddha can go to heaven.

Jainism

Another religion also came to India at this time. It is called **Jainism.** Its main teacher was Mahavira. Mahavira's title was "the Jina," or "the Conqueror." His followers are called Jains. Much of Jainism is like Buddhism. Both taught that people should stop wanting worldly things. Their goal was to stop the process of being reborn and reach nirvana.

Jainism has one main teaching: Never harm any living creature. The name of this teaching is *ahimsa*. *Ahimsa* means that a person should not kill even insects or worms.

Centuries later, in the early 1900s, an Indian man named Mohandas Gandhi led a movement to free his nation from the rule of the British. Instead of using weapons, Gandhi followed the example of *ahimsa*. He and his followers used nonviolent ways of protesting. Through peaceful ways, the nation of India gained its independence.

Glue Foldable here

Check for Understanding

List one important belief or practice of each religion.

1. Hinduism ______________________
2. Buddhism ______________________
3. Jainism ______________________

Reading Check

8. Where is Buddhism practiced today and in what forms?

____

____

____

____

Reading Check

9. What is the belief of *ahimsa*?

____

____

____

FOLDABLES®

10. Place a three-tab Foldable along the dotted line to cover the Check for Understanding. Label the anchor tab *How did they develop?* Label the three tabs *Hinduism*, *Buddhism*, *Jainism*. On the back of the tabs, write a sentence about each religion based upon what you remember.

NAME ____________________ DATE ____________ CLASS __________

networks

Ancient India

Lesson 3 The Mauryan Empire

ESSENTIAL QUESTION

What makes a culture unique?

GUIDING QUESTIONS

1. *How did religion affect the development of the Mauryan Empire?*
2. *Why did the Gupta Empire become powerful?*
3. *What were the cultural contributions of the Mauryan and Gupta Empires?*

Terms to Know

stupa a special, dome-shaped building meant to honor the Buddha

pilgrim a person who travels to places of religious importance

Bhagavad Gita part of a famous long poem; it is about the Hindu god Krishna

When did it happen?

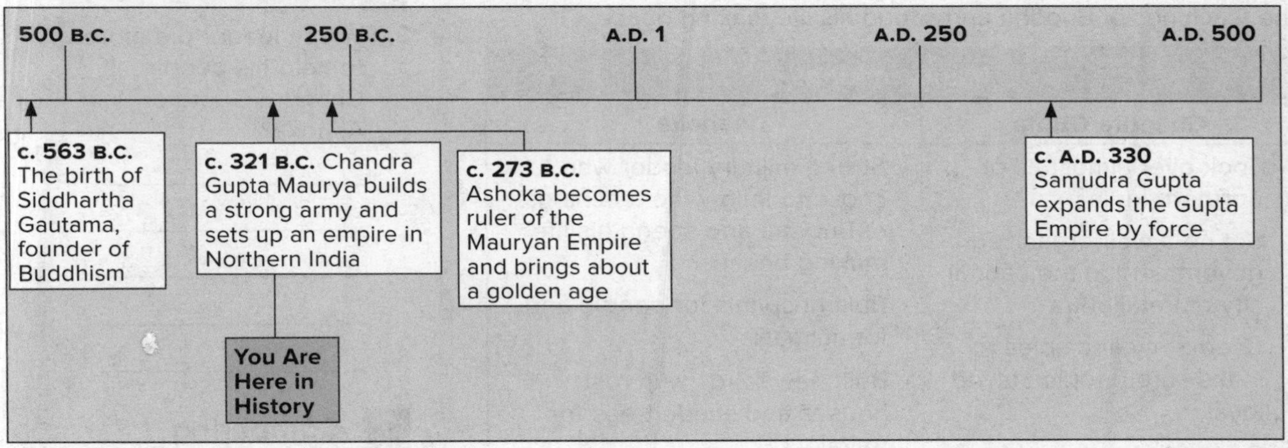

500 B.C.
250 B.C.
A.D. 1
A.D. 250
A.D. 500
c. 563 B.C. The birth of Siddhartha Gautama, founder of Buddhism
c. 321 B.C. Chandra Gupta Maurya builds a strong army and sets up an empire in Northern India
c. 273 B.C. Ashoka becomes ruler of the Mauryan Empire and brings about a golden age
c. A.D. 330 Samudra Gupta expands the Gupta Empire by force
You Are Here in History

What do you know?

Write a short definition of each term using your own words.

empire ____________________

Sanskrit ____________________

Hinduism ____________________

Buddhism ____________________

Lesson 3 The Mauryan Empire, *Continued*

Origin of an Empire

India had many small kingdoms by the 500s B.C. Around 325 B.C., an Indian military leader named Chandra Gupta Maurya built a strong army. He took over almost all of northern India.

In 321 B.C., the Mauryan dynasty began. A dynasty is a group of rulers from the same family. Chandra Gupta set up a well-organized government in the capital city of Pataliputra. To keep control, Chandra Gupta also set up a strong army and a spy system to make sure his subjects were loyal.

Many historians think that the greatest king of the Mauryan Empire was Chandra Gupta's grandson, Ashoka. Ashoka ruled from about 273 B.C. to 232 B.C. He was a strong military leader who grew to hate war. After one bloody fight, he decided to follow the teachings of Buddha and spend his life making peace.

Mauryan Kings

Chandra Gupta	Ashoka
• Took over almost all of northern India • Set up a well-organized government in the capital city of Pataliputra • Used army and spies to make sure people stayed loyal • Created a postal system to have fast communications throughout the empire	• Strong military leader who chose to follow the teachings of Buddha and spend his life making peace • Built hospitals for people and for animals • Built new roads with rest houses and shade trees for travelers • Sent teachers to spread Buddhism throughout India and Asia • Tolerant of other religions such as Hinduism

Ashoka sent teachers to spread Buddhism throughout India and Asia. He had workers carve the Buddha's teachings on pillars, or large, tall stones. He also had workers build thousands of **stupas,** or Buddhist shrines. Unlike most rulers of the time, Ashoka was tolerant of other religions such as Hinduism.

When there is a good road system and a strong ruler, trade is good. Trade was very good under Ashoka. India became the center of a huge trade network. It stretched all the way to the Mediterranean Sea.

Identifying

1. Fill in the blanks. Write three things that Ashoka did for his people after he became a Buddhist.

A. ____________________

B. ____________________

C. ____________________

Comparing

2. Which leader did more to help his people, Chandra Gupta or Ashoka?

____

____

____

____

____

Comparing

3. What did both Chandra Gupta and Ashoka do to increase communication in the empire?

____

____

____

Reading Check

4. What caused Ashoka to denounce violence? What was the result?

____

____

____

____

Reading Check

5. How did the Gupta Empire profit from trade routes?

____

____

____

Identifying

6. In what language were Indian epic poems written?

____

Ashoka died in 232 B.C. The kings who followed him were not good leaders. They forced merchants to pay heavy taxes. They took the peasants' crops without paying them. The empire grew weak. The people turned against these rulers. In 183 B.C., the last Mauryan king was killed by one of his own generals. After that, the Mauryan Empire split into small warring kingdoms.

The Gupta Empire

For the next 500 years, the small kingdoms fought each other. Then, a prince from the Ganges River valley rose to power. His name was Chandra Gupta, just like the founder of the Mauryan Empire. This Chandra Gupta founded the Gupta dynasty in A.D. 320. He ruled from the old capital city, Pataliputra, for ten years. Then, his son Samudra Gupta took over. Samudra Gupta gained new lands for the empire. He became a patron, or gave money, for people to make art and literature. India began a golden age.

Merchants used a network of trade routes to buy and sell. They gained wealth for themselves and the empire. Cities grew along the trade routes and made travel easier.

The Guptas practiced and supported Hinduism. They built fine temples and created beautiful works of art to honor the Hindu gods. **Pilgrims**—people who travel to holy places—used the trade routes to get to these popular places. These travelers made the cities rich.

Culture in Ancient India

Artists, builders, scientists, and writers were busy under the Mauryan and Gupta empires. After Sanskrit developed under the Aryans, the Hindu Vedas were written down. Another kind of popular text was the epic. These were long poems that taught important lessons about right and wrong. The most famous epic poems are the *Mahabharata* and the *Ramayana*.

Epic Poem: The *Mahabharata*

- the longest poem in any written language
- contains about 90,000 verses
- best-known section is the *Bhagavad Gita*
- hero learns that he should do his duty and follow his dharma

The best-known section of the poem *Mahabharata* is the ***Bhagavad Gita***. The name means "Song of the Lord."

Lesson 3 The Mauryan Empire, *Continued*

The hero in the poem learns that he should do his duty and follow his dharma, no matter how difficult it is.

Music was important in the religious and social lives of the ancient Indians. Religious poems, such as the *Bhagavad Gita*, were probably sung in group settings.

Early art that has survived is mostly religious art carved in stone. Many sculptures are of the Buddha, some carved as early as the A.D. 100s. The most important buildings in early India were those used for religious worship.

Mathematicians invented a way to show nothing by using the number zero. The Indian number symbols for 0 through 9 are the same ones we use today. Arab traders adopted these "Arabic numerals" and Europeans later borrowed them. By about the A.D. 1200s, these numerals had replaced Roman numerals.

Indian scientists mapped the movements of the planets and stars. They knew that the Earth was round and that it moved around the sun. Metal workers used steel and iron to make tools and weapons.

Gupta doctors set broken bones and performed operations. They invented medical tools, such as scalpels, and used herbs to treat illnesses. A doctor named Shushruta even performed an early type of plastic surgery.

Mathematics	Science	Medicine

Glue Foldable here

Check for Understanding

List one accomplishment of each Indian leader.

1. Chandra Gupta Maurya ______
2. Ashoka ______
3. Samudra Gupta ______

Listing

7. In the graphic organizer, list some of the advances in mathematics, science, and medicine.

Reading Check

8. What lasting achievement did Indian mathematicians make?

______

______

______

FOLDABLES®

9. Place a 3-tab Venn diagram Foldable along the dotted line to cover the Check for Understanding. Label the top tab *Mauryan Empire* and the bottom tab *Gupta Empire*. Label the center tab *Both*. On the top and bottom tabs, list words or phrases that describe each empire. On the middle tab, write what they had in common.

NAME _______________ DATE _______ CLASS _______

networks

Early China

Lesson 1 The Birth of Chinese Civilization

ESSENTIAL QUESTION

What makes a culture unique?

GUIDING QUESTIONS

1. *How have rivers, mountains, and deserts shaped the development of China's civilization?*
2. *Why did China's Shang rulers become powerful?*
3. *How did the Zhou claim the right to rule China?*

Terms to Know

warlord a leader who has his own army

aristocrat a person who belongs to the highest class of society

ancestor a family member who is no longer living

pictograph a symbol in a writing system based on pictures

ideograph a symbol in a writing system that represents a thing or an idea

bureaucracy a group of non-elected government officials

hereditary having title or possession by reason of birth

Mandate of Heaven belief that the Chinese king's right to rule came from the gods

Dao Chinese system of beliefs that describes the way a king must rule

Where in the world?

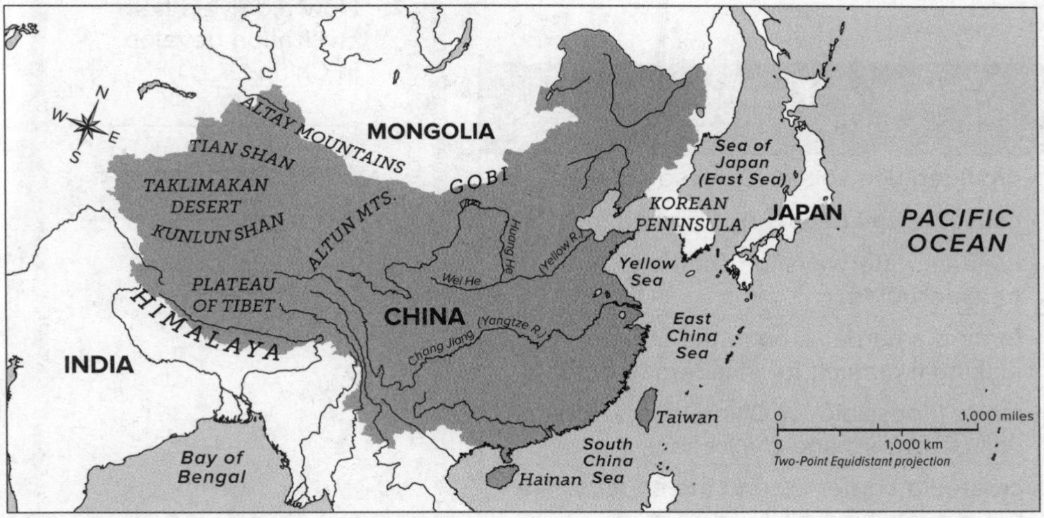

When did it happen?

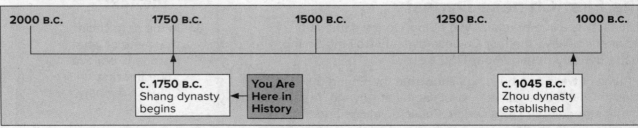

2000 B.C. — 1750 B.C. — 1500 B.C. — 1250 B.C. — 1000 B.C.

c. 1750 B.C. Shang dynasty begins ← **You Are Here in History**

c. 1045 B.C. Zhou dynasty established

The Land of China

Two powerful rivers have helped shape Chinese history. The Huang He, or Yellow River, flows across China. As it flows, it carries large amounts of rich soil. The soil spreads along the banks of the river. This makes the land more fertile, or a high quality for farming. Farmers along the Huang He are able to grow more food. However, the Huang He often floods. Millions of people have died because of these floods.

The Chang Jiang, or Yangtze River, is another important waterway in China. Like the Huang He, the Chiang Jiang provides rich soil for farming. It also serves as a way of trade and transportation.

Mountains and deserts cover much of China. They were difficult to cross, acting like walls around the country. These natural barriers limited contact between China and other civilizations. The high mountains and vast deserts helped China develop a unique culture. Chinese civilization was different from other civilizations.

Geographic Feature	Effect on Chinese Civilization
rivers	• provided rich soil for Chinese farmers • caused many deaths by flooding • used as waterways for trade and transportation
mountains	• formed a barrier around the country making it difficult for invaders to enter • made it possible for China to develop a unique culture and civilization
deserts	• created a barrier around the country, like the mountains did

The First Chinese Dynasty

A dynasty is a line of rulers who belong to the same family. Historians believe the first Chinese dynasty was the Shang. The Shang dynasty began about 1750 B.C.

Ruins of walls and buildings show that the Shang built the first cities in China. One was the royal capital at Anyang. A palace and temple stood at the city's center. Public buildings and the homes of government officials were nearby. Beyond these stood workshops and other homes.

Explaining

1. How did mountains and deserts affect China's civilization?

____

____

____

____

Reading Check

2. How did rivers help civilization develop in China?

____

____

____

Marking the Text

3. In the text, circle the name of what historians believe to be the first Chinese dynasty.

Defining

4. What is a *warlord*?

____

____

Identifying

5. Which group of people made up most of Chinese society?

____

Contrasting

6. What is the difference between a pictograph and an ideograph?

____

____

____

Reading Check

7. Why did Shang kings have questions scratched on oracle bones?

____

____

The king was the political, religious, and military leader of Shang China. Over time, the Shang conquered nearby areas. Kings began to rule more land and people. Warlords helped the Shang kings control territories throughout the country. A **warlord** is a military leader who has his own army.

Warlords and other royal officials were aristocrats. **Aristocrats** are people in an upper class of society. Their wealth comes from the land they own. Most Chinese people, however, were farmers. They farmed the land owned by aristocrats. A small number were merchants, artisans, and enslaved people.

People in Shang China:

- worshiped many gods
- believed the gods could bring good or bad fortune
- honored their **ancestors**, or long-dead family members.
- believed their ancestors would bring them good luck
- made offerings to the gods and their ancestors

Kings looked to their ancestors for help in making important decisions. They had priests scratch questions on oracle bones such as, "Will I win the battle?" Priests heated the bones until they cracked. Answers were found in the pattern of the cracks.

Early Chinese writing used pictographs and ideographs. **Pictographs** are characters that represent objects. **Ideographs** are another kind of character. They link two or more pictographs to express an idea.

The Zhou: China's Longest Dynasty

According to legend, the last Shang ruler was a wicked tyrant. Rebels overthrew the Shang government and declared a new dynasty called the Zhou. The Zhou ruled China for more than 800 years. The king led the government. He was helped by a **bureaucracy.** A bureaucracy is a group of selected officials who do different government jobs.

Under Zhou rulers, China grew larger. The king divided the country into territories. Each territory was ruled by an aristocrat. When an aristocrat died, his son or another member of his family governed the territory. This means these positions were **hereditary**.

Zhou kings believed that the gods gave them the right to rule China. This idea is known as the **Mandate of Heaven**. The Mandate said that the king must rule by the proper "Way," known as the **Dao**. The king's duty was to honor and please the gods.

Lesson 1 The Birth of Chinese Civilization, *Continued*

During the Zhou dynasty, new technology helped farmers. The Chinese developed better ways to bring water to their fields. With a better irrigation system, farmers were able to grow more food than ever before. Under the Zhou, China's trade expanded also. Silk from the Zhou dynasty has been found as far away as Greece.

The aristocrats became more powerful under the Zhou. They began to ignore the king. They each took control of their own territory, or states. Aristocrats began to fight each other for power. These battles lasted for nearly 200 years. This time in Chinese history is known as the "Period of the Warring States."

Check for Understanding

List two different landforms and explain how each one helped shape Chinese history.

1. ______________________

2. ______________________

List one accomplishment of the Shang dynasty and one accomplishment of the Zhou dynasty.

3. ______________________

4. ______________________

Glue Foldable here

Defining

8. What does *hereditary* mean?

____

____

____

Reading Check

9. What technology was developed in China during the Zhou dynasty?

____

____

FOLDABLES®

10. Place a two-tab Foldable along the dotted line to cover the Check for Understanding. Label the tabs—*Shang Dynasty* and *Zhou Dynasty*.

Use both sides to list facts about each family of Chinese kings, their beliefs, and how they governed the people. Use this Foldable and the chart on Geographic Features to complete the lists in the Check for Understanding.

NAME ______________________ DATE __________ CLASS __________

networks

Early China

Lesson 2 Society and Culture in Ancient China

ESSENTIAL QUESTION

How do new ideas change the way people live?

GUIDING QUESTIONS

1. ***How did Chinese thinkers influence society and government?***
2. ***How was early Chinese society organized?***

Terms to Know

Confucianism a system of beliefs based on the teachings of Confucius; duty is central idea

Daoism a Chinese philosophy focused on obtaining long life and living in harmony with nature

legalism a Chinese philosophy based on the importance of laws

social class a group of people at a similar cultural, economic, or educational level

filial piety the responsibility children have to respect, obey, and care for their parents

When did it happen?

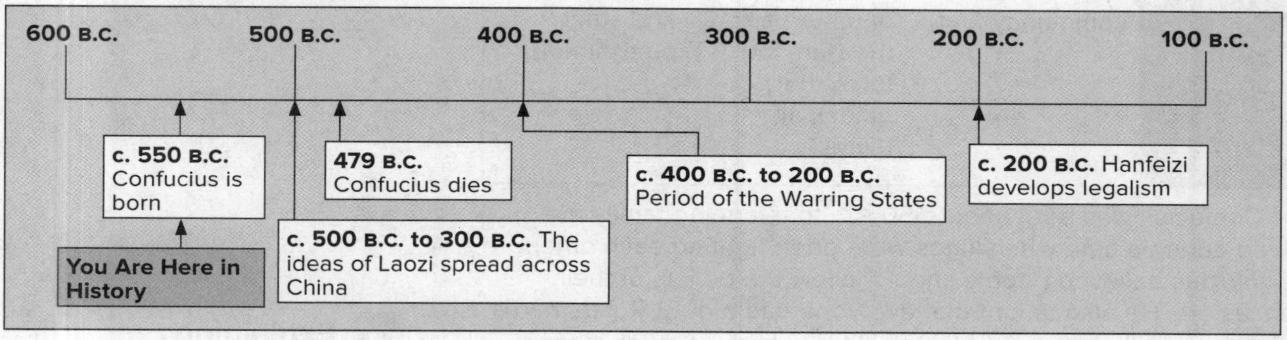

600 B.C.
500 B.C.
400 B.C.
300 B.C.
200 B.C.
100 B.C.
c. 550 B.C. Confucius is born
You Are Here in History
479 B.C. Confucius dies
c. 500 B.C. to 300 B.C. The ideas of Laozi spread across China
c. 400 B.C. to 200 B.C. Period of the Warring States
c. 200 B.C. Hanfeizi develops legalism

What do you know?

In the first column, answer the questions based on what you know before you study. After this lesson, complete the last column.

Now...		Later...
	Who was Confucius?	
	What is legalism?	
	Who owned most of the land, farmers or aristocrats?	
	Were wealthy merchants respected?	
	What did Chinese philosophy say that children owed to their parents?	

Chinese Philosophies

Between 500 B.C. and 200 B.C. Chinese thinkers developed three major philosophies. They were Confucianism, Daoism, and legalism. The philosophies were different from each other. However, they had the same goal. Each philosophy aimed to create a well-run and peaceful society.

	Confucianism	Daoism	Legalism
Founder	Confucius	Laozi	Hanfeizi
Key Ideas	People should put the needs of their family and community first.	People should give up worldly desires in favor of nature and the Dao, the force that guides all things.	Society needs a system of harsh laws and strict punishment.

Confucius was born about 550 B.C. to a farming family. He lived during a time when kings were often fighting each other. Confucius believed people should follow the beliefs of their ancestors. He also taught that everyone had a duty. Rulers had a duty to lead their people wisely. Children had a duty to respect their parents. Parents had a duty to love their children.

Confucius believed that if everyone did their duty and followed traditional beliefs, there would be peace. He also believed that all men should be able to serve in the government. This led to a system of examinations to choose government officials.

Confucius was honored as a great teacher. After his death, his teachings, called **Confucianism,** spread across China.

Like Confucianism, **Daoism** aimed to create a peaceful society. It began with the ideas of Laozi. Confucius thought people should work hard to make the world better. Daoism taught people to turn away from society and live in harmony with nature. Dao means "the Way." Laozi and his followers believed Daoism was the way, or path, to a better life. Many Chinese followed both Confucianism and Daoism.

Hanfeizi introduced the ideas of **legalism** during the 200s B.C. Unlike Confucious and Laozi, he believed that humans are naturally evil. He thought only strict laws and harsh punishment would get people to do what they should do.

Marking the Text

1. In the text, circle the names of the founders of each Chinese philosophy. Underline the name of the philosophy they founded. Draw an arrow from the name of the founder to his philosophy.

Explaining

2. Why is a system of examinations a good way to choose government officials?

____

____

____

____

Lesson 2 Society and Culture in Ancient China, *Continued*

Explaining

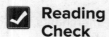

3. Why did aristocrats and kings like legalism?

Reading Check

4. How are the ideas of Confucius and Laozi similar? How are they different?

FOLDABLES®

Summarizing

5. Place a two-tab Foldable along the dotted line to cover the chart titled *Chinese Society*. Cut the tabs in half to form four tabs. Write *Chinese Social Classes* on the anchor tab. Label the tabs: *Aristocrats, Farmers, Artisans*, and *Merchants*. Write on both sides what you learn about the four social classes.

Many aristocrats supported legalism because it emphasized force. Under legalism, rulers did not have to think of the needs or wishes of their people. The ideas led to harsh punishments for even small crimes.

Chinese Life

Chinese society was made up of four social classes. A **social class** is a group of people in a society with the same economic and social position.

Glue Foldable here

Chinese Society	
Aristocrats	• small number of people • wealthy • owned large plots of land and lived on large estates
Farmers	• most people • worked on land owned by aristocrats • paid rent in the form of crops • paid taxes • served as soldiers in wartime • worked one month per year on public projects, such as roads
Artisans	• skilled workers who made useful objects, such as tools and silk cloth • learned skills from fathers and taught them to sons
Merchants	• shopkeepers and traders • lived in towns • provided goods and services to aristocrats • some wealthy, but not respected because merchants made money only for themselves

Lesson 2 Society and Culture in Ancient China, *Continued*

Aristocratic families in China were wealthy. They lived on estates with walls surrounding their homes for protection. They owned large amounts of land. After a father died, his estate was divided equally among his sons. This meant that sons and grandsons ended up with much less land.

Most Chinese were farmers. They lived in villages surrounded by mud walls. Outside these walls were the fields that farmers rented from aristocrats. They paid rent by giving some of their harvest to the aristocrats.

Artisans are skilled workers who make useful objects. Merchants provided goods and services to the aristocrats. Some merchants grew wealthy, but they were not respected. People believed that merchants acted only for their own gain and not for the good of society.

The family was at the center of Chinese society. Chinese families practiced filial piety. **Filial piety** is the responsibility children have to respect, obey, and take care of their parents.

Men and women had very different roles in early China. Men grew crops, ran the government, and fought wars. Women raised children and saw to their education. They also managed the household and family finances.

Marking the Text

6. Underline the work done by men. Circle the work done by women.

Reading Check

7. Why were merchants not respected in ancient China?

____

____

____

FOLDABLES®

8. Place a two-tab Foldable along the dotted line. Label the anchor tab *Philosophies*. Label the top tab *Confucianism* and the bottom tab *Daoism*.

Make a memory map by drawing three arrows below each title. Write words or phrases you remember about each. Use these notes and the *Chinese Social Classes* Foldable to help you answer the questions under the tabs.

Glue Foldable here

Check for Understanding

What is a major difference between Confucianism and Daoism?

1. ______________________

____

List the four classes of early Chinese society.

2. ______________________

3. ______________________

4. ______________________

5. ______________________

Early China

Lesson 3 The Qin and the Han Dynasties

ESSENTIAL QUESTION

How do governments change?

GUIDING QUESTIONS

1. ***How did the Qin Emperor unite China?***
2. ***What improvements did the Chinese make under Han rulers?***
3. ***How did the Silk Road benefit China and the rest of the world?***
4. ***Why did Buddhism become a popular religion in China?***

Terms to Know

censor an official who made sure that government workers did their jobs

currency something that is used as money

civil service government work

tenant farmer a farmer who works land owned by someone else

acupuncture a Chinese practice of inserting fine needles through the skin to treat disease or relieve pain

Where in the world?

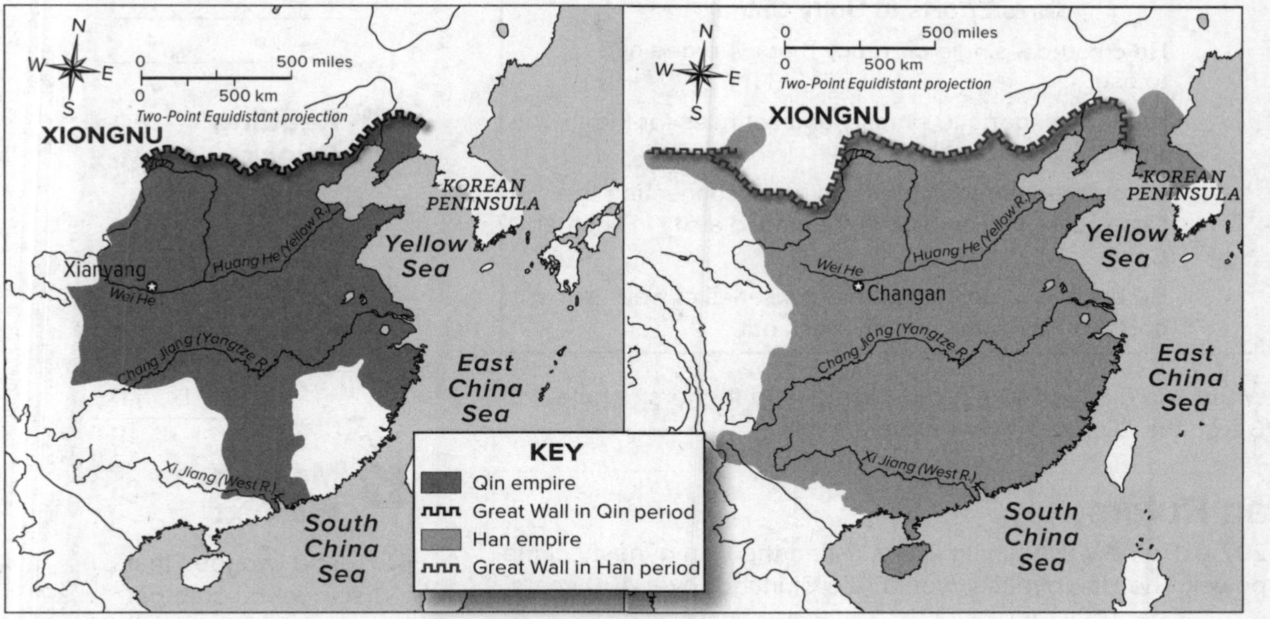

When did it happen?

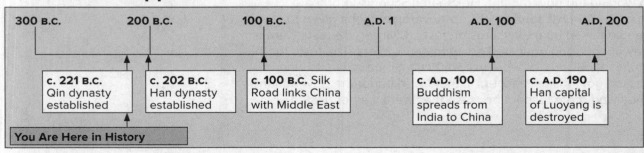

300 B.C. — 200 B.C. — 100 B.C. — A.D. 1 — A.D. 100 — A.D. 200

- **c. 221 B.C.** Qin dynasty established
- **c. 202 B.C.** Han dynasty established
- **c. 100 B.C.** Silk Road links China with Middle East
- **c. A.D. 100** Buddhism spreads from India to China
- **c. A.D. 190** Han capital of Luoyang is destroyed

You Are Here in History

The Qin Emperor

In 221 B.C. the ruler of the Chinese state of Qin took control of China and ended the Zhou dynasty. The new ruler called himself Qin Shihuangdi, which means "the First Qin Emperor." Qin brought many changes to China.

Qin wanted to unify China. He took control of China's provinces. Before then, the provinces were ruled by aristocrats. The aristocrats passed control to their sons when they died. Instead, Qin now appointed the governors.

Qin's rule was harsh. Anyone who disagreed with him was punished or killed. He burned writings that did not agree with him. He appointed **censors** to make sure government officials did their work.

Qin's Efforts to Unify China

- He created a single **currency** that everyone had to use.
- He hired experts to simplify and set rules for the Chinese writing system.
- He ordered farmers to build a canal connecting the Chang Jiang River in central China to a city in southern China.
- He began a project to connect a series of walls across northern China to keep invaders out.

When Qin died in 210 B.C., aristocrats and farmers revolted. By 206 B.C., the Qin dynasty was over.

Han Rulers

In 202 B.C. a new dynasty in China called the Han dynasty came to power. The Han dynasty would rule China for over 400 years.

The first strong Han emperor was Han Wudi. Han Wudi ruled from 141 B.C. to 87 B.C. He wanted dedicated and talented people to work in the government. He created schools to prepare students for **civil service** jobs, or government jobs given to people based on their scores on tests. Civil service tests were a way of choosing educated government workers. The tests for the Chinese civil service were very difficult. Some students who passed got jobs as teachers. Others worked for the government. They won great respect because they were well-educated.

Marking the Text

1. Underline two examples that show Qin's rule was harsh.

Analyzing

2. Do you think Qin's rule helped to unite the country? Why or why not?

____

____

____

Reading Check

3. How would you describe Qin as a ruler?

____

____

____

Marking the Text

4. Circle two jobs that someone could get after passing the civil service examination.

Lesson 3 The Qin and the Han Dynasties, *Continued*

Reading Check

5. Why did Han rulers create civil service examinations?

____

____

____

Explaining

6. Why did Han Wudi encourage trade with the West?

____

____

FOLDABLES®

Listing

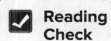

7. Place a two-tab Foldable along the dotted line. Write *Silk Road* on the anchor tab. Label the first tab *to China* and the second tab *from China*. Draw arrows from one tab to the other to illustrate the flow of trade to and from China. On the reverse sides, list facts about the trade routes.

During the Han dynasty, many farmers became tenant farmers. A **tenant farmer** works land that belongs to someone else. Most tenant farmers were very poor. As the population grew, the Han empire took in new areas. Han armies conquered lands to the north, including Korea, and moved south into Southeast Asia. They went west as far as India. The Chinese lived peacefully for nearly 150 years.

During this time, ideas, art, literature, and science blossomed. The ideas of Confucius influenced more people. New paintings and sculptures were created. Writers wrote about current events. They made copies of old works.

New technology helped Chinese farmers produce more food.

- The cast-iron plow was developed. It could break up soil better than wooden plows.
- Waterwheels ground more grain.
- Silk manufacturing improved.
- Paper, a Chinese invention, was used to keep written records.
- The rudder and a new way to move a ship's sails allowed the Chinese to travel farther.

Doctors discovered that certain foods prevented disease. They learned to treat some illnesses with herbs. Chinese doctors relieved their patients' pain with acupuncture. **Acupuncture** is the practice of inserting thin, short needles into a patient's skin at certain points to relieve pain.

On the Silk Road

/ / / / / / / / / / / / Glue Foldable here / / / / / / / / / / / /

During the Han period, Chinese traders grew rich by delivering expensive goods to other parts of the world. Both sea and land routes led to an exchange of goods and ideas.

In A.D. 139 Han Wudi sent a general named Zhang Qian to explore areas west of China. Zhang's mission was to find allies to help China fight their enemies. He returned 13 years later. He had not found allies. However, he told about the people and places he had seen.

He told Han Wudi about the strong horses of the West. Han Wudi wanted these horses for his soldiers. To get them, the emperor encouraged trade between China and the West. Chinese merchants traded silk, spices, and other luxury goods. This trade route to the West would later be called the Silk Road.

The Silk Road was a network of trade routes. When it was completed, it stretched from China to the Mediterranean. Travel on the Silk Road was difficult and dangerous. Traders had to cross high mountains and vast deserts. Robbers and thieves also traveled the roads. Over the years, China came into contact with other civilizations. Chinese inventions, such as paper, traveled along the Silk Road to civilizations in the West.

Buddhism Reaches China

The Silk Road also served as a way to spread ideas. Buddhism spread from India to China along the Silk Road. At first, Buddhism attracted few followers. However, the long period of unrest after the fall of the Han dynasty helped the spread of Buddhism.

Many of the Han emperors after Han Wudi were weak and dishonest. Greedy aristocrats took over more of the land. They forced many farmers to give up their property. Finally, the people rebelled against the Han rulers. In A.D. 190, rebels destroyed the Han capital city, Luoyang. By A.D. 220, civil war divided China. For the next 400 years, China was divided into many small kingdoms.

The long years of civil war made many Chinese feel unsafe. Many turned to Buddhism. Buddhist ideas appealed to people dealing with fear and worry. By the A.D. 400s, Buddhism had become one of China's major religions.

Check for Understanding

List two acts by Qin Shihuangdi to unify China.

1. ______________________________

2. ______________________________

Name one way in which life for farmers worsened during the Han dynasty and one way in which it improved.

3. ______________________________

4. ______________________________

Glue Foldable here

Reading Check

8. What developments led to the creation of the Silk Road?

____

____

____

Reading Check

9. Why did the fall of the Han dynasty help Buddhism spread in China?

____

____

____

FOLDABLES®

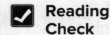

10. Place a two-tab Foldable along the dotted line. Label the anchor tab *Powerful Dynasties*. Label the two tabs—*Qin Dynasty* and *Han Dynasty*. Make a memory map by drawing three arrows below each title. Write three words or phrases that you remember about each on the front of the tabs.

NAME _______________ DATE ________ CLASS ________

networks

Rome: Republic to Empire

Lesson 1 The Founding of Rome

ESSENTIAL QUESTION

How does geography influence the way people live?

GUIDING QUESTIONS

1. ***What effect did geography have on the rise of Roman civilization?***
2. ***How did Rome become a great power?***

Where in the world?

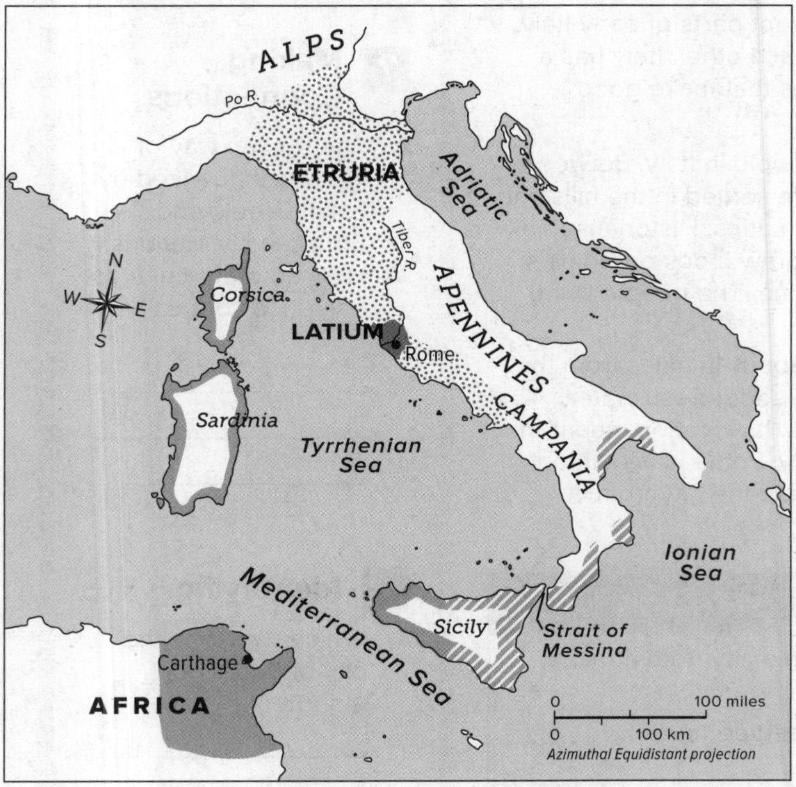

Terms to Know

republic a form of government in which citizens elect their leaders

legion a large group of Roman soldiers

When did it happen?

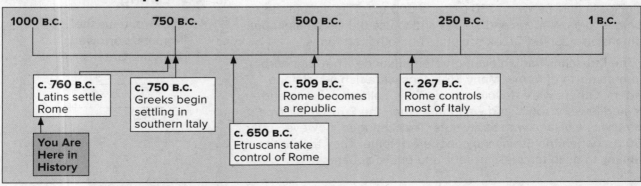

1000 B.C. — 750 B.C. — 500 B.C. — 250 B.C. — 1 B.C.

c. 760 B.C. Latins settle Rome

You Are Here in History

c. 750 B.C. Greeks begin settling in southern Italy

c. 650 B.C. Etruscans take control of Rome

c. 509 B.C. Rome becomes a republic

c. 267 B.C. Rome controls most of Italy

The Beginning of Rome

Italy is a peninsula in the Mediterranean Sea. It is shaped like a boot. The heel points toward Greece. The toe points toward the island of Sicily.

The Alps cross the top of Italy and separate it from the rest of Europe. Another mountain range, called the Apennines, runs down Italy, from north to south. Passes, which run through the mountains, helped link people from different parts of early Italy. They could trade ideas and goods with each other. Italy has a mild climate, rich soil, and large, flat plains that make good farmland.

Historians know little about the first people in Italy. Between 2000 B.C. and 1000 B.C., groups of people settled in the hills and on the plains. These people included the Latins. Historians think that a group of Latins tended herds and grew crops on Rome's hills. Their community developed into Rome. The people living there became known as the Romans.

Rome was built along the Tiber River about 15 miles from the Mediterranean Sea. The river could be used for fresh water, transportation, and the shipping of goods. Its location meant that sea-going pirates could not attack the city. Rome was built on seven hills. The hills made it easy to protect the city from attackers.

Tiber River	Seven Hills
15 miles from Mediterranean Sea	Protected city from attacks
Used for fresh water, transportation, and shipping	Latins settled here

Roman history does not just involve the Latins. Around 800 B.C., the Greeks and the Etruscans came to Italy. The Greeks built many colonies in Italy between 750 B.C. and 500 B.C. They taught the Romans to grow olives and grapes and to use the Greek alphabet. Romans also copied Greek sculpture and other art forms.

The Etruscans had an even greater influence. They came from the area north of Rome. Many Etruscans were rich miners and traders. Others were devoted to art. They painted pictures and created jewelry, tools, and weapons. When the Etruscans came, Rome was a village with straw huts. That changed, however, after 650 B.C. when the Etruscans conquered Rome. They taught the Romans to build temples, streets, and public squares.

Marking the Text

1. Underline two features of Italy's geography.

Making Connections

2. The Roman way of life was influenced by Latin, Greek, and Etruscan civilizations. How do other cultures influence your daily life?

____

____

____

Identifying

3. Which river was the city of Rome built along?

____

____

Listing

4. List two items the Romans borrowed from the Greeks.

____

____

Lesson 1 The Founding of Rome, *Continued*

Reading Check

5. How did the Etruscans influence early Rome?

____

____

____

Contrasting

6. How did Romans rule differently from the Etruscans?

____

____

FOLDABLES®

Describing

7. Assemble a Foldable booklet to be placed along the dotted line. At the top of a one-tab Foldable, write *Republic of Rome.* Glue a two-tab Foldable behind the one-tab. Cut the tabs in half to make four tabs. Label the tabs—*Soldiers*, *Legions*, *Towns and Roads*, and *Conquered People*. Write facts about each category to describe the early days of the republic.

The Etruscans introduced togas and short cloaks. A toga is like a sheet wrapped around your body, with one end over your shoulder. Most importantly, the Etruscans showed the Romans how an army could be more effective. Later, the Romans copied the Etruscan army and conquered an empire.

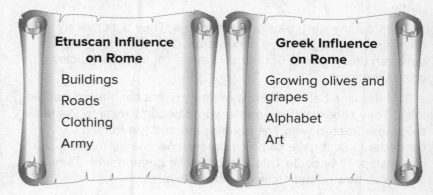

Etruscan Influence on Rome

Buildings

Roads

Clothing

Army

Greek Influence on Rome

Growing olives and grapes

Alphabet

Art

Becoming a Republic

The Etruscans ruled Rome for more than 100 years. The people benefited from Etruscan culture and ideas, but they got tired of Etruscan rulers. According to Roman tradition, in 509 B.C., the Romans rebelled and set up a **republic.** A republic is a form of government in which citizens elect their leaders.

Rome was still a small city when it became a republic. It had enemies all around it. Over the next 200 years, Rome fought many wars. By 267 B.C., the Romans had taken over the Greek colonies in what is now known as Italy. By then, the Romans ruled almost all of the Italian peninsula.

The Roman Republic grew because of its strong army. Roman soldiers were well trained. At the beginning of the republic, every male citizen who owned land had to join the army. Men who ran away, or deserted the army, were killed. This turned Romans into loyal fighters.

The Romans also thought of better ways to organize their army in battle. At first, the soldiers marched next to each other, moving in one large group. They attacked their enemy from only one direction. This way of fighting was slow. Then the generals changed the style of battle.

The Roman generals divided their armies into groups of soldiers called **legions.** Each legion had about 6,000 men. Legions were broken into even smaller groups of 60 or 120 men. These small groups could move very quickly in battle.

Glue Foldable here

Lesson 1 The Founding of Rome, *Continued*

Roman soldiers used a short sword called a *gladius* and an iron spear called a *pilum*. Each group also had a *standard*. A standard was a tall pole with a symbol on top—sometimes an eagle or other animal. One soldier would hold up the standard so others could see it. This helped the group stay together during battle.

The Romans were also smart planners. They built military towns in every region they conquered. Then they built roads between these towns. Soon their armies could travel quickly across the land.

The Romans believed they needed to treat conquered people fairly. They stressed that people would become loyal to Rome if they were treated well. The Romans created the Roman Confederation. It gave some conquered people full Roman citizenship. They could vote and be in the government. They were also treated the same as other citizens by law.

The Romans made other people allies. Allies could run their own towns, but they had to pay taxes to Rome. Allies also had to fight in Rome's armies. With these procedures, the Romans hoped to keep peace. If an area did rebel, Rome was ready to squash it. As a result, the Roman republic grew stronger.

Check for Understanding

List four characteristics of Rome and its people.

1. _______________

2. _______________

3. _______________

4. _______________

Glue Foldable here

? Drawing Conclusions

8. How do you think the people conquered by the Romans felt about their new rulers?

____

____

____

✓ Reading Check

9. Why were the Romans able to expand their control of Italy?

____

____

____

FOLDABLES®

10. Place a two-tab Foldable along the dotted line to cover the Check for Understanding. Label the anchor tab *Roman Civilization*. Label the two tabs—*Rome* and *Romans*. Write at least three words or phrases that you remember about each on the front and back of the tabs. Use your notes to help you complete the Check for Understanding.

NAME________________________________ DATE _____________ CLASS ________

networks

Rome: Republic to Empire

Lesson 2 Rome As a Republic

ESSENTIAL QUESTION

How do governments change?

GUIDING QUESTIONS

1. ***How did conflict between classes change Rome's government?***
2. ***How did Rome conquer the Mediterranean region?***

Terms to Know

patrician a member of the ruling class
plebeian an ordinary citizen
consul head of government
veto to reject or say no to
praetors government officials who interpret the law and serve as judges
tribune an elected official who protects the rights of ordinary citizens
dictator a person given total power
civic duty the idea that citizens have a duty to help their country

Where in the world?

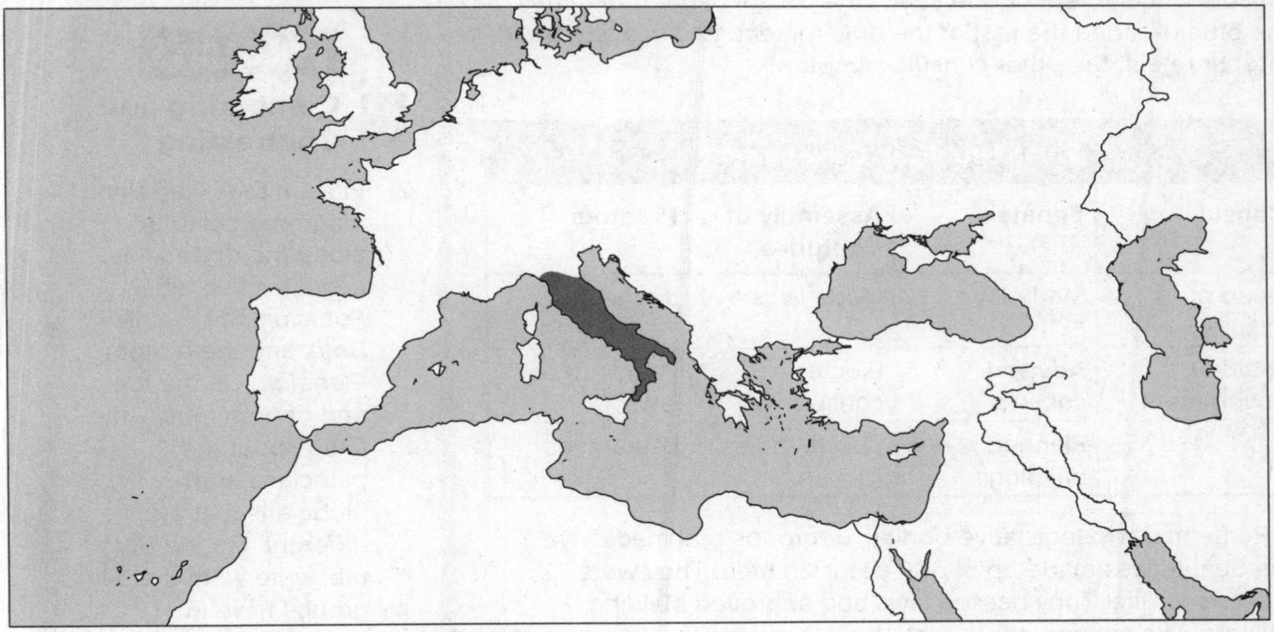

When did it happen?

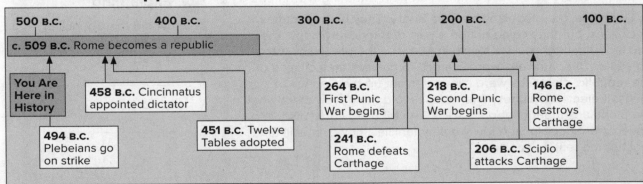

500 B.C. — **400 B.C.** — **300 B.C.** — **200 B.C.** — **100 B.C.**

- **c. 509 B.C.** Rome becomes a republic
- You Are Here in History
- **494 B.C.** Plebeians go on strike
- **458 B.C.** Cincinnatus appointed dictator
- **451 B.C.** Twelve Tables adopted
- **264 B.C.** First Punic War begins
- **241 B.C.** Rome defeats Carthage
- **218 B.C.** Second Punic War begins
- **206 B.C.** Scipio attacks Carthage
- **146 B.C.** Rome destroys Carthage

Lesson 2 Rome As a Republic, *Continued*

Governing Rome

There were two main social classes in early Rome: **patrician** and **plebeian.** Patricians were wealthy landowners who held government offices. Most people were plebeians—shopkeepers, artisans, and small farmers. Patricians and plebeians could not marry each other.

All patrician and plebeian men were citizens and had the right to vote. They had to pay taxes and join the army, but only patricians could be in the government.

The Roman government had three parts. This was to stop any one part from getting too strong. The top leaders were two **consuls** who served for one year. One consul headed the army. The other headed the rest of the government. Each consul could **veto,** or reject, the other consul's decision.

The Republican Government			
Consul	**Senate**	**Assembly of Centuries**	**Praetors**
Head of military	Made laws	Made laws	Judges
Head of government	Advised consuls	Elected consuls	Interpreted laws
	Planned buildings		Led armies

Rome had two legislative bodies, or groups that made laws. The Senate was made up of 300 patrician men. They were senators for life. They passed laws and approved building projects. The second group that made laws was the Assembly of Centuries. It also elected consuls and **praetors** (or judges). Roman praetors could lead armies and help run the government.

Over time, the plebeians became angry. They had the duties of citizens, but they could not be a part of the government. They wanted equal rights. As a result, in 494 B.C., the plebeians went on strike. The patricians were scared. To prevent the collapse of the republic, plebeians were allowed to set up the Council of Plebs. It elected **tribunes.** The tribunes told the government what the plebeians thought about issues. The tribunes could also veto government decisions. A few wealthy families, however, still held most of the real power.

Glue Foldable here

Making Connections

1. How is the structure of the Roman government similar to that of the U.S.?

____

____

____

FOLDABLES®

Comparing and Contrasting

2. Place a three-tab Venn diagram Foldable along the dotted line. Label the top tab *Patrician*, the middle *Both*, and the bottom *Plebeian.* On the top and bottom tabs, write facts about the patricians and plebeians that are different. On the *Both* tab, write what the two groups have in common.

Explaining

3. How did the Council of Plebs change life for the plebeians?

____

____

____

Lesson 2 Rome As a Republic, *Continued*

Summarizing

4. What was the job of the dictators in the early Roman Republic?

____

____

____

Drawing Conclusions

5. How do you think poor Romans felt about the rule of law?

____

____

____

Reading Check

6. What was the emergency that caused Cincinnatus to be appointed dictator?

____

____

____

The Roman Republic included **dictators.** Today, a dictator is a cruel ruler who controls everything. In early Rome, dictators were chosen by the Senate to rule during emergencies. As soon as the emergency ended, the dictator's rule ended.

Tribunes	Dictators
• elected by the Council of Plebs • told leaders what plebeians thought about issues • could veto government decisions	• chosen by the Senate • ruled during an emergency • rule ended when the emergency was over

In 458 B.C. the Roman army was attacked. The Senators chose a farmer named Cincinnatus to be dictator. He had been a respected Roman consul. Cincinnatus gathered an army, which easily defeated the enemy. Afterward, he went home to his farm. Cincinnatus was famous for doing his **civic duty** by serving his government when he was needed.

Plebeians demanded that Rome's laws be written down. That way, everyone could know the laws and make sure the judges followed them. In 451 B.C. Rome adopted its first written laws, known as the Twelve Tables. They were carved on bronze tablets and placed in the marketplace where everyone could see them. The Twelve Tables were based on the idea that all citizens should be treated equally under the law.

When Rome began taking over other nations, they made a new set of laws called the Law of Nations. The Law of Nations listed principles, or ideas, for justice. We still use some of these ideas today. For example, American law says that people are innocent until they are proven guilty.

Rome's legal system was based on the idea that everyone should be treated equally. This is called "the rule of law." Many rich people did not like the rule of law. They were used to having special privileges. In fact, many rich people were not used to obeying the law at all. The rule of law changed that.

The Punic Wars

Rome continued to grow. It wanted to control the entire Mediterranean world, but so did an empire named Carthage. Carthage was a trading empire on the coast of North Africa. It was the largest and richest city in the western Mediterranean.

Lesson 2 Rome As a Republic, *Continued*

Carthage was built around 800 B.C. by the Phoenicians, who were skilled sailors and traders.

In 264 B.C. Rome and Carthage both wanted to rule the island of Sicily. The First Punic War was fought between Rome and Carthage. This war lasted 20 years until Rome won in 241 B.C. Carthage had to leave Sicily and pay a huge fine to the Romans.

Carthage then conquered southern Spain. The Romans helped the Spanish people rebel. In 218 B.C. Carthage sent their great general, Hannibal, to attack Rome. This started the Second Punic War.

Hannibal sailed his army from Carthage to Spain. His men rode horses and elephants across the Alps and into Italy. Hannibal's army beat the Romans at Cannae and began raiding Italy. In response, the Roman general Scipio captured Spain and attacked Carthage. Hannibal and his army had to return home to defend their people. Finally, Scipio's army defeated Hannibal's forces. Carthage was forced to give up its navy and give its Spanish territory to Rome. Rome now ruled the western Mediterranean region.

Carthage was no longer a military power, but it was still a rich trading center. In 146 B.C. during the Third Punic War, Roman soldiers burned Carthage to stop it from getting stronger. Many people in Carthage were enslaved.

In the 140s B.C., Rome conquered all of Greece. Twenty years later, it took its first province in Asia. Romans began to call the Mediterranean Sea *mare nostrum*, which means "our sea."

/ / / / / / / / / / / / / / Glue Foldable here / / / / / / / / / / / / / /

Check for Understanding

Explain the role or importance of each group of people in Rome.

1. consuls ____________________
2. dictators ____________________
3. patricians ____________________
4. plebeians ____________________
5. praetors ____________________
6. tribunes ____________________

Identifying

7. What happened to Carthage after the Third Punic War?

____

____

____

Reading Check

8. How did Hannibal lose the Second Punic War?

____

____

____

FOLDABLES®

9. Place a one-tab Foldable along the dotted line to cover the Check for Understanding. Label the anchor tab *Conflict Between Classes*. Write *Changes in Government* at the top of the tab. Draw three arrows from the title and list three changes that were the result of conflict between different classes in Rome.

NAME________________________ DATE ____________ CLASS ________

networks

Rome: Republic to Empire

Lesson 3 The End of the Republic

ESSENTIAL QUESTION

Why does conflict develop?

GUIDING QUESTIONS

1. *What factors led to the decline of the Roman Republic?*
2. *How did Julius Caesar rise to power in Rome?*
3. *How did Rome become an empire?*

Terms to Know

latifundia large farming estates

triumvirate three rulers who share equal power

Where in the world?

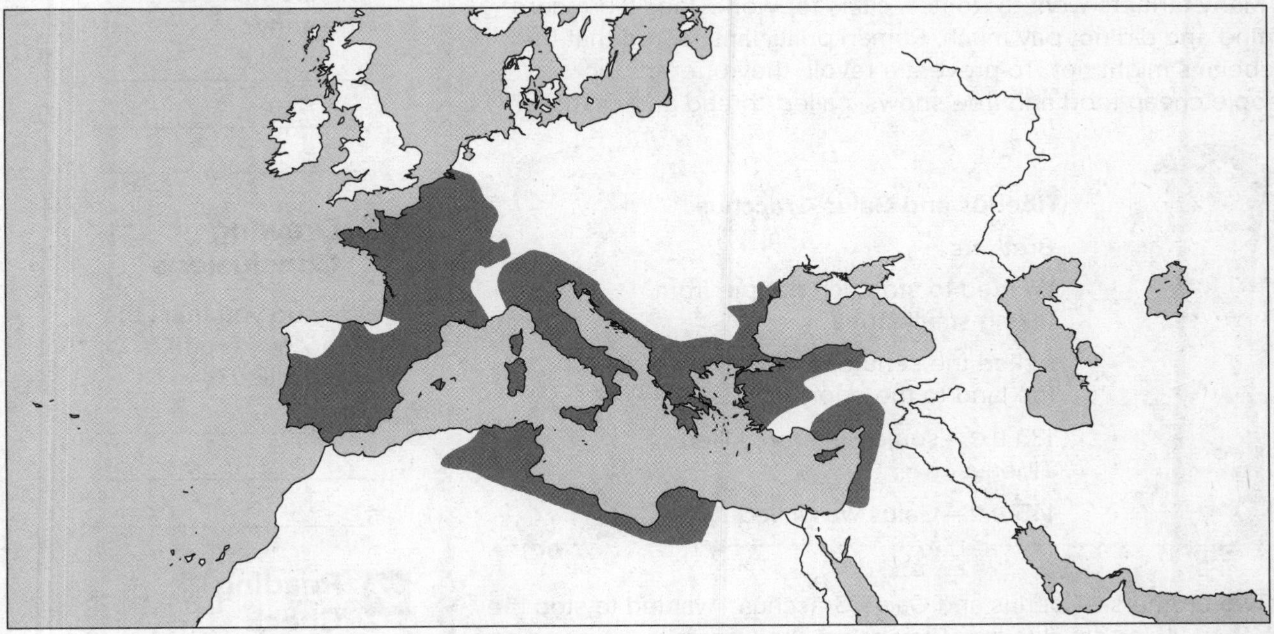

When did it happen?

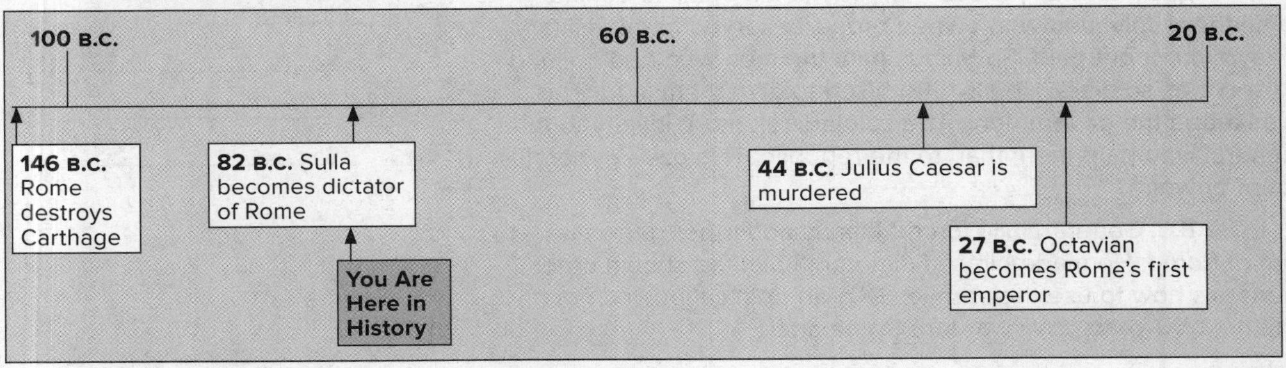
100 B.C.
60 B.C.
20 B.C.
146 B.C. Rome destroys Carthage
82 B.C. Sulla becomes dictator of Rome
You Are Here in History
44 B.C. Julius Caesar is murdered
27 B.C. Octavian becomes Rome's first emperor

Lesson 3 The End of the Republic, *Continued*

Problems in the Republic

Even though Rome's armies were doing well in other parts of the world, Rome had problems at home. By 100 B.C., many plebeian farmers could not work on their farms because they were in the army. Others had watched the Carthaginian army destroy their small farms.

At the same time, rich Romans were buying land. They formed large farming estates called **latifundia.** Enslaved people from Carthage worked the land. As a result, the rich charged less for their crops than the plebeian farmers did. This caused plebeian farmers to go out of business.

Many farmers went to Rome's cities for work. Jobs were hard to find and did not pay much. Roman politicians feared that the plebeians might riot. To prevent a revolt, they offered poor people cheap food and free shows, called "bread and circuses."

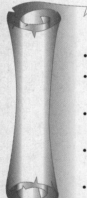

Tiberius and Gaius Gracchus

- Brothers
- Wanted to stop rich people from taking small farms
- Asked the senate to return some of the land to the poor
- 133 B.C.—some Senators killed Tiberius
- 145 B.C.—Gaius was killed

Two brothers—Tiberius and Gaius Gracchus—wanted to stop the rich from taking small farms. They asked the Senate to return some of the land to the poor. Many Senators were against the idea.

In 107 B.C., a military leader named Marius became consul. Until then, only men who owned property served in the military. They did not get paid. So Marius paid the men who had no land to serve as soldiers. He also promised to give them land. This weakened the government. The soldiers felt more loyalty to the general who paid them than to the republic. This gave generals a lot of power.

In 82 B.C. General Sulla forced Marius and other generals out of Rome. He made himself dictator. Sulla had shown other generals how to use their armies to grab political power. For the next 50 years, civil war tore Rome apart.

Defining

1. What is a *latifundia*?

____

____

____

Identifying

2. What change did Marius make to the army?

____

____

____

Drawing Conclusions

3. Why do you think the Gracchus brothers were killed?

____

____

____

Reading Check

4. What was the purpose of "bread and circuses?"

____

____

____

Lesson 3 The End of the Republic, *Continued*

Defining

5. What is a *triumvirate*?

____

____

____

Cause and Effect

6. What did Caesar do after he made himself dictator for life?

____

____

____

Reading Check

7. Why did some Romans oppose Caesar?

____

____

____

The Rise of Julius Caesar

By 60 B.C., three men emerged as the most powerful in Rome. They were three generals: Crassus, Pompey, and Julius Caesar. They formed the First Triumvirate. A **triumvirate** is a political partnership of three people.

After Crassus died in battle, the Senators thought that Caesar was becoming too popular. The Senators ordered Caesar to give up his army. Instead, Caesar and his soldiers captured all of Italy.

In 44 B.C. Caesar made himself dictator for life. He also filled the Senate with people who supported him. Caesar knew many reforms were needed. He started new colonies so that farmers and soldiers would have land. He forced patricians to hire free workers instead of using slave labor.

60 B.C.—Three generals formed the First Triumvirate: Crassus, Pompey, and Julius Caesar.

↓

The Senators thought Caesar was too popular.

↓

The Senators ordered Caesar to give up his army.

↓

Caesar and his soldiers captured all of Italy.

↓

44 B.C.—Caesar made himself dictator for life.

Caesar's supporters thought he was a strong leader who brought peace to Rome. His enemies thought that he wanted to be king. On March 15, 44 B.C., Caesar's enemies, led by Cassius and Brutus, stabbed him to death.

From Republic to Empire

After Caesar was killed, civil war broke out. Octavian, Antony, and Lepidus won the civil war. Octavian was Caesar's 18-year-old grandnephew. Antony and Lepidus had been Caesar's best generals. In 43 B.C. they formed the Second Triumvirate.

The Second Triumvirate did not last long. Lepidus retired from politics. Antony fell in love with the Egyptian queen, Cleopatra. The two made an alliance. Octavian thought they wanted to take over Rome. Many Romans were upset by this news. Octavian declared war on Antony.

Lesson 3 The End of the Republic, *Continued*

In 31 B.C. the navies of Antony and Cleopatra fought those of Octavian at the Battle of Actium. Octavian's forces crushed the couple's army and navy. Antony and Cleopatra later killed themselves. Octavian became Rome's only ruler.

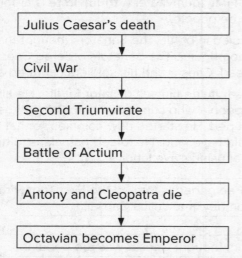

Julius Caesar's death
↓
Civil War
↓
Second Triumvirate
↓
Battle of Actium
↓
Antony and Cleopatra die
↓
Octavian becomes Emperor

Cicero, a writer, political leader, and speaker, strongly supported the republican government. Octavian, however, believed that a republic was too weak to solve Rome's problems. He wanted power for himself. The senate finally agreed to his wishes and declared Octavian commander-in-chief.

Octavian took the title of Augustus. *Augustus* means "the majestic one." In 27 B.C. Caesar Augustus became Rome's first emperor.

Check for Understanding

Number the events in the order that they happened.

_____ **1.** Octavian became emperor.

_____ **2.** Marius reformed the military.

_____ **3.** Julius Caesar was murdered.

_____ **4.** Julius Caesar declared himself "dictator for life."

_____ **5.** The First Triumvirate was formed.

_____ **6.** Octavian fought a civil war against Antony and Cleopatra.

Glue Foldable here

Explaining

8. What happened at the Battle of Actium?

____

____

____

Reading Check

9. How do you think Cicero might have reacted when the senate named Octavian the first emperor of Rome?

____

____

____

FOLDABLES®

10. Place a two-tab Foldable along the dotted line. Label the anchor tab *Conflict and Change*. Label the two tabs—*Rome as a Republic* and *Rome as an Empire*. On both sides of the tabs, list events that you remember occurring during each time period. Use your notes to help you with the activity under the tabs.

NAME ______________________ DATE ____________ CLASS ________

networks

Rome: Republic to Empire

Lesson 4 Rome Builds an Empire

ESSENTIAL QUESTION

What are the characteristics of a leader?

GUIDING QUESTIONS

1. ***How did Augustus create a new age of prosperity for Rome?***
2. ***How did the Roman Empire become rich and prosperous?***

Terms to Know

Pax Romana Roman peace; a long period of peace and prosperity in Roman history

proconsul governor

Where in the world?

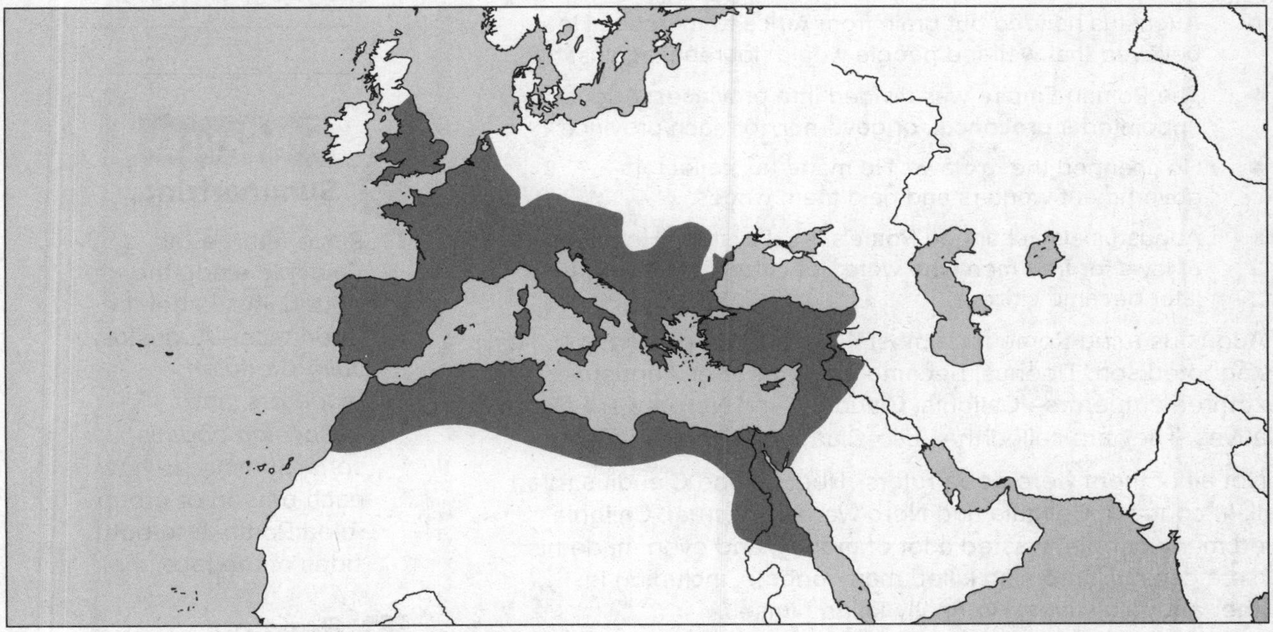

When did it happen?

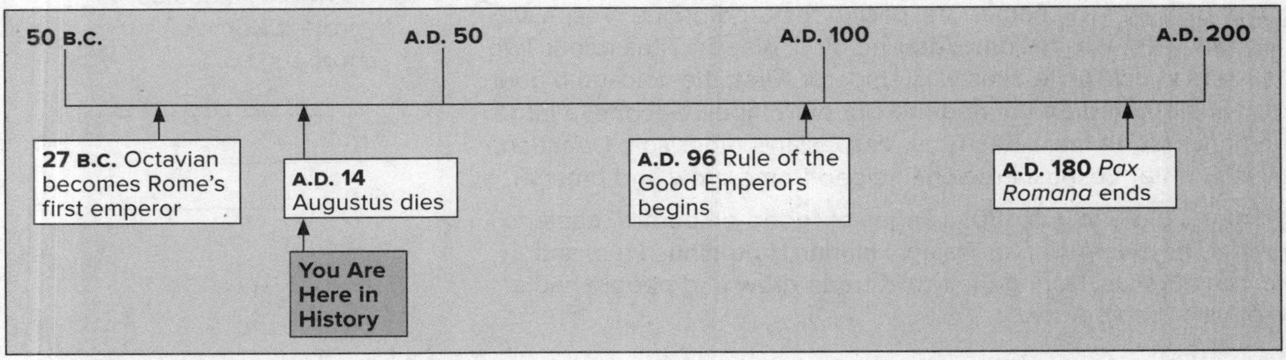

50 B.C.
A.D. 50
A.D. 100
A.D. 200
27 B.C. Octavian becomes Rome's first emperor
A.D. 14 Augustus dies
You Are Here in History
A.D. 96 Rule of the Good Emperors begins
A.D. 180 Pax Romana ends

The Rule of Augustus

For hundreds of years, there had been fighting in the area around the Mediterranean Sea. Caesar Augustus (formerly called Octavian) ended the fighting. He took control of the whole area. That brought ***Pax Romana,*** or "Roman peace." This peace lasted about 200 years.

- Augustus wanted to make the empire strong and safe.
- He wanted Rome's borders to be easier to defend, so he made the natural physical features of the land the empire's borders.
- Augustus built beautiful buildings out of marble.
- Augustus handed out grain from Africa to the poor. He believed that well-fed people would not rebel against him.
- The Roman Empire was divided into provinces. Augustus appointed a **proconsul,** or governor, for each province.
- He changed the tax laws. He made tax collectors government workers and paid them wages.
- Augustus also changed Rome's legal system. He made a set of laws for free men who were not citizens. Many of them later became citizens.

Augustus ruled Rome for almost 40 years. He died in A.D. 14. His adopted son, Tiberius, became emperor after Augustus. The next three emperors—Caligula, Claudius, and Nero—were also relatives. They are called the Julio-Claudian emperors.

Not all of them were good rulers. Tiberius and Claudius ruled well. In contrast, Caligula and Nero were very cruel. Caligula killed many people, wasted a lot of money, and even made his horse a consul. Nero also killed many people, including his mother and two wives. He finally killed himself.

Glue Foldable here

The Roman Peace

In A.D. 69 a general named Vespasian restored peace. Vespasian stopped several rebellions. After he died, his son Titus ruled. Two disasters struck while Titus was emperor. First, the volcano Mount Vesuvius erupted and buried the city of Pompeii. Second, a large fire damaged Rome. After Titus, Vespasian's other son, Domitian, ruled. Both of Vespasian's sons helped Rome grow and prosper.

From A.D. 96 to A.D. 180, a series of "good emperors" came to power. They were Nerva, Trajan, Hadrian, Antoninus Pius, and Marcus Aurelius. During their rule, trade grew and people had a better life than before.

Marking the Text

1. Underline how long the *Pax Romana* lasted.

Defining

2. What was a *proconsul*?

____

____

____

FOLDABLES®

Summarizing

3. Place a three-tab Foldable along the dotted line. Label the three tabs—*Augustus, Julio-Claudian emperors*, and *Vespasian and his sons.* Summarize how each person or group ruled Rome. Use both sides of the tabs.

Reading Check

4. How did Augustus protect Rome's borders?

____

____

____

Lesson 4 Rome Builds an Empire, *Continued*

Comparing

5. What did all five of the Good Emperors build?

Identifying

6. Which emperor passed laws to help orphans?

Listing

7. Which emperors improved Rome by building things?

Explaining

8. Why was Trajan's empire hard to rule well?

The Five Good Emperors ruled wisely. All five built roads, bridges, monuments, harbors, and aqueducts. An aqueduct is a channel that carries water for long distances.

The Five Good Emperors

Emperor	Good Works
Nerva A.D. 96–98	• Changed land laws to help the poor • Revised taxes
Trajan A.D. 98–117	• Expanded the empire to its largest size • Built many new public works
Hadrian A.D. 117–138	• Built Hadrian's Wall in Britain • Made Roman laws easier to understand
Antoninus Pius A.D. 138–161	• Promoted art and science • Built new public works • Passed laws to help orphans
Marcus Aurelius A.D. 161–180	• Helped unite the empire economically • Reformed Roman law

The empire was biggest in size when Trajan ruled. It spread from the Mediterranean to Britain in the northeast and Mesopotamia in the east. This made the empire too big to rule well. Many rulers after Trajan pulled troops out of areas they could not defend well. For example, Hadrian pulled troops out of Mesopotamia. He made the empire's boundaries at the Rhine and the Danube Rivers stronger.

By the A.D. 100s, the Roman Empire was one of the largest empires in history. It had 3.5 million square miles (9.1 million square km) of land. The empire was united because people thought of themselves as Romans. Even if they spoke different languages, they had the same laws, rulers, and culture. By A.D. 212, every free person was thought of as a Roman citizen.

Lesson 4 Rome Builds an Empire, *Continued*

Agriculture was the most important part of the empire's economy. Some cities became centers for making pottery, cloth, and brass. Traders came from all over the world to ports in Italy. They brought silk from China, spices from India, tin from Britain, lead from Spain, and iron from Gaul.

The Roman Empire had a good system of paved roads. This helped trade grow. The Roman navy kept pirates off the Mediterranean Sea. This made it safer for ships to bring goods in and out of the empire's ports.

By A.D. 100, everyone in the empire used a common currency, or money. This made it easy to trade. It meant that a merchant in Greece could sell to a person in Italy or Egypt. People also used a system of weights and measures to set prices, trade, and ship goods.

Many people became wealthy. However, most people in the cities and on the farms were still poor. Many other people were still enslaved.

/ / / / / / / / / / / / / / Glue Foldable here / / / / / / / / / / / / / /

Check for Understanding

List at least one accomplishment of each Roman emperor.

1. Augustus ______________________
2. Vespasian ______________________
3. Trajan ______________________
4. Hadrian ______________________

Listing

9. List three products that traders brought into Rome's ports.

____

____

____

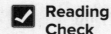

Reading Check

10. Why were five of Rome's rulers known as the "good emperors?"

____

____

____

FOLDABLES®

11. Place a one-tab Foldable along the dotted line to cover the Check for Understanding. Label the anchor tab *Characteristics of …* and write … *Roman emperors* in the middle of the tab. Make a memory map by drawing five arrows around the title. Write five words or phrases about Roman emperors. Use your notes to help you answer the questions under the tabs.

NAME________________________________ DATE ____________ CLASS ________

networks

Roman Civilization

Lesson 1 The Roman Way of Life

ESSENTIAL QUESTION

What makes a culture unique?

GUIDING QUESTIONS

1. ***What was daily life like for the Romans?***
2. ***How did the Greeks influence Roman culture?***

Terms to Know

gladiator a person who fought people and animals for public entertainment

satire writing that pokes fun at human weaknesses

ode poem that expresses strong emotions about life

vault a curved ceiling

anatomy the study of the body's structure

Where in the world?

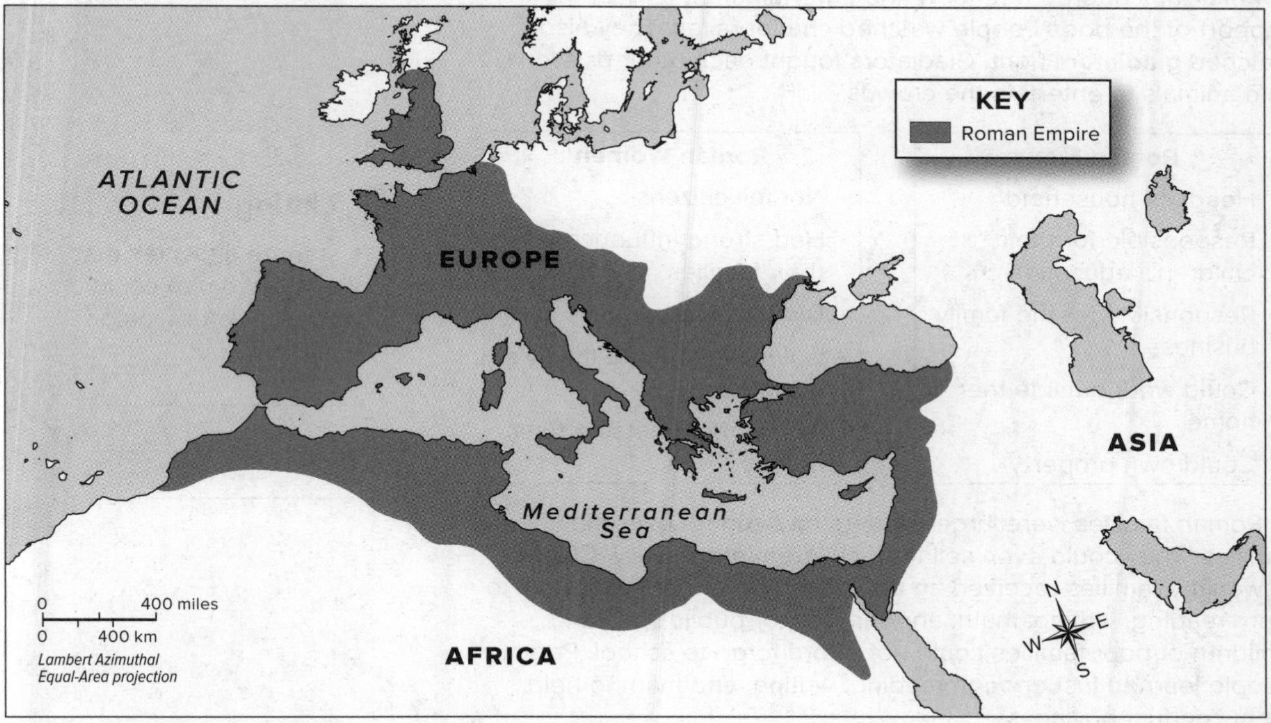

When did it happen?

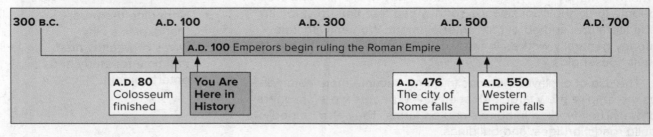

300 B.C. — A.D. 100 — A.D. 300 — A.D. 500 — A.D. 700

A.D. 100 Emperors begin ruling the Roman Empire

A.D. 80 Colosseum finished

You Are Here in History

A.D. 476 The city of Rome falls

A.D. 550 Western Empire falls

Lesson 1 The Roman Way of Life, *Continued*

Daily Life

Rome was one of the largest and most carefully planned cities in the ancient world. More than a million people lived in Rome by about A.D. 1. It had a public square called the Forum. Romans shopped, conducted business, played games, and visited with friends in this area.

Wealthy people lived in big houses built around courtyards. Most Romans were poor and did unskilled labor. They lived in apartment buildings. Those neighborhoods were crowded, noisy, and dirty.

Politicians offered free food and entertainment to gain the support of the poor. People watched chariot races. They also watched **gladiators** fight. Gladiators fought each other or even wild animals to entertain the crowds.

Roman Men

- Heads of household
- Responsible for their children's education
- Responsible for the family business
- Could work outside the home
- Could own property

Roman Women

- Not full citizens
- Had strong influence on their families
- Did the housework
- Could work in the family's business
- Few worked outside their homes

Roman families were large. Fathers had control over their families. They could even sell their children into slavery. Children of wealthy families received an education. Sons went to school to learn reading, writing, math, and rhetoric, or public speaking. Children of poor families could not afford to go to school. Poor people learned just enough reading, writing, and math to help them conduct business.

Wives of wealthy, powerful men had more freedom than those with less money. They could own land. They could hire enslaved people to do their housework, so they had free time to study art and literature, and go out for entertainment. Women with little money generally worked in the family business and took care of their households.

The use of enslaved persons in Rome became more common as the empire grew larger. Most enslaved people were prisoners of war. They worked in homes and on farms. They also helped build roads, bridges, and buildings.

Explaining

1. What did politicians do to make people like them?

____

____

____

Listing

2. List three activities that wealthy women could do that poorer women could not.

____

____

____

Marking the Text

3. Underline the phrase that explains why wives of wealthy men had time for study and entertainment.

Lesson 1 The Roman Way of Life, *Continued*

Reading Check

4. Why was the family important in Roman society?

____

____

____

FOLDABLES®

Listing

5. Cut a two-tab Foldable in half to make four tabs. On the anchor tab, write *Romans Borrowed from Greeks.* Label the four tabs *Religion and Culture*, *Art*, *Science*, and *Architecture*.

Use both sides of the tabs to list examples of each category.

Contrasting

6. How were satires different from odes?

____

____

____

Glue Foldable here

Romans believed that gods and spirits controlled all parts of life. Greek gods and goddesses were popular in Rome, but the Romans gave them new names. The Roman Senate declared that the emperors were gods. The Romans worshiped their gods by praying and offering food to them.

Romans borrowed ideas such as Stoicism from the Greeks and changed them to fit their culture. For Greeks, Stoicism meant finding happiness through reason. For the Romans, it meant living in a practical way. Roman Stoics urged people to do their civic duty and participate in government. These ideas are still important to us today.

Science and Art

The Romans used many features of Greek writing, art, and architecture, but changed them to fit Roman style. Like the Greeks, Roman artists created statues. Greek statues showed perfect and beautiful people. Roman statues, on the other hand, showed people that looked more realistic.

Greeks	Romans
Greeks believed in gods and goddesses.	Romans gave Greek gods and goddesses new names.
Stoicism taught people to find happiness through reason.	Stoicism taught people to do their duties as citizens and participate in government.
Statues made people look perfect and beautiful.	Realistic statues showed details like warts and wrinkles.
Writers honored their gods and praised their generals' successes.	Writers wrote comedies about their gods' mistakes. Writers also wrote about the failures of their generals.

Some Roman writers based their work on Greek models. The Roman poet Virgil borrowed some of the ideas for his poem the *Aeneid* from the Greek poem called the *Odyssey.* The poet Horace based his **satires** and **odes** on Greek works. Satires poke fun at human weakness, like comedians do today. Odes are poems that express strong emotions about life.

Other Romans wrote plays. Unlike the Greeks, however, Romans wrote comedies about their gods as well as plays that honored them.

Lesson 1 The Roman Way of Life, *Continued*

Romans added new ideas to architecture. Architecture is the art of making structures, such as buildings. Romans built with concrete. They added arches. By putting many arches together, they could form a **vault**, or curved ceiling. Curved ceilings created beautiful domes. Using domes, the Romans were able to build large, open rooms.

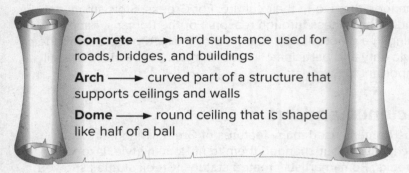

Concrete ⟶ hard substance used for roads, bridges, and buildings

Arch ⟶ curved part of a structure that supports ceilings and walls

Dome ⟶ round ceiling that is shaped like half of a ball

Romans also learned science from the Greeks. They studied the work of a Greek doctor named Galen. Galen studied **anatomy** to learn about the body's structure.

Roman engineers built practical things such as bridges, buildings, and roads. Roads connected the city of Rome to every part of the empire. This allowed soldiers to travel quickly. Traders used the roads so trade grew. The Romans also built aqueducts that carried fresh water into the cities.

The Romans influenced future generations. Concrete and other elements of Roman architecture are still used today. Until about A.D. 1500, Latin, the language of the Romans, was the official language of European government, trade, and learning. Latin is the basis of many modern languages, such as Italian, French, and Spanish.

/ / / / / / / / / / / / Glue Foldable here / / / / / / / / / / / / /

Check for Understanding

List two facts that describe what life was like for the Romans.

1. ______________________

2. ______________________

List two things the Romans borrowed from the Greeks and then adapted to meet their needs.

3. ______________________

4. ______________________

Explaining

7. How did engineers change and improve the lives of people throughout the empire?

____

____

Reading Check

8. Describe Roman improvements to Greek architecture.

____

____

____

FOLDABLES®

9. Place a one-tab Foldable to cover the Check for Understanding. Label the anchor tab *Culture and Influences.* In the center of the Foldable, write *Roman Daily Life*.

Make a memory map by drawing five arrows out from the title. Write five words or phrases about Roman daily life. Use your notes to help you with the lists under the tab.

NAME________________________ DATE______________ CLASS___________

networks

Roman Civilization

Lesson 2 Rome's Decline

ESSENTIAL QUESTION

Why do civilizations rise and fall?

GUIDING QUESTIONS

1. ***What problems led to Rome's decline?***
2. ***What effect did Germanic invaders have on the Roman Empire?***
3. ***What are the key achievements and contributions of Roman civilization?***

Term to Know

reforms political changes to bring about improvement

Where in the world?

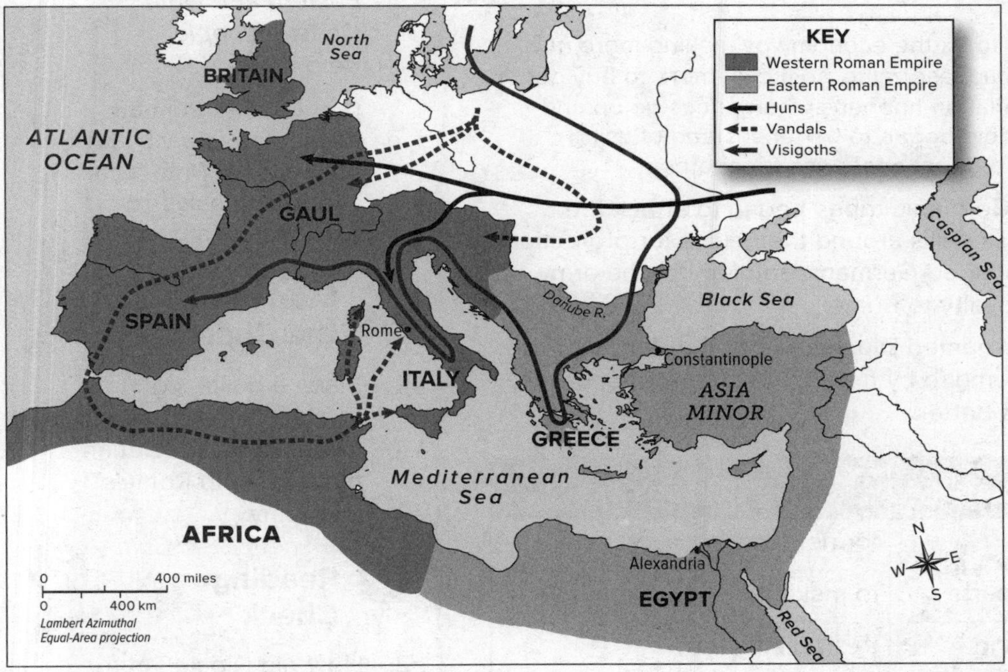

When did it happen?

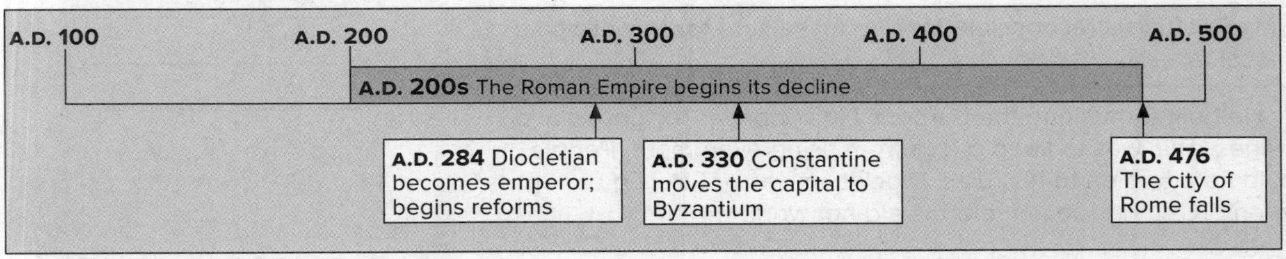

A Troubled Empire

/ / / / / / / / / / / / , Glue Foldable here / / / / / / / / / / / / /

The peace of the *Pax Romana* was followed by a century of confusion and violence. Roman government grew weak while the army grew strong and independent. The legions of the army fought each other to put new emperors on the throne. Rome had 22 emperors in a period of 50 years.

This period of civil war caused great suffering, including:

- Food shortages
- High prices
- Decreased support for education
- Unpaid taxes

The government tried to fix the economy by making more new coins. These new coins had less value, so it cost more to buy goods. This is called inflation. Inflation happens when prices go up and money is worth less. People began to barter. Instead of using money, they traded one product or service for another.

As Rome struggled, Germanic tribes began to attack the empire. The Romans built walls around their cities for protection. The Roman government hired Germanic soldiers for the army, but these soldiers had no loyalty to Rome.

In A.D. 284, a general named Diocletian became emperor. He tried to strengthen the empire by making many **reforms**, or changes to make things better.

Diocletian's Reforms	Reasons
Built forts on borders	for defense
Split empire into four parts	to make it easier to rule
Set prices for goods and wages	to stop inflation
Ordered workers to keep their jobs until they died	to improve the amount of goods being made
Made officials responsible for local taxes	to make sure taxes were paid

He built forts along the borders. He set prices for goods and wages. This was to keep prices from rising even more. People paid no attention to his rules. Diocletian was not strong enough to enforce them, so his reforms did not work.

FOLDABLES®

Explaining

1. Place a two-tab Foldable along the dotted line. On the anchor tab, write *Roman Empire*. Label the left tab *Western* and write *Rome* below it. Label the right tab *Eastern* and write *Constantinople* below it.

   Draw arrows from the anchor tab to each label on the tabs. Write facts about both halves of the Roman Empire.

Marking the Chart

2. Place a dollar sign to the left of the three reforms that Diocletian made to help Rome's economy.

Reading Check

3. How did Diocletian try to improve Rome's economy?

____

____

____

Identifying

4. Which phrase tells what Constantine finally did when his reforms failed to help Rome?

____

Explaining

5. Why did some Germanic tribes want land?

____

Drawing Conclusions

6. Why did the Visigoths rebel?

____

Reading Check

7. Why do historians consider A.D. 476 an important date?

____

The Fall of Rome

The next emperor was Constantine. He tried to make Diocletian's reforms work so the empire would grow strong again. Constantine made the military stronger. Nothing seemed to help Rome improve. In A.D. 330, he moved the capital from Rome to Byzantium in the east. Then he changed the name of the new capital to Constantinople. That name lasted many years. Today the city is known as Istanbul in present-day Turkey. Constantine's reforms helped the empire, but not enough.

After Constantine died, Theodosius took power. He realized that the empire had grown too big to rule. When Theodosius died, he left a will that instructed the Romans to divide the empire into eastern and western parts. When the Romans divided the empire, they also divided the army. The western half of the empire was now too weak to stop invaders.

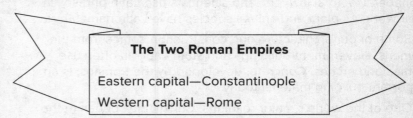

The Two Roman Empires

Eastern capital—Constantinople

Western capital—Rome

In the A.D. 300s and A.D. 400s, many Germanic tribes took over Roman land. Some wanted better land for raising crops and farm animals. Many were running away from the Huns, a fierce group of warriors. A tribe called the Visigoths asked Rome for protection. The Romans let the Visigoths live just inside the empire's border. Later, the Romans treated the Visigoths badly so the tribe fought back. The Visigoths captured Rome in A.D. 410.

Then, another Germanic tribe, the Vandals, invaded the Western Roman Empire. They burned buildings and took valuable things. The Germanic people now had entered every part of Roman society. Many held high government positions.

The last Western Roman emperor was a 14-year old boy name Romulus Augustulus. He did not have strong power or support.

In A.D. 476, a Germanic general named Odoacer overthrew the emperor. He took control of Rome. No Roman emperor ever again ruled from Rome. This is considered the end of the Western Roman Empire.

Rome's Legacies

Roman ideas still influence our lives in the United States today. We read Roman literature. Modern buildings use Roman arches, domes, and concrete.

We share Roman ideas about justice and the law. Like the Romans, we believe that everyone is equal under the law and that a person is considered innocent until proven guilty. We also require judges to decide court cases fairly.

Our government, too, is similar to the Roman republic. In a republic, citizens elect their leaders. As in Rome, our republic works best when citizens get involved.

The Romans also influenced how we speak. The Italian, French, Spanish, Portuguese, and Romanian languages come from Latin. Many English words have Latin roots. We use the Latin alphabet. Doctors, lawyers, and scientists use Latin phrases in their work. All plant and animal species have Latin names.

Some of our architecture and construction comes from the Romans. Government buildings and state capitols often use domes and arches. Concrete, developed by the Romans, is an important building material today.

One of the world's major religions, Christianity, began in the Roman Empire. It spread with the help of the Roman road system. When Roman emperors adopted Christianity in the A.D. 300s, they also helped spread the new religion.

/ / / / / / / / / / / / / / Glue Foldable here / / / / / / / / / / / / / /

Check for Understanding

List four contributions or achievements of Roman civilization that influence our lives today.

1. ______________________

2. ______________________

3. ______________________

4. ______________________

Marking the Text

8. Underline the Roman ideas that tell how the language of the Romans influenced languages used today.

Reading Check

9. What Roman contributions still influence our lives today?

____

____

____

FOLDABLES®

10. Place a one-tab Foldable along the dotted line to cover the Check for Understanding. Label the anchor tab *Positive and Negative Aspects*. Write *The Roman Empire* in the center.

Make a memory map by drawing five arrows around the title and writing words about Rome. Use your map to list the information in the Check for Understanding.

Roman Civilization

Lesson 3 The Byzantine Empire

ESSENTIAL QUESTION

How does geography influence the way people live?

GUIDING QUESTIONS

1. ***How did the Byzantine Empire become rich and powerful?***
2. ***How did Emperor Justinian and Empress Theodora strengthen the Byzantine Empire?***

Terms to Know

mosaics patterns or pictures made from small pieces of colored glass or stone

saints Christian holy people

When did it happen?

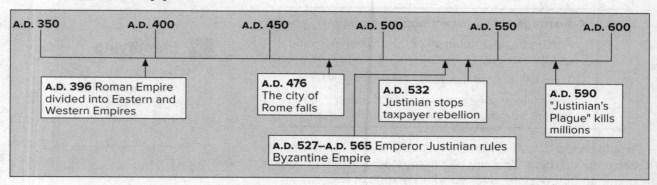

A.D. 350 — A.D. 400 — A.D. 450 — A.D. 500 — A.D. 550 — A.D. 600

- **A.D. 396** Roman Empire divided into Eastern and Western Empires
- **A.D. 476** The city of Rome falls
- **A.D. 527–A.D. 565** Emperor Justinian rules Byzantine Empire
- **A.D. 532** Justinian stops taxpayer rebellion
- **A.D. 590** "Justinian's Plague" kills millions

What do you know?

In the K column, list what you already know about the Byzantine Empire. In the W column, list what you want to know. After reading the lesson, fill in the L column with the information that you learned.

K	W	L

Lesson 3 The Byzantine Empire, *Continued*

The New Rome

The Eastern Roman Empire became known as the Byzantine Empire. It was at its most powerful in the A.D. 500s. The empire stretched east to Arabia, south to Egypt, and west to Italy.

Constantinople was the capital of the empire. The location of the city gave it special advantages. The city sat on a peninsula between the Black Sea and the Aegean Sea. It was surrounded on three sides by water. This made the city easy to defend. Because the city sat between Europe and Asia, it became a crossroads for trade. Merchants from far away did business there and trade grew. Constantinople became the wealthiest part of the Roman Empire.

Advantages of Constantinople's Location

- Fishing boats, trading ships, and warships could use its harbors.
- The seas around it made it easy to defend.
- Two major trade routes crossed through it, so traders from Asia to Europe sold goods there.

People called Constantinople the "New Rome." Many wealthy Romans moved there. The city had many Roman-style buildings, including an outdoor arena for sporting events. It was called the Hippodrome. Like Rome, officials gave free food and entertainment to the poor.

People from many lands settled in the Byzantine Empire. Their different customs blended together to form a new culture. Over time, the empire became less Roman and more Greek. Most Byzantines spoke Greek, so officials and emperors learned to speak Greek too. Between A.D. 500 and A.D. 1200, the Byzantines developed one of the most advanced civilizations in the world.

Byzantine Achievements A.D. 500 to A.D. 1200

- Passed on Greek culture and Roman law to other peoples
- Brought Christianity to people in Eastern Europe

Visualizing

1. On the time line for this lesson, shade in the hundred-year period when the Byzantine Empire was strongest.

Identifying

2. What language did Byzantine officials and emperors learn to speak and why?

____

____

____

Reading Check

3. Why was Constantinople important to the Byzantine Empire?

____

____

____

____

? Analyzing

4. Why was Theodora an important part of Justinian's rule?

____

____

FOLDABLES® Making Connections

5. Place a two-tab Foldable along the dotted line. On the anchor tab, write *Byzantine Empire*. Label the first tab *Emperor Justinian* and the second tab *Empress Theodora*.

On the back sides, explain how the contributions of each have influenced life today.

? Critical Thinking

6. Why do you think so many countries have used the Justinian Code as the basis of their laws?

____

____

____

Justinian's Rule

Emperor Justinian ruled the Byzantine Empire when it was at its most powerful. He was a skilled general and a strong leader. He controlled the military and made the laws.

Justinian was married to Empress Theodora. She helped Justinian rule the empire. Theodora helped her husband choose government officials. She helped women gain more legal rights. She urged Justinian to grant women the right to own land. This reform helped widowed women earn money to take care of their children.

When angry taxpayers rebelled in A.D. 532, Empress Theodora's wisdom helped stop the crisis. The people threatened the government. Justinian's advisers told him he should leave the city to be safe. Theodora told him he would not like his life if he ran away. She said he should stay and fight to protect the empire. He took her advice and stayed. Justinian's army stopped the riot and brought order back to the capital. This victory made him a more powerful ruler.

One of the most important things Justinian did was in the area of law. He ordered a group of scholars to organize the laws and make them simpler and better. The new laws were easier for people to understand and follow. The Justinian Code is still the basis of legal systems in many countries today.

Glue Foldable here

Justinian's Contributions

- Improved women's rights
- Created the Justinian Code
- Constructed the Hagia Sophia

Many Byzantine emperors ordered workers to build forts, government buildings, and churches all over the empire. The emperors supported the work of artists and architects. Justinian ordered the building of a church called the Hagia Sophia. The Hagia Sophia has gold and silver decoration inside. It is also decorated with **mosaics**, pictures or patterns made from small pieces of colored glass or stone. This church became the religious center of the empire. It still stands today as a museum.

The Byzantines also became famous for their mosaics. This Byzantine art usually showed figures of **saints**. Saints are Christian holy people.

Lesson 3 The Byzantine Empire, *Continued*

Justinian's Military Conquests

- Began using a cavalry in the army
- Conquered Italy and parts of Spain and northern Africa
- Protected the eastern border from Persia

Justinian knew the empire had once been much larger. He wanted his army to be strong so they could take back the lands that had once been part of the empire. He wanted his army to protect the borders of the empire.

A general named Belisarius reorganized the Byzantine army and made it stronger. He created cavalry—groups of soldiers on horses. The cavalry wore armor and carried bows and long spears.

Justinian's army fought in Italy, Spain, and northern Africa. It conquered the invaders who had taken lands from the Western Roman Empire. The army also defeated the Persians. It was able to secure the eastern border again.

However, these conquests did not last long. A deadly disease, known as "Justinian's Plague," moved through Asia and Europe. It killed millions of people, including Roman soldiers. There were not enough soldiers to protect the large empire. There also was not enough money to pay them. After Justinian died, the empire again lost control over most of the western lands.

Check for Understanding

List five of Justinian's accomplishments.

1. ______________________
2. ______________________
3. ______________________
4. ______________________
5. ______________________

Glue Foldable here

Explaining

7. Why did Justinian make his army stronger?

____

____

____

Reading Check

8. What effect did Theodora have on Justinian's rule?

____

____

____

FOLDABLES®

9. Cut a two-tab Foldable to make four tabs. Place the Foldable over the Check for Understanding. Label the four tabs *Who*, *What*, *When*, *Where*.

On both sides of the tabs, write facts about Emperor Justinian: what he did, when he did it, and where. Use your notes to help you list his accomplishments under the tabs.

NAME________________________ DATE ____________ CLASS ________

networks

The Rise of Christianity

Lesson 1 Early Christianity

ESSENTIAL QUESTION

What are the characteristics of a leader?

GUIDING QUESTIONS

1. ***How did the Jews respond to Roman rule?***
2. ***Why were the life and death of Jesus of Nazareth important to his followers?***
3. ***How did early Christianity spread throughout the Roman Empire?***

Terms to Know

parables short stories that teach a lesson about good, or honorable, behavior

resurrection coming back to life from the dead

apostle Christian leader chosen by Jesus to spread his message

salvation the act of being saved from the effects of wrongdoing, or sin

Where in the world?

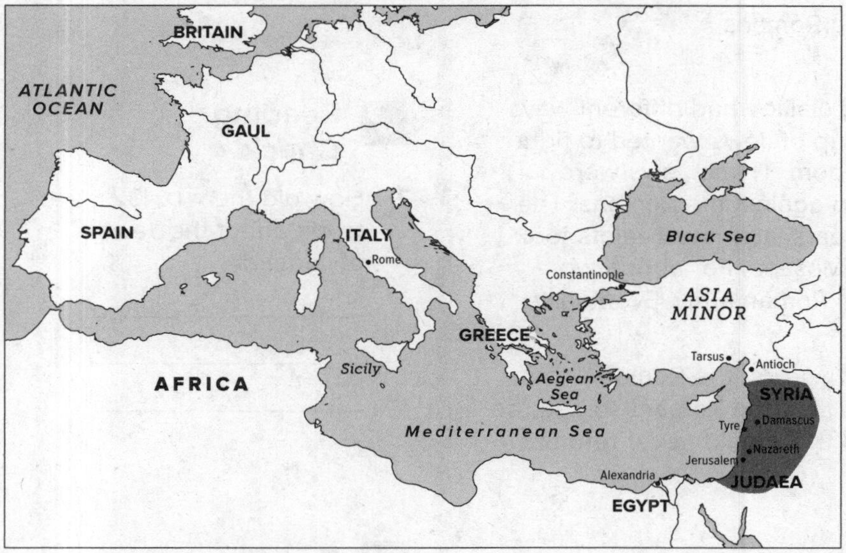

When did it happen?

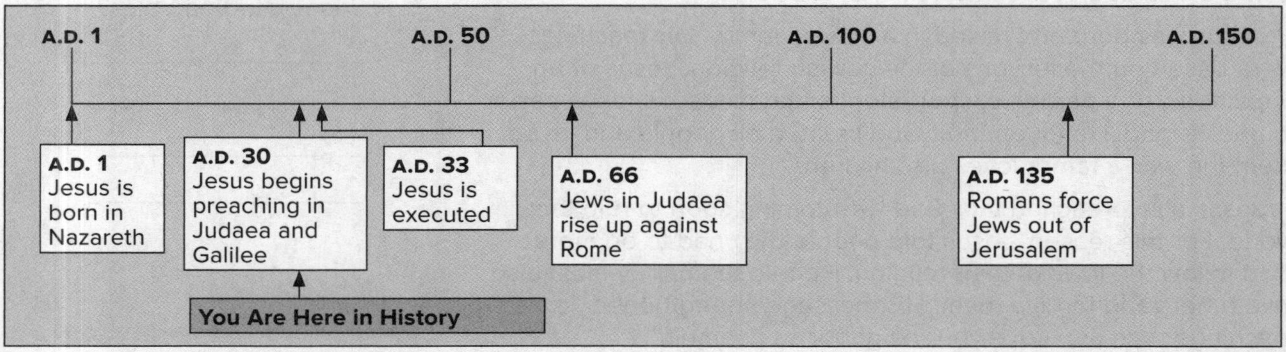

Lesson 1 Early Christianity, *Continued*

Judaism and Rome

The Roman Empire allowed Jews to practice their religion. However, in Judaea and Galilee, the Romans made life very difficult for Jews. The Romans replaced the Jewish king with a Roman governor. Many Jews hoped God would send someone to free them from Roman rule.

Different ways the Jews responded to Roman rule:

- avoided the Romans
- tried to get along with Romans
- set up their own communities and lived apart
- fought against the Romans

The Jews who lived in Judaea and Galilee had different ways of dealing with the Romans. One group of Jews wanted to fight the Romans in order to win their freedom. These Jews were called Zealots. In A.D. 66 they rose up against the Romans. The Romans crushed the uprising. Four years later, the Zealots took over an ancient mountain fort called Masada. For about two years, the Zealots held off a powerful Roman army. Eventually, the Romans defeated the Zealots.

In A.D. 132, the Jews again rose up against the Roman rulers. Once again they were defeated. This time the Romans forced the Jews out of Jerusalem and told them they could never return.

Jesus of Nazareth

Jesus was born in the small town of Nazareth in Galilee. In about A.D. 30, he began to preach in Galilee and Judaea. He traveled with a group of close followers called disciples.

Jesus was born and raised in a Jewish family. His teachings were based on the lessons of the Jewish religion. Jesus often preached using **parables,** short stories that made his ideas easier to understand. He taught that God created all people and loved them the way a father loves his children.

Jesus also preached that God was coming soon to rule the world. For this reason, Jesus told people they had to do more than follow the laws of their religion. He told them they must also love others and forgive them. His message strengthened Jewish teachings such as, "Love your neighbor as yourself."

Listing

1. List 3 ways the Jews responded to Roman rule.

____

____

____

Reading Check

2. How did the A.D. 132 revolt affect the Jews of Judaea?

____

____

____

Explaining

3. Why do you think Jesus used parables?

____

____

____

____

Lesson 1 Early Christianity, *Continued*

Analyzing

4. Why did leaders in Jerusalem arrest Jesus?

____

____

____

Drawing Conclusions

5. Why do you think Jesus traveled to Jerusalem when there was already so much tension between the Romans and the Jews?

____

____

____

Reading Check

6. How did Jesus reinforce traditional Jewish teachings?

____

____

____

Marking the Text

7. Underline the word *apostles* and its definition.

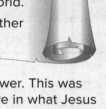

Some teachings of Jesus:

- People should love God.
- God loves people the way a father loves his children.
- God is coming to rule the world.
- People should love one another the way God loves them.

The Romans saw Jesus as a threat to their power. This was because more and more people began to believe in what Jesus was saying. The more his influence grew, the more dangerous he became in the eyes of Roman rulers.

In about A.D. 33, Jesus traveled with his disciples to the city of Jerusalem to celebrate the Jewish holy days of Passover. The Jews were tired of Roman rule and high taxes. The Romans were angry because the Jews would not worship statues of the Roman emperor.

Jesus celebrated the Passover meal with his disciples. This event has come to be known as the Last Supper. After the meal, leaders in Jerusalem arrested Jesus. Jesus was accused of disloyalty to the Roman government. He was sentenced to death by crucifixion. This meant he would be hung from a wooden cross until he died.

According to Christian belief, three days after Jesus died, he rose from the dead and appeared to some of his followers. The disciples of Jesus still thought of themselves as Jews. However, the message of his **resurrection,** or coming back from the dead, led to the birth of Christianity.

Who Were the Apostles?

The **apostles** were early Christian leaders who spread the teachings of Jesus after his death. People who accepted these teachings came to be known as Christians. Early Christians met in people's homes. These gatherings were the first churches.

Two of the most influential leaders of the early Christian church were Peter and Paul. Tradition says that after Jesus died, Peter went to Rome and set up a Christian church.

Lesson 1 Early Christianity, *Continued*

Paul was an educated Jew. At first, he tried to stop Christianity from spreading. Then one day, according to Christian writings, Paul saw a great light and heard the voice of Jesus. After this experience, Paul became a Christian. He spent the rest of his life spreading the message of Jesus.

Facts about the Apostles Peter and Paul	
Peter	**Paul**
• A fisher • Became a disciple of Jesus • Went to Rome and set up a Christian church	• An educated Jew • Opposed Christianity • Became a Christian after seeing a light and hearing the voice of Jesus

Christianity grew out of Judaism. Christians believe in the God of Israel. However, they came to believe in God in a new way.

First, Christians believe that Jesus is the Son of God. Another Christian belief concerns **salvation.** Christians believe that people who accept Jesus will be saved from their sins, or wrongdoings. After they die, they will one day be resurrected the way Jesus was and enter heaven. Another Christian belief is the Trinity, which means "three." In Christian teaching, this refers to the three persons of God: the Father, Son, and Holy Spirit.

Check for Understanding

List two different ways the Jews responded to Roman rule.

1. ______________________

2. ______________________

List the names of two early Christian leaders who helped spread Christian teachings.

3. ______________________

4. ______________________

Glue Foldable here

Contrasting

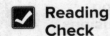

8. Describe two basic Christian beliefs.

____

____

____

____

Reading Check

9. Why were the apostles important to early Christians?

____

____

____

FOLDABLES®

10. Place a two-tab Foldable to cover the Check for Understanding. On the anchor tab, write *Memory Map.* Label the tabs *Jews under Roman Rule* and *Early Christian Leaders.*

In words or short phrases, record what you remember about each. Use your notes to answer the Check for Understanding.

NAME ______________________ DATE ______________ CLASS ________

networks

The Rise of Christianity

Lesson 2 The Early Church

ESSENTIAL QUESTION

How do religions develop?

GUIDING QUESTIONS

1. *How did Christianity change over time?*
2. *How did early Christians organize their church and explain their beliefs?*

Terms to Know

martyr someone who is willing to die rather than give up his or her beliefs

hierarchy an organization with different levels of authority

clergy church officials

laity regular church members

doctrine official church teaching

gospel an account of the life and teaching of Jesus, written by the apostles

pope the title for the bishop of Rome, who is the head of the Roman Catholic Church

When did it happen?

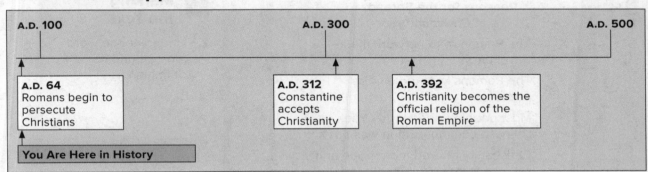

A.D. 100 — A.D. 300 — A.D. 500

A.D. 64 Romans begin to persecute Christians

A.D. 312 Constantine accepts Christianity

A.D. 392 Christianity becomes the official religion of the Roman Empire

You Are Here in History

What do you know?

In the first column, answer the questions based on what you know before you study. After this lesson, complete the last column.

Now...		Later...
	Why did the Romans punish people who became Christians?	
	How did Christians pass on the teachings of Jesus?	
	How is the Christian Church organized?	

Christianity and the Empire

The first followers of Jesus taught his messages to Jews and non-Jews in the Mediterranean region. From there Christianity spread throughout the Roman Empire. This happened for many reasons. A network of roads made long-distance travel fairly safe and easy. The people who lived under Roman rule spoke Latin or Greek. This made it easier for Christians to share their ideas.

Another reason for the spread of Christianity was that it appealed to people. Christianity promised a better life after death. It gave people hope, which the Roman religion did not do. Christian communities took care of the needs of their members.

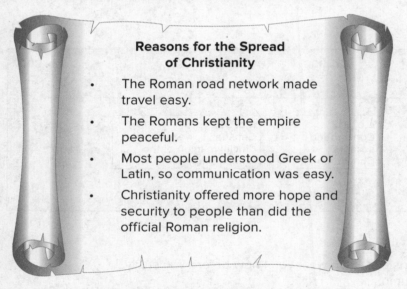

Reasons for the Spread of Christianity

- The Roman road network made travel easy.
- The Romans kept the empire peaceful.
- Most people understood Greek or Latin, so communication was easy.
- Christianity offered more hope and security to people than did the official Roman religion.

The Romans tried to stop Christianity from spreading. Rome saw the new religion as a dangerous threat to its empire. Christians refused to worship the emperor as a god. They also refused to serve in the Roman army and were against war. For these and other reasons, Christians were arrested, beaten, and sometimes killed. Some Christians became **martyrs,** people who are willing to die rather than give up their beliefs.

In the early A.D. 300s, the emperor Diocletian made one last attempt to destroy Christianity. He failed because Christianity had grown very strong.

In A.D. 312 the new religion took a major turn. The night before an important battle, the Emperor Constantine had a dream. In the dream he saw a flaming cross in the sky. The next day he had his soldiers paint the cross on their shields. After his army won the battle, Constantine believed the Christian God had helped him.

Explaining

1. Why did Christianity appeal to many people more than the old Roman religion?

____

____

____

Marking the Text

2. Underline the word *martyrs* and its definition.

Summarizing

3. Why did the Romans mistreat Christians?

____

____

____

____

____

Lesson 2 The Early Church, *Continued*

Reading Check

4. How did Constantine support Christianity?

Defining

5. How is a *hierarchy* organized?

Explaining

6. How was Church doctrine decided?

Constantine became a strong supporter of Christianity. He built churches in Jerusalem and Rome. He let Christians serve in the government. Constantine also excused Christians from paying taxes. Soon, Christians began to join the military. In A.D. 313, Constantine issued the Edict of Milan. This important order gave religious freedom to all religions in the empire, including Christianity.

After Constantine's rule, the emperor Theodosius outlawed Greek and Roman religions. In A.D. 392, he made Christianity the official religion of the Roman Empire. During this time, Christianity also spread to the Kingdom of Axum in East Africa.

Organizing the Church

The early Christian church had to become better organized in order to unite its many followers. It also had to make sure that Christian communities shared similar beliefs and practices. Early church leaders used the Roman Empire as a model. Like the empire, the church was ruled by a **hierarchy** of officials. A hierarchy is an organization with different levels of authority.

Leaders of the church were known as the **clergy.** Regular church members were called the **laity.** In the hierarchy of clergy, archbishops had the most authority. Priests had the least. Each of the five most powerful archbishops were in charge of an entire city. These leaders were called patriarchs.

Hierarchy of the Early Christian Church

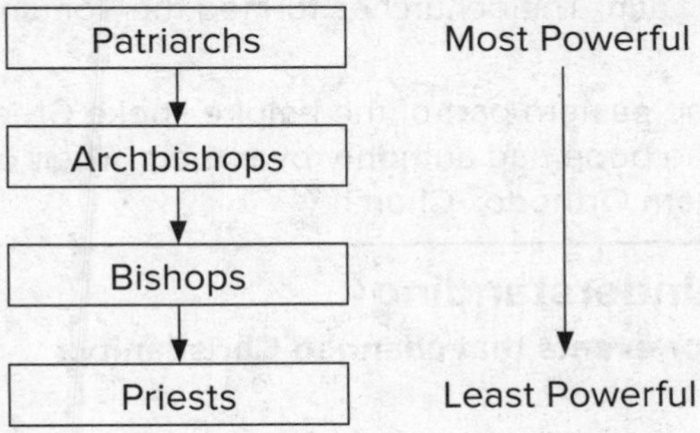

The bishops decided the true teachings of the Church. Accepted teachings became **doctrine.** Teachings that went against the Christian faith were called heresies.

Lesson 2 The Early Church, *Continued*

Church leaders also preserved stories about Jesus and the writings of the apostles. By A.D. 300 there were four accepted accounts of the life and teachings of Jesus. Christians believed four apostles of Jesus wrote these accounts, or **gospels.** The word gospel means "good news." The New Testament includes all four gospels and the writings of early Christians. What Christians call the Old Testament is the Greek version of the Jewish sacred writings. The Christian Bible consists of the Old Testament and the New Testament.

OLD TESTAMENT		NEW TESTAMENT		CHRISTIAN BIBLE
Greek version of sacred Jewish Writings	+	Gospels and writings of early Christians	=	

Two of the most influential early Christian writers were Paul and Augustine. Paul's writings are part of the New Testament. Augustine is one of the Church Fathers. These writers and thinkers played an important role in explaining and defending the teachings of Christianity.

As the Church grew, the bishop of Rome came to believe he had authority over all the other bishops. By A.D. 600, the bishop of Rome had the title of **pope.** *Pope* is from a Latin word that means "father." Christians in the western part of the Roman Empire accepted the pope as the head of all the churches. These Christians spoke Latin. Their churches formed the Roman Catholic Church.

Christians in the eastern part of the empire spoke Greek. They did not believe the pope had authority over them. Their churches became the Eastern Orthodox Church.

Check for Understanding

List two major events that changed Christianity.

1. ______________________________

2. ______________________________

List two ways early Christians explained their beliefs and teachings.

3. ______________________________

4. ______________________________

Glue Foldable here

? Drawing Conclusions

7. The four gospels were written many years after the death of Jesus. How were people able to remember what Jesus did and said before the gospels were written?

____

____

____

____

Reading Check

8. What writings are included in the New Testament?

____

____

FOLDABLES®

9. Place a two-tab Foldable to cover the Check for Understanding. Label the top tab *The Government and Christianity* and the bottom tab *Explaining Christianity.*

Use both sides of the tabs to record words or phrases about each.

NAME ____________________ DATE __________ CLASS ________

networks

The Rise of Christianity

Lesson 3 A Christian Europe

ESSENTIAL QUESTION

How do new ideas change the way people live?

GUIDING QUESTIONS

1. *What issues divided the western and eastern Christian churches?*
2. *How did Christianity spread across Europe?*

Terms to Know

icon a painting of Jesus, Mary (the mother of Jesus), saints, or Christian holy people

iconoclast originally: a person who destroys icons; today: someone who criticizes traditional beliefs or practices

excommunicate to declare that a person or group no longer belongs to the church

schism separation or division

monastery a religious community

Where in the world?

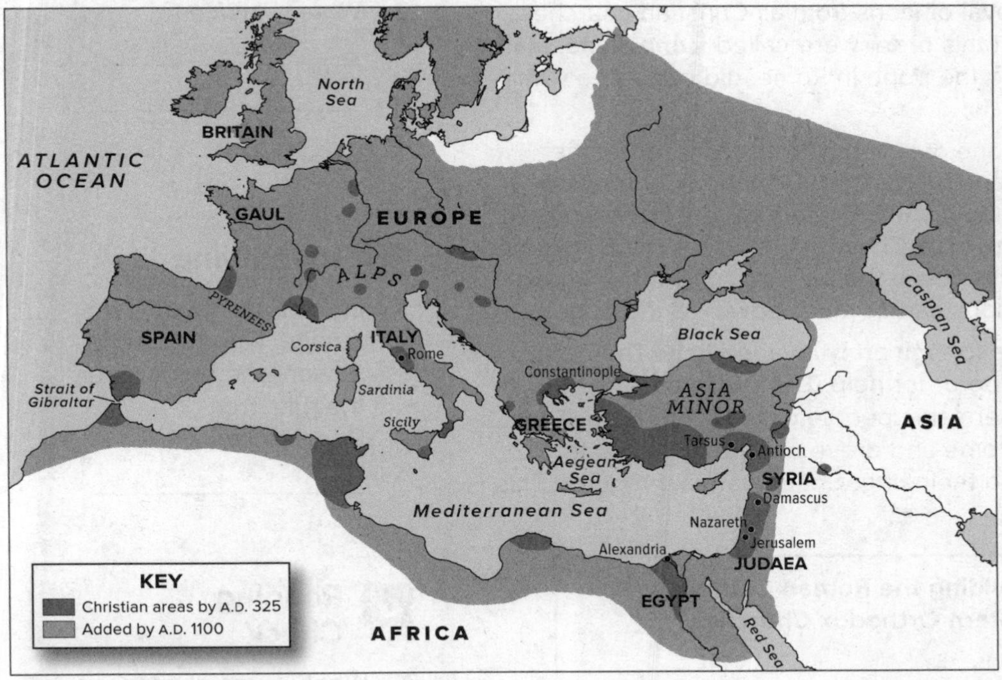

When did it happen?

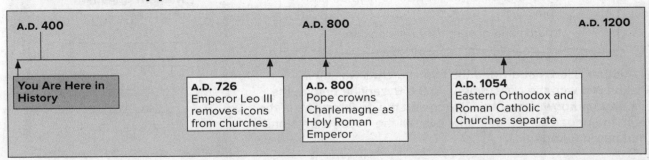

A.D. 400 | A.D. 800 | A.D. 1200

You Are Here in History

A.D. 726 Emperor Leo III removes icons from churches

A.D. 800 Pope crowns Charlemagne as Holy Roman Emperor

A.D. 1054 Eastern Orthodox and Roman Catholic Churches separate

Two Christian Churches

The eastern part of the Roman Empire became known as the Byzantine Empire. The Byzantine church was Christian. It was called the Eastern Orthodox Church. The Eastern Orthodox Church and the Byzantine government worked together. The Byzantine emperor was in charge of the Church. He was seen as God's representative on Earth.

Within the Eastern Orthodox Church, there was conflict over the use of **icons.** Icons are paintings of Jesus, the apostles, and Christian holy people called saints. Some people thought icons helped explain Church teachings. Others felt that the icons were a form of idol worship forbidden by God. In A.D. 726, Emperor Leo III ordered the removal of icons from all Christian churches. Officials who carried out this order were called **iconoclasts.** Many church leaders, including the pope in Rome, did not agree with Leo's actions.

The use of icons was one of several issues that divided the Roman Catholic Church and the Eastern Orthodox Church. The most serious issue was about church authority. The pope in Rome believed he was in charge of all Christian churches. The Byzantines did not accept this. They believed the patriarch of Constantinople and other Byzantine bishops had as much power as the pope.

In the late A.D. 700s, a foreign army invaded Italy. The pope asked the Byzantine emperor for help. The emperor refused. The pope then turned to a Germanic people called the Franks. They successfully defended Rome and drove out the invaders. In return, the pope crowned their king, Charlemagne, emperor. This angered the Byzantines.

Issues Dividing the Roman Catholic and Eastern Orthodox Churches

- Use of icons
- Authority of the pope
- Byzantine emperor's refusal to help defend Rome
- Church and government relationship.

Another issue that divided the two churches was their relationship with the government. In the Byzantine Empire the emperor had power over the church and the government. In the West, the pope claimed authority over all the governments and churches in Europe.

Identifying

1. Identify three characteristics of the Byzantine church.

____

____

____

Defining

2. What is an *icon*?

____

____

____

Identifying

3. In the Byzantine Empire, who had more power—the emperor or the patriarch of Constantinople?

____

Reading Check

4. What issues divided the eastern and western Christian churches?

____

____

____

____

Explaining

5. What did monks and nuns do?

____

____

____

Comparing

6. How were Basilian Rule and Benedictine Rule similar?

____

____

____

____

Identifying

7. How did monks and nuns help spread Christianity?

____

____

____

____

The differences between the two churches were so serious that in A.D. 1054 their leaders **excommunicated,** or cast out, each other. This resulted in a **schism,** or separation, between the two churches that remains today.

The Spread of Christianity

During the A.D. 300s, Christians in the Eastern Roman Empire formed **monasteries.** These were religious communities where men called monks spent much of their days praying and studying. They also worked outside the monasteries. In nearby towns and villages, monks ran schools and hospitals and helped the poor.

Christian women could join convents, which were similar to monasteries. As nuns, these women served the poor and also spent time in prayer and study.

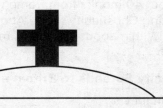

In the A.D. 300s, monks and nuns:

- Studied and prayed in their religious communities
- Ran schools and hospitals in towns and villages
- Helped the poor
- Helped spread Christianity in Europe

Eastern monasteries and convents followed a set of rules created by the Greek bishop Basil. The Basilian Rule told men and women how they were supposed to live in their religious communities. Western monasteries and convents followed the Benedictine Rule, which was created by an Italian monk named Benedict. In general, monks and nuns were expected to pray, study, live simple lives, and perform good deeds.

One of their major duties was to help spread Christianity. They did this by working as missionaries. Missionaries teach their religion to people who are not believers.

Two Byzantine missionaries, brothers Cyril and Methodius, wanted to bring Christianity to the Slavs in Eastern Europe. The Slavs spoke very different languages. Cyril invented a new alphabet that made it possible to translate the Bible into Slavic languages. It is called the Cyrillic alphabet in honor of Cyril. It is still used today by people who speak Slavic languages, such as Russian.

In Western Europe, Christian missionaries did much of their work in Britain and Ireland. After the Romans left Britain, Germanic tribes invaded from present-day Germany and Denmark. The tribes included people called the Angles and the Saxons. Over time, they became the Anglo-Saxons. They lived in Angleland, or England.

The people who were already living in Britain were the Celts. Many of them were driven across the sea to Ireland after the Anglo-Saxons arrived. A priest named Patrick spread Christianity to Ireland. He set up churches and monasteries and converted many people to Christianity.

In A.D. 597, about 40 monks from Rome went to Britain. Their mission was to bring Christianity to the Anglo-Saxons of Britain. They succeeded. Within about 100 years, most of England had become Christian.

Christianity Spreads to Britain and Ireland

1. Romans begin leaving Britain.
2. Germanic tribes invade Britain.
3. Celts in Britain flee to Ireland.
4. Patrick teaches Christianity to the Celts in Ireland.
5. Monks bring Christianity to Anglo-Saxons in Britain.

Check for Understanding

List two major issues that divided the Eastern and Western Christian churches.

1. ______________________

2. ______________________

How did Christianity spread to Britain and Ireland?

3. ______________________

____

Examining Details

8. How did the missionary brothers Cyril and Methodius spread Christianity to the Slavs?

____

____

____

Reading Check

9. Why were monasteries and convents important in Christian Europe?

____

____

____

FOLDABLES®

10. Place a two-tab Foldable along the dotted line to cover Check for Understanding. Label the top tab *Church Division* and the bottom tab *Missionaries.*

Use both sides of the Foldable to record words or phrases about each.

Glue Foldable here

NAME ______________________ DATE ____________ CLASS __________

networks

Islamic Civilization

Lesson 1 A New Faith

ESSENTIAL QUESTION

How do religions develop?

GUIDING QUESTIONS

1. *How did physical geography influence the Arab way of life?*
2. *What message did Muhammad preach to the people of Arabia?*
3. *How does Islam provide guidance to its followers?*

Terms to Know

Islam a religion based on the teachings of Muhammad
oasis a green area in a desert fed by underground water; a water hole in the desert
sheikh the leader of an Arab tribe
caravan a group of traveling merchants and animals, usually camels
Quran the holy book of Islam
shari'ah Islamic code of law

Where in the world?

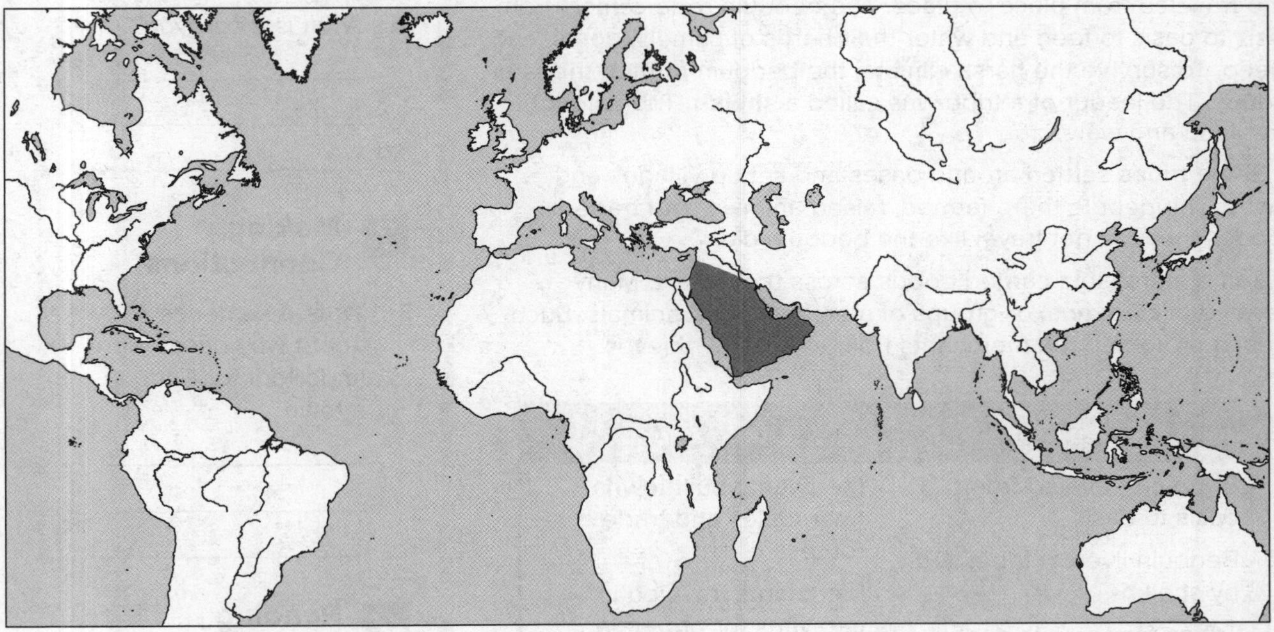

When did it happen?

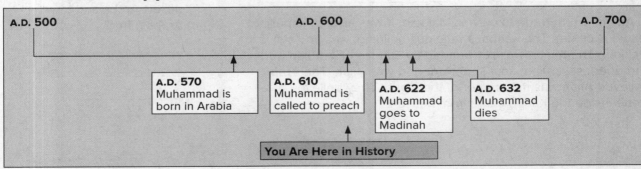

A.D. 500 — **A.D. 600** — **A.D. 700**

- **A.D. 570** Muhammad is born in Arabia
- **A.D. 610** Muhammad is called to preach
- **A.D. 622** Muhammad goes to Madinah
- **A.D. 632** Muhammad dies

You Are Here in History

Arab Life

In the 600s, people on the Arabian peninsula built an empire in Southwest Asia. The empire was based on the religion of Islam. The land in Arabia is mostly desert. It also has dry, sandy plains. It is very hot. The temperatures in summer can rise above 122° F (50° C). The desert had no cities and few towns.

The very hot weather and the dry, sandy land made it difficult to live in the desert. The towns that existed were built around water. In the desert, water can be found only at an oasis. An **oasis** is a spring or water hole.

A group of Arab people called bedouin, however, learned to live in the difficult environment. They were nomads, or people who traveled from place to place. The bedouin rode camels from oasis to oasis to feed and water their herds of camels, goats, and sheep. To survive the harsh climate, the bedouin formed tribes or groups. The leader of a tribe was called a **sheikh.** Tribes fought over land and water.

Some tribes settled around oases and set up villages and towns. The people there farmed, raised animals, and traded goods. They did not travel like the bedouin did.

Some merchants carried goods across the desert. Many traveled in **caravans,** or groups of merchants and animals. Such groups protected the merchants from attacks by thieves.

Life in the desert	Life in towns
• Bedouin traveled from oasis to oasis. • Bedouin lived in tribes led by sheikhs. • Tribes fought with each other over land and water.	• Merchants built towns near oases and trade routes. • Merchants traveled in caravans for protection. • Makkah was an important religious center.

An important trade town was Makkah. It was also an important religious center. The Kaaba, a religious building, was and still is in Makkah. The Kaaba was surrounded by statues of Arabian gods and goddesses. The most important god was Allah. The Arabs believed Allah was the creator of the world. They believed a stone inside the Kaaba came from heaven.

Explaining

1. How did the bedouin learn to live in the desert of the Arabian peninsula?

____

____

____

Defining

2. What is a *caravan*?

____

____

____

Making Connections

3. Write a sentence about why oases were important for living in a town.

____

____

____

Reading Check

4. How did the lives of desert Arabs and town Arabs differ?

____

____

____

FOLDABLES®

Explaining

5. Place a two-tab Foldable along the dotted line. Write *Muhammad* on the anchor tab. Label the two tabs *Who* and *What*.

Use both sides of the tabs to write key words and facts to explain who Muhammad was and what his message taught.

Glue Foldable here

Explaining

6. How did Makkah become a holy city of Islam?

____

____

____

Reading Check

7. Why did Makkah's merchants and religious leaders oppose Muhammad and his message?

____

____

____

Muhammad and His Message

Muhammad was born in Makkah in A.D. 570. Both his parents died. He grew up in his grandfather's house and became a successful merchant. Muhammad was troubled by the way of life in Makkah, especially by the lifestyles of Makkah's wealthy citizens. He saw greed, dishonesty, and neglect of the poor. People did not care about family life.

Muhammad prayed about this. In A.D. 610, according to tradition, he was called by God to preach Islam. The word **Islam** means "to surrender to the will of Allah."

Muhammad preached that there was only one God, Allah. The statues of the gods and goddesses around the Kaaba in Makkah should be destroyed. He also taught that Allah valued people's good deeds instead of their wealth. He said that rich people should share their wealth with the poor.

Many people started following Muhammad, especially the poor. Rich merchants and leaders of the existing religions did not accept Muhammad's teachings. They believed Muhammad was trying to take away their power.

In A.D. 622 Muhammad and his followers believed they were in danger from these enemies. They left Makkah and went to Yathrib. The people of Yathrib accepted Muhammad as a prophet of God. They changed the name of the town to Madinah, which means "the city of the prophet."

In Madinah, Muhammad was a political leader and a religious leader. Muhammad used government power to support Islam. He formed an army. With his army, he took over Makkah and made it a holy city of Islam.

Muhammad was born.

↓

Muhammad became a successful merchant.

↓

Muhammad was called to preach Islam.

↓

Muhammad and his followers went to Madinah.

Beliefs and Practices of Islam

Islam shares some beliefs with Christianity and Judaism. For example, all three religions believe that there is only one God. They believe that God is all-powerful and created the universe. Each religion has a holy book.

Lesson 1 A New Faith, *Continued*

The holy book of Islam is the **Quran.** Muslims believe the Quran is the written word of God. The Quran describes events that are important to Islam. The Quran also includes teachings and instructions.

The Quran teaches people to:

- be honest
- treat others fairly
- respect their parents
- be kind to their neighbors
- be kind to the poor
- not commit murder
- not steal
- not tell a lie

Islam teaches people to worship Allah in five ways. They are called the Five Pillars of Islam. A pillar is a basic belief. The Five Pillars include belief, prayer, charity (giving to the poor), and fasting. Fasting means to eat very little or no food. The fifth pillar is pilgrimage. Muslims are encouraged to travel to the holy city of Makkah to see the Kaaba.

To guide believers, Islam also has a set of laws called the ***shari'ah.*** *Shari'ah* applies the teachings of the Quran to family, business, and government. The shari'ah says Muslims may not gamble or eat pork.

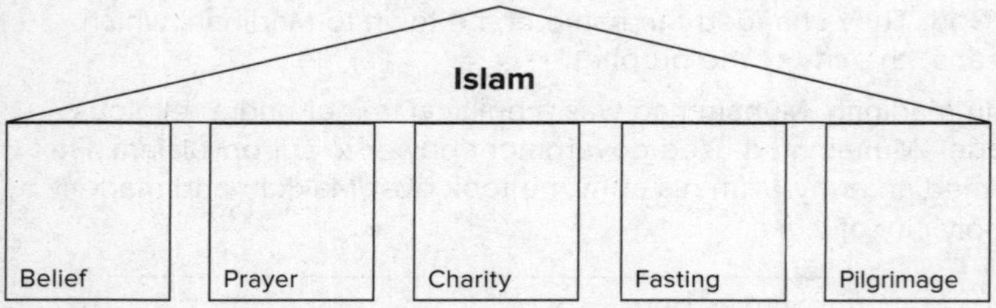

Check for Understanding

List two ideas from the Quran that are presented as guidelines for how to live.

1. ______________________________

2. ______________________________

What is a pilgrimage and why is it important to Islam?

3. ______________________________

____

Marking the Text

8. Circle the five ways that Muslims can worship Allah.

Defining

9. What is *shari'ah*?

____

____

Reading Check

10. Why is the Quran important in the daily life of Muslims?

____

____

____

FOLDABLES®

11. Place a three-tab Foldable along the dotted line. Write Islam on the anchor tab. Label the three tabs *Quran*, *Five Pillars of Islam*, and *Shari'ah*.

Use both sides of the tabs to write key words and facts that you remember about each.

Glue Foldable here

NAME ______________________ DATE ____________ CLASS ________

networks

Islamic Civilization

Lesson 2 The Spread of Islam

ESSENTIAL QUESTION

How does religion shape society?

GUIDING QUESTIONS

1. ***How did the Arabs spread Islam and create an empire?***
2. ***How did the Arab Empire change after the Umayyads?***
3. ***How did the Turks, Safavids, and Moguls rule their empires?***

Terms to Know

caliph a Muslim leader seen as a successor to Muhammad

Shia a group of Muslims who believed the descendants of Ali should rule

Sunni a group of Muslims who accepted the rule of the Umayyad caliphs

sultan a Seljuk ruler

Where in the world?

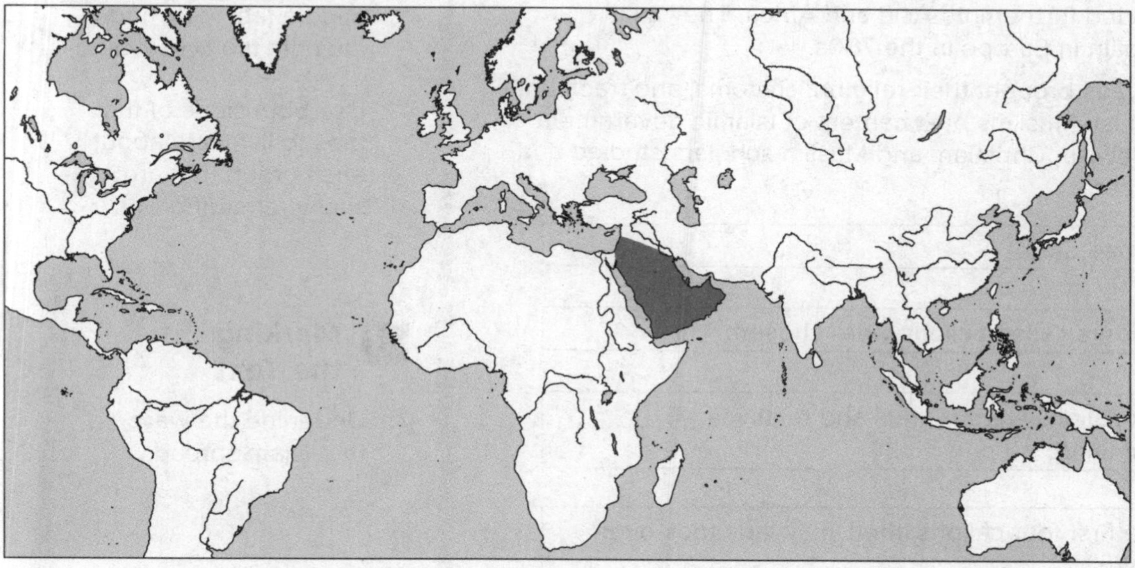

When did it happen?

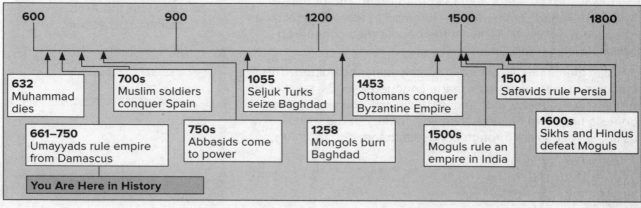

600 — 900 — 1200 — 1500 — 1800

632 Muhammad dies

661–750 Umayyads rule empire from Damascus

700s Muslim soldiers conquer Spain

750s Abbasids come to power

1055 Seljuk Turks seize Baghdad

1258 Mongols burn Baghdad

1453 Ottomans conquer Byzantine Empire

1500s Moguls rule an empire in India

1501 Safavids rule Persia

1600s Sikhs and Hindus defeat Moguls

You Are Here in History

Founding an Empire

Muhammad died in 632. He left no directions about choosing the leader who should come after him. A group of Muslim leaders selected a new kind of leader. They called this leader the **caliph,** or the successor. The caliph was the successor to Muhammad.

The first four caliphs were relatives or friends of Muhammad. Their goal was to protect and to spread Islam. Their armies conquered many lands beyond the Arabian peninsula. They conquered lands in Southwest Asia and Africa.

After the first four caliphs, a new group of caliphs ruled. They were called the Umayyads. They ruled the empire from the city of Damascus in Syria. Their goal also was to spread Islam. Their armies expanded further into Asia and Africa. They also conquered Spain in Europe in the 700s.

The Umayyads brought their religion, customs, and traditions to Spain. Spanish Muslims built centers of Islamic government and culture. Jewish, Christian, and Muslim scholars studied and worked together.

Glue Foldable here

Muhammad died.

↓

New leaders called caliphs were chosen.

↓

The first caliphs were friends and relatives of Muhammad.

↓

After the first four caliphs, the Umayyads took over the empire.

The Muslims were good warriors and fought well in battle. They believed they had a duty to spread Islam. The people of other empires had sometimes been forced to follow the religion of their leaders. The Muslims let the people they conquered practice their own religions.

Muslim merchants also spread Islamic faith and culture. The merchants built trading posts in the conquered lands, such as Southeast Asia. Today, in Southeast Asia, the country of Indonesia has more Muslims than any country in the world. Muslims spread Islam through conquest, trade, and teaching.

FOLDABLES®

Comparing and Contrasting

1. Place a three-tab Venn diagram Foldable along the dotted line. Write *Founding an Empire* on the anchor tab. Label the left tab *First Four Caliphs*, the middle tab *Both*, and the right tab *Umayyads*.

   Use both sides of the tabs to list facts about each group that are similar and different.

Marking the Text

2. Underline the ways that Islam spread.

Reading Check

3. Why was the Arab military successful?

   ____

   ____

   ____

Lesson 2 The Spread of Islam, *Continued*

Marking the Text

4. Circle the name for people who believe that only Muhammad's descendants could be caliphs.

Defining

5. What is a *sultan*?

Analyzing

6. Who do you think had more power in the Islamic world, the sultan or the Abbasid caliph? Be sure to give a reason for your thinking.

Reading Check

7. How did the Sunni and Shia differ? What beliefs did they share?

Division and Growth

There were groups in Islam that argued about who had the right to be caliph. Muslims divided into two groups over the issue. The **Shia** believed only people descended from Muhammad's son-in-law, Ali, should be caliphs. The **Sunni,** a larger group than the Shia, disagreed. They did not think caliphs had to be related to Muhammad.

Today the two groups are still divided over this question. They do both agree, however, on the basic beliefs of Islam.

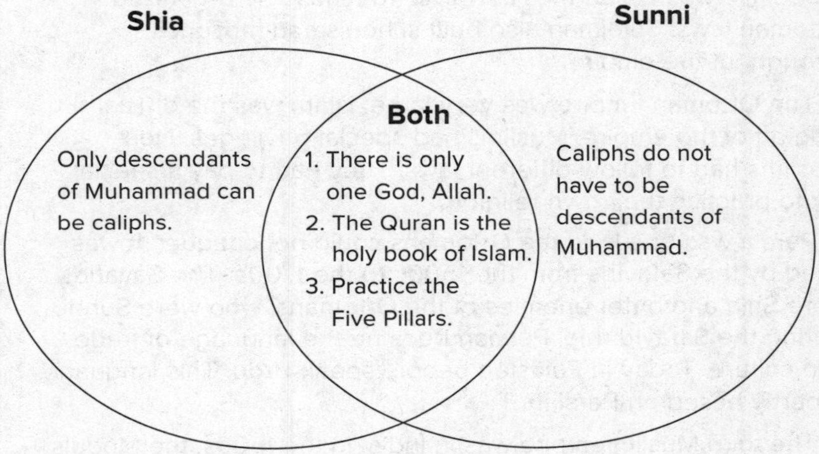
Shia
Sunni
Both
Only descendants of Muhammad can be caliphs.
1. There is only one God, Allah.
2. The Quran is the holy book of Islam.
3. Practice the Five Pillars.
Caliphs do not have to be descendants of Muhammad.

Around 750, the Shia Muslims rebelled and took over the rule from the Umayyad caliphs. The new caliphs were called Abbasids.

The Abbasid caliphs focused on improving trade and culture. They built the city of Baghdad. It became the new capital of the Arab Empire. All the trade routes passed through Baghdad. It was a beautiful and wealthy city.

In 1055 Baghdad was seized by people called the Seljuk Turks. They came from central Asia and invaded the Arab Empire. The Seljuk Turks and Abbasids ruled together. The leader of the Turks was called a **sultan.** The sultan controlled the military and the government. The Abbasid caliphs managed religious matters. They ruled for 200 years this way.

In 1258 people from central Asia, called Mongols, quickly moved into the empire. The Mongols burned Baghdad and killed thousands of people. The Arab Empire was over.

Three Muslim Empires

After the Arab Empire ended in 1258, other Muslim groups built their own empires. The Ottomans were based in what is now the country of Turkey. They built the largest Islamic empire. It lasted until the early 1900s. The Ottomans conquered much of the Byzantine Empire and expanded further into Europe, Southwest Asia, and North Africa.

Rulers of the Ottoman Empire were also called sultans. The most famous Ottoman sultan was Suleiman I. He ruled during the 1500s. He was called the "Lawgiver" because he organized Ottoman laws. Suleiman also built schools and mosques throughout the empire.

The Ottoman Empire was very large. Islam was the official religion of the empire. Muslims had special privileges. Non-Muslims had to follow different laws. They had to pay a special tax to practice their own religion.

Persia was one land the Ottomans could not conquer. It was ruled by the Safavids from the 1500s to the 1700s. The Savafids were Shia and bitter enemies of the Ottomans, who were Sunni. During the Safavid rule, Persian became the language of trade and culture. Today in Pakistan people speak Urdu. This language is partly based on Persian.

The third Muslim empire was in India. In the 1500s, the Moguls conquered India. Under a Mogul emperor named Akbar, non-Muslims were treated fairly. Later Mogul rulers treated Hindus and Sikhs cruelly. The religion of Sikhism started in the 1500s. The Sikhs believe in one God and rely on one holy book called the *Adigranth*. Today, sikhism is the fifth largest religion in the world.

/ / / / / / / / / / / / / / Glue Foldable here / / / / / / / / / / / / / /

Check for Understanding

Define the major belief of each of the following groups: Shia and Sunni.

1. ______________________

2. ______________________

What were the three major Muslim Empires?

3. ______________________

____

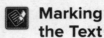

Marking the Text

8. Circle two things that Suleiman I did.

Identifying

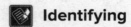

9. Which group built the largest Muslim empire?

____

____

____

Reading Check

10. What is *Urdu*?

____

FOLDABLES®

11. Place a three-tab Venn diagram Foldable along the dotted line to cover the Check for Understanding. On the anchor tab, write *Two Groups in Islam*. Write *Shia* on the left tab, *Both* on the middle tab, and *Sunnis* on the right tab.

On both sides of the tabs, list what you remember about each and determine what they have in common.

NAME ____________________ DATE __________ CLASS ________

networks

Islamic Civilization

Lesson 3 Life in the Islamic World

ESSENTIAL QUESTION

How do ideas change the way people live?

GUIDING QUESTIONS

1. *How did people live and trade in the Islamic world?*
2. *What were Muslim contributions in mathematics, science, and the arts?*

Terms to Know

mosque a Muslim house of worship
bazaar a marketplace of shops
astrolabe a tool that helps sailors find their way at sea by using the stars
minaret a tower of a mosque from which a person calls Muslims to prayer

When did it happen?

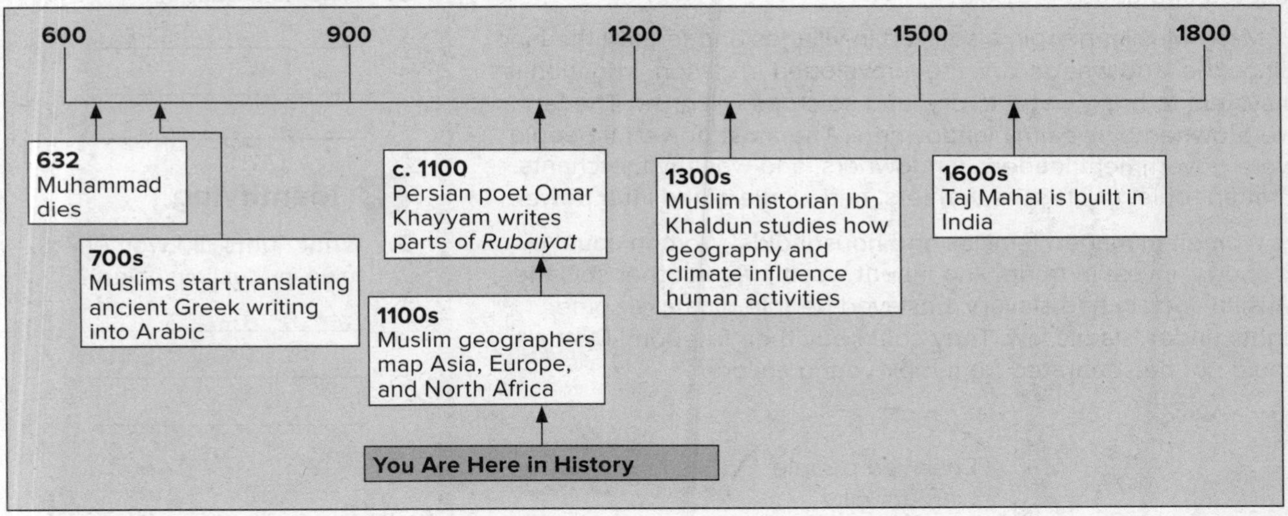
600
900
1200
1500
1800
632 Muhammad dies
700s Muslims start translating ancient Greek writing into Arabic
c. 1100 Persian poet Omar Khayyam writes parts of *Rubaiyat*
1100s Muslim geographers map Asia, Europe, and North Africa
1300s Muslim historian Ibn Khaldun studies how geography and climate influence human activities
1600s Taj Mahal is built in India
You Are Here in History

What do you know?

Think about what you already know about the Islamic world. Write it down in the K column. In the W column, list what you want to know about the Islamic world. After reading this lesson, fill in the L column with a list of what you learned.

K	W	L

Lesson 3 Life in the Islamic World, *Continued*

Daily Life and Trade

From 700 to the 1400s, Muslims controlled trade in much of Asia and Africa. Muslim merchants spread Islam and the Arabic language. Muslim merchants developed a money system that made trading easier. They also kept detailed records. This led to the development of banking.

As trade increased, cities grew. Muslim cities always had **mosques.** People worshiped in the mosques. Schools and courts were located in the mosques. The mosques were learning centers. Muslim cities also had **bazaars.** A bazaar is a marketplace. It is a place in a city or town where shops are located and goods are sold.

Many Muslim people also lived in villages and farmed the land. Since the land was so dry, they developed irrigation. Irrigation is a system to bring water to dry land so crops will grow. The farms were owned by wealthy landowners. The most powerful people were government leaders, landowners, and wealthy merchants. Craftspeople, or artisans, farmers, and workers had little power.

Women managed families and households. Women could own property, invest in trade, and inherit wealth. As in other societies, Muslim society had slavery. Enslaved people did have some rights under Islamic law. They could buy their freedom. Mothers could not be separated from their young children.

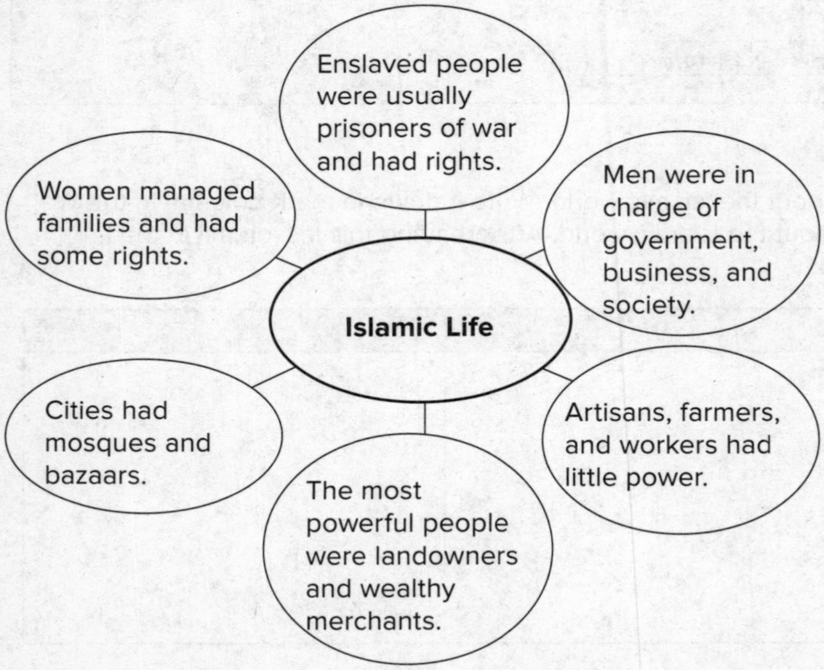
Islamic Life
Enslaved people were usually prisoners of war and had rights.
Men were in charge of government, business, and society.
Artisans, farmers, and workers had little power.
The most powerful people were landowners and wealthy merchants.
Cities had mosques and bazaars.
Women managed families and had some rights.

Listing

1. List three functions of a mosque.

____

____

____

Defining

2. What is a *bazaar*?

____

____

____

Identifying

3. What rights did women have in Muslim society?

____

____

____

Reading Check

4. Why were Muslim merchants successful?

____

____

____

Marking the Text

5. Circle the name of the language that allowed Europeans to learn about ancient Greek ideas.

Making Inferences

6. How might the use of Arabic numerals be connected to Islamic trade?

____

____

Analyzing

7. Why might the Quran be considered the most important book written in Arabic?

____

____

____

Explaining

8. Why does Islamic art not show people?

____

____

____

Muslim Contributions

The Arabic language was the common language throughout the Islamic world. That helped promote trade and the exchange of ideas. Muslim scholars and doctors made many contributions in science, mathematics, medicine, literature, art, and architecture. Many of these contributions are still used today.

Muslim scholars in Spain translated many ancient Greek works into Arabic. Later, the Arabic versions were translated into Latin. That is when Europeans learned about ancient Greek ideas.

Many ancient Greek works were lost in Europe.	→	Muslim scholars translated ancient Greek works into Arabic.	→	The Arabic versions were translated into Latin.	→	Europeans learned about ancient Greek ideas.

In science, Muslims improved the Greek **astrolabe.** Sailors used this tool to study the stars and chart their location. Muslims used the improved astrolabe to measure the distance around the Earth. By studying the skies, they also proved that the moon affects the Earth's ocean tides.

Muslim scientists began what we know today as the study of chemistry. They studied metals. A Muslim chemist, al-Razi, identified chemical substances.

In mathematics, Muslim scholars invented algebra. They also used the Hindu number symbols to develop a number system called Arabic numerals. We use Arabic numerals today as our numbering system.

In the field of medicine, Muslim doctors discovered that blood moves to and from the heart. They learned to diagnose diseases and explained how diseases spread from one person to another person. Muslims were the first to establish medical schools for training and testing doctors. They also built clinics where the sick could go for medicine.

Muslims made major contributions in literature, the arts, and architecture. The Quran was the first and the most important piece of Arabic writing. A well-known work of literature is *The Arabian Nights*. The Muslim poet Omar Khayyam wrote the *Rubaiyat*. It is widely read today.

Islamic art included detailed designs of flowers, leaves, stars, and fancy lettering, but images of people and animals were forbidden. Muslim leaders believed that images of living things encouraged idol worship.

Lesson 3 Life in the Islamic World, *Continued*

They felt that idol worship meant that people were being unfaithful to Allah. Because of this, Islamic art does not show images of people.

Many examples of Muslim architecture still stand today. Throughout the world mosques have a **minaret,** or tower. From this tower, an announcer calls Muslims to prayer five times a day. Other Muslim buildings that still stand today include the Taj Mahal, a beautiful building in India that was built in the 1600s.

Muslim Contributions	
Science	• improved the astrolabe • proved that the Earth is round • learned that the moon affects the ocean • developed chemistry
Mathematics	• developed Arabic numbers • developed algebra
Medicine	• discovered how blood moves to and from the heart • diagnosed and explained the spread of diseases • established medical schools and tests for doctors
Literature	• *The Arabian Nights* • the *Rubaiyat*
Art	• detailed designs of flowers, leaves, stars, fancy lettering • did not show images of people • decorated walls, books, buildings, and rugs
Architecture	• mosques with minarets • Taj Mahal

/ / / / / / / / / / / / / Glue Foldable here / / / / / / / / / / / / /

Check for Understanding

List two ways you think a common language throughout the Islamic world helped the spread of knowledge, culture, and religion.

1. ______________________________

2. ______________________________

Using Vocabulary

9. Write a sentence that describes how a *minaret* is used at a *mosque*.

____

____

____

Reading Check

10. What achievements were made by Muslims in medicine?

____

____

____

FOLDABLES®

11. Place a three-tab Foldable along the dotted line to cover the Check for Understanding. On the anchor tab, write *Muslim Contributions*. Label the three tabs *Mathematics*, *Science*, and *Literature and the Arts*.

Write words and phrases about Muslim contributions in each field.

NAME______________________________ DATE ____________ CLASS ________

networks

African Civilizations

Lesson 1 The Rise of African Civilizations

ESSENTIAL QUESTION

Why do people trade?

GUIDING QUESTIONS

1. ***How did early peoples settle Africa?***
2. ***How did trade develop in Africa?***
3. ***Why did West African trading empires rise and fall?***
4. ***How did trade affect the development of East African kingdoms?***

Terms to Know

savannas tropical grasslands with small trees and bushes
plateau an area of high, mostly flat land
griot a traditional African storyteller
dhow a sailboat with a special triangle-shaped sail

Where in the world?

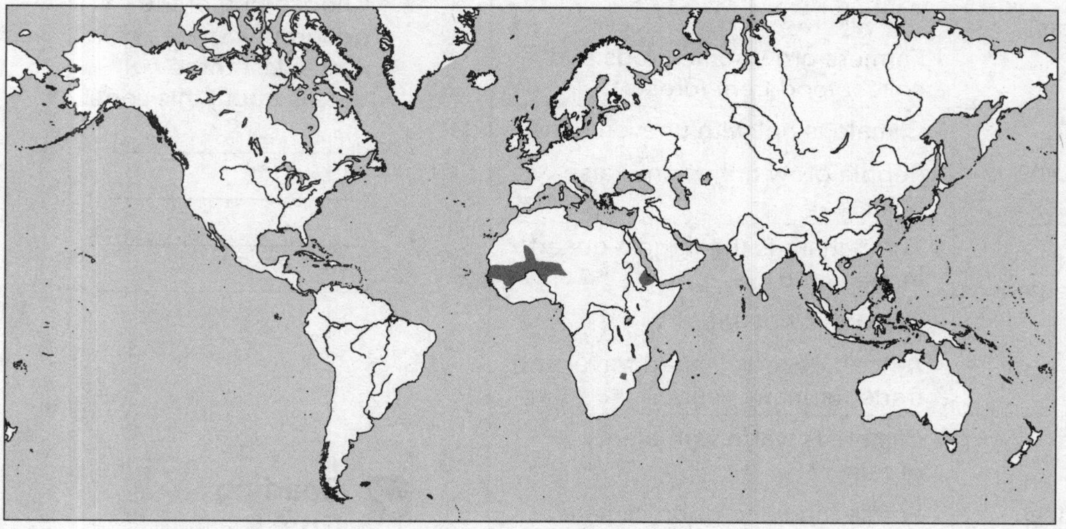

When did it happen?

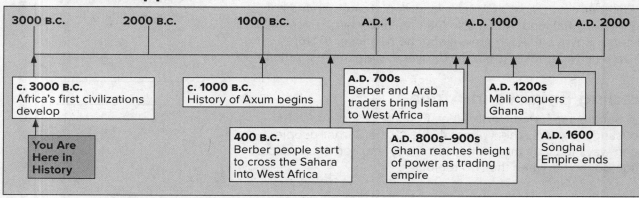

3000 B.C. | **2000 B.C.** | **1000 B.C.** | **A.D. 1** | **A.D. 1000** | **A.D. 2000**

c. 3000 B.C. Africa's first civilizations develop

You Are Here in History

c. 1000 B.C. History of Axum begins

400 B.C. Berber people start to cross the Sahara into West Africa

A.D. 700s Berber and Arab traders bring Islam to West Africa

A.D. 800s–900s Ghana reaches height of power as trading empire

A.D. 1200s Mali conquers Ghana

A.D. 1600 Songhai Empire ends

Lesson 1 The Rise of African Civilizations, *Continued*

African Beginnings

Scientists believe the first humans lived in Africa more than 150,000 years ago. About seven or eight thousand years ago, groups of people began to stay in one place. They tamed animals, grew crops, and formed villages. Later, these villages became more organized. Africa's first civilizations developed. They were called Egypt and Kush.

The geography of Africa affected its early people. Africa is the second largest continent on Earth. It has four geographic zones and climates. These differ a great deal from one another.

Geographic Zone	Description
Rain forests (lush, tropical forests)	• Climate is warm with heavy rainfall. • Farmers grow some crops and collect food from forests.
Savannas (grasslands; cover about 40 percent of Africa)	• Climate is hot with uneven rains. • People grow grains and raise animals.
Deserts (cover about 40 percent of Africa)	• The Sahara is the largest desert in the world. • Climate is hot and dry. • Africa's deserts limited travel and trade for many years.
Mild climate areas (on northern coast and southern tip of Africa)	• Climate is warm with plenty of rain. • Fertile land and good climate enable farmers to grow many crops.

Plateaus cover most of Africa's land. A **plateau** is an area of high, mostly flat land. Africa also features many large river systems. Egypt and Kush grew along the Nile River in North Africa. The Niger River is the major river system in West Africa.

Trading Empires in Africa

The Sahara separated North Africa from the rest of Africa for thousands of years. Then, about 400 B.C., the Berber people found ways to cross this vast desert. They reached West Africa. Trade began between the two regions.

Marking the Text

1. Underline the information about the first humans in Africa.

Examining Details

2. Choose one of the geographic zones of Africa. List three details about this zone.

Zone: ____________

• ____________

• ____________

• ____________

Reading Check

3. How did Africa's climate zones affect people's ability to raise crops?

____

____

____

FOLDABLES®

Describing

4. Place a one-tab Foldable along the dotted line to cover the text to the right. Label the anchor tab *Trade*. From memory, sketch the outline of North Africa on the front of the tab. Label the Sahara, North Africa, and West Africa on your sketch. On the back of the tab, write about the importance of crossing the Sahara to trade.

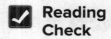

Reading Check

5. Why were camels essential for the Sahara trade?

____

____

____

Identifying

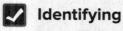

6. How did Islam arrive in Ghana?

____

____

____

Glue Foldable here

Berbers used donkeys and horses to cross the Sahara, but these animals often died because of the heat. In A.D. 200, the Romans introduced the camel to North Africa. Camels could better handle the hot, dry conditions. They can travel days without water. The use of camels increased trade between North Africa and West Africa.

Berber traders formed caravans made up of many camels. The caravans carried trade goods, such as ivory, spices, and leather, across the Sahara. At times, the caravans also transported enslaved people who were captured in wars. Merchants sent the enslaved people to the Mediterranean region and Southwest Asia. In these locations, they were forced to serve as soldiers and household servants.

Early slave trade in Africa

Africa: Traders bring enslaved people to merchants.

↓

Africa: Merchants send enslaved people to other regions.

↓

Mediterranean and Southwest Asia: Enslaved people arrive and are forced to serve as soldiers and servants.

West African Kingdoms

Caravans traveled from North Africa to West Africa. One of the important goods they carried was salt. This salt came from mines located in the Sahara. Traders also brought Islam to West Africa in the A.D. 700s. Many merchants in West Africa became Muslims.

Ghana was the first great trading empire in West Africa. It grew powerful during the A.D. 400s as a center of trade. Ghana was located between the salt mines of the Sahara and the gold mines of West Africa. Ghana's kings became wealthy by taxing traders who passed through the empire. Muslim Arabs and Berber traders brought Islam to Ghana. Many people converted to Islam.

The power of Ghana slowly declined in the A.D. 1100s. One group separated from the empire and formed the empire of Mali. In the A.D. 1200s, Mali conquered what was left of Ghana. **Griots** told how Sundiata Keita ruled well and made Mali great. Griots are traditional African storytellers. Sundiata united people under a strong government. He also conquered new lands that put Mali in control of gold mines in West Africa. The empire built its wealth and power on the gold and salt trade.

Lesson 1 The Rise of African Civilizations, *Continued*

Mali began to weaken in A.D. 1337. The state of Songhai eventually gained control of the gold and salt trade. By A.D. 1492, Songhai had become the largest empire in West Africa. This empire lasted about 100 more years.

Effects of Trade on West Africa

- Trade brought wealth to West Africa.
- The population of West Africa grew.
- Powerful African city-states developed. Rulers of these city-states began to build empires.
- African empires became larger and richer than most European kingdoms from the A.D. 500s to A.D. 1300s.

East African Kingdoms

The East African kingdom of Axum became an important stop on trade routes that connected Africa, the Mediterranean world, and India. In A.D. 334 King Ezana made Christianity the official religion. Islam was introduced later. Both religions had a major impact.

Arab traders had sailed to East Africa for many years. They traveled in sailboats called **dhows.** These ships used a special triangle-shaped sail to catch the wind. In the A.D. 700s, many Arab Muslim traders settled along the Indian Ocean in East Africa. The Indian Ocean trade also reached inland. During the A.D. 900s, Zimbabwe became one of the important inland trading states. Many large stone buildings still stand at the site of the empire's capital, Great Zimbabwe.

Check for Understanding

List the two important trading regions separated by the Sahara.

1. ______________________

2. ______________________

List two ways that trade affected African kingdoms.

3. ______________________

4. ______________________

Glue Foldable here

Reading Check

7. What were two valuable products traded through Ghana?

____

Reading Check

8. Why did Axum become a prosperous trading center?

____

FOLDABLES®

9. Use a one-tab Foldable. Cut the tab into quarters to make four tabs. Label the tabs *West African Kingdoms*, *Rain Forest Kingdoms*, *East African Kingdoms*, and *Central and South Africa*.

On both sides of the tabs, write about the effects of trade in each kingdom or area. Use your Foldable to help you complete the lists under the tabs.

NAME ______________________ DATE ______________ CLASS __________

African Civilizations

Lesson 2 Africa's Governments and Religions

ESSENTIAL QUESTION

How does religion shape society?

GUIDING QUESTIONS

1. ***How did African rulers govern their territories?***
2. ***How did traditional religions influence African life?***
3. ***How did Islam spread in Africa?***

Terms to Know

clan a group of people who all share the same ancestor

Swahili the unique culture of Africa's East Coast and the language spoken there

When did it happen?

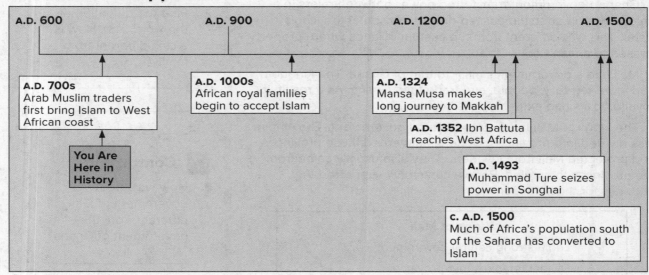

A.D. 600 — **A.D. 900** — **A.D. 1200** — **A.D. 1500**

- **A.D. 700s** Arab Muslim traders first bring Islam to West African coast
  - **You Are Here in History**
- **A.D. 1000s** African royal families begin to accept Islam
- **A.D. 1324** Mansa Musa makes long journey to Makkah
- **A.D. 1352** Ibn Battuta reaches West Africa
- **A.D. 1493** Muhammad Ture seizes power in Songhai
- **c. A.D. 1500** Much of Africa's population south of the Sahara has converted to Islam

What do you know?

Write two facts that you have already learned about each African kingdom.

Axum ____

Ghana ____

Mali ____

Songhai ____

Zimbabwe ____

Lesson 2 Africa's Governments and Religions, *Continued*

African Rulers and Society

Africans developed different ways to rule their growing empires. Powerful empires such as Ghana and Mali had strong, central governments. Rulers settled disputes, controlled trade, and defended the empire. In return, they expected total loyalty from their people. This relationship was good for everyone.

Ghana had a council of ministers to help the king govern. Kings divided Ghana into provinces as the empire grew. Lesser kings ruled these provinces. Chiefs ruled smaller districts. A district included all the villages in a chief's **clan,** those who shared the same ancestor as the chief.

Ghana's government transferred power between rulers in a unique way. Leadership passed only to the son of the king's sister. This was different from the custom in lands where property passed to a man's sons.

Mali had a government similar to that of Ghana. The kingdom had more territory, people, and trade than Ghana. As a result, its royal officials had extra responsibilities.

The kings of Mali led a strong central government. The empire was divided into provinces. Generals governed these provinces and protected Mali from invaders. They also usually came from the provinces they ruled. People commonly supported the generals for those reasons.

Kings of Mali

- Led a strong central government
- Divided empires into provinces
- Hired generals to govern provinces and protect Mali from invaders
- Had the support of the people

The richest and most famous king of Mali was Mansa Musa. He ruled from A.D. 1312 to A.D. 1337. Mansa Musa won people's loyalty by giving them gifts like gold, property, and horses.

Songhai built its government on the political traditions of Ghana and Mali. The empire was at its most powerful under Muhammad Ture, a general and devout Muslim. He divided Songhai into provinces. A governor, a tax collector, a court of judges, and a trade inspector were in charge of each province. Muhammad Ture used a navy and soldiers on horseback to keep peace.

Summarizing

1. What were some of the duties of African rulers?

____

____

____

Analyzing

2. Find the definition of the word *clan*. How is a clan different from a family?

____

____

____

Contrasting

3. How was the government of Mali different from the government of Ghana?

____

____

____

Reading Check

4. Why did people in Mali mostly support the generals who ruled the provinces?

____

____

____

Listing

5. List the people who governed each province of Songhai.

1. ______________
2. ______________
3. ______________
4. ______________

Identifying

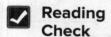

6. List two important purposes that religious beliefs served in Africa.

____

____

Reading Check

7. What was the role of diviners in African religions?

____

____

____

Marking the Text

8. Underline the text that explains how Islam reached West Africa.

Traditional African Religions

Most African societies shared some common religious beliefs. Many shared a belief in a single creator god. Some wanted to keep their own religious practices. These practices varied in different places.

Traditional African Religion	Location	Belief
Igbo	West Africa	a single creator god
Yoruba	West Africa	chief god sent his son from heaven in a canoe; this son created the first humans
Ashanti	Ghana	a supreme god whose sons were lesser gods

Even though religious beliefs differed, they served similar purposes. They provided rules to live by. They also helped people remember their history. Africans believed that religion could protect them from danger and help them succeed in life. Some believed that a group of people called diviners could foretell the future. Kings hired diviners to guarantee good harvests and protect their kingdoms.

Islam Arrives in Africa

The arrival of Islam began to challenge traditional religions starting in the A.D. 700s. Berber and Arab merchants took Islam to West Africa as they traded.

African rulers welcomed the Muslim traders. They allowed their people to accept Islam. During the A.D. 1000s, African rulers themselves finally began to accept Islam. Much of Africa's population south of the Sahara converted to Islam by the end of the 1400s.

Mansa Musa became Mali's most famous ruler. He worked hard to spread Islam. He used his wealth to build mosques. He also set up libraries in the capital, Timbuktu.

Mansa Musa became well-known for his journey to the Muslim holy city of Makkah. In Makkah, Mansa Musa made sure the people knew he was the ruler of a great empire. He brought a large caravan of camels carrying gold. Mansa Musa gave this gold to the poor he met along his journey.

Lesson 2 Africa's Governments and Religions, *Continued*

In Makkah, Mansa Musa met Muslim scholars. He talked them into returning to Mali with him. These scholars helped spread Islam in West Africa.

A young Arab lawyer from Morocco named Ibn Battuta was impressed by Mansa Musa. In 1325 he set out to see the Muslim world. In West Africa, he discovered many people were Muslims. However, some people still followed traditional African religions.

Islam spread slowly in East Africa. A new society called **Swahili** helped it spread beginning in the 1100s and 1200s. The Swahili culture and language are a mixture of African and Muslim cultures. The Muslim influences came from Arab and Persian settlers. Swahili comes from an Arabic word meaning "people of the coast." Swahili culture and language remain important in modern Africa.

Islam had a major impact on Africa. Many people accepted the laws and ideas of Islam. Muslim schools introduced the Arabic language. Islam also had an effect on art and architecture in Africa. Muslim builders created beautiful mosques and palaces in African cities such as Timbuktu.

Check for Understanding

List two facts that describe the government of Ghana.

1. ______________________________

2. ______________________________

List two facts that describe the kingdom of Mali.

3. ______________________________

4. ______________________________

Glue Foldable here

Critical Thinking

9. How did Mansa Musa help spread Islam in West Africa?

____

____

____

Reading Check

10. What caused a unique brand of Islam to develop in Africa?

____

____

____

FOLDABLES®

11. Glue a three-tab Foldable along the dotted line to cover the Check for Understanding. Label the anchor tab *West Africa Kingdoms*. On the three tabs write *Ghana*, *Mali*, and *Songhai*.

Use both sides to describe each kingdom.

NAME ______________________ DATE ____________ CLASS ________

networks

African Civilizations

Lesson 3 African Society and Culture

ESSENTIAL QUESTION

How do religions develop?

GUIDING QUESTIONS

1. ***Why do people in different parts of Africa have similar traditions and cultures?***
2. ***How did the slave trade affect Africans?***
3. ***Why were art forms important to Africans?***

Terms to Know

extended family a family made up of several generations

matrilineal tracing family history through mothers instead of fathers

oral history stories told out loud and passed down from generation to generation

sugarcane a grassy plant that is grown as a source of sugar

spiritual a gospel song

Where in the world?

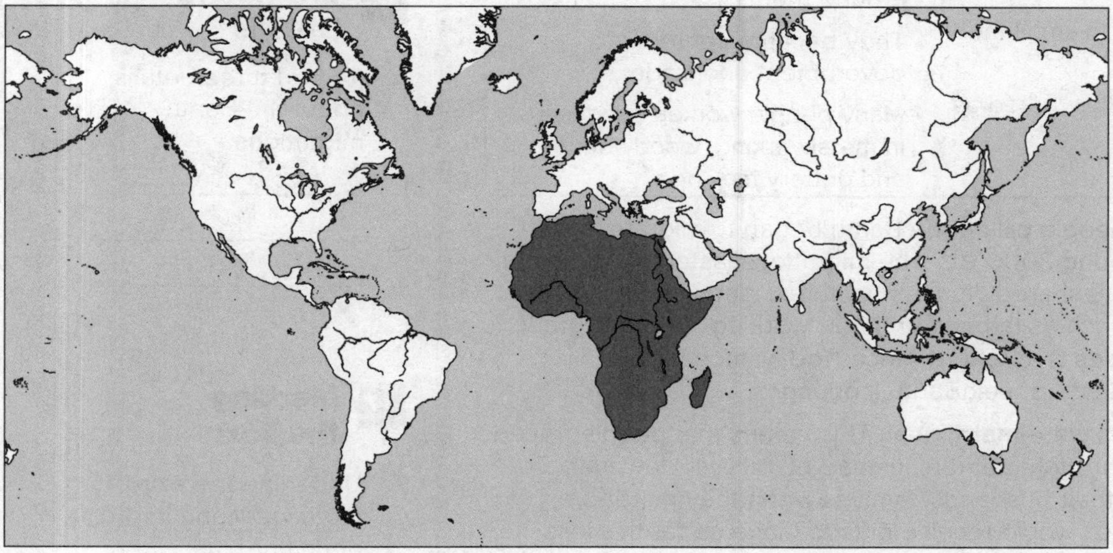

When did it happen?

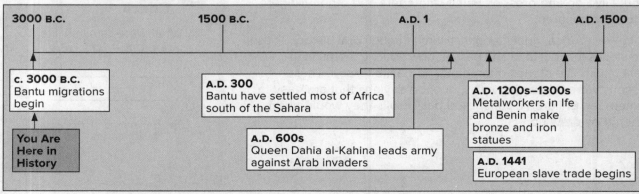

3000 B.C. — **1500 B.C.** — **A.D. 1** — **A.D. 1500**

c. 3000 B.C. Bantu migrations begin

You Are Here in History

A.D. 300 Bantu have settled most of Africa south of the Sahara

A.D. 600s Queen Dahia al-Kahina leads army against Arab invaders

A.D. 1200s–1300s Metalworkers in Ife and Benin make bronze and iron statues

A.D. 1441 European slave trade begins

African Society

Family was the basis of African society. Many people lived in **extended families.** These were families made up of several generations. Extended families belonged to larger groups of people called lineage groups. All of the people in a lineage group could trace their family history to one common relative. Members of these groups supported and cared for each other.

Rural villages	Cities and towns
• Most people in early Africa lived in communities in the countryside. • People lived in small mud homes. • People usually worked as farmers.	• Cities and towns often grew from smaller villages. • They often had protective walls around them. • They became centers of government and trade. • Many people worked as artisans in metalworking, woodworking, and pottery making.

A group of people called the Bantu began to migrate from West Africa around 3000 B.C. The migrations lasted hundreds of years. The Bantu shared common cultures, languages, and technologies, such as farming and iron-working. These migrations spread similarities throughout Africa. Today, more than 200 million Africans speak Bantu languages.

Many villages were **matrilineal.** This means that people traced family history through mothers instead of fathers. However, women joined their husbands' families when they married. Women's families would receive gifts to make up for this loss. Gifts might include cattle, metal tools, goats, or cloth.

African families valued children. Children meant that families would live on and prosper. Family members and other villagers educated children.

In West Africa, griots taught children through **oral history.** These are stories told out loud and passed down from generation to generation. The stories often contained a life lesson. These lessons were told as proverbs, or short sayings that are easy to remember. Children also learned basic skills they would need when they grew up.

Contrasting

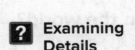

1. What are two ways in which rural villages in Africa differed from towns and cities?

____

____

____

Examining Details

2. Record three details about the Bantu migrations.

1. ______________________
2. ______________________
3. ______________________

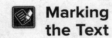

Marking the Text

3. Underline the word *matrilineal* and its definition.

Reading Check

4. What were families like in early Africa?

____

____

____

Lesson 3 African Society and Culture, *Continued*

Identifying

5. What are some jobs enslaved people were forced to work for African rulers?

____

____

Drawing Conclusions

6. Why do you think European plantation owners wanted to force enslaved Africans to work for them?

____

____

Explaining

7. What caused the slave trade to grow in Africa?

____

____

Reading Check

8. How did increased contact with other parts of the world affect the slave trade in Africa?

____

____

____

African women acted mostly as wives and mothers. They had fewer rights than men. However, some women served as soldiers and rulers. Queen Dahia al-Kahina led an army to fight off Arab invaders who attacked her kingdom. Another woman ruler was Queen Nzinga. She spent many years fighting Europeans and the slave trade.

The Slave Trade

Slavery had existed in Africa since ancient times. It was a common practice in many parts of the world. Bantu warriors often raided villages for captives. These people were forced to work for African rulers as laborers, servants, or soldiers. Their lives were hard, but enslaved Africans could win their freedom. Sometimes they were able to work for their freedom or they might marry a free person.

People who were enslaved included:

- enemies captured during war
- people who owed money
- criminals

Enslaved people became part of the African trade. This trade grew as contact with the Muslim world increased. The Quran forbid Muslims to enslave other Muslims. They could, however, enslave non-Muslims. This caused Arab Muslim merchants to trade goods for enslaved Africans who were not Muslim.

The arrival of Europeans caused the slave trade to grow even more. The European slave trade began in 1441 when African captives were taken to Portugal. Most enslaved Africans were forced to work as laborers in Portugal at first.

Portugal later settled islands in the Atlantic Ocean. On these islands, they grew crops such as **sugarcane** on huge farms called plantations. Sugarcane is a grassy plant used to make sugar. Harvesting this crop was hard work. The enslaved workers received no pay.

Other European countries began to join Portugal in the slave trade. These countries started to settle in the Americas during the late 1400s. They brought enslaved Africans to the Americas to help grow crops such as sugar, tobacco, rice, and cotton.

Culture in Africa

African works of art had a religious purpose. Artists made these works to help people connect with gods, spirits, or ancestors. Art also helped teach people about their history.

African Art Forms

- painting
- weaving
- woodcarving
- poetry
- dancing
- metalworking

Rock paintings were the earliest form of art in Africa. Later, woodcarvers made masks and statues. In the A.D. 1200s and 1300s, people in Benin made statues of bronze and iron.

Music and dance in Africa related to everyday life. These arts could express religious feelings. Enslaved Africans used music to remember their homeland. In America, songs that told of hard times became known as the blues. **Spirituals** are gospel songs. They developed from songs of religious faith and hope for freedom. Ragtime, jazz, rock and roll, and rap are all forms of African-based music.

Dance offered a way for Africans to communicate with the spirits. Dance also reflected community life and marked important stages of life.

Africans also kept alive their storytelling tradition. Some enslaved Africans shared their stories after they escaped. Those who heard the stories told them again and again.

Check for Understanding

List two common beliefs or customs that the Bantu introduced to Africa.

1. ____________________

2. ____________________

List two ways that the slave trade affected Africans.

3. ____________________

4. ____________________

Glue Foldable here

Identifying

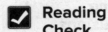

9. What were two important purposes of African works of art?

____

____

____

Reading Check

10. What role did music and dance play in the everyday lives of early Africans?

____

____

____

FOLDABLES®

11. Place a three-tab Foldable to cover the Check for Understanding. Write *Slave Trade* on the anchor tab. Label the tabs *Bantu*, *Muslims*, and *Europeans*.

Use both sides to write key points you remember about each group. Use your Foldable to help you complete the lists under the tabs.

NAME______________________ DATE ____________ CLASS ________

networks

The Americas

Lesson 1 The First Americans

ESSENTIAL QUESTION

How does geography affect the way people live?

GUIDING QUESTIONS

1. ***How did geography shape the ways people settled in the Americas?***
2. ***How did prehistoric people reach the Americas and form settlements?***
3. ***How did farming make civilization possible in the Americas?***
4. ***Why did a large number of societies develop in North America?***

Where in the world?

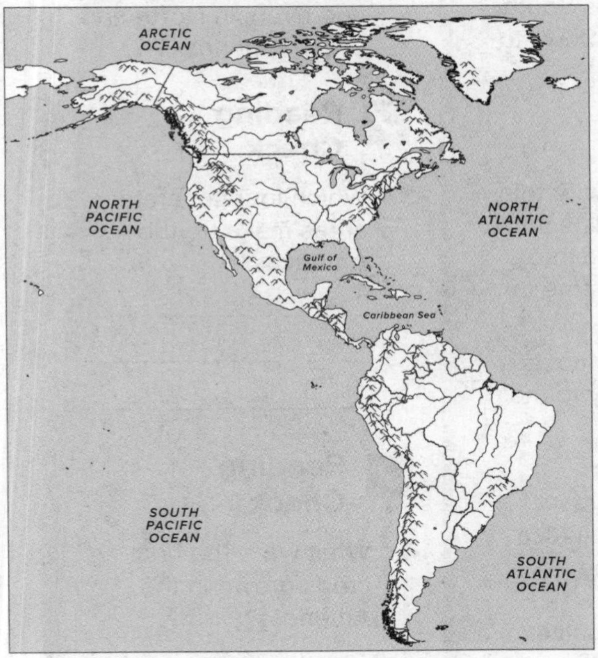

Terms to Know

isthmus a narrow piece of land that connects two larger areas of land

maize corn

When did it happen?

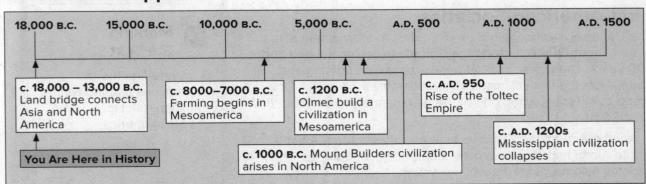

18,000 B.C. | 15,000 B.C. | 10,000 B.C. | 5,000 B.C. | A.D. 500 | A.D. 1000 | A.D. 1500

- **c. 18,000 – 13,000 B.C.** Land bridge connects Asia and North America
- **You Are Here in History**
- **c. 8000–7000 B.C.** Farming begins in Mesoamerica
- **c. 1200 B.C.** Olmec build a civilization in Mesoamerica
- **c. 1000 B.C.** Mound Builders civilization arises in North America
- **c. A.D. 950** Rise of the Toltec Empire
- **c. A.D. 1200s** Mississippian civilization collapses

Geography of the Americas

The Americas is a vast region. It includes North America, Central America, South America, and the Caribbean. Central America is an isthmus. An **isthmus** is a narrow piece of land that connects two larger areas of land. Central America connects North and South America.

The Americas have many different geographic features. The Rocky Mountains are in western North America. The Appalachians run along eastern North America. The Andes stretch along the Pacific coast of South America.

The Mississippi is the largest river system in North America. It runs from Minnesota to the Gulf of Mexico. The Amazon is South America's largest river system. It starts in the Andes and flows to the Atlantic Ocean.

Settling the Americas

About 15,000 to 20,000 years ago, ocean levels were low. A thin strip of land linked Asia and North America. Some scientists think that early people walked across this land bridge from Asia into North America. Other scientists believe the first people came to America by boat.

The first Americans were hunters and gatherers. They moved from place to place looking for food. They used what they found for food, clothing, and shelter.

When the last Ice Age ended, the climate grew warmer. Farming began in Mesoamerica around 9,000 to 10,000 years ago. Mesoamerica is the land from central Mexico to Costa Rica in Central America. The land in Mesoamerica was rich. The climate was mild. Crops grew well there. Early people grew squash, peppers, potatoes, and beans. Later, they grew **maize,** or corn. Maize became the most important crop in the Americas.

First American Societies

The Olmec civilization might be the oldest in Mesoamerica. It began about 1200 B.C. along the Gulf of Mexico and lasted about 800 years. The Olmec civilization was based on farming and trade. After the Olmec, inland civilizations grew powerful. One group built Teotihuacán, one of the first planned cities. More than 100,000 people lived there.

Another group, the Zapotec, built the city of Monte Albán. Monte Albán had stone temples, monuments, and tombs. The Zapotec also developed a writing system.

Defining

1. What is an *isthmus*?

____

____

Marking the Text

2. Circle the names of the major mountain ranges and rivers in North and South America.

Reading Check

3. Which four separate areas make up the Americas?

____

____

____

Reading Check

4. What were the first crops grown in the Americas?

____

____

Marking the Text

5. Underline the two reasons farming was successful in Mesoamerica.

Comparing

6. What were some of the similarities among the Mesoamerican cultures?

____

____

Marking the Text

7. Circle the achievement that allowed the Moche to farm in their desert homeland.

Reading Check

8. Why did early American cultures decline?

____

____

____

Examining

9. What made it possible for new civilizations to develop in North America?

____

____

____

The Maya civilization began in the rain forests of Mexico. From there, the Maya spread deeper into southern Mexico and Central America. Like the Zapotec, the Maya built cities. These civilizations declined around the A.D. 500s. Historians are not sure why. Perhaps there was too little rain to grow food or local people may have revolted. Whatever the reason, people left the cities.

Civilizations of Mesoamerica
1200 B.C. to A.D. 800

- Olmec
- Teotihuacán
- Zapotec
- Maya

Soon after this, the Toltec came to power. The Toltec conquered much of central Mexico and northern Central America. The Toltec built pyramids and palaces. Around A.D. 1125, the Toltec Empire began to decline. For 200 years there was no ruling group in central Mexico.

In South America, the Chavín lived in the coastal areas of present-day Peru and Ecuador. They used stones from nearby hills to build a temple. A new group called the Moche settled in the dry coastal desert of Peru. They built canals to bring water from the Andes to the desert so they could grow food. The Chavín and the Moche did not build empires. The first empire in South America was built by the Inca.

Early Cultures in North America

Many groups of people in North America learned how to farm from the people of Mesoamerica. As farming spread across North America, new cultures developed.

The Hohokam lived in the desert of the American Southwest. They dug canals to bring river water to their fields. They grew corn, cotton, beans, and squash. Another group, called the Anasazi, collected water that ran off cliffs. They sent the water through canals to their fields.

The Anasazi built stone buildings called pueblos. They also built dwellings in the walls of cliffs. The Anasazi and Hohokam both faded in the early A.D. 1000s. A lack of rain caused their crops to die. The large settlements broke up and people formed smaller communities.

NAME________________________ DATE ____________ CLASS ________

networks

Lesson 1 The First Americans, *Continued*

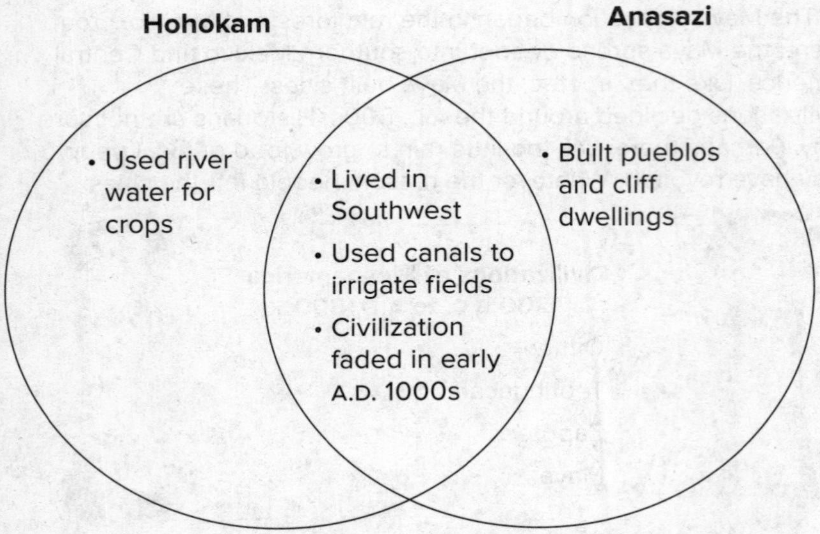

• Used river water for crops

• Used canals to irrigate fields

• Built pueblos and cliff dwellings

East of the Mississippi River, another civilization arose—the Mound Builders. The Mound Builders built huge mounds of earth. The mounds were used as tombs or for ceremonies. Mound Builders were mostly hunters and gatherers. They also practiced some farming. Corn was a popular crop. This civilization began about 1000 B.C. and ended about A.D. 400.

A new group of people settled in the Mississippi River Valley by A.D. 700. The Mississippians were farmers. They also built mounds. Their largest city may have had more than 16,000 people. The Mississippian society collapsed during the A.D. 1200s. Historians are not sure why. The downfall may have been caused by too little food or attacks by other groups.

Glue Foldable here

Check for Understanding

Name two cultures that developed in North America.

1. ____________________

2. ____________________

Name two reasons that civilizations developed in North America.

3. ____________________

4. ____________________

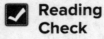

Reading Check

10. How were early Americans able to grow crops in desert areas of the Southwest?

____

____

____

FOLDABLES®

11. Place a two-tab Foldable along the dotted line to cover the Check for Understanding. Cut the tabs in half to form a four-tab Foldable. Label the four tabs *Hohokam*, *Anasazi*, *Mound Builders*, and *Mississippians*.

Use both sides of the tabs to list words and phrases that you remember about each civilization. Use your Foldable to help you answer the questions under the tabs.

NAME_______________________________ DATE ______________ CLASS __________

networks

The Americas

Lesson 2 Life in the Americas

ESSENTIAL QUESTION

What makes a culture unique?

GUIDING QUESTIONS

1. ***How did the Maya live in the rain forests of Mesoamerica?***
2. ***How did the Aztec establish their society in central Mexico?***
3. ***How did the Inca organize their government and society?***
4. ***What were the societies of North American peoples like?***

Terms to Know

sinkholes areas where the soil has collapsed into a hollow or depression

hogans square, wooden homes built by the Navajo

When did it happen?

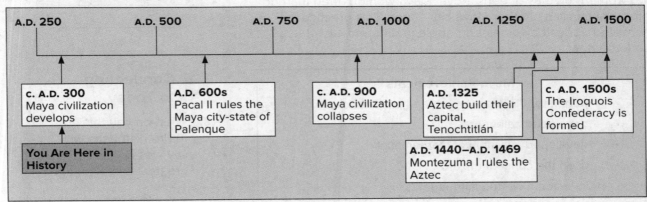

A.D. 250 — A.D. 500 — A.D. 750 — A.D. 1000 — A.D. 1250 — A.D. 1500

- **c. A.D. 300** Maya civilization develops
  - **You Are Here in History**
- **A.D. 600s** Pacal II rules the Maya city-state of Palenque
- **c. A.D. 900** Maya civilization collapses
- **A.D. 1325** Aztec build their capital, Tenochtitlán
- **A.D. 1440–A.D. 1469** Montezuma I rules the Aztec
- **c. A.D. 1500s** The Iroquois Confederacy is formed

What do you know?

In the first column, answer the questions based on what you know before you study. After this lesson, complete the last column.

Now ...		Later ...
	Where did the Maya, Aztec, and Inca establish their empires?	
	How did early Americans in North America adapt to their environments?	

Lesson 2 Life in the Americas, *Continued*

The Maya

Around A.D. 300, the Maya developed a civilization in southern Mexico and Central America. They settled in an area of swampy forests. The swamps gave the Maya a source of water. The Maya also used sinkholes to reach water underground. **Sinkholes** are areas where the land has fallen and formed a hollow.

The Maya cleared forests to plant corn and build cities. They set up more than 50 city-states. A king ruled each city-state. Each king claimed the sun god was his ancestor.

Maya city-states had a strict class system. Kings, nobles, and priests were at the top. Below them were farmers, artisans, and hunters. These people had to pay taxes. They also had to work on large building projects.

Women played an important role in Maya city-states. At least two women ruled as queens. Royal Maya women often married into royal families of other Maya city-states. This practice increased trade. It also helped people in different city-states work together.

Maya Achievements

- understood astronomy, able to predict eclipses
- developed calendars
- developed a system of mathematics
- used the concept of zero
- invented a written language

The Maya had two major calendars. They used one with 260 days for religious events. They used another calendar with 365 days for agriculture. The Maya also developed a system of mathematics. They invented a written language using hieroglyphics.

Around A.D. 900, the Maya civilization collapsed. Historians are not sure why. Evidence shows that conflict and warfare increased among the city-states. Also, erosion caused food production to fall. Too little food would have led to diseases and starvation.

The Aztec

In A.D. 1325, the Aztec began building a city in central Mexico. The city was on an island in the middle of a lake. The Aztec called the city Tenochtitlán. It would become the largest city in Mesoamerica. It was the center of Aztec life.

Marking the Text

1. Underline the two places where the Maya got water.

Evaluating

2. What do you think was the greatest achievement of the Maya?

____

____

____

Connecting to Today

3. What do you think future historians will say was our society's greatest achievement?

____

____

____

Reading Check

4. How were the Maya governed?

____

____

Lesson 2 Life in the Americas, *Continued*

FOLDABLES®

Explaining

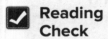

5. Place a one-tab Foldable along the dotted line. Write *Aztec Civilization* on the anchor tab. Write words and short phrases to explain the Aztec civilization.

Reading Check

6. Why did the Aztec develop two different calendars?

____

____

Reading Check

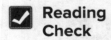

7. What building projects did the Inca carry out?

____

____

Evaluating

8. Do you think everyone in a society should have to serve in the military? Why or why not?

____

____

/ / / / / / / / / / / / Glue Foldable here / / / / / / / / / / / /

Aztec rulers claimed to be descended from the gods. A council of priests, nobles, and warriors chose the emperor. Montezuma I was a powerful Aztec emperor. He ruled from A.D. 1440 to A.D. 1469. Montezuma expanded the Aztec Empire. He built temples and roads.

There were four classes of people under the emperor. These were nobles, commoners, unskilled workers, and enslaved people. Most of the Aztec were commoners. They worked as farmers, artisans, or merchants.

Priests played an important role in Aztec society. Some sacrificed captives to the gods. Aztec priests also recorded Aztec knowledge in books that historians refer to today. They used two calendars. One was for important ceremonies and festivals. The other was for everyday use.

The Inca

In the A.D. 1400s, the Inca created a powerful empire in the valleys of the Andes. Strong rulers created a strong central government. They set up legal courts and collected taxes. The government stored extra food from good harvests to give to people when harvests were poor.

The Inca emperors demanded that everyone in the empire learn Quechua, the language of the Inca. People also had to work on government projects. One project was a system of roads that connected all parts of the empire. The Inca were skilled builders. They built Machu Picchu, a retreat for Inca emperors, without wheels or iron tools.

Inca emperors were the head of Inca society. Army leaders also had a high place in society. The Inca Empire was built on war. All young men had to serve in the army.

North American Peoples

By A.D. 1500 many different groups of Native Americans lived in North America. People adapted to the different environments they lived in.

The Inuit settled just south of the Arctic Circle. The land was harsh, cold, and treeless. The Inuit built homes from stone and blocks of earth. They also made shelters from blocks of hard-packed snow, called igloos. They hunted seals, walruses, and polar bears.

Many different groups of Native Americans lived along the Pacific coast. The climate was mild. People could hunt and fish. They used the trees to build houses and canoes.

The Hopi, the Acoma, and the Zuni lived in the Southwest. They built apartment-like homes from adobe bricks made of dried mud. They dug canals to bring water to their fields. They grew corn, beans, squash, and melons.

Types of Native American Buildings

Igloos →	Far North: homes made of pressed snow
Pueblos →	Southwest: homes made of adobe, or sun-dried brick
Hogans →	Southwest: homes made of wood
Tepees →	Great Plains: tents made from animal skins

In the A.D. 1500s, the Apache and Navajo settled in the Southwest. At first, they were hunters and gatherers. Later, the Navajo began to farm and settled in villages. They built square wooden homes called **hogans.**

Native Americans on the Great Plains were nomads. They lived in tepees. Men hunted antelope, deer, and bison. Plains people used every part of the bison. They made clothing from the skins and tools from the bones.

People of the Eastern Woodlands farmed and hunted. They formed governments that linked different groups. The Iroquois Confederacy was made up of five Native American groups. Its purpose was to keep peace. The league also created a constitution, or plan of government. This was the first constitution in what would become the United States.

Check for Understanding

List two things North American civilizations had in common.

1. ____________________

2. ____________________

Name two accomplishments of the Iroquois Confederacy.

3. ____________________

4. ____________________

Drawing Conclusions

9. How did the people in the Southwest use the resources of their environment?

____

Reading Check

10. Why did the Iroquois form a confederacy?

____

FOLDABLES®

11. Place a three-tab Foldable along the dotted line. Cut each of the tabs in half to form six tabs. Label the six tabs *Arctic*, *Pacific Coast*, *Southwest*, *Great Plains*, *Eastern Woodland*, and *Iroquois Confederacy.*

Use both sides of the Foldable to write words and short phrases to record what you remember about each.

Glue Foldable here

NAME______________________ DATE ____________ CLASS ________

networks

Imperial China

Lesson 1 China Reunites

ESSENTIAL QUESTION

How does geography influence the way people live?

GUIDING QUESTIONS

1. ***How did China rebuild its empire after years of war?***
2. ***Why did Buddhism become popular in Tang China?***
3. ***How did Confucian ideas shape China's government?***

Terms to Know

neo-Confucianism a new understanding of Confucianism that included some Daoist and Buddhist beliefs

Where in the world?

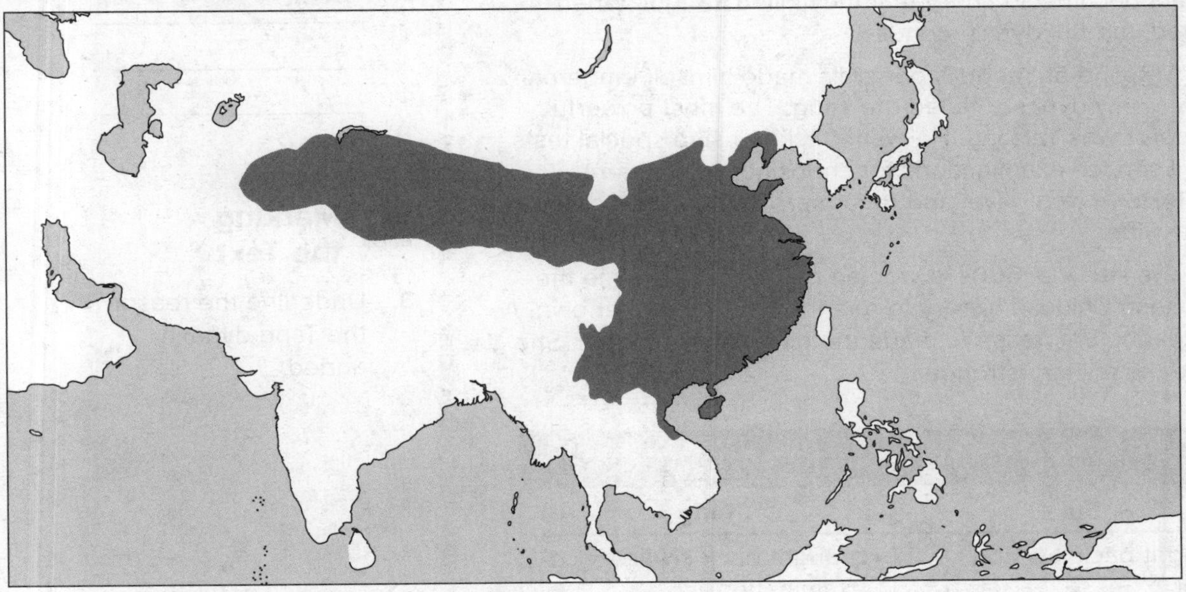

When did it happen?

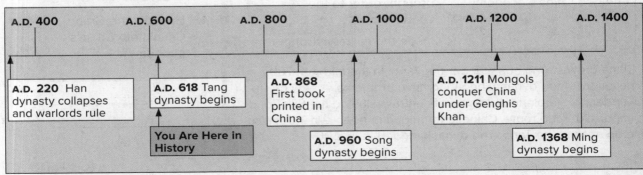

A.D. 400 | **A.D. 600** | **A.D. 800** | **A.D. 1000** | **A.D. 1200** | **A.D. 1400**

- **A.D. 220** Han dynasty collapses and warlords rule
- **A.D. 618** Tang dynasty begins
- **You Are Here in History**
- **A.D. 868** First book printed in China
- **A.D. 960** Song dynasty begins
- **A.D. 1211** Mongols conquer China under Genghis Khan
- **A.D. 1368** Ming dynasty begins

China Rebuilds Its Empire

China's Han empire ended in A.D. 220. For the next 300 years, Chinese warlords fought with each other. China finally unified again under a general named Wendi. He set up a new dynasty called the Sui in which emperors ruled.

After Wendi died, his son Yangdi became emperor. Yangdi rebuilt the Great Wall. Yangdi's biggest accomplishment, however, was building the Grand Canal. The Grand Canal was used to ship products between northern and southern China. It helped make China's economy stronger.

Yangdi made life very hard for the Chinese people, however. He made farmers work on the Great Wall and the Grand Canal. The people also had to pay for these projects with high taxes. The farmers became so angry that they killed Yangdi. When Yangdi died, the Sui dynasty ended.

In A.D. 618, one of Yangdi's generals made himself emperor. He set up a new dynasty called the Tang. The most powerful Tang emperor was Taizong. He went back to using special tests called civil service examinations for choosing government officials. Taizong also gave land to farmers and brought order to the countryside.

During the late A.D. 600s, a woman named Wu became the only woman in Chinese history to rule the country on her own. As a strong leader, Empress Wu made the government bigger. She also made the military stronger.

Improvements and Reforms

Sui	Tang
• brought back law and order • built Grand Canal • helped China's economy grow	• brought back civil service examination • gave land to farmers • brought order to the countryside • made the military stronger

China grew strong again under the Tang. In the mid-A.D. 700s, however, the Tang dynasty began to have problems. A new group of wandering people took control of central Asia and the Silk Road, an important trade route. Chinese farmers and people in Tibet also rose up against the Tang. The dynasty ended in A.D. 907.

Defining

1. What is a *dynasty*?

____

____

Contrasting

2. How were Yangdi and Taizong different as rulers?

____

____

____

Marking the Text

3. Underline the reason the Tang dynasty ended.

Reading Check

4. How did the Grand Canal help China's economy?

____

____

____

Lesson 1 China Reunites, *Continued*

Eventually, a general named Song made himself emperor. The Song dynasty was a time of great wealth and rich culture, but Song rulers did not have enough soldiers to control their large empire. Nomads took over land in northern China. The Song moved their capital south to the city of Hangzhou for safety.

Buddhism in China

Traders and missionaries from India had brought Buddhism to China in about A.D. 150. A short time later, a civil war started. Many people suffered greatly. Buddhism taught that people could escape their suffering. Many Chinese who were looking for peace and comfort became Buddhists.

Early Tang rulers were not Buddhists, but they allowed people to practice Buddhism and build Buddhist temples. Many Chinese Buddhist nuns and monks ran schools. They also provided rooms and food for travelers. Buddhist monks served as bankers and gave medical care.

Civil war breaks out.
↓
Chinese people suffer.
↓
Many become Buddhists.
↓
Buddhists help the poor and needy.
↓
Buddhists gain wealth and power.
↓
Tang rulers try to destroy Buddhism.

Some Chinese did not like Buddhism. Many thought the monasteries were gaining too much wealth. Others thought that monks and nuns did not encourage respect for families because they did not marry. In A.D. 845, the Tang destroyed many Buddhist monasteries and temples. Buddhism in China would never be the same.

Korea broke free from China when the Han dynasty fell. Chinese Buddhists brought their religion to Korea. In about A.D. 660, the Koreans came together to form one country. The new government supported Buddhism in Korea and even spread to the islands of Japan.

Drawing Conclusions

5. Why was Buddhism first accepted and then ended by Tang rulers?

____

____

____

Examining

6. How did the civil war affect the people of China?

____

____

____

Making Connections

7. Where in Asia do you think Buddhism is practiced today? Why?

____

____

____

Reading Check

8. How did Buddhist monks and nuns help the Chinese?

____

____

Revival of Confucian Ideas

Confucius and his followers believed that a good government depended on wise leaders. The Tang dynasty supported **neo-Confucianism,** a new kind of Confucianism. It taught that life in this world was just as important as life in the next one. Neo-Confucianism became more than a list of rules. It became a religion.

Neo-Confucianism also helped make the government stronger. In the past, jobs had been given to people because of their wealth, family, or friends. Now the government hired people based on their knowledge and ability to think. People taking civil service examinations had to show how much they knew about Confucian writings.

Only men could take the tests, and only rich people had enough money to help their sons study for the tests. It took years of study and only one out of every five men passed. Those who failed could become teachers, but they could never get a government job.

Neo-Confucianism

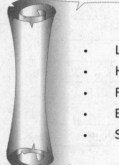

- Live in this world.
- Help others.
- Find peace.
- Enjoy nature.
- Serve your community.

/ / / / / / / / / / / / / / Glue Foldable here / / / / / / / / / / / / / /

Check for Understanding

Name the two types of people who spread Buddhism to China.

1. ______________________________

2. ______________________________

Name one condition in China that opened people to the teachings of Buddhism.

3. ______________________________

____

Making Connections

9. What do people today spend years of training to do?

____

____

____

Reading Check

10. How did the civil service examinations affect Chinese society?

____

____

____

FOLDABLES®

11. Place a one-tab Foldable along the dotted line to cover the Check for Understanding. Write *Buddhism: Tang China* on the anchor tab. Label the tab *Rise and Decline*.

Draw arrows to indicate a rise and decline. On both sides of the tabs, describe the rise and decline of Buddhism.

Imperial China

Lesson 2 Chinese Society

ESSENTIAL QUESTION

How do new ideas change the way people live?

GUIDING QUESTIONS

1. ***How did China's economy change under the Tang and Song dynasties?***
2. ***How did new inventions change China's society?***
3. ***Why were the Tang and Song dynasties a golden age of literature and the arts?***

Terms to Know

porcelain a ceramic made of fine clay baked at very hot temperatures

calligraphy artistic or elegant handwriting

When did it happen?

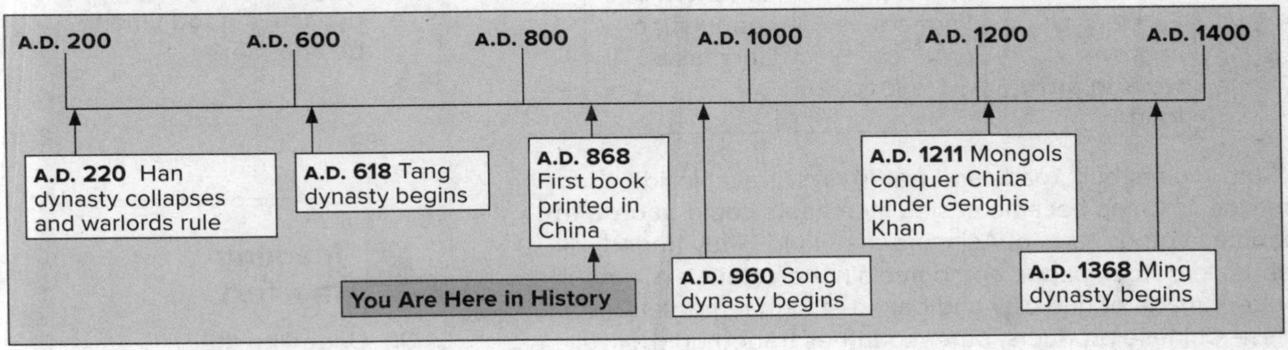
A.D. 200
A.D. 600
A.D. 800
A.D. 1000
A.D. 1200
A.D. 1400
A.D. 220 Han dynasty collapses and warlords rule
A.D. 618 Tang dynasty begins
A.D. 868 First book printed in China
You Are Here in History
A.D. 960 Song dynasty begins
A.D. 1211 Mongols conquer China under Genghis Khan
A.D. 1368 Ming dynasty begins

What do you know?

Put a check mark (✓) next to each true statement.

_______ **1.** Tang rulers made Chinese government stronger.

_______ **2.** Tang rulers did not allow people to practice Buddhism.

_______ **3.** China grew weaker under the Song rulers.

_______ **4.** Neo-Confucianism taught that people should care about this life as much as the next one.

_______ **5.** People who wanted to work for the Chinese government had to pass difficult tests.

Economic Growth

China's economy suffered when the Han dynasty ended in the A.D. 200s. Widespread fighting ruined cities and farms. People had little food and few goods to trade.

The Tang rulers took power in A.D. 618. They brought peace to the countryside and gave more land to farmers. This allowed farmers to improve ways of watering and growing crops. They also grew new kinds of rice. Because farmers produced more food, the number of people in China grew. People moved to new areas. Farmers moved south where they could grow even more rice.

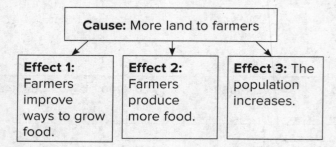

Cause: More land to farmers

Effect 1: Farmers improve ways to grow food.	**Effect 2:** Farmers produce more food.	**Effect 3:** The population increases.

Tang rulers built roads and waterways. Travel inside and outside of China became easier. Merchants could trade with people in other parts of Asia and the world. They traded silk fabric, tea, steel, paper, and porcelain. **Porcelain** is a kind of pottery made of fine clay and baked at high temperatures. For these Chinese products, other countries traded gold, silver, precious stones, and fine woods.

Technological Advances

During the Tang and Song dynasties, people made new discoveries and inventions that changed life in China. These developments soon would spread to other parts of the world.

For a long time, people burned wood to keep warm and cook food. Eventually, too many trees were cut down and wood was hard to get. The Chinese then learned that coal could be burned to heat things. When heated in a furnace, the melted iron mixed with carbon from the coal. It became a new, stronger metal known as steel.

The Chinese made strong armor, swords, and helmets for their army with steel. They also used steel to make stoves, farm tools, drills, nails, and sewing needles. These changes made the army stronger and helped workers do more work.

Determining Cause and Effect

1. What was the cause of China's economic problems in the A.D. 200s?

____

____

Analyzing

2. Why was the Tang dynasty a good time to be a farmer?

____

____

____

Marking the Text

3. Underline the improvements that helped Chinese traders during the Tang dynasty.

Reading Check

4. How did advancements in farming affect China's population?

____

____

____

Making Connections

5. Which Chinese inventions or ideas do we still use today?

____

____

____

Drawing Conclusions

6. What do you think happened when armies were given steel weapons and armor?

____

____

____

Reading Check

7. Why was the Chinese invention of printing important?

____

____

____

Explaining

8. What is a golden age?

____

____

The Chinese found a way to print books. Before this, people had to copy books by hand. This was expensive, so few books were made. The Chinese cut the characters of an entire page onto a block of wood. Then they put ink on the wood block and pressed a piece of paper on top of it to print a page. Cutting a block took a long time. Once it was cut, however, it could be used to make many copies.

The first known printed book is from about A.D. 868. Printing made it easier to make books. However, once a block was carved, changes could not be made.

In the A.D. 1000s, a Chinese printer named Pi Sheng invented a new way to print. He used movable type. This meant that each character—instead of each page—was a separate piece, made of clay. These pieces could be moved around to make sentences. Pieces could be used again and again. Printing also led to another Chinese invention—paper money. Paper money helped the economy grow.

The Chinese made gunpowder for use in weapons and fireworks. One weapon was the fire lance. It was like an early gun. It helped make the Chinese army a strong force. The Chinese also built large ships with sails and rudders for steering. Chinese sailors also began using the magnetic compass to help them find their way. The compass allowed ships to sail farther from land.

Chinese Inventions That Changed the World

- coal
- steel
- printing
- movable type
- gunpowder
- ships with rudders
- magnetic compass

Literature and the Arts

The years of the Tang and Song dynasties were some of the best for Chinese culture. That is why those years are called "a golden age." Chinese rulers supported art and literature. They invited artists and poets to live and work in the capital city of Changan.

The Tang dynasty was the great age of poetry in China. Chinese poetry often showed an appreciation of the world. Li Bo was one of the most popular Tang poets. He wrote about nature. For years, the Chinese have studied and memorized his poems.

Lesson 2 Chinese Society, *Continued*

Another favorite Tang poet was Du Fu. Civil war in China made life hard. Food was difficult to find. Du Fu almost died of hunger. These experiences helped him see the suffering of people. Du Fu often wrote about the unfairness of life for the poor and the wastefulness of war.

China's Golden Age of Literature and the Arts	
Ideas in Poetry	**Ideas in Landscape Painting**
• the beauty of nature • the joys of friendship • the unfairness of life • the shortness of life	• Nature is bigger than people. • People cannot control nature. • People can only try to live in harmony with nature.

During the Song dynasty, Chinese artists painted large nature scenes called landscapes. These paintings were not realistic. Instead, they showed the power of the mountains and lakes. As a result, people appeared to be small in the paintings, much smaller than the nature around them. Chinese painters often wrote poetry on their works. They used a brush and ink to write beautiful characters called **calligraphy.**

During the Tang period, Chinese artisans, or skilled workers, made very fine porcelain. Because porcelain comes from China, people around the world call it by the name "china." Porcelain can be made into plates, cups, figurines, and vases.

Check for Understanding

List four inventions that changed Chinese society.

1. ______________________

2. ______________________

3. ______________________

4. ______________________

Making Connections

9. Is today a golden age for the arts? Why or why not?

____

____

____

Reading Check

10. What themes did Chinese poets often write about?

____

____

____

FOLDABLES®

11. Place a three-tab Foldable along the dotted line. On the anchor tab, write *Importance of ....* Label the three tabs *Coal and Steel, Printing*, and *Gunpowder.*

Write words and short phrases to describe the changes each brought during the Tang and Song dynasties.

Glue Foldable here

networks

Imperial China

Lesson 3 The Mongols in China

ESSENTIAL QUESTION

What are the characteristics of a leader?

GUIDING QUESTIONS

1. ***Why were the Mongols able to build a vast empire so quickly?***
2. ***How did the Mongols rule the Chinese?***

Terms to Know

steppe flat, dry grasslands

terror violent acts that are meant to cause fear in people

Where in the world?

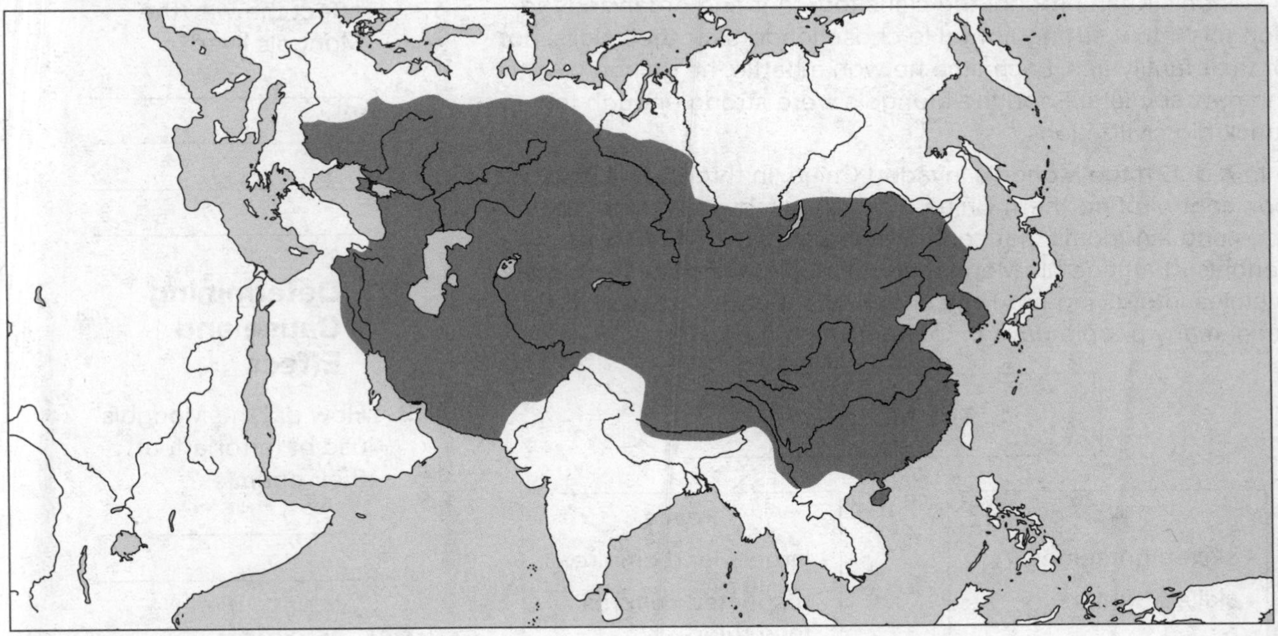

When did it happen?

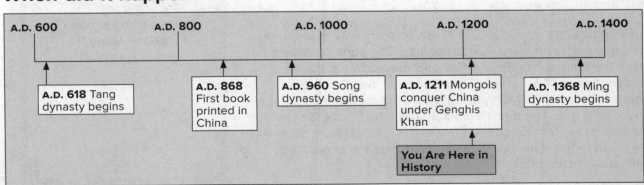

A.D. 600 — A.D. 800 — A.D. 1000 — A.D. 1200 — A.D. 1400

- **A.D. 618** Tang dynasty begins
- **A.D. 868** First book printed in China
- **A.D. 960** Song dynasty begins
- **A.D. 1211** Mongols conquer China under Genghis Khan
  - **You Are Here in History**
- **A.D. 1368** Ming dynasty begins

Mongol Expansion

The Mongols lived in an area north of China called Mongolia. They lived in clans, or groups of loosely-related families. The Mongols raised sheep, horses, and yaks, a kind of long-haired oxen. They moved as the animals fed on Mongolia's great **steppes.** Steppes are wide, grassy lands. The Mongols were excellent horseback riders and skilled fighters.

Mongol leaders came together in A.D. 1206 in the Gobi, a desert covering parts of Mongolia and China. At that meeting, they elected a young warrior named Temujin to be Genghis Khan, which means "strong ruler."

Genghis Khan brought the clans together and organized the Mongols into a strong army. He chose leaders for their skills, not for their family ties. Each time he won a battle, he gained wealth and new soldiers. Soon the Mongols were strong enough to attack big civilizations.

In A.D. 1211 the Mongols invaded China. In three years, they took control of northern China. Then they moved west to attack cities and kingdoms that controlled parts of the Silk Road. Genghis Khan and his Mongol fighters used **terror** to scare their enemies into giving up. They attacked, robbed, and burned cities. Soon, many people gave in to them without fighting.

The Mongols

War	Peace
• skilled horsemen • skilled fighters • used terror • adopted gunpowder and fire lance	• largest land empire • respected cultures they ruled • protected trade

Genghis Khan died in A.D. 1227. His territory was split among his sons. Each one ruled a different area. The sons continued to make the empire bigger. The Mongols moved into parts of eastern and central Europe. They also took over Persia in Southwest Asia. The Mongols brought all of these lands together under their rule. The empire reached from the Pacific Ocean in the east to eastern Europe in the west. It reached from Siberia in the north to the Himalaya in the south. It was the largest land empire ever created.

Identifying

1. Who were the Mongols?

____

____

Explaining

2. How did the geography of Mongolia affect the way the Mongols lived?

____

____

____

____

Determining Cause and Effect

3. How did the Mongols' use of terror affect their enemies?

____

____

Marking the Text

4. Underline the description of how large the Mongol empire was.

Reading Check

5. How were the Mongols influenced by their opponents?

____

____

____

Describing

6. How did the rulers of the Yuan dynasty change Chinese government?

____

____

____

FOLDABLES®

Recalling

7. Place a two-tab Foldable along the dotted line. Title the anchor tab *Yuan Dynasty.* Label the two tabs *Who* and *What*.

Use both sides of the tabs to list words and phrases that you remember about the Mongols and what they did.

Glue Foldable here

The Mongols brought peace to their lands. Peace was good for trade, and the Mongols now had control of many of Asia's trade routes. They gained great wealth by taxing the goods that were traded. The Mongols had great respect for the cultures they now ruled. Sometimes they took on the beliefs and customs of the people. For example, the Mongols in Southwest Asia accepted Islam. The Mongols also learned from their enemy, the Chinese. They learned about gunpowder and the fire lance and began to use them. With these new weapons, their enemies were even more afraid of the Mongols.

Mongol Conquest of China

In A.D. 1260 Genghis Khan's grandson, Kublai Khan, became ruler. Kublai Khan took over more of China. Kublai moved his capital from Karakorum in Mongolia to Khanbaliq in northern China. Today the city of Beijing stands in the same place.

The Mongols in China

- ruled for 100 years
- did not mix with the Chinese
- stopped giving tests for government jobs
- allowed others to practice their own faiths
- brought China its greatest wealth and power

In A.D. 1279 Kublai Khan made himself China's new emperor and started the Yuan dynasty. Yuan means "beginning." However, the Yuan dynasty lasted for only about 100 years. Kublai Khan ruled for 30 of those years.

The Yuan rulers stopped using the civil service examinations for government jobs. They let non-Chinese work in the government. The Mongol and Chinese cultures were different in many ways. The Mongols had their own language, laws, and customs. This separated them from the Chinese people they ruled. The two groups lived apart and did not mix socially.

Lesson 3 The Mongols in China, *Continued*

Many Mongols were Buddhists, but they respected other religions. For example, Kublai Khan allowed Christians, Muslims, and Hindus to practice their faiths.

China reached its greatest wealth and power under Mongol rule. People from other countries were attracted to China. These visitors traveled the Silk Road to get there.

A famous European traveler who came to China was Marco Polo. He was from Italy. The capital city of Khanbaliq impressed Polo with its wide streets, beautiful palaces, and nice homes. Kublai Khan liked the stories Polo told about his travels. For many years, Kublai Khan sent Polo on trips to gather information. When Polo went back to Europe, he wrote a book about his adventures. His stories of China amazed Europeans.

The Mongols ruled a large empire, from the Pacific Ocean to eastern Europe. China grew wealthy from being able to trade with many parts of the world. The Chinese traded tea, silk, and porcelain for silver, spices, carpets, and cotton from Europe and other parts of Asia. Europeans and Muslims took Chinese discoveries like steel, gunpowder, and the compass back to their homes.

The Mongols made China's empire larger. They took over Vietnam and northern Korea. The Koryo rulers of Korea were allowed to stay in power because they accepted Mongol rule. The Mongols forced the Koreans to build warships. The Mongols tried to use these ships two times to take over Japan. Both times, huge storms destroyed the Mongol fleet.

Glue Foldable here

Check for Understanding

List two events that led to the growth of the Mongol Empire.

1. ______________________

2. ______________________

Explain two ways the Mongols were good for the regions they conquered.

3. ______________________

4. ______________________

Explaining

8. Why did China grow wealthy under the Mongol rulers?

____

____

____

Reading Check

9. What was Marco Polo's reaction to seeing China's cities?

____

____

FOLDABLES®

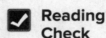

10. Place a one-tab Foldable along the dotted line. Write *Mongol Empire* in the middle of the tab.

Make a memory map by drawing five arrows around the title. Then, write five things you remember about this empire and its expansion.

NAME_______________________________________ DATE ______________ CLASS ________

networks

Imperial China

Lesson 4 The Ming Dynasty

ESSENTIAL QUESTION

How do new ideas change the way people live?

GUIDING QUESTIONS

1. ***How did Ming rulers bring peace and prosperity to China?***
2. ***How did Chinese contact with the outside world change during the Ming dynasty?***

Terms to Know

census a count of the number of people living in a place

novel a long fictional story

barbarian an uncivilized person

Where in the world?

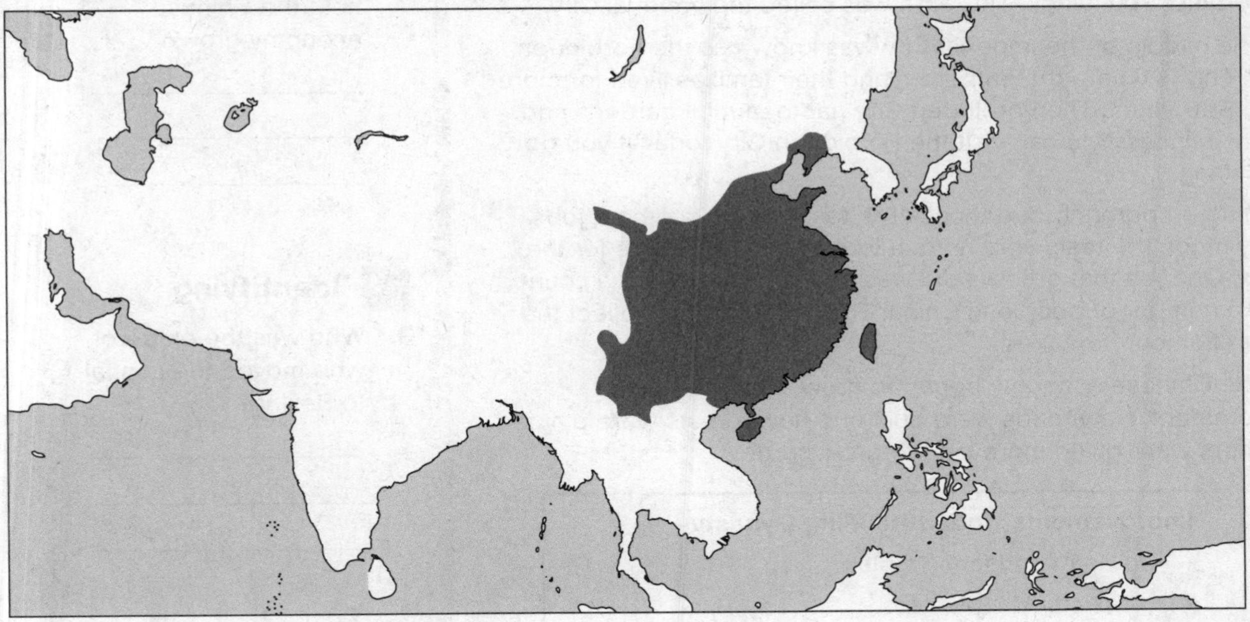

When did it happen?

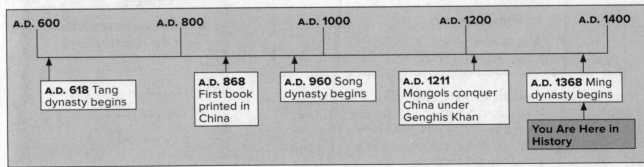

A.D. 600 — A.D. 800 — A.D. 1000 — A.D. 1200 — A.D. 1400

- **A.D. 618** Tang dynasty begins
- **A.D. 868** First book printed in China
- **A.D. 960** Song dynasty begins
- **A.D. 1211** Mongols conquer China under Genghis Khan
- **A.D. 1368** Ming dynasty begins
  - **You Are Here in History**

The Ming Dynasty

Kublai Khan died in A.D. 1294. The weak Mongol emperors who followed him began to lose power. At the same time, the Chinese wanted to rule themselves. The Chinese fought against Mongol control and won.

In A.D. 1368, a leader named Zhu Yuanzhang became emperor. He took the name Hong Wu, or "military emperor." Hong Wu set up his capital at Nanjing. He started the Ming, or "brilliant," dynasty. Hong Wu brought back order, yet he was also a cruel leader.

Hong Wu's son became emperor in A.D. 1398. He took the name Yong Le. To show his power as emperor, Yong Le moved the capital north to Beijing. He built a large area of palaces and government buildings. This area was called the Imperial City.

The middle of the Imperial City was known as the Forbidden City. This is where the emperors and their families lived for more than 500 years. The Forbidden City had beautiful gardens and many palaces. You can visit the Forbidden City today if you go to China.

Ming emperors brought back the tests for government jobs. They made the tests very hard. It took years to prepare for the tests. One job that officials did was taking a **census,** or a count of the number of people in China. This helped them collect the correct amount of taxes.

The Chinese economy began to grow under the Ming government. New roads were built and new forests were planted. Farmers were given more land to grow crops.

Improvements Under the Ming Dynasty

- Canals and farms rebuilt
- New forests planted
- New roads built
- Farming grew
- Silk industry supported
- Arts and culture grew
- Forbidden City built

Ming rulers repaired the Grand Canal and made it bigger. Rice and other goods could again be shipped throughout China. Farmers planted new types of rice that grew faster. More food could be sent to the growing number of people living in cities. Ming rulers also helped the silk industry.

Defining

1. What is a *census*?

____

____

____

Describing

2. How did Ming rulers help the Chinese economy grow?

____

____

____

Identifying

3. Who was the emperor who moved the capital to Beijing?

____

____

____

Reading Check

4. What was the purpose of the Imperial City?

____

____

____

Lesson 4 The Ming Dynasty, *Continued*

Explaining

5. Why did people want to read novels and go to the theater?

___

___

___

Listing

6. Give two reasons why Ming emperors wanted to send ships on overseas trips.

___

___

___

Describing

7. What did Zheng He (Chengho) bring back from his sea trips?

___

___

___

___

Chinese culture grew under the Ming. Traders and skilled workers became wealthy. They wanted to be entertained and now could pay for it. During the Ming period, Chinese writers wrote many **novels,** or long, made-up stories. The Chinese also liked seeing dramas on stage. Actors used words, songs, dances, and costumes to perform stories.

Chinese Exploration

Early Ming emperors were curious about the world outside of China. So they built a large group of ships to sail along China's coast and on the open sea to other countries.

From A.D. 1405 to 1431, Ming emperors sent the ships on seven trips. They wanted to trade with other kingdoms. They also wanted other rulers to see China's power and make weaker kingdoms pay money to China. A Chinese Muslim named Zheng He led these trips. He was also known as Chengho.

Reasons for Sea Voyages

- to show China's power
- to collect tribute, or money
- to learn about other cultures
- to trade with new places

Zheng He took his first ships to Southeast Asia. Later, he went to India and East Africa. Zheng He traded Chinese silk, paper, and porcelain. He brought back items the Chinese had never seen. For example, he brought giraffes and other animals from Africa for the emperor's zoo.

After these trips, Chinese merchants settled in Southeast Asia and India. They traded goods there and spread Chinese culture. Merchants earned a lot of money and added to China's wealth. Many good things came from these trips, yet people in the Chinese government thought the trips cost too much.

They also said that the trips were bad for China because they would bring unwanted ideas from the outside world and help merchants become rich. This went against the teachings of Confucius. He taught that people's desires should come after loyalty to their community. Officials believed that rich people were only concerned with themselves.

Lesson 4 The Ming Dynasty, *Continued*

After the death of Zheng He, government officials stopped the trips. No more ships were built. Existing ships were even taken apart. As a result, China's trade with other countries decreased.

Ming officials were not able to cut off China from the outside world for good. In A.D. 1514, ships from the European country of Portugal came to China. It was the first direct contact between China and Europe since the time of Marco Polo. The Portuguese wanted China to trade with them. They also wanted the Chinese to become Christians.

China's rulers did not think that the outsiders were a threat. In fact, the Chinese thought the Europeans were **barbarians,** or uncivilized people. At first, the Chinese said they would not trade with the Portuguese. By A.D. 1600, however, Portugal had built a trading post. Still, trade between China and Europe was limited.

Even with little contact, ideas from Europe came to China. Highly educated Christian missionaries arrived on European ships. Their knowledge of science impressed the Chinese. However, not many Chinese became Christians.

After many years of wealth and growth, the Ming dynasty became weak. Dishonest officials took over the country. They made farmers pay high taxes. The farmers revolted. Without law and order, people from north of China attacked. These people, called the Manchus, defeated the Chinese armies. In A.D. 1644, they set up a new dynasty.

Check for Understanding

List two reasons Chinese officials thought exploration and contact with the outside world was bad for China.

1. ________________________

2. ________________________

Name two examples of China's relationship with Europe.

3. ________________________

4. ________________________

Glue Foldable here

Explaining

8. Why did the Portuguese want to be in China?

____

____

____

Reading Check

9. Why did Chinese officials oppose overseas voyages?

____

____

____

FOLDABLES®

10. Place a two-tab Foldable along the dotted line to cover the Check for Understanding. Title the anchor tab *Chinese Exploration.* Write *Rise* on the first tab and *Decline* on the second tab.

Use both sides of the tabs to write what you remember about the rise and decline of Chinese exploration.

NAME_______________________________ DATE _____________ CLASS _______

networks

Civilizations of Korea, Japan, and Southeast Asia

Lesson 1 Korea: History and Culture

ESSENTIAL QUESTION

Why do people form governments?

GUIDING QUESTIONS

1. ***Why is Korea described as a bridge between China and Japan?***
2. ***How did Korea build a civilization?***

Terms to Know

shamanism belief in gods and spirits; shamans communicate with these spirits

Where in the world?

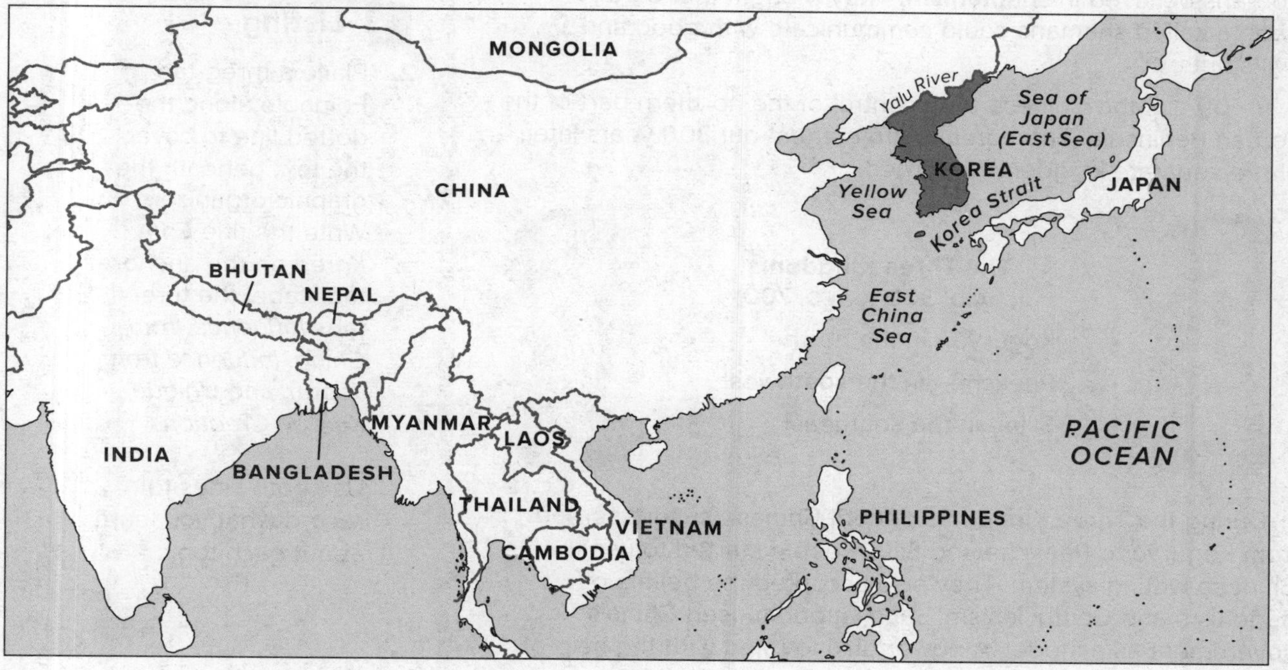

When did it happen?

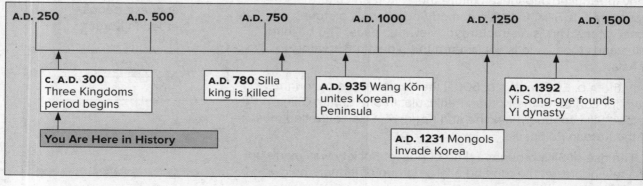

A.D. 250 — A.D. 500 — A.D. 750 — A.D. 1000 — A.D. 1250 — A.D. 1500

- **c. A.D. 300** Three Kingdoms period begins
- You Are Here in History
- **A.D. 780** Silla king is killed
- **A.D. 935** Wang Kŏn unites Korean Peninsula
- **A.D. 1231** Mongols invade Korea
- **A.D. 1392** Yi Song-gye founds Yi dynasty

Lesson 1 Korea: History and Culture, *Continued*

Location of Korea

The mountainous Korean Peninsula lies between China and Japan. Korea has been called a bridge between China and Japan. The Chinese and Japanese civilizations have influenced Korea in many ways. The Koreans have mixed these influences with their own traditions to create a unique culture.

The first Koreans were nomads. They came from northern or central Asia. The early Koreans lived in villages with no central government. They grew rice and made tools and weapons of bronze. Later, they used iron to make these items. The early Koreans believed in **shamanism.** They thought that certain people called shamans could communicate with good and evil spirits.

In 109 B.C. the Chinese took control of the northern part of the Korean Peninsula. The Koreans drove them out 300 years later. Three separate kingdoms emerged.

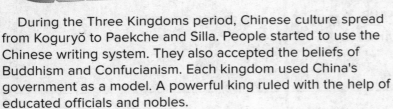

The Three Kingdoms
(c. A.D. 300 to A.D. 700)

- Koguryŏ - in the north
- Paekche - in the southwest
- Silla - in the southeast

During the Three Kingdoms period, Chinese culture spread from Koguryŏ to Paekche and Silla. People started to use the Chinese writing system. They also accepted the beliefs of Buddhism and Confucianism. Each kingdom used China's government as a model. A powerful king ruled with the help of educated officials and nobles.

Japanese merchants, artisans, and scholars settled in Paekche. They introduced Japanese culture there. Korean culture also blossomed. In Silla, a queen named Sondok built a stone observatory. This is a structure for viewing space. The building still stands today and is considered the oldest observatory in Asia.

In the A.D. 500s and A.D. 600s, the three kingdoms fought wars for control of the Korean Peninsula. In one battle, China helped Silla conquer Paekche and Koguryŏ. Silla controlled most of the Korean Peninsula.

The rise of Silla brought a time of peace. Society was made up of a few nobles at the top and a large group of farmers below.

Glue Foldable here

Defining

1. What is *shamanism*?

____

____

FOLDABLES®

Listing

2. Place a three-tab Foldable along the dotted line to cover the text beneath the graphic organizer. Write the title *Early Korea* on the anchor tab. Label the three tabs *Influence from China*, *Influence from Japan*, and *Unique Korean Creations*.

   Use both sides to record what you learn about each topic.

Identifying

3. Which types of Japanese people settled in Korea?

____

____

____

Reading Check

4. How did outside influences affect early Korea?

____

____

____

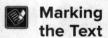

Determining Cause and Effect

5. What was the effect of giving land to the farmers and building irrigation systems during the Silla kingdom?

____

____

____

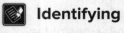

Marking the Text

6. Underline the names of the generals responsible for founding Korean dynasties.

Identifying

7. Name two of Sejong's achievements.

____

____

The government gave land to farmers. It also built irrigation systems for rice fields. More food was produced, trade increased, and the economy grew.

Silla kings also encouraged the arts, mainly the building of Buddhist temples. One temple was a nine-story wooden tower, one of the tallest structures in East Asia at the time. Another achievement by the Silla was printing Buddhist sacred writings with wooden blocks.

Korean Civilization

After years of conflict, the Silla kingdom collapsed. Nobles in the north fought to claim power. By A.D. 935, a general named Wang Kŏn had won. He was the first Korean ruler to unite all of Korea. He founded the Koryŏ dynasty. It stayed in power for 400 years.

The Koryŏ rulers set up a code of laws. Like China, they based their civil service system on examinations. Buddhism continued to spread under their leadership. Korean artisans developed movable metal type. They printed one of the world's oldest books using metal type. They also perfected the art of making celadon, a fine porcelain pottery known for its green color.

In A.D. 1231, the Mongols invaded the northern part of Korea. After 25 years of struggle, the royal family surrendered to Mongol rule. The Korean people suffered greatly under the rule of the Mongols. Thousands of Koreans were forced to build ships for Kublai Khan's attempts to invade Japan.

Korea Under the Mongols

- Invaded northern Korea in A.D. 1231
- Royal family surrendered after 25 years of conflict
- Korean people suffered greatly under Mongol rule
- Forced to build ships for Kublai Khan's attempts to invade Japan

In 1392, the Korean general Yi Song-gye founded a new dynasty. The new ruling family was known as the Yi dynasty. It lasted for over 500 years. Yi rulers set up their capital at Hanseong. This site is now Seoul, the modern capital of South Korea.

One of the greatest Yi kings was Sejong. He ruled from 1394 to 1450. Sejong was interested in science and technology. He used bronze to make the first instruments that people used to measure the amount of rainfall. He was also involved in producing sundials and globes. The globes showed the position and motion of the planets.

Lesson 1 Korea: History and Culture, *Continued*

Sejong and his advisers worked to spread literacy, or the ability to read, among the Korean people. They created an alphabet called *hangul*. The Chinese and Japanese alphabets use thousands of characters. *Hangul* uses one letter for each sound, similar to the English alphabet. *Hangul* is still the standard writing system in Korea today.

In 1592 Japanese forces attacked Korea. With Chinese help, the Koreans were able to win the land battles. They were also successful at sea because of their new invention: the world's first iron-covered ships called turtle ships.

In the early 1600s, the Koreans were attacked by a Chinese dynasty known as the Manchus. The Yi dynasty was defeated. It had to pay tribute to show that it surrendered to the Manchu rulers.

Invasions of Korea

Year	Invaders	Result
1231	Mongols	Mongols defeated the Koryŏ dynasty and ruled Korea.
1592	Japanese	Koreans defeated the Japanese, but were weakened as a result.
early 1600s	Chinese (Manchu Dynasty)	The Manchus defeated the Yi Dynasty and forced the Koreans to pay tribute.

Check for Understanding

List two aspects of life in early Korea.

1. ______________________

2. ______________________

Name two improvements during the Silla kingdom.

3. ______________________

4. ______________________

Glue Foldable here

Contrasting

8. How does *hangul* differ from the writing systems of China and Japan?

____

____

____

Reading Check

9. How did the building of turtle ships help the Koreans?

____

____

____

FOLDABLES®

10. Place a two-tab Foldable along the dotted line to cover the Check for Understanding. Write the title *Korea* on the anchor tab. Label the top tab *Early Korea* and the bottom tab *Silla Kingdom*.

Use both sides of the tabs to write what you remember about each. Use your notes to help answer Check for Understanding.

NAME______________________ DATE __________ CLASS ________

networks

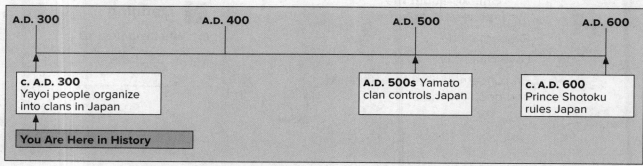

Civilizations of Korea, Japan, and Southeast Asia

Lesson 2 Early Japan

ESSENTIAL QUESTION

How does geography influence the way people live?

GUIDING QUESTIONS

1. ***How did geography shape Japan's early society?***
2. ***Why did the early Japanese believe that nature was important?***
3. ***How did Prince Shotoku reform Japan's government?***
4. ***How did Chinese ways influence Japan during the Nara period?***

Terms to Know

archipelago an expanse of water with many scattered islands

animism belief in spirits that are outside the body

constitution set of basic laws that define the role of government

Where in the world?

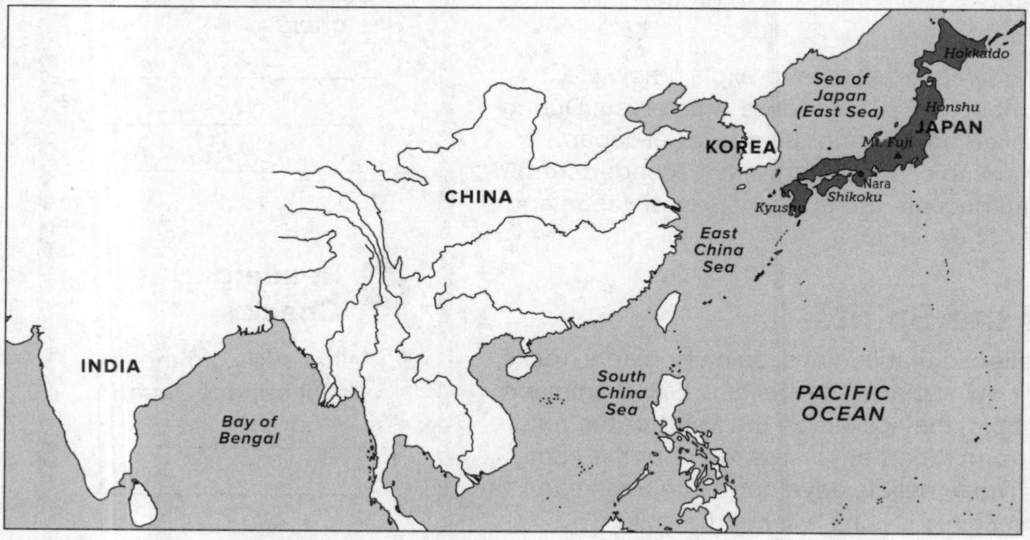

When did it happen?

A.D. 300 — A.D. 400 — A.D. 500 — A.D. 600

c. A.D. 300 Yayoi people organize into clans in Japan

You Are Here in History

A.D. 500s Yamato clan controls Japan

c. A.D. 600 Prince Shotoku rules Japan

Lesson 2 Early Japan, *Continued*

Geography and Settlement

Japan is an **archipelago,** or a chain of islands, in the Pacific Ocean near Korea. Most Japanese live on the four largest islands: Hokkaido, Honshu, Shikoku, and Kyushu. The islands are actually the tops of mountains that come up from the ocean floor. Earthquakes often strike Japan because it lies above an unstable part of the earth's crust.

The Japanese turned to the sea to make a living. They also traveled by ship among the islands. The seas kept the people separated from the rest of Asia. That forced Japan to develop as an independent civilization.

The first people came to Japan more than 10,000 years ago. About 300 B.C., the Yayoi arrived in Japan. They brought farming with them. They made pottery and grew rice. They were also skilled metalworkers. By A.D. 300, each Yayoi clan was headed by a small group of warriors. It was their job to protect the people.

The early Japanese developed stories to explain how life began. One myth described the sun goddess Amaterasu. During the A.D. 500s, a clan called the Yamato ruled most of Japan. Legend says that the Yamato chief Jimmu was descended from the sun goddess. Jimmu became the first emperor of Japan and took the title "emperor of heaven."

Shinto: Way of the Spirits

The early Japanese believed that humans, animals, plants, rocks, and rivers all have their own spirits. This belief is called **animism.** When people needed help, they called on the *kami*, or the nature spirits. They would perform rituals at shrines to honor the *kami* and ask for their help. These beliefs developed into a religion called *Shinto*. The word Shinto means "way of the spirits."

Shinto Taught the Japanese People To:

- Respect nature
- Love simplicity
- Be concerned about cleanliness and good manners

Identifying

1. How did the first settlers in Japan make a living?

____

____

Determining Cause and Effect

2. Why did the early Japanese develop stories?

____

____

____

Reading Check

3. What skills did the Yayoi bring to Japan?

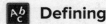

____

____

____

Defining

4. What is *animism*?

____

____

Reading Check

5. How did the Japanese show respect to the *kami*?

____

____

____

Identifying

6. What clan was Prince Shotoku from?

____

____

Drawing Conclusions

7. Why did Shotoku model the Japanese government on that of China?

____

____

____

Reading Check

8. What was the goal of Shotoku's constitution?

____

____

____

Shinto became closely linked to Japan's monarchy. The emperor's duties included taking part in Shinto rituals. These actions were intended to help protect Japan and make sure the country was successful.

Shinto still affects the Japanese people. Because of it, they have a love of nature. It also has influenced their desire for simplicity, cleanliness, and good manners.

Prince Shotoku

About A.D. 600, a Yamato prince named Shotoku ruled Japan. He wanted to give Japan a strong, well-organized government. He created a **constitution,** or a plan of government. The constitution made the emperor an all-powerful ruler.

The Japanese were expected to obey the emperor. The constitution laid out specific rules about how people should do their duties. These were based on the writings of Confucius.

Shotoku admired Chinese civilization. He wanted the Japanese to learn from it. Officials and students studied Buddhism as well as Chinese art, philosophy, and medicine.

Shotoku's Reforms

- Created a constitution
- Made emperor an all-powerful ruler
- Modeled government on that of China

Even after Shotoku died, Japanese officials used China as a model. In A.D. 646, the Yamato began the Taika. *Taika* is a word that means Great Change.

Under this plan, Japan was divided into provinces, or regional districts. Officials in the provinces reported to the emperor. All farmland was placed under the emperor's control.

While clan leaders could still direct farmer's work, they could no longer collect taxes. Government officials took over that job. The Taika reforms created the first strong central government in Japan.

The Nara Period

In the early A.D. 700s, the Nara Period began. Japanese emperors built a new capital city called Nara. Nara had broad streets, large public squares, Buddhist temples, and Shinto shrines. The families in the noble class lived in large, Chinese-style homes.

During the Nara period, emperors organized government officials by level of importance, from highest to lowest. This organization is called a hierarchy. The emperor gave positions to nobles from powerful families. In return for their services, leading government officials received estates, or large farms. The emperor's control of the land gave him great power.

Buddhist teachings reached Japan from Korea in the A.D. 500s. Buddhism became powerful. In A.D. 770, a Buddhist monk tried and failed to take power in Japan. As a result, the emperor decided to leave Nara for a new capital.

Glue Foldable here

Check for Understanding

Name two effects the lack of farmland had on Japan.

1. ____________________

2. ____________________

List two studies Shotoku wanted officials to learn in China.

3. ____________________

4. ____________________

Identifying

9. Buddhism reached Japan from what country?

____

Reading Check

10. What was Nara?

____

FOLDABLES®

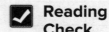

11. Glue two one-tab Foldables together along the anchor tabs. Place the Foldable booklet along the dotted line to cover the Check for Understanding. Title the top tab *Geography of Japan* and the bottom tab *China as a model.*

Record what you have learned by writing words or phrases about each. Use the Foldable to complete the activity under the tabs.

NAME ______________________ DATE ____________ CLASS ________

networks

Civilizations of Korea, Japan, and Southeast Asia

Lesson 3 Medieval Japan

ESSENTIAL QUESTION

How do new ideas change the way people live?

GUIDING QUESTIONS

1. *Why did military leaders rise to power in Japan?*
2. *Why did Japan experience disunity from the 1300s to the 1500s?*
3. *How were the Japanese affected by their country's growing wealth?*
4. *How did religion and the arts relate to each other under the shoguns?*

Terms to Know

samurai a warrior who served a Japanese daimyo, or lord

shogun a military governor who ruled Japan

vassal a person who serves a feudal lord

feudalism the system of service based on the relation of lord to vassal

guild a group of merchants or craftspeople during medieval times

sect a religious group

martial arts sport involving combat and self-defense

meditation mental exercise to reach a greater spiritual awareness

When did it happen?

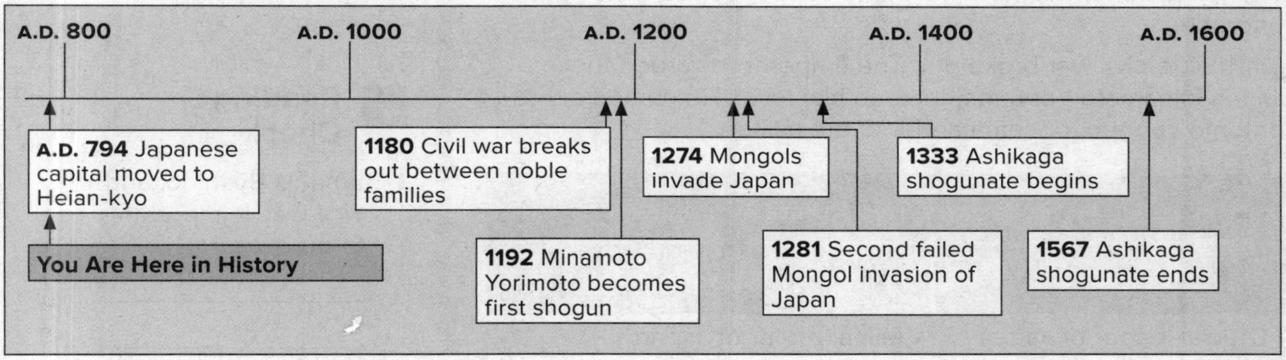
A.D. 800
A.D. 1000
A.D. 1200
A.D. 1400
A.D. 1600
A.D. 794 Japanese capital moved to Heian-kyo
You Are Here in History
1180 Civil war breaks out between noble families
1192 Minamoto Yorimoto becomes first shogun
1274 Mongols invade Japan
1281 Second failed Mongol invasion of Japan
1333 Ashikaga shogunate begins
1567 Ashikaga shogunate ends

What do you know?

In the K column, list what you already know about medieval Japan. In the W column, list what you want to know. After reading the lesson, fill in the L column with the information that you learned.

K	W	L

Samurai and Shoguns

In A.D. 794, the Japanese capital was moved from Nara to a new city called Heian-kyo. This city later became known as Kyoto. It looked a lot like important Chinese cities.

During the A.D. 800s, Japan was ruled by a number of weak emperors. Court officials known as regents governed for them. A regent rules for an emperor who is too young or too sick to rule. As a result, Japan's emperors had little power. Emperors pursued literature or the arts instead of governing.

Other nobles also grew powerful. They formed their own armies to guard their lands and enforce the law. They gave warriors called **samurai** land in exchange for service. Samurai wore armor and fought on horseback. They lived by a code of conduct called Bushido. This required a samurai to be loyal to his master. A loyal samurai would rather die than betray his master or be taken prisoner. Samurai were also supposed to be brave and honorable.

In 1180, a civil war broke out. The emperor rewarded the winner, Minamoto Yoritomo, to keep him loyal. He named Yoritomo **shogun,** or commander of the military.

Japan's Two Rulers	
Emperor	**Shogun**
• Official leader of Japan • Had no real power	• Military ruler of Japan • Controlled military government called shogunate that had most of the power

In the late 1200s, Japan was invaded two times by China's Mongol emperor. During both attempts, violent storms called typhoons destroyed many ships. The Mongols who made it to shore were defeated by the Japanese.

A Divided Japan

A general named Ashikaga Takauji made himself the new shogun in 1333. The shoguns from the new government were weak leaders, however. As a result, Japan became divided into small territories. Powerful military lords, known as daimyo, ruled these independent lands. To guard their lands, the daimyo used armies of samurai warriors.

Defining

1. What is a *samurai*?

____

____

Explaining

2. Why was the shogun important?

____

____

____

Reading Check

3. What is Bushido, and why was it important to the samurai?

____

____

____

Marking the Text

4. Circle the name of Japan's powerful military lords who ruled the smaller territories.

Defining

5. What is a *vassal*?

Reading Check

6. Why did feudalism develop in Japan?

Drawing Conclusions

7. Why do you think only a few people enjoyed the wealth of Japan?

Reading Check

8. Why did Japan's wealth increase under the rule of the shoguns?

Many samurai became **vassals** of a daimyo. This meant that the samurai gave an oath of loyalty to serve his daimyo in battle. In return, the daimyo gave land to his samurai. This system is known as **feudalism.**

Feudalism

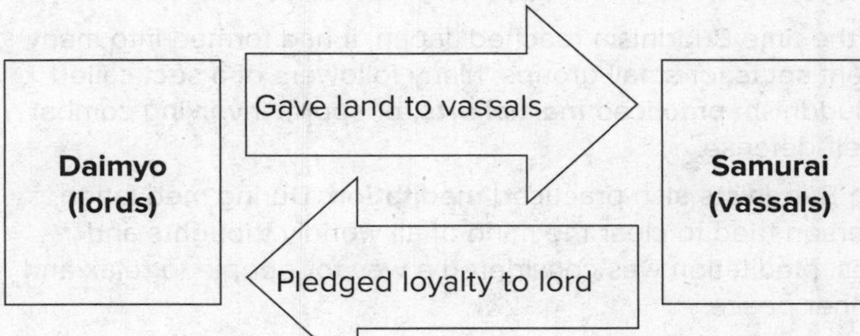

Fighting spread and the violence finally ended the Ashikaga shogunate in 1567. By that time, only a few powerful daimyo were left.

Society Under the Shoguns

Under the shoguns, Japan grew richer. Still, only a few Japanese enjoyed this wealth. This group included the emperor and his family, noble families, and military leaders. Merchants and traders also benefited.

Most Japanese were poor farmers. They created most of Japan's wealth. Their lives improved with a better irrigation system for crops. Artisans on the daimyo estates made armor, weapons, and tools. Merchants sold these items.

Heian-kyo, now called Kyoto, became a major center of production and trade. Artisans and merchants formed **guilds.** These groups protected their jobs and increased profits. The Japanese traded with Korea, China, and Southeast Asia.

A typical Japanese household included grandparents, parents, and children. A man had complete control over family members. Upper class women lost many freedoms when Japan became a warrior society.

Women in farming families had more say in choosing husbands. They worked long hours in the fields, however. They cooked, wove cloth, and cared for their children. In the towns, the wives of artisans and merchants helped run businesses. Some talented women became famous artists, writers, and entertainers.

Lesson 3 Medieval Japan, *Continued*

Religion and the Arts

During the rule of shoguns, most people in Japan believed in both Shinto and Buddhism. Each religion met different needs. Shinto linked people to nature and their homeland. Buddhism offered spiritual peace. Many Japanese wrote religious poems and plays, produced paintings, and built shrines and temples.

By the time Buddhism reached Japan, it had formed into many different **sects,** or small groups. Many followers of a sect called Zen Buddhism practiced **martial arts,** or sports involving combat and self-defense.

Zen Buddhists also practiced **meditation.** During meditation, the person tried to clear the mind of all worldly thoughts and desires. Meditation was considered a way for people to relax and find inner peace.

The Japanese borrowed the Chinese writing system. However, they changed it by adding symbols that stood for sounds. This made it much easier to read and write. Lady Murasaki Shikibu wrote *The Tale of Genji* around A.D. 1000. Some scholars call this work the world's first novel.

The Japanese also wrote plays. The oldest type of play in Japan is called Noh. Noh plays taught Buddhist ideas. Many Noh plays are still performed in Japan today.

Japanese architecture and art focused on simplicity and beauty. Shinto shrines were usually simple wooden buildings with a straw roof. Buddhist temples were built in the Chinese style. They were richly decorated. They had many altars, paintings, and statues.

To create beauty inside buildings, Japanese artisans made wooden statues, furniture, and household items.

Check for Understanding

List two methods of fighting used by samurai.

1. ______

2. ______

Name two characteristics of Japanese art and architecture.

3. ______

4. ______

Glue Foldable here

Contrasting

9. How were Buddhist temples different from Shinto shrines?

______

Reading Check

10. How did meditation play a part in Buddhism?

______

FOLDABLES®

11. Place a two-tab Foldable along the dotted line to cover the Check for Understanding. Title the anchor tab *Japan*. Label the top tab *Samurai* and the bottom tab *Arts*.

Write words or phrases to record what you remember about each topic. Use this information to help answer the Check for Understanding.

NAME ______________________ DATE ____________ CLASS ________

networks

Civilizations of Korea, Japan, and Southeast Asia

Lesson 4 Southeast Asia: History and Culture

ESSENTIAL QUESTION

What makes a culture unique?

GUIDING QUESTIONS

1. ***How did geography affect settlement and early ways of life in Southeast Asia?***
2. ***Why did powerful kingdoms and empires develop in Southeast Asia?***

Terms to Know

volcano a mountain that may release melted rocks from inside the Earth

tsunami a huge ocean wave caused by an undersea earthquake

maritime related to the sea or seafaring

Where in the world?

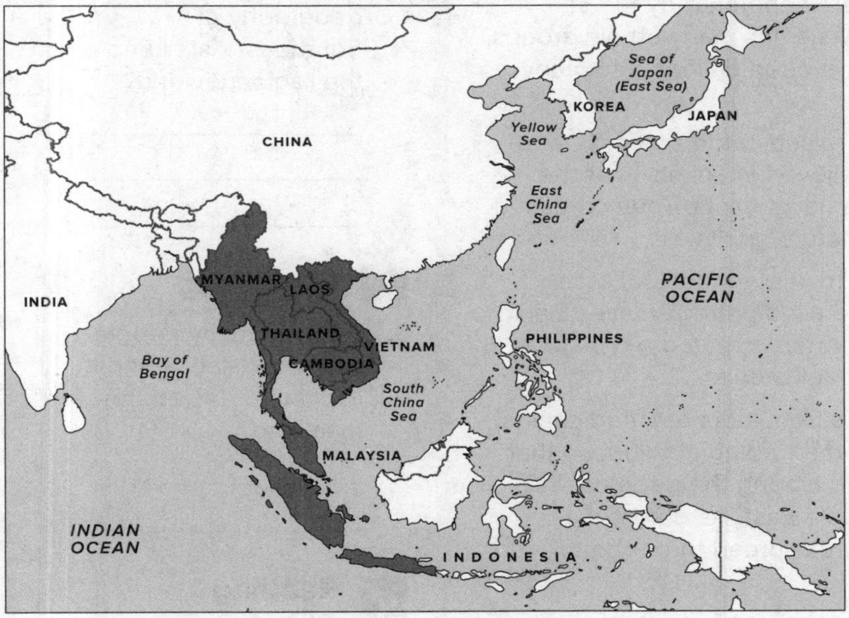

When did it happen?

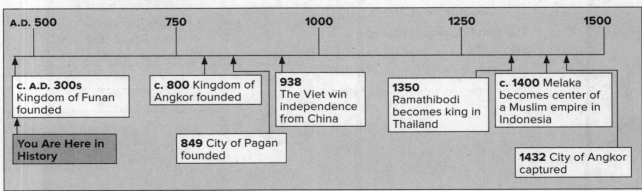

A.D. 500 — 750 — 1000 — 1250 — 1500

- **c. A.D. 300s** Kingdom of Funan founded
- **You Are Here in History**
- **c. 800** Kingdom of Angkor founded
- **849** City of Pagan founded
- **938** The Viet win independence from China
- **1350** Ramathibodi becomes king in Thailand
- **c. 1400** Melaka becomes center of a Muslim empire in Indonesia
- **1432** City of Angkor captured

Early Civilization

Southeast Asia lies south of China and east of India. It has long peninsulas and a large chain of islands. Mountain ranges cross the mainland. The lowlands between them have rich soil. The island soil is also fertile. Many people settled in the lowlands and on the islands because the farming was good.

The area also has dangers. The islands have many active **volcanoes.** The lowland areas on the coast may be struck by **tsunamis.** A tsunami is a huge ocean wave caused by an undersea earthquake. This happened in Japan in 2011.

People in the lowlands were cut off from each other by the mountains. People on the islands were separated by the sea. As a result of its geography, Southeast Asia has many ethnic groups, languages, and religions. It has always been divided into many different empires and kingdoms.

Early Southeast Asians grew rice, raised cattle and pigs, and made metal goods. These people believed in animism, or the belief that living and nonliving things have spirits. They practiced rituals to honor their ancestors and nature spirits.

Southeast Asians also developed their own forms of art. Artisans made a type of cloth with detailed patterns called batik. Musicians played many instruments. Artists created a type of theater that used shadow puppets to tell stories.

During the A.D. 100s, Hindu traders from India reached coastal areas of Southeast Asia. They created a trading network so that goods and ideas could be exchanged among the peoples of Southeast Asia, India, and the Middle East. As different people came into contact, their cultures spread throughout Southeast Asia.

Musical Instruments of Southeast Asia

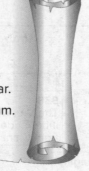

- The *dan bau* was similar to a xylophone
- The *dan day* was a type of guitar.
- The *rammana* was a kind of drum.

Defining

1. What is a *tsunami*?

____

____

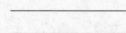

Identifying Cause and Effect

2. How did the geography of Southeast Asia keep the region divided?

____

____

____

Explaining

3. Why did many people settle on islands and in lowland areas on the mainland?

____

____

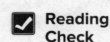

Reading Check

4. Why did outside influences have a powerful effect on early Southeast Asia?

____

____

____

Contrasting

5. How did land-based and sea-based economies differ?

____

____

____

Marking the Text

6. Circle the examples of China's influence on the government of Dai Viet.

Explaining

7. Why was Angkor Wat built?

____

____

____

Describing

8. What influences did Thai culture adopt from Hinduism?

____

____

____

____

Kingdoms and Empires

Southeast Asian states in inland areas relied mainly on farming. States along the coast relied more on trade. They became **maritime,** or seafaring, powers based on shipping.

In 938, the people who lived in what is now Vietnam won independence from China. Their new state was called Dai Viet, or Great Viet. It was based on China's government. Confucianism became its official religion. Viet rulers used Chinese court ceremonies. Government officials were selected through Chinese-style civil service examinations.

Present-day Cambodia was once the home of the Khmer people. Khmer kings based their rule on Hindu and Buddhist ideas from India. They had architects design Indian-style buildings. The most magnificent of these structures was Angkor Wat.

Angkor Wat served as a Hindu and Buddhist temple, a royal tomb, and an observatory for stars and planets. The expense of building Angkor Wat weakened the Khmer Empire. In 1432 the Thai, a neighboring people, captured Angkor. The Khmer Empire faded from history.

The first Thai kingdom was called Sukhothai. It became a center of learning and arts. The Thai developed a writing system. Monks from India converted many Thai people to Buddhism. The Thai were also influenced by Hinduism in their political practices, dance, and literature.

Sukhothai	Ayutthaya
Center of learning and arts	Controlled large areas of Southeast Asia
Monks converted people to Buddhism	Center of Buddhist learning and culture
Influenced by Hinduism	Traded with China and other Asian kingdoms

In 1350 a new Thai kingdom called Ayutthaya was formed. Ayutthaya controlled large areas of Southeast Asia. It was also an important center of Buddhist learning and culture. The people of Ayutthaya traded teak wood and spices with China and other nearby Asian kingdoms.

West of the Thai kingdom, the Burmese developed their own civilization. In 849 they set up a capital city called Pagan. It, too, became a center of Buddhist learning. In the late 1200s, Mongol attacks weakened Pagan. Many Burmese people moved south to escape the Mongols.

Lesson 4 Southeast Asia: History and Culture, *Continued*

New states grew around seaport cities on the Malay Peninsula and the islands of Indonesia. The people living on Southeast Asian islands were Malays. They were divided into separate communities because of the distance and trade rivalries. In the 700s, a Malay state called Srivijaya developed on the islands of Java and Sumatra. Srivijaya controlled the major trade route.

Southeast Asian Kingdoms		
Name	**Location**	**Year Founded (A.D.)**
Srivijaya	Java and Sumatra	700s
Angkor	Cambodia	c. 800
Pagan	Burma	849
Dai Viet	Vietnam	938
Khmer Empire	Cambodia, Laos, Thailand, Vietnam	1100s
Ayutthaya	Thailand	1350
Melaka	Malay Peninsula	1400

Muslim traders and missionaries brought their religion to Southeast Asia in the 800s. Eventually, Islam began to spread. The port of Melaka became the first major Islamic center in the region.

Islam spread from Melaka, on the Malay Peninsula, to the islands of Indonesia. The only island to remain outside of Muslim influence was Bali. It kept its Hindu religion and culture at the time and still does today.

Check for Understanding

Name two religions that were practiced in the Thai kingdoms.

1. ______________________

2. ______________________

List the two geographical features that separated early Southeast Asian states.

3. ______________________

4. ______________________

Glue Foldable here

Reading Check

9. How did the culture of China affect Southeast Asian states?

____

____

____

____

FOLDABLES®

10. Glue two one-tab Foldables together along the anchor tabs. Place the Foldable booklet along the dotted line. On the top tab, write *Religions of Southeast Asian States* and on the bottom tab *Geography of Southeast Asia.*

On both sides of the tabs, list two or more facts that you remember about each. Use the Foldable to help answer the Check for Understanding.

NAME________________________ DATE ____________ CLASS ________

networks

Medieval Europe

Lesson 1 The Early Middle Ages

ESSENTIAL QUESTION

Why does conflict develop?

GUIDING QUESTIONS

1. ***How did geography shape life in Europe after the fall of Rome?***
2. ***How did Germanic groups build kingdoms in Western Europe?***
3. ***How did the Catholic Church influence life in early medieval Europe?***

Terms to Know

fjord a narrow body of water between steep cliffs where the sea cuts into the land

missionary a person who is sent by a religious organization to teach the religion

concordat an agreement between the pope and the ruler of a country

Where in the world?

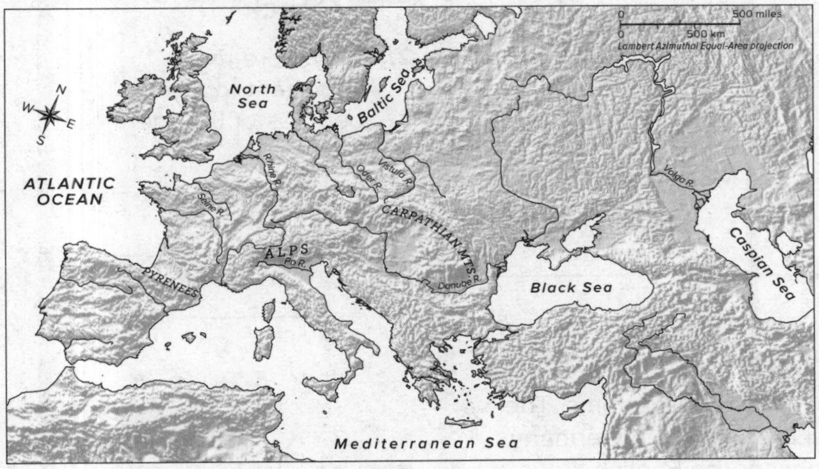

When did it happen?

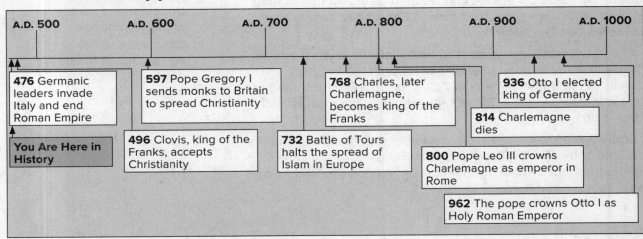

A.D. 500 — A.D. 600 — A.D. 700 — A.D. 800 — A.D. 900 — A.D. 1000

476 Germanic leaders invade Italy and end Roman Empire

You Are Here in History

496 Clovis, king of the Franks, accepts Christianity

597 Pope Gregory I sends monks to Britain to spread Christianity

732 Battle of Tours halts the spread of Islam in Europe

768 Charles, later Charlemagne, becomes king of the Franks

800 Pope Leo III crowns Charlemagne as emperor in Rome

814 Charlemagne dies

936 Otto I elected king of Germany

962 The pope crowns Otto I as Holy Roman Emperor

Geography of Europe

Europe's geography played an important role in shaping how Europeans lived. Europe is a continent. It is also a very large peninsula. A peninsula is land surrounded on three sides by water. As a result, most of Europe is within 300 miles (483 km) of an ocean or a sea. Europe also has many rivers, such as the Rhine, Danube, Seine, and Po. Access to rivers and seas often made it easy to travel and trade in other parts of the world. This helped Europe's economy grow.

Large bodies of water, such as the English Channel, also separated Europe into distinct regions. Mountains played a similar role. Regions cut off from each other developed independent kingdoms and cultures.

Oceans, Seas, and Rivers

- Provided transportation
- Made it easier to trade
- Separated some areas
- Provided protection

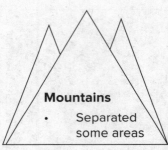

Mountains

- Separated some areas

Kingdoms in Western Europe

After Rome fell, Western Europe broke into many kingdoms. The Angles and Saxons invaded Britain from Denmark and Germany. They became known as the Anglo-Saxons, or the English.

The strongest Germanic people were called the Franks. They settled in what is now France and western Germany. In 496 King Clovis of the Franks accepted Catholic Christianity. Nearly all of the Franks became Catholic too.

After Clovis died, power passed from kings to government officials. A leader named Charles Martel defeated invading Muslims at the Battle of Tours in 732. This stopped the spread of Islam in Western Europe. Christianity remained the main religion in the region.

After Charles Martel died, his son Pepin eventually became the new king of the Franks. Pepin forced a Germanic group called the Lombards to leave Rome. He then gave the pope the land he had taken from the Lombards.

Defining

1. What is a *peninsula*?

____

____

____

Reading Check

2. Why were rivers important to the peoples of Europe?

____

____

____

Marking the Text

3. Underline the names of the Germanic groups that invaded and settled in Britain during the Middle Ages.

FOLDABLES®

Listing

4. Place a two-tab Foldable along the dotted line. Title the anchor tab *Charlemagne*. Label the two tabs *Who* and *What*.

   Use both sides of the Foldable to list words and short phrases that describe Charlemagne's life.

Summarizing

5. How were the Catholic Church and Roman emperors connected to each other?

___

___

___

Reading Check

6. What impact did the Battle of Tours have on European history?

___

___

___

Glue Foldable here

After Pepin died, his son Charles became king. Charles won many battles against neighboring kingdoms. By 800, Charles's kingdom was an empire covering much of western and central Europe. He was called Charlemagne, which means "Charles the Great."

The pope made Charlemagne the new Roman emperor. Charlemagne used local officials to help him govern. He started a school for the children of government officials. Students studied religion, Latin, literature, and math.

When Charlemagne died, his empire broke into separate kingdoms. Muslims, Magyars, and Vikings attacked these kingdoms in the 800s and 900s.

The Vikings came from Scandinavia in northern Europe. Scandinavia's coast has many **fjords.** Fjords are strips of water between steep slopes, where the water cuts into the land. Vikings depended on the sea for food and trade.

In 911 a group of nobles tried to unite small territories in Germany by electing a king. Otto I was one of the strongest kings of Germany. He defeated the Magyars and freed the pope from the control of Roman nobles. To reward Otto, the pope named him Roman emperor in 962.

Germanic Ruler	Accomplishments
Clovis	Became a Christian in 496
Charles Martel	Stopped invasion of Muslims in 732
Charlemagne	United Europe in one empire; crowned Roman emperor by pope
Otto I	United Germans; became Roman emperor

The Church and Its Influence

The Roman Catholic Church became very important during the Middle Ages. Monks became **missionaries** and spread Christianity over the next several hundred years. By 1050 most people in Western Europe had become Catholic.

Monks and monasteries were important. They provided schools and hospitals. Monks taught carpentry and weaving. They invented better ways to farm. They also helped save knowledge. Monks copied ancient works of Romans and Greeks and Christian writings such as the Christian Bible.

Duties of Monks During the Middle Ages

- to become missionaries and spread Christianity
- to build churches
- to teach
- to help the poor and sick
- to copy important papers and books

Disagreements grew between popes and kings over who had greater authority. In 1073 Pope Gregory VII and Holy Roman Emperor Henry IV fought over this issue.

Henry wanted to keep his power to name high-ranking Church officials called bishops. Gregory declared that only the pope could choose bishops. He cast Henry out of the Catholic Church. German nobles chose a new king, but Henry took over Rome and replaced the pope. Still, the dispute was not settled.

In 1122 a new pope and king agreed that only the pope could choose bishops. However, they decided that only the emperor could give government jobs to bishops. This deal was called the *Concordat of Worms*. A **concordat** is an agreement between the pope and the ruler of a country.

When Innocent III became pope in 1198, he wanted to make sure that only the Church could appoint bishops. He was able to control kings. If a king did not obey, he would be punished.

Glue Foldable here

Check for Understanding

List two ways monasteries were important in early medieval Europe.

1. ______________________

2. ______________________

European kings and popes disagreed over who had greater authority during the Middle Ages. What were the two positions?

3. ______________________

4. ______________________

Reading Check

7. What major issue did kings and popes disagree on?

____

____

____

FOLDABLES®

8. Place a three-tab Foldable along the dotted line to cover the Check for Understanding. Label the anchor tab *Christianity*. Label the three tabs *How it spread*, *Role of the monastery*, and *Who has ultimate authority*.

On the tabs, write what you remember about the spread of Christianity, its influence on life, and who had greater authority—European monarchs or the pope. Use the front and back of each tab as needed.

NAME ______________________ DATE ____________ CLASS ________

networks

Medieval Europe

Lesson 2 Feudalism and the Rise of Towns

ESSENTIAL QUESTION

What are the characteristics that define a culture?

GUIDING QUESTIONS

1. ***How did Europeans try to bring order to their society after the fall of Charlemagne's empire?***
2. ***How did most Europeans live and work during the Middle Ages?***
3. ***How did increased trade change life in medieval Europe?***

Terms to Know

feudalism a political order where nobles governed and protected people in return for services

vassal a low-ranking noble under the protection of a feudal lord

fief the land granted to a vassal by a noble

knight a warrior on horseback who fought for a superior

chivalry the system of rules and customs of being a knight

serf a peasant who was tied to the land and its owner

guild a group of merchants or craftspeople

When did it happen?

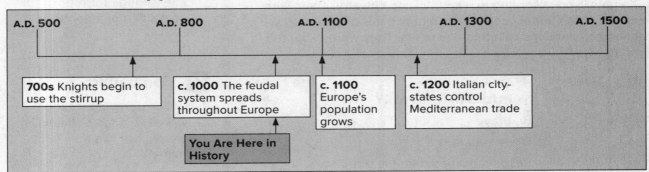

A.D. 500 — A.D. 800 — A.D. 1100 — A.D. 1300 — A.D. 1500

- **700s** Knights begin to use the stirrup
- **c. 1000** The feudal system spreads throughout Europe — **You Are Here in History**
- **c. 1100** Europe's population grows
- **c. 1200** Italian city-states control Mediterranean trade

What do you know?

In the first column, answer the questions based on what you know before you study. After this lesson, complete the last column.

Now...		Later...
	What is feudalism?	
	What were the knights' responsibilities?	
	What was life like in a medieval city?	

NAME ______________________________ DATE ______________ CLASS ________

networks

The Feudal Order

When Charlemagne's empire fell, Europe no longer had a powerful central government. Nobles who owned land became more powerful than kings. This led to a new system called **feudalism.** Under feudalism, nobles ruled and protected the people. In return, the people worked for the nobles. They fought in the noble's army or farmed the noble's land. By 1000, the kingdoms of Europe were divided into thousands of areas ruled by nobles. Most of these feudal territories were very small.

Feudalism was based on loyalty and duty. A lord was a high-ranking noble who had power. A **vassal** was a low-ranking noble who served a lord. The lord rewarded him with land. The land given to a vassal was called a **fief.** Many vassals were **knights,** or warriors in armor who fought on horseback.

Knights lived according to a code called **chivalry.** They were expected to be honest and loyal. Knights trained for battle by holding competitions called tournaments. They were expected to fight fairly.

RULES OF CHIVALRY

- Be brave
- Obey your lord
- Respect women of noble birth
- Honor the Church
- Help people in need

Nobles lived in castles—tall, stone buildings that served as forts and as homes. High stone walls surrounded the castle. Its buildings contained a storage area, stables for the horses, a kitchen, a great hall for eating and receiving guests, bedrooms, and a chapel. When nobles were away at war, their wives or daughters ran the estates.

The Medieval Manor

The fiefs of the Middle Ages were divided into farming communities called manors. The lord ruled the manor. Peasants worked the land.

There were two groups of peasants—freemen and serfs. Freemen paid the nobles for the right to farm the land.

Defining

1. What is the difference between a *vassal* and a *knight*?

____

____

Marking the Text

2. Circle what people did in exchange for the protection of a noble.

Comparing

3. Which parts of a castle were like a fort? Which were more like a home?

____

____

____

Reading Check

4. What were the rules of behavior that knights followed?

____

____

____

Defining

5. What is a *serf*?

____

____

Analyzing

6. Why might a serf run away from a manor?

____

____

____

Marking the Text

7. Circle the inventions or changes that helped medieval peasants grow more food.

Reading Check

8. How did the lives of freemen and serfs differ?

____

____

____

They had legal rights and could move when and where they wished. Most peasants were **serfs.** *Serfs could not* leave the manor, *own property*, or marry without the lord's permission. However, lords could not sell the serfs.

Lords protected their serfs. In return, serfs worked long hours and gave their lord part of their own crops. It was not easy for serfs to gain freedom. They could run away to the towns. If a serf stayed in a town for more than a year without being captured, he or she was considered free. By the end of the Middle Ages, many serfs were allowed to buy their freedom.

Freemen	Serfs
• paid nobles for the right to farm land • had rights under the law • could move when and where they wished	• *could not own property* or go to court • could not leave or marry without permission • had to give part of their crops to their lord • at first could not buy freedom

New inventions made farming better. The most important was a heavy-wheeled plow with an iron blade. It easily cut through thick clay soil. The horse collar let a horse pull a plow. Horses could pull plows much faster than oxen, so peasants could plant more crops and grow more food. In addition, peasants learned to rotate their crops. They planted only two of their three fields at a time. This kept the soil healthy, and more food could be grown.

The Growth of Towns and Cities

When the Roman Empire fell, almost all trade in Western Europe stopped. By 1100, feudalism had made Europe safer. Trade began again. As trade increased, towns grew. Many cities became wealthy. Venice and other Italian cities began trading with the Byzantine Empire. Soon Italian cities became the centers of trade in the Mediterranean.

Towns in Flanders were the centers of trade for northern Europe. Flanders is a region in Belgium today. Merchants from all over western Europe met there to trade their goods for fine wool.

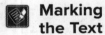

Lesson 2 Feudalism and the Rise of Towns, *Continued*

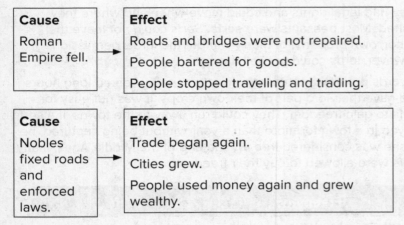

Cause	Effect
Roman Empire fell. →	Roads and bridges were not repaired. People bartered for goods. People stopped traveling and trading.
Nobles fixed roads and enforced laws. →	Trade began again. Cities grew. People used money again and grew wealthy.

Towns were usually built on land owned by nobles. They tried to control town business. Townspeople wanted to make their own laws. As people grew wealthier, they forced nobles to give them basic rights. Over time, medieval towns set up their own governments.

Trade encouraged people to make things. Soon these craftspeople organized **guilds,** or business groups. Each craft had its own guild. Guilds set standards of quality for products, and they set prices. They also decided who could join a trade and what training was involved.

Medieval cities could be unpleasant and even dangerous places to live. The streets were narrow and often dirty and smelly. If a fire started, a medieval city easily could be destroyed. Yet a city was also a place where people could earn a living. In addition to running their households, city women often helped their husbands. Sometimes when a master craftsperson died, his wife continued his trade.

Check for Understanding

List two characteristics of serfs.

1. ______________________

2. ______________________

List two ways that increased trade changed life in medieval Europe.

3. ______________________

4. ______________________

Glue Foldable here

Explaining

9. Why did trade resume after feudalism began?

____

____

____

Reading Check

10. How did guilds affect the way medieval townspeople made a living?

____

____

____

FOLDABLES®

11. Place a two-tab Foldable along the dotted line to cover the Check for Understanding. Write the title *Medieval* on the anchor tab. Label the top tab *Manors* and the bottom tab *Trade*.

On both sides of the tabs, list words and short phrases that describe each aspect of medieval life.

NAME________________________ DATE ____________ CLASS ________

networks

Medieval Europe

Lesson 3 Kingdoms and Crusades

ESSENTIAL QUESTION

How do governments change?

GUIDING QUESTIONS

1. ***How was the king's power strengthened and then limited in medieval England?***
2. ***How did the kings of France increase their power?***
3. ***How did the cities of Kiev and Moscow become centers of powerful Slavic states?***
4. ***Why did Western Europeans go on crusades?***

Terms to Know

grand jury a group of citizens that decides if a person should be accused of a crime

trial jury a group of citizens that decides whether an accused person is innocent or guilty

Where in the world?

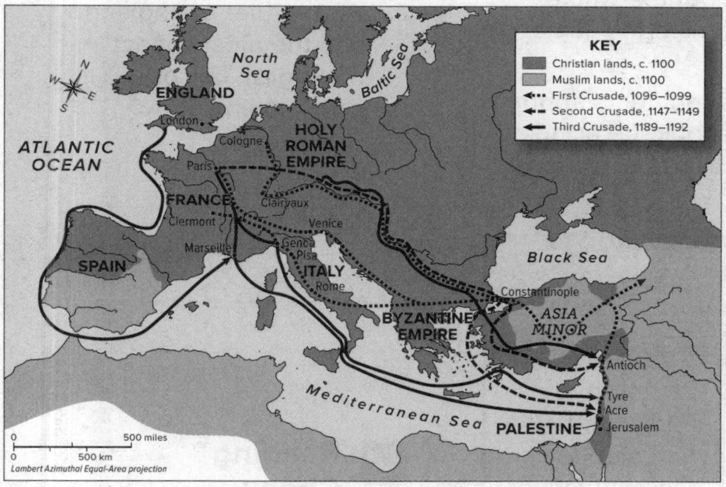

When did it happen?

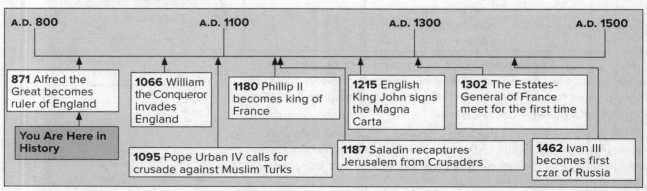

A.D. 800 — A.D. 1100 — A.D. 1300 — A.D. 1500

- **871** Alfred the Great becomes ruler of England
- **You Are Here in History**
- **1066** William the Conqueror invades England
- **1095** Pope Urban IV calls for crusade against Muslim Turks
- **1180** Phillip II becomes king of France
- **1187** Saladin recaptures Jerusalem from Crusaders
- **1215** English King John signs the Magna Carta
- **1302** The Estates-General of France meet for the first time
- **1462** Ivan III becomes first czar of Russia

Lesson 3 Kingdoms and Crusades, *Continued*

Royal Power in England

When Vikings attacked Britain, King Alfred of Wessex united the Anglo-Saxons to drive away the Vikings. Alfred's kingdom became known as "Angleland," or England.

William was the ruler of Normandy and a cousin of the king of England. In 1066 William and his army invaded England and won the Battle of Hastings. William then became king of England. He was known as William the Conqueror and became a powerful ruler.

William brought many customs from Normandy, but he also kept many of the Anglo-Saxon ways of running the government. He allowed Anglo-Saxons to keep their language, which later became English. As Normans and Anglo-Saxons married, they created a new English culture.

Henry II ruled England from 1154 to 1189. He set up a court system with lawyers and judges. This helped create a body of common law, or law that was the same throughout the whole kingdom. The courts were fair because they applied the same laws to everyone.

Henry also set up juries of citizens to settle arguments about land. A **grand jury** decided whether a person should be accused of a crime. A **trial jury** decided whether an accused person was innocent or guilty.

Contributions to Law and Government by Early Kings of England

Henry II	John	Edward I
• Established a court system and common law	• Signed the Magna Carta—limited the power of the king and established certain rights for nobles and freemen	• Established Parliament—the first step toward representative government in England

Henry's son John became king of England in 1199. King John raised taxes. He also punished enemies without trials. A group of angry nobles forced King John to sign the Magna Carta in 1215. Magna Carta means "Great Charter."

This document limited the king's powers. It said the king and vassals had certain rights and duties. Over time, the Magna Carta strengthened the idea all people have rights and that the powers of government should be limited.

Defining

1. What is the difference between a *grand jury* and a *trial jury*?

____
____
____
____

Drawing Conclusions

2. Which ruler of England had the most impact on English law or government? Why?

____
____
____
____

Reading Check

3. How did the common law help unite England?

____
____
____

Lesson 3 Kingdoms and Crusades, *Continued*

FOLDABLES

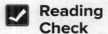

4. Place a two-tab Foldable along the dotted line. Write *France* on the anchor tab. Write *Divided* on the top tab and *Unified* on the bottom tab.

Write key phrases to describe how France was divided and how it became unified.

Glue Foldable here

Reading Check

5. How was the Estates-General of France different from England's Parliament?

______
______
______

Reading Check

6. Why did the rulers of Moscow work with the Mongols?

______
______
______

In the late 1200s, Edward I gathered people from different parts of England to help him make laws. This group was called Parliament.

Monarchy in France

In 843 Charlemagne's empire was split into three parts. The western part became the kingdom of France. In 987 Hugh Capet became king, but he controlled little land.

Philip II became king of France in 1180. At that time, England ruled part of western France. Philip regained these lands. Having more land gave French kings more power.

Philip IV was called Philip the Fair. He met with people from three classes, or estates, of French society. This meeting of the estates was France's first parliament. It was called the Estates-General. The Estates-General never became as strong as the English Parliament.

Eastern States of the Slavs

A people called the Slavs organized villages in Eastern Europe. In time, Slavs divided into three major groups: the southern, western, and eastern Slavs.

In the 800s, the eastern Slavs began to expand the city of Kiev. The state of Kievan Rus grew around the city. About 1240, Mongols from Central Asia conquered Kievan Rus. Many Slavs left and founded the city of Moscow in present-day Russia.

Why Moscow Was Important →

- Had power to tax and conquer new land
- Wealthy trade center
- Headquarters of Eastern Orthodox Church in Russia
- Became the center of a new Russian empire

The rulers of Moscow learned to work with the Mongols. They let Moscow collect taxes from nearby Slav areas. If the Slavs could not pay the tax, Moscow could take over their territory. Moscow used this method to expand its power.

In 1462 Ivan III became the ruler of Moscow. Ivan called himself a czar, Russian for "emperor." By 1480 he had driven the Mongols out of Russia. By then, the people of Moscow, now known as Russians began to build a great empire.

European Crusaders

In 1095 Pope Urban II asked Europe's lords to launch a crusade, or holy war, to take Jerusalem from the Muslim Turks. Thousands of soldiers left western Europe to join the First Crusade. After many more crusades, Muslims won back all of the territory they had lost.

The Crusade	Success or Failure?	Why?
First	Success	Crusaders captured Jerusalem and formed four Christian states.
Second	Failure	Muslims recaptured Jerusalem.
Third	Failure	Muslims kept Jerusalem.
Fourth	Failure	Crusaders attacked Byzantine capital.
Fifth—Tenth	Failure	Muslims recaptured all lands held by Crusaders.

The Crusades changed Europe. Western Europeans gained new knowledge from Byzantines and Muslims, such as how to build better ships. Feudalism broke down because nobles who joined the Crusades sold their lands and freed their serfs. This meant the nobles had less power. As a result, kings were able to build stronger governments. The Crusades also caused bitter feelings between Christian western Europe and the Muslims.

Check for Understanding

List two reasons why you think Pope Urban II might have launched the Crusades.

1. ______________________________

2. ______________________________

Name two regions set up by Crusaders in the eastern Mediterranean area.

3. ______________________________

4. ______________________________

Glue Foldable here

Identifying

7. What was the goal of the First Crusade?

____
____
____

Reading Check

8. What was one way the Crusades changed Christian Europe?

____
____
____

FOLDABLES®

9. Place a two-tab Foldable along the dotted line to cover the Check for Understanding. Cut the tabs in half to form four tabs. Title the anchor tab *European Crusades*.

Label the four tabs *What*, *When*, *Where*, and *Why*. Use both sides of the tabs to explain each.

NAME________________________ DATE ____________ CLASS ________

networks

Medieval Europe

Lesson 4 Culture and the Church

ESSENTIAL QUESTION

What is the role of religion in government?

GUIDING QUESTIONS

1. ***What types of learning and art developed during the Middle Ages?***
2. ***How did the Catholic Church affect the lives of medieval Europeans?***

Terms to Know

theology the study of religious faith, practice, experience

scholasticism a way of thinking that combined faith and reasoning

vernacular the everyday spoken language of a region

mass Catholic religious worship service

heresy ideas that go against Church teachings

anti-Semitism hatred and mistreatment of Jews

When did it happen?

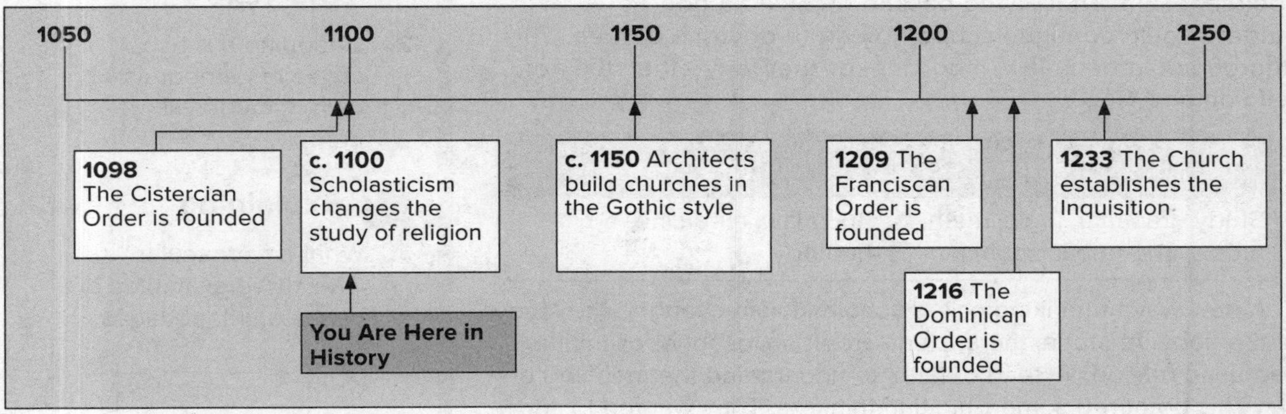

1050
1100
1150
1200
1250
1098 The Cistercian Order is founded
c. 1100 Scholasticism changes the study of religion
You Are Here in History
c. 1150 Architects build churches in the Gothic style
1209 The Franciscan Order is founded
1216 The Dominican Order is founded
1233 The Church establishes the Inquisition

What do you know?

Put a check mark (✓) next to each true statement.

_______ 1. Romanesque churches are tall and have large stained glass windows.

_______ 2. Universities of today trace their origins back to the Middle Ages.

_______ 3. One popular form of vernacular literature is troubadour poetry.

_______ 4. Friars were monks who preached and served as missionaries.

_______ 5. In the 1100s, rulers in western Europe drove out their Jewish subjects.

European Culture in the Middle Ages

By the 1100s, people in medieval Europe felt safer because of stronger governments. Trade, banking, and business grew. People valued religion. Church leaders, merchants, and nobles had cathedrals, or large churches, built.

Cathedrals were built in two styles. Romanesque was a mix of Roman and Byzantine styles. These rectangular buildings had long, rounded ceilings and small windows. Gothic cathedrals, on the other hand, were tall. Large stained glass windows showed scenes from the Bible.

Universities were first created during the Middle Ages. Universities educated and trained scholars. University students studied for four to six years before taking an oral, or spoken, exam. Those who passed received a degree. A student could continue school to earn a doctor's degree. This degree could be in law, medicine, or **theology**—the study of religion and God.

Basic Degree	Doctor's Degree
Study grammar, logic, math, music, and public speaking	Study law, medicine, or theology

A new way of thinking called **scholasticism** changed the study of theology. Aristotle, the ancient Greek philosopher or thinker, had used reason, instead of faith, to understand the meaning of life. This bothered some Christian thinkers. They wanted to show that ideas accepted by faith did not have to oppose ideas developed by reason.

An Italian priest named Thomas Aquinas helped spread the ideas of scholasticism. Aquinas wrote *Summa Theologica,* a summary of what was known about theology. He also wrote about government and the concept of natural law, or laws that come from human nature. Aquinas claimed that natural law gave people certain rights that the government should not take away.

Latin was the language of the Church and of educated people throughout Europe. Each region of Europe also had its own language. This everyday language is called **vernacular.** Over time, vernacular languages became the languages of Spanish, French, English, Italian, and German.

During the 1100s, new literature was written using vernacular language. Educated people enjoyed vernacular writings, especially poetry told by troubadours.

Identifying

1. What type of degree could a student in a medieval university earn for studying music?

____

____

____

Marking the Text

2. Underline the two styles of cathedrals built in medieval Europe.

Explaining

3. What is vernacular? Give three examples of vernacular languages.

____

____

____

Reading Check

4. Why was it important that literature was written in everyday language?

____

____

____

Explaining

5. Why were many new religious orders founded beginning in the 1000s?

____

____

____

Defining

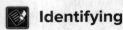

6. Explain what a *mass* is.

____

____

____

Marking the Text

7. Underline the definition of *heresy*.

Identifying

8. What happened to people who were found guilty of heresy?

____

____

____

Troubadours were poets who sang love stories, especially about the love of a knight for a lady. Another type of vernacular writing was the heroic epic. In epics, brave knights fight for kings and lords. *The Song of Roland* is an example of a heroic epic.

Religion Affected Society

Beginning in the 1000s, a wave of religious feeling swept through Europe. As a result, new groups of priests, monks, and nuns were formed. These were called religious orders.

New Religious Orders		
Cistercians	**Franciscan Friars**	**Dominicans**
• founded in 1098 • farmed land, worshipped, and prayed • invented new ways of farming that helped grow more crops • helped the poor	• founded in 1209 • went out into the world to preach • lived by begging • could not own anything • loved nature	• founded in 1216 • went out into the world to preach • lived by begging • defended Church teachings • studied for years

The Cistercian order was based in rural monasteries. Its members invented new ways of farming that helped grow more crops. They also helped the poor. Francis of Assisi started a new order called Franciscans. They preached Christianity in the towns. They also were known for their cheerfulness and love of nature. A Spanish monk named Dominic de Guzmán started the Dominicans. Its main goal was to defend Church teachings.

The Catholic Church affected almost every part of people's lives. On Sundays and holy days, people went to **mass**, which is the Catholic worship service. People prayed to the saints to ask for help from God. Mary, the mother of Jesus, was the most honored saint.

The Catholic Church used its power to try to stop **heresy**, or religious beliefs that did not agree with Church teaching. In 1233 the pope created a special court to deal with heretics. It was called the Inquisition. Its job was to question heretics, or people who were accused of heresy. People who were found guilty could confess and ask for forgiveness. Those who refused to confess were punished.

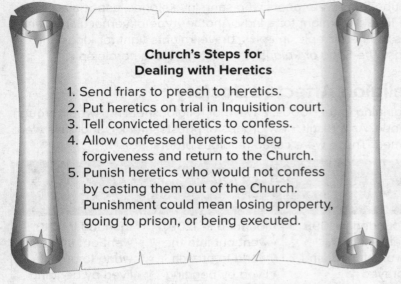

Church's Steps for Dealing with Heretics

1. Send friars to preach to heretics.
2. Put heretics on trial in Inquisition court.
3. Tell convicted heretics to confess.
4. Allow confessed heretics to beg forgiveness and return to the Church.
5. Punish heretics who would not confess by casting them out of the Church. Punishment could mean losing property, going to prison, or being executed.

Many church leaders and church members also practiced **anti-Semitism**, or the hatred of Jews. Many European Christians unfairly blamed Jews for problems in society, such as famine or economic decline. Christian mobs attacked and killed thousands of Jews. Many Jews had to wear special badges or clothing. In some places, they had to live in separate neighborhoods known as ghettos. Jews also could not own land or work at certain jobs.

In the 1100s, Western European rulers began driving out their Jewish subjects. Many of these Jews went to countries in eastern Europe. There they formed thriving communities that were based on their religious traditions.

Glue Foldable here

Check for Understanding

Name two reasons large cathedrals and churches were built during this time.

1. ______________________________

2. ______________________________

List two ways the Catholic Church influenced the lives of medieval Europeans.

3. ______________________________

4. ______________________________

Listing

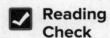

9. List three examples of how European Christians mistreated Jews.

____

____

____

Reading Check

10. Why did Church officials set up the Inquisition?

____

____

____

FOLDABLES®

11. Place a three-tab Foldable along the dotted line to cover the Check for Understanding. Title the anchor tab *Catholic Church.* Label the three tabs *Daily Life*, *Saints*, and *Power.*

Use words and short phrases to record what you remember about the effects of the Catholic Church on each.

NAME________________________________ DATE ______________ CLASS ________

networks

Medieval Europe

Lesson 5 The Late Middle Ages

ESSENTIAL QUESTION

How do governments change?

GUIDING QUESTIONS

1. ***How did the Black Death affect Europe during the Late Middle Ages?***
2. ***How did disputes and wars change societies in Europe during the Late Middle Ages?***

Terms to Know

plague a disease that spreads quickly and kills many people

Reconquista the Christian "reconquest" of the Iberian peninsula from the Muslims

Where in the world?

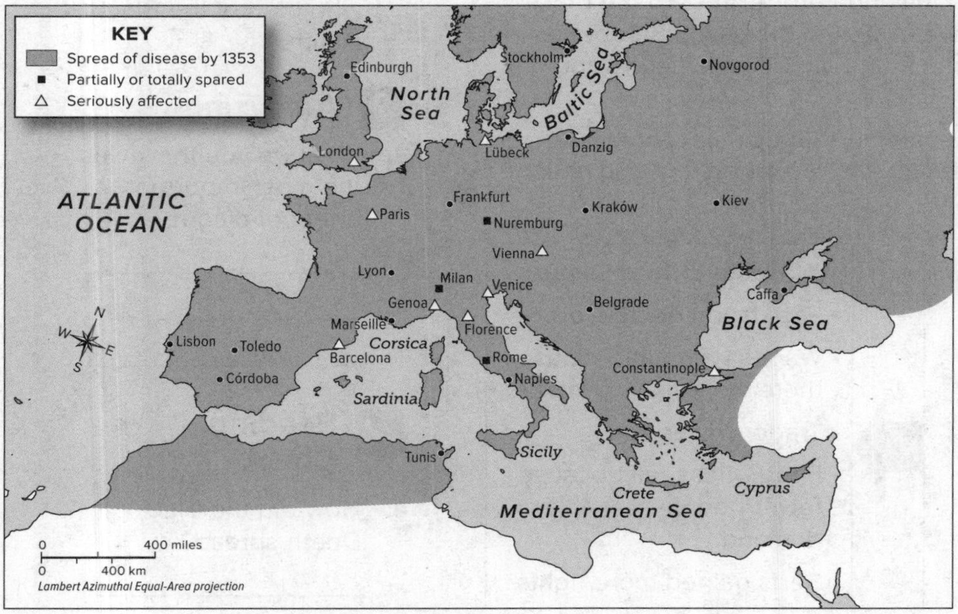

When did it happen?

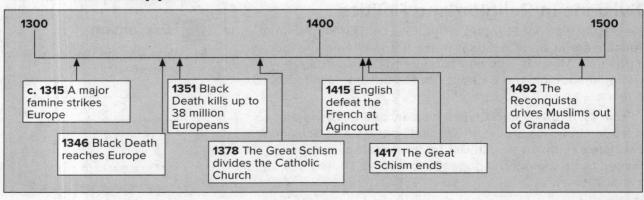

1300 — 1400 — 1500

- **c. 1315** A major famine strikes Europe
- **1346** Black Death reaches Europe
- **1351** Black Death kills up to 38 million Europeans
- **1378** The Great Schism divides the Catholic Church
- **1415** English defeat the French at Agincourt
- **1417** The Great Schism ends
- **1492** The Reconquista drives Muslims out of Granada

Famine and Plague

In the 1300s, disaster struck western Europe. Bad weather and disease killed the crops. Livestock died from diseases. The result was a seven-year famine, or lack of food.

Then, a terrible **plague** swept across Europe and Asia. A plague is a disease that spreads quickly and kills many people. The plague was called the Black Death. Most scientists think that a type of bacteria carried by fleas was the source of the plague. Rats from boats and trading caravans carried the fleas to places all over the world.

The Black Death probably began in China and spread along the trade routes between China and Europe. In 1346 the Black Death reached Europe. Between 19 and 38 million Europeans died of the Black Death in just four years. That is nearly one out of every two people.

The deaths of so many people hurt Europe's economy. As a result, the plague helped weaken the feudal system and change European society.

Causes of the Plague		Effects of the Plague
• Fleas carried bacteria or germs. • Rats carried fleas on ships and caravans. • Trade routes spread rats and fleas around the world.	→	• Population decreased. • Wages went up because there were fewer workers. • Trade slowed. • Food prices fell because fewer people meant less demand. • Serfs gained more rights. • Feudalism weakened.

Divisions in Religion and Politics

The plague was not Europe's only problem. The English and French were at war. Christians in the Iberian Peninsula fought to drive out Muslims who had conquered them centuries before. In addition, the Catholic Church became divided over its leadership.

From 1378 to 1417, the Church was divided by disputes over its leadership. This argument was called the Great Schism. A schism is a break or a split. During this time, several men claimed to be the rightful pope. Each wanted church members to support him.

Defining

1. What is a *plague*?

____

____

Marking the Text

2. Circle the number of western Europeans who died of the Black Death.

Analyzing

3. What do you think was the most important effect of plague?

____

____

____

Reading Check

4. How did the Black Death spread?

____

____

____

Explaining

5. What was the Great Schism?

____

____

____

____

Lesson 5 The Late Middle Ages, *Continued*

Cause and Effect

6. Why did the Hundred Years' War happen?

Identifying

7. Who was Joan of Arc?

Explaining

8. What was the *Reconquista*?

In 1417 a council of church officials chose a pope that everyone agreed on. Many educated people, however, wanted to change the Church. They wanted the Church to be less worldly and more spiritual.

Europe also experienced political divisions. For centuries, the English ruled areas of France. In 1337 English king Edward III claimed to be king of all of France. He invaded France, beginning a war between England and France that lasted more than 100 years.

The English won two important battles, at Crécy in 1346 and at Agincourt in 1415. They had better weapons than the French: longbows and an early form of the cannon.

In 1429 a French peasant girl named Joan visited Prince Charles of France. She told him that saints had spoken to her and wanted her to free France. He let her lead a French army. Joan's faith inspired the French soldiers, and they took back the city of Orléans from the English.

Shortly after, Charles was named king. A few months later, the English captured Joan. They handed her over to the Inquisition. She was burned at the stake. She later became known as Joan of Arc, a French national hero.

Joan of Arc

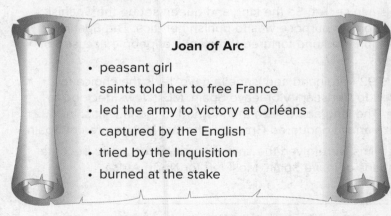

- peasant girl
- saints told her to free France
- led the army to victory at Orléans
- captured by the English
- tried by the Inquisition
- burned at the stake

The French finally defeated the English in the Hundred Years' War. England's loss in the war was hard on the English nobles. Soon, they were fighting a civil war. It was known as the War of the Roses and fought over who should be king. The winner, Henry Tudor, became King Henry VII.

During the early Middle Ages, Muslims ruled much of the Iberian Peninsula, the area that is now Spain and Portugal. They developed a rich culture. However, over time, Christians drove out most of the Muslims. The struggle was known as the **Reconquista,** or "reconquest." By the 1200s, Christians ruled most of the peninsula.

Lesson 5 The Late Middle Ages, *Continued*

In 1469 Princess Isabella of Castile married Prince Ferdinand of Aragon. They became king and queen and joined their lands into one country called Spain. Ferdinand and Isabella wanted all of Spain to be Catholic.

Jews in Spain

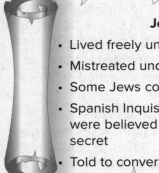

- Lived freely under the Muslims
- Mistreated under Christian rule
- Some Jews converted to Christianity
- Spanish Inquisition sought Jews who were believed to be practicing Judaism in secret
- Told to convert or leave Spain in 1492

When Muslims ruled, Iberian Jews mostly lived freely. As Christians took over Spain, they mistreated the Jews. To avoid persecution, some Jews became Christians. Ferdinand and Isabella, however, believed many of these people practiced Judaism in secret. So the king and queen set up the Spanish Inquisition. Its purpose was to punish heretics. The Spanish Inquisition tried and tortured thousands of people accused of heresy.

In 1492 Ferdinand and Isabella gave Jews the choice to convert to Christianity or leave Spain. Most Jews decided to leave. The king and queen then turned to the Muslims. In 1492 Spain's army conquered Granada, the last Muslim area of Spain.

Muslims were given the same choice as the Jews: become Christians or leave Spain. Most left for North Africa.

Check for Understanding

List four ways that disputes and wars changed societies in Europe during this time.

1. ______________________________

2. ______________________________

3. ______________________________

4. ______________________________

Identifying

9. What was the Spanish Inquisition?

____

____

____

Reading Check

10. How did Ferdinand and Isabella treat those of Muslim and Jewish faiths?

____

____

____

FOLDABLES®

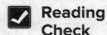

11. Place a two-tab Foldable along the dotted line to cover the text titled Check for Understanding. Title the anchor tab *Europe*. Label the two tabs *Religious Division* and *Political Division*.

Use both sides of the tabs to write words and short phrases that you remember to explain the divisions in Europe.

Glue Foldable here

NAME _______________ DATE _______ CLASS _______

networks

Renaissance and Reformation

Lesson 1 The Renaissance Begins

ESSENTIAL QUESTION

Why do people make economic choices?

GUIDING QUESTIONS

1. ***Why did the states of Italy become leading centers of culture during the Renaissance?***
2. ***How did Italy's states become wealthy and powerful?***
3. ***Who controlled the states of Italy?***

Terms to Know

Renaissance "rebirth"; period in European history from 1350 to 1650 when people became interested again in art and learning

secular related to worldly things

urban related to cities, not the countryside

mercenary a soldier who fights for money

diplomacy making agreements with other countries

Where in the world?

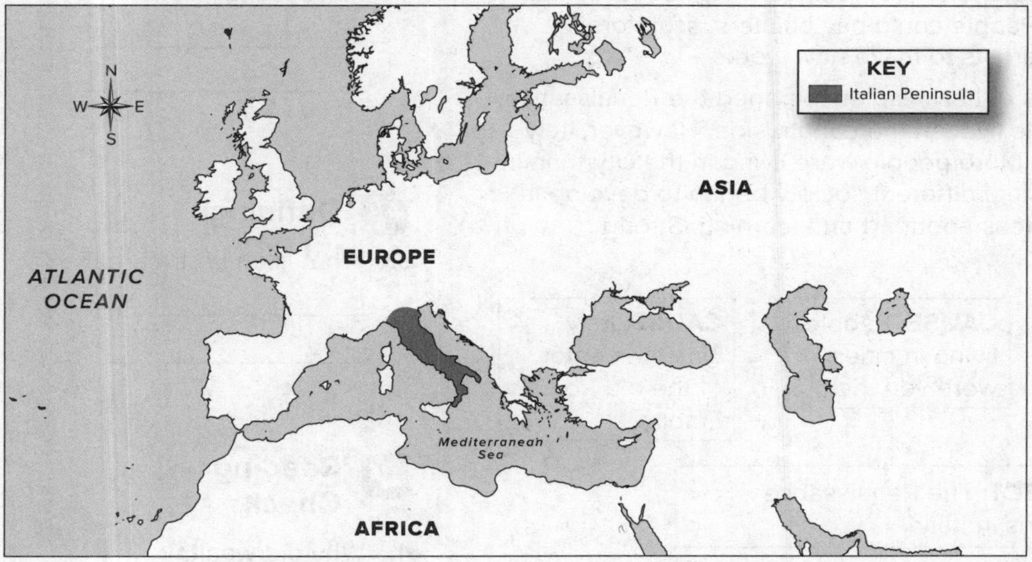

When did it happen?

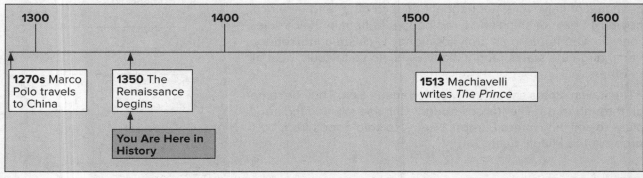

1300 — 1400 — 1500 — 1600

1270s Marco Polo travels to China

1350 The Renaissance begins

You Are Here in History

1513 Machiavelli writes *The Prince*

The Renaissance in Italy

In European history, the years from about 1350 to 1650 were called the **Renaissance.** The word *renaissance* means "rebirth." During this time period, people became interested again in art and learning.

After the hard years of the Black Death, Europeans became interested in the knowledge of the ancient Greeks and Romans. People became more **secular.** This meant that, even though religion was still important, people were interested in worldly ideas and events.

The Renaissance began in Italy, the center of the old Roman Empire. Italians were surrounded by Roman ruins and art. These ancient examples inspired the Italians in their own art.

Another reason the Renaissance was born was because Italian cities were very rich. People could pay painters, sculptors, architects, and other artists to make new works.

The powerful states of Italy also encouraged the Renaissance. In Europe, most people lived in the countryside. However, Italy was becoming **urban.** More people were living in the city than in the country. As a result, a different society began to develop in Italy. People shared ideas about art and learning. Strong economies developed.

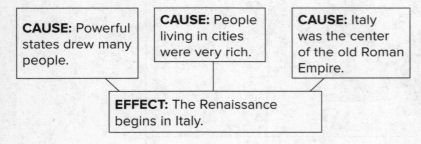

CAUSE: Powerful states drew many people.

CAUSE: People living in cities were very rich.

CAUSE: Italy was the center of the old Roman Empire.

EFFECT: The Renaissance begins in Italy.

The States of Italy

The states of Italy were independent of each other and very rich. They built fleets of ships and hired people to fight in their armies. A person who fights in an army for money is called a **mercenary.** Even though the states fought many wars, no state could beat all the others.

The Italian states sat on the Mediterranean Sea. They became rich through trade. The Italians bought Chinese silk and Indian spices to sell in Western Europe. They also sold goods from Europe in the Middle East.

Marking the Text

1. Underline the reason this period of time is called the Renaissance, or "rebirth."

Identifying

2. Where did the Renaissance begin?

____

____

Defining

3. What is an *urban* area?

____

____

Reading Check

4. Why did wealthy Italians support artists during the Renaissance?

____

____

____

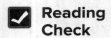

Making Connections

5. Why did Europeans want Asian goods?

____

____

Identifying

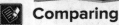

6. Which city was the most famous Renaissance city?

____

Reading Check

7. How did the travels of Marco Polo affect Europeans?

____

____

____

FOLDABLES

Comparing

8. Place a two-tab Foldable along the dotted line to cover the text about Florence. Title the anchor tab *City-States*. Label the top tab *Florence* and the bottom tab *Venice*.

List facts about each and use them to compare the two city-states.

Marco Polo was a merchant from Venice. In the 1270s, he traveled to China. There he met Kublai Khan, the ruler of the Mongol Empire. The emperor sent Marco Polo on trips all over China. Marco wrote a book about his travels. After reading his stories, many people wanted to buy China's goods.

How did Italian states get rich?

- Traded Chinese silk and Indian spices at high prices in Europe
- Sold Western European goods in the Middle East
- Met increasing demand for Asian goods

Glue Foldable here

Florence was the most famous city of the Renaissance. It was the first city to grow rich. It had many famous artists. Florence became rich from trading cloth, mainly wool from England. In Florence, the wool was woven into fine fabrics.

Banking was another way people in Florence made money. Merchants needed to know how much the coins from different countries were worth. Florentine bankers set up a system to do this. They used the florin, the gold coin of Florence, to measure the value of other money. Florence's richest family was the Medici family. They owned banks as far away as Flanders, which is today part of Belgium.

The people of Venice built their city on many small islands. Long wooden poles in the mud supported their buildings. Instead of making roads, the Venetians built canals and waterways. They used boats to move around the city. Venice also became a major shipbuilding center.

Glue Foldable here

A New Ruling Class

In Italy, old noble families moved to the cities. Rich merchants tried to live like noble families. The sons and daughters of nobles and rich merchants married each other. Their families blended together, and they became the upper class of the city-states.

Many city-states were republics at first. A republic is a government controlled by its citizens. Only merchants and artisans could be citizens. When city-states faced war or rebellion, they often gave power to a single person. Some leaders ruled harshly. Others used a more gentle approach.

Lesson 1 The Renaissance Begins, *Continued*

In Venice, the ruler was the duke, or doge. He was the official leader, but a small group of wealthy merchants held the real power.

In Florence, the Medici family controlled the government for many years. Lorenzo de' Medici ruled the city from 1469 to 1492. He was known as "the Magnificent."

Lorenzo the Magnificent

- part of the rich Medici family
- ruled Florence from 1469 to 1492
- supported artists, architects, and writers

Politics in Italy were not simple. The rulers of each city had to stop other rich people from taking power by force. They also had to get along with leaders from other states. To work with others, the Italians developed **diplomacy.** This is the art of making agreements with other countries. Today's ideas about diplomacy first began in Italy.

Niccolò Machiavelli was an official in Florence. He wrote a book called *The Prince* in 1513. He wrote that rulers should do anything they could to keep power and protect their city. This included killing and lying. Today when we say someone is being Machiavellian, we mean he or she is being tricky or sly and acting without morals.

Glue Foldable here

Check for Understanding

List two reasons why Italy was an ideal location for the Renaissance to begin.

1. ______________

2. ______________

List two ways Italian states helped fuel the Renaissance.

3. ______________

4. ______________

Analyzing

9. Niccolò Machiavelli said rulers should do whatever they need to in order to keep power. Why?

____

Reading Check

10. Why did the Italian states develop diplomacy?

____

FOLDABLES®

11. Place a one-tab Foldable along the dotted line to cover the Check for Understanding. Title the anchor tab *The Renaissance*. Draw five arrows from the title and write five words or phrases about the Renaissance.

Use your Foldable to complete the Check for Understanding.

NAME_______________ DATE _________ CLASS _______

networks

Renaissance and Reformation

Lesson 2 New Ideas and Art

ESSENTIAL QUESTION

How do new ideas change the way people live?

GUIDING QUESTIONS

1. *How did Renaissance writers rely on the past to develop new ideas?*
2. *How did Renaissance artists learn to make their art look natural and real?*
3. *How did the Renaissance change as it moved from Italy into northern Europe?*

Term to Know

humanism an emphasis on worldly concerns; a belief that reason leads to knowledge

When did it happen?

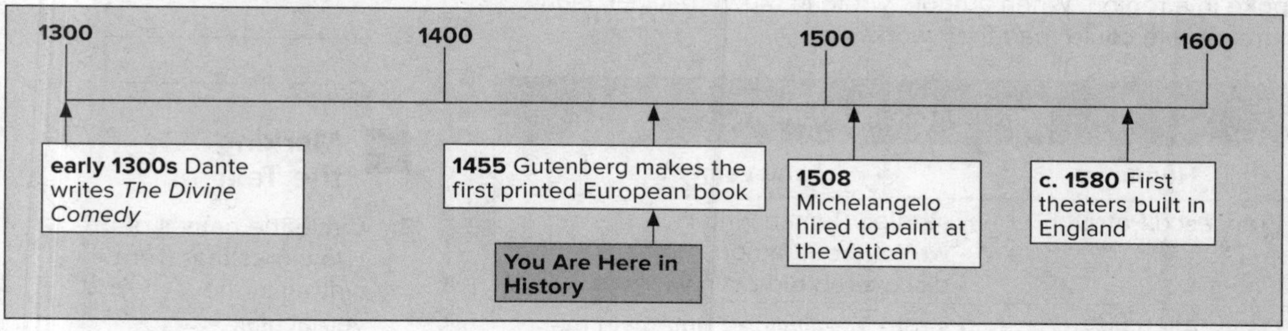

1300
1400
1500
1600
early 1300s Dante writes The Divine Comedy
1455 Gutenberg makes the first printed European book
You Are Here in History
1508 Michelangelo hired to paint at the Vatican
c. 1580 First theaters built in England

What do you know?

In the K column, list what you already know about life in the Renaissance. In the W column, list what you would like to know. After reading the lesson, fill in the L column with the information that you learned.

K	W	L

Lesson 2 New Ideas and Art, *Continued*

Renaissance Humanism

In the 1300s, European scholars created a new way of understanding the world. It was called **humanism**, and it was based on ancient Greek and Roman ideas. Humanists believed that individuals were important. They wanted to use reason, not just religion, to gain knowledge.

During the Crusades, Arab Muslims passed on what they knew about Greek and Roman works to western Europeans. Italians found old Latin writings in monasteries. They also studied old buildings and statues to understand what made them beautiful. Humanist scholars studied mathematics, medicine, biology, and astronomy.

Educated people wrote in the classical Latin. They also began to write in the vernacular, or the everyday language that people spoke in a region. When authors wrote in the vernacular, many more people could read their works.

Renaissance Humanists

Humanist	Achievements
Francesco Petrarch	• studied Roman writers • wrote about famous Romans • discovered old Latin writings
Dante Alighieri	• wrote *The Divine Comedy* in the vernacular
Geoffrey Chaucer	• wrote in the vernacular • wrote *The Canterbury Tales* in English
Johannes Gutenberg	• printed the Christian Bible using movable type
Leonardo da Vinci	• created great works of art • drew sketches of scientific ideas and artistic projects

In the early 1450s, Johannes Gutenberg invented a printing press that used movable metal type. It could print books quickly. More books were available so more people learned to read. Scholars read one another's works and wrote letters to discuss their thoughts. These changes helped ideas spread more quickly than ever before.

Leonardo da Vinci was one of the most important Renaissance scientists and artists. Most of what we know about him comes from his drawings of scientific projects.

Defining

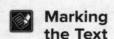

1. Define the term *humanism*.

____

____

Analyzing

2. Why might humanism have appealed to people after the Black Death?

____

____

____

Marking the Text

3. Circle the names of two works that were written in the vernacular.

Reading Check

4. How did Gutenberg's printing press bring change to Europe?

____

____

____

____

Identifying

5. Who paid artists to create works during the Renaissance?

____

____

Making Connections

6. How could studying science have helped Renaissance artists?

____

____

____

Comparing

7. What was similar about the work of da Vinci and Michelangelo?

____

____

____

Reading Check

8. What is the technique of chiaroscuro?

____

____

____

____

Italy's Renaissance Artists

Rich Italian families and church leaders paid artists to make paintings, sculptures, and buildings. Renaissance artists followed examples of the ancient Romans and Greeks. They also expressed new humanist ideas.

Renaissance painters painted in new ways. They used perspective, a way of showing things as they appear at different distances. Artists studied the human body to help them draw more accurately. They used light and shadows instead of hard outlines to separate objects. This is called chiaroscuro. *Chiaro* means "clear or light" in Italian and *oscuro* means "dark."

Renaissance Art

New Techniques
- Perspective gives three-dimensional look
- Chiaroscuro adds drama and emotion

New Ideas
- Show how people look in real life
- Show people's feelings

The golden age of Renaissance art lasted from 1490 to 1520. Famous artists of the time were Leonardo da Vinci, Michelangelo Buonarroti, and Raphael Sanzio.

One of da Vinci's most famous works is the *Mona Lisa*. He also painted *The Last Supper*, which shows Jesus with his disciples. Da Vinci showed the feelings of the disciples through their positions and gestures.

Michelangelo painted and sculpted. He tried to show realistic human beings with feelings and emotions. Michelangelo also painted the ceiling of the Sistine Chapel in Rome with images from the Christian Bible. The figures he painted have muscular bodies that show their power.

Raphael was one of the best painters in Italy. He is best known for a fresco called the *School of Athens*. It shows many Greek philosophers.

Some women, like the daughters of nobles, contributed to the arts. Artemisia Gentileschi was one of the first women to paint important historical and religious scenes.

The Northern Renaissance

In the late 1400s, the Renaissance spread to northern Europe and later to England. War, trade, travel, and the printing press spread humanist ideas.

The Northern Renaissance took place in present-day Belgium, Luxembourg, Germany, and the Netherlands. Northern artists painted with oil paints. Oils created richer colors and allowed more detail. Jan van Eyck was a Flemish painter. His best-known painting is *The Arnolfini Portrait*. It shows a newly married couple. Every fold in their rich clothes and every detail in the room are visible.

Albrecht Dürer was an important Renaissance artist from Germany. He is best known for his engravings. An engraving is made from an image carved in metal, wood, or stone. Ink is put on the surface, then the image is printed on paper. Dürer's *Four Horsemen of the Apocalypse* shows four men on horses who announce the end of the world.

In England, the Renaissance theater was very popular. Playwrights, or writers of plays, wrote about people's strengths, weaknesses, and feelings.

The greatest playwright of the time was William Shakespeare. He wrote comedies, historical plays, and tragedies. A tragedy is a play in which the main character suffers great loss or pain. Some of Shakespeare's most famous works are *Hamlet*, *Macbeth*, and *Romeo and Juliet*. Shakespeare's plays are still very popular.

Check for Understanding

List three features of Renaissance art.

1. ______________________

2. ______________________

3. ______________________

For each of these categories, name three Renaissance artists.

4. Writers ______________________

5. Painters ______________________

Glue Foldable here

Explaining

9. How did Renaissance ideas arrive in northern Europe?

____

____

Reading Check

10. How did northern Renaissance painters differ from Italian Renaissance painters?

____

____

____

FOLDABLES®

11. Place a two-tab Foldable along the dotted line to cover the Check for Understanding. Title the anchor tab *Renaissance Changes.* Label the top tab *writers and their work* and the bottom tab *artists and their work.*

Write what you remember about important writers and artists during this time and their works.

NAME ______________________ DATE ____________ CLASS ________

networks

Lesson 3 The Reformation Begins

ESSENTIAL QUESTION

How do religions develop?

GUIDING QUESTIONS

1. ***Why was the Church under pressure to reform itself?***
2. ***How did Luther's reforms lead to a new form of Christianity?***
3. ***How did the teachings of Protestant reformers shape the western world?***
4. ***How did the Reformation shape England and later its American colonies?***

Terms to Know

Reformation a religious movement that changed the Catholic Church and created Protestant churches
indulgence a pardon, or forgiveness, of sin
predestination a religious belief that God has already decided who will go to heaven
annul to declare not valid

Where in the world?

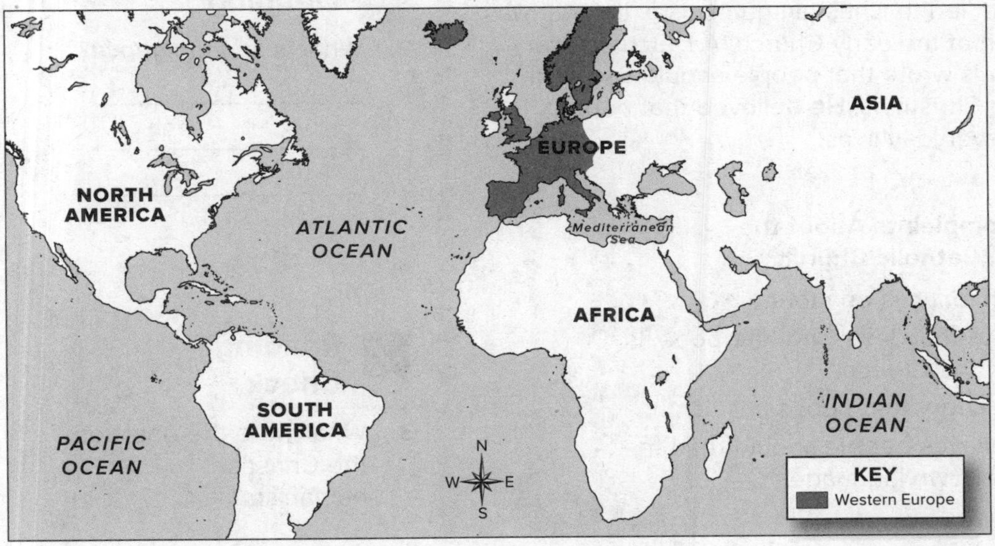

When did it happen?

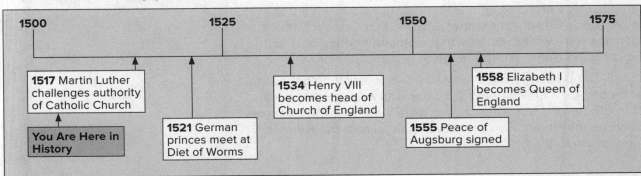

1500 — 1525 — 1550 — 1575

- **1517** Martin Luther challenges authority of Catholic Church
- **You Are Here in History**
- **1521** German princes meet at Diet of Worms
- **1534** Henry VIII becomes head of Church of England
- **1555** Peace of Augsburg signed
- **1558** Elizabeth I becomes Queen of England

Lesson 3 The Reformation Begins, *Continued*

Early Calls for Reform

In 1517 a German monk named Martin Luther challenged the Catholic Church. At first, Martin Luther wanted only to reform, or change, the Catholic Church. This is why these events are called the **Reformation.** By the end of the Reformation, Europe had many new Christian churches.

Church officials had grown rich by selling indulgences. An **indulgence** was a certificate that said a person would not be punished for his or her sins. Many Catholics became angry at the Church for focusing on money.

In the 1370s, an English priest named John Wycliffe said that Jesus was the head of the Church, not the pope. Wycliffe wanted everyone to read the Bible, so he translated parts of it from Latin into English. After he died, his followers finished translating it.

Renaissance humanism led to Christian humanism. Its goal was to restore the simple faith of the early Church. A Dutch scholar named Desiderius Erasmus wrote that people should use their reason to become better Christians. He believed that people should be good in their everyday lives.

Complaints About the Catholic Church

- The Church focuses on money.
- Wycliffe says that Jesus, not the pope, is the head of the Church.
- Erasmus is angry that popes are rich.
- Wycliffe believes people should read the Bible in their own language.

Luther's Reformation

Martin Luther's disagreement with the Catholic Church led to a big change in Christianity. Luther decided that Catholic Church teachings were wrong. He said that a person needed only faith, and not good works, in order to go to heaven.

In 1517 Pope Leo X told Church leaders to sell indulgences to get money for a new cathedral. Luther was angry. He wrote a list of 95 reasons why indulgences were wrong. The list became known as the Ninety-Five Theses. People across the German kingdoms read them.

Summarizing

1. What was the major complaint people had about the Catholic Church?

____

____

____

____

Defining

2. What is an *indulgence*?

____

____

____

Reading Check

3. What were the goals of the Christian humanists?

____

____

____

Summarizing

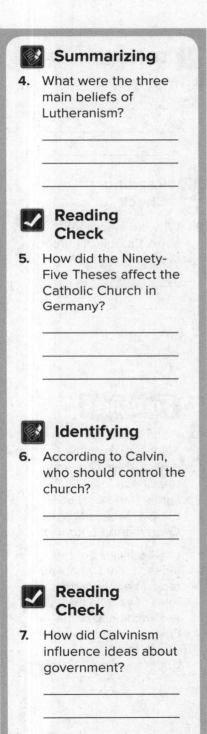

4. What were the three main beliefs of Lutheranism?

___

___

___

Reading Check

5. How did the Ninety-Five Theses affect the Catholic Church in Germany?

___

___

___

Identifying

6. According to Calvin, who should control the church?

___

___

Reading Check

7. How did Calvinism influence ideas about government?

___

___

___

Luther began to attack other Catholic beliefs. He said popes could make mistakes when they taught about Christianity. He argued that all Christians had a right to read the Bible. He said Christians could confess their sins to God without the help of a priest.

Pope Leo X thought Luther was dangerous. He made Luther leave the Catholic Church. Luther's ideas led to a new branch of Christianity, called Lutheranism. It was the first Protestant church. It was based on three main ideas.

- Belief in Jesus, not good works, brings a place in heaven.
- The Bible is the final source for truth about God.
- The church includes all believers, not just the clergy.

Many German rulers made their kingdoms Lutheran. They took land from Catholic monasteries. In addition, rulers could set their own church taxes and keep the money for themselves. Protestant rulers became stronger. The Catholic Church became weaker.

These changes angered the Holy Roman Emperor Charles V. Charles V went to war with the Lutheran German rulers, but could not defeat them. Finally, an agreement named the Peace of Augsburg made most of northern Germany Protestant territory. The south stayed Catholic. This division still exists today.

The Reformation Spreads

Martin Luther's reformation spread across Europe. John Calvin agreed with Martin Luther and added other ideas, too. Calvin's main idea was that God has decided who will go to heaven and who will not. This belief is called **predestination.** This means that no matter what people do, God has decided the final outcome of all events.

Another important idea of Calvinism is that kings and bishops should not control the church. The people of the church should choose their own elders and ministers. His ideas influenced people in England, Scotland, and the Netherlands. Calvinism began to give people the idea that they could elect government leaders.

Important Ideas from Calvin

- God has already decided who is going to heaven.
- Kings and bishops should not control the church.
- People should choose the clergy.

The Reformation in England

In England, King Henry VIII was stubborn and impatient. He wanted a son to rule after him. Unfortunately, he had only a daughter with his wife Catherine. Henry wanted to **annul,** or end, his marriage. An annulment says that the marriage never happened. Then he could remarry.

The pope refused. So Henry had the highest-ranking church official in England end his marriage to Catherine. He then married Anne Boleyn. Because of that, the pope excommunicated Henry from the Catholic Church. Henry had Parliament pass the Act of Supremacy. This made the king, not the pope, the head of the Church of England.

- Henry ordered all priests and bishops to accept him as the new head of the church.
- Some who refused were killed.
- Henry took the Catholic Church's land in England.
- He gave some of the land to his nobles so they would stay loyal to him.

When Henry's oldest daughter Mary became queen, she wanted to make England a Catholic country again. Mary arrested or executed many Protestants. When she died, her half-sister Elizabeth became queen. She was a Protestant, so she brought back the Anglican Church.

A group of Protestants called Puritans wanted to purify the Anglican Church of its Catholic ways. Queen Elizabeth I put up with the Puritans, but James I did not. James I and the king who came after him, Charles I, mistreated the Puritans. Many Puritans moved to America so they could practice their religion freely. These colonies became the states of Massachusetts, Connecticut, New Hampshire, and Rhode Island.

Check for Understanding

List two contributions of Martin Luther.

1. ______________________

2. ______________________

Name two facts about the Puritans.

3. ______________________

4. ______________________

Glue Foldable here

Defining

8. What was a *Puritan*?

____

____

____

Reading Check

9. Why did Henry VIII seize Catholic Church lands in England?

____

____

____

FOLDABLES®

10. Place a two-tab Foldable along the dotted line to cover the Check for Understanding. Label the two tabs *Lutheran Church* and *Puritanism*.

Use both sides of the tabs to record what you remember about the roles of each in the Reformation. Use the Foldable to help answer Check for Understanding.

NAME ______________________ DATE ____________ CLASS ________

networks

Lesson 4 Catholics and Protestants

ESSENTIAL QUESTION

Why does conflict develop?

GUIDING QUESTIONS

1. *How did the Catholic Church respond to the spread of Protestantism?*
2. *How did wars of religion affect Europe?*

Terms to Know

seminary a school for religious training

heresy a religious belief that goes against what the church says is true

When did it happen?

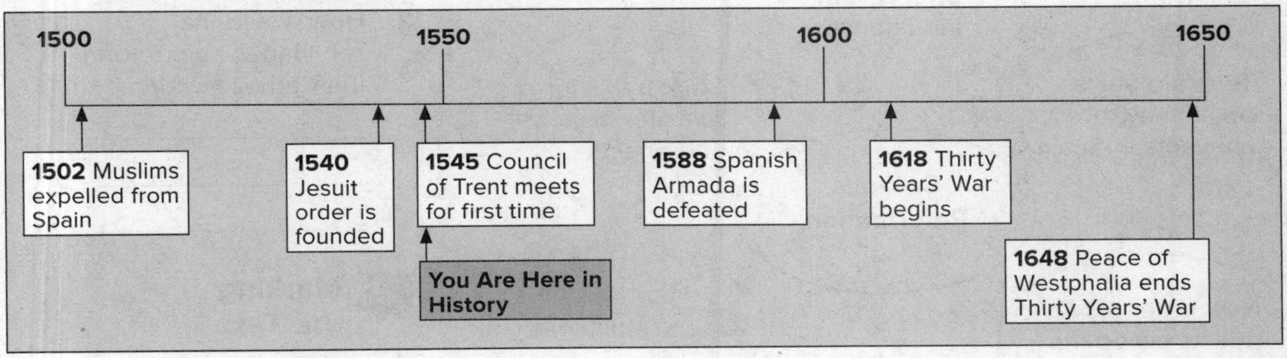
1500
1550
1600
1650
1502 Muslims expelled from Spain
1540 Jesuit order is founded
1545 Council of Trent meets for first time
You Are Here in History
1588 Spanish Armada is defeated
1618 Thirty Years' War begins
1648 Peace of Westphalia ends Thirty Years' War

What do you know?

Read each statement. Circle T if you think the statement is true. Circle F if you think the statement is false.

1. A priest could learn about the Bible at a seminary.	T	F
2. The Spanish Armada defeated the English navy.	T	F
3. The Catholic Church lost members after the Reformation.	T	F
4. All countries in Europe became Protestant.	T	F
5. The Reformation led to war between the countries of Europe.	T	F

The Catholic Reformation

In the 1500s and 1600s, the Catholic Church tried to stop Protestantism. This was called the Catholic Reformation.

The Catholic Church knew it needed to change. Pope Paul III called a church meeting at Trent, Italy. The Council of Trent made Catholic beliefs clear. It also ended many abuses. For example, the Catholic church stopped selling indulgences. The council set up strict rules for how bishops and priests should act. They were told to work harder at teaching the faith. The Catholic church set up seminaries to train priests. A **seminary** is a special school for educating priests.

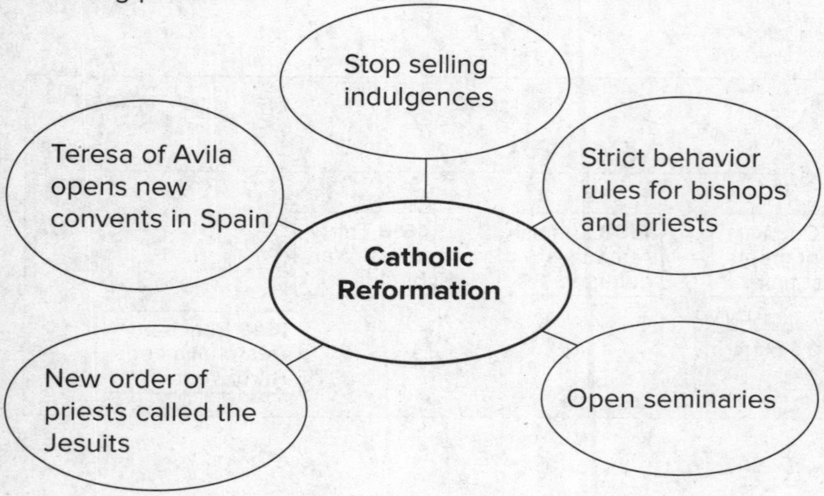

Spain was formed in 1469 when King Ferdinand and Queen Isabella married and joined their two kingdoms. They wanted a strong nation. They thought if everyone in Spain were Catholic, Spain would be united and loyal.

Muslims had ruled much of Spain during the Middle Ages. Catholics, Jews, and Muslims lived together with few problems at that time. Christians and Jews had to pay special taxes and had limited rights, but they were allowed to practice their own religions.

This religious harmony ended when Catholics took over Spain. Jews and Muslims were no longer welcome. Spain's rulers set up the Spanish Inquisition to find out people's religious beliefs. The Spanish Inquisition was a Catholic court. It was designed to uncover **heresy,** or beliefs that oppose church teachings. The Spanish Inquisition used torture and executions. About 2,000 Spaniards were killed.

Explaining

1. What did Catholic leaders discuss at the Council of Trent?

____

____

____

Drawing Conclusions

2. How would the seminaries help reform the Catholic Church?

____

____

____

Marking the Text

3. Circle the names of three religions that lived side by side in Spanish kingdoms before the marriage of Ferdinand and Isabella.

Identifying

4. What was the Spanish Inquisition?

____

____

____

Lesson 4 Catholics and Protestants, *Continued*

Reading Check

5. What was the goal of the Spanish Inquisition?

______

______

______

Paraphrasing

6. How did war between Spain and England start?

______

______

______

Marking the Text

7. Underline the description of the ships in the Spanish Armada.

Explaining

8. Why did French nobles rebel against the Catholic king?

______

______

______

In 1492 Ferdinand and Isabella ordered all Jews to become Catholic or leave the country. Ten years later, they ordered Muslims to do the same.

Church and government controls did not stop writers and artists in Catholic Spain. Miguel de Cervantes was a writer. He wrote the novel *Don Quixote* about a funny knight and his servant.

Events in Catholic Spain after 1469

Isabella and Ferdinand marry and form a united Catholic country.
↓
Spain forces Jews to leave the country.
↓
Spain forces Muslims to leave the country.
↓
Spain begins Inquisition to uncover heresy.

Religious Wars

By the mid-1500s, Christians in Europe were divided. Most northern Europeans were Protestant. Most southern Europeans were Catholic. Differences in religions led to wars in Europe. These wars lasted until about 1650.

During the rule of Queen Elizabeth I, England was the strongest Protestant power in Europe. Spain, led by King Philip II, was the strongest Catholic power. When Elizabeth helped the Protestant Dutch rebel against Spain, Philip grew angry. He decided to invade England.

In 1588 Philip sent a huge fleet, called the Spanish Armada, to England through the English Channel. This is the narrow body of water between England and Europe. The Spanish ships were large and had many guns. However, they were hard to steer. The smaller English ships moved faster. They drove back the Armada. Then there was a great storm and many Spanish ships were lost. The Protestant English had defeated the Catholic Spanish.

During the 1500s, most people in France were Catholic. Wealthy people, though, became Protestant. They were called Huguenots. They followed the ideas of John Calvin.

Many French nobles wanted to be able to practice their religion freely. They also wanted to weaken the power of the king of France.

Lesson 4 Catholics and Protestants, *Continued*

A civil war broke out between Protestants and Catholics in France. The Huguenots were led by Henry of Navarre who became King Henry IV of France. He wanted people to be loyal to him. He decided to change his religion, or **convert,** to Catholicism. He thought that being the king of France was more important than being Protestant.

Henry worked to end the religious war in France. He issued an edict, or order, when he visited the city of Nantes. The Edict of Nantes said that Catholicism was the official religion of France. However, it also gave Huguenots the right to worship as they wanted.

Catholic and Protestant Conflicts

- England destroyed the Spanish Armada.
- The Huguenots fought the Catholic rulers of France.
- The Thirty Years' War started in Bohemia and spread through Europe.

The worst religious war of the Reformation began when Protestant nobles in Bohemia turned against their Catholic king. The war lasted for 30 years. France, Sweden, and Denmark sent troops to help the Protestants. Spain and the Holy Roman Empire supported the Catholics. Even though France was a Catholic country, it helped the Protestants in order to win territory and wealth. The war was not just about religion.

The German people suffered greatly in the war. Finally, in 1643, the Holy Roman Emperor asked for peace. To end the war, the countries signed the Peace of Westphalia. After the war, Spain and the Holy Roman Empire were weaker. France was a stronger nation.

/ / / / / / / / / / / / / / Glue Foldable here / / / / / / / / / / / / / /

Check for Understanding

List two responses the Catholic Church had toward the Reformation.

1. ______________________

2. ______________________

List two events that led to the end of the Reformation.

3. ______________________

4. ______________________

Marking the Text

9. Underline the name of the agreement that ended the Thirty Years' War.

Reading Check

10. Why was the Edict of Nantes important in the history of France?

____

____

____

FOLDABLES®

11. Place a two-tab Foldable along the dotted line. Title the anchor tab *Reformation*. Label the first tab *Beginning* and the next tab *End*. Draw an arrow from left to right, across both tabs.

Write words or short phrases to record what you remember about the beginning and end of the Reformation.

NAME_________________________ DATE ______________ CLASS ________

networks

Age of Exploration and Trade

Lesson 1 The Age of Exploration

ESSENTIAL QUESTION

How does technology change the way people live?

GUIDING QUESTIONS

1. ***Why did Europeans begin to explore the world?***
2. ***Which leaders were responsible for European exploration of the world?***

Terms to Know

conquistadors Spanish soldiers who conquered people in other lands

circumnavigate to go completely around something, such as the world

Where in the world?

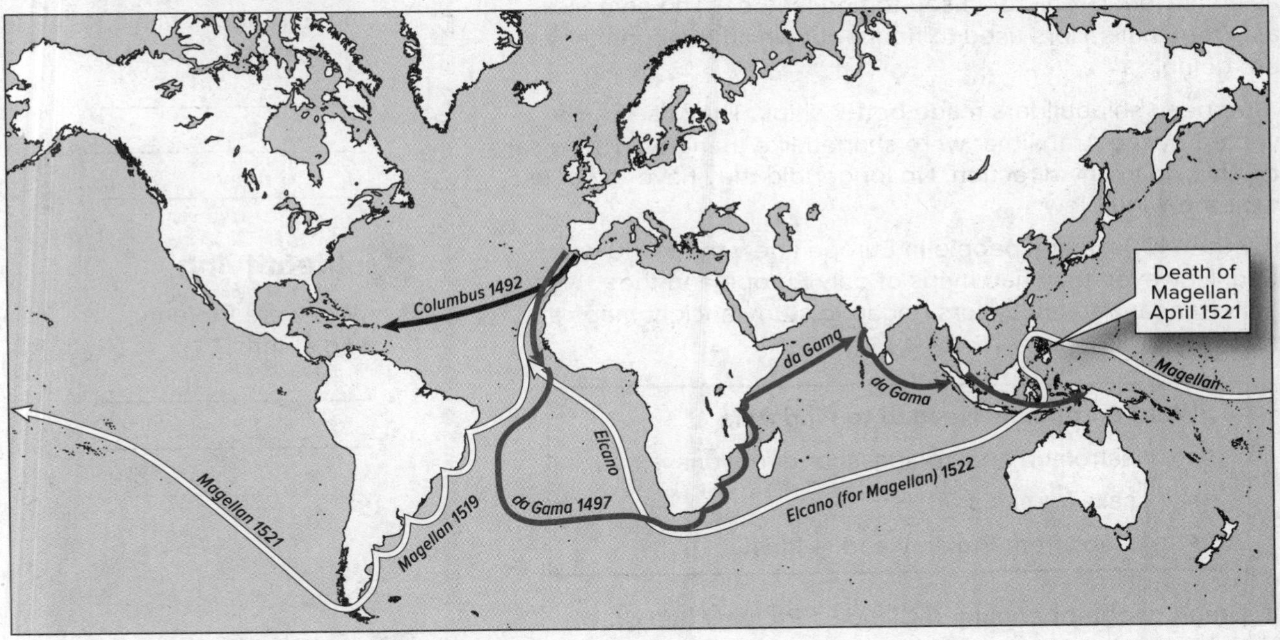

When did it happen?

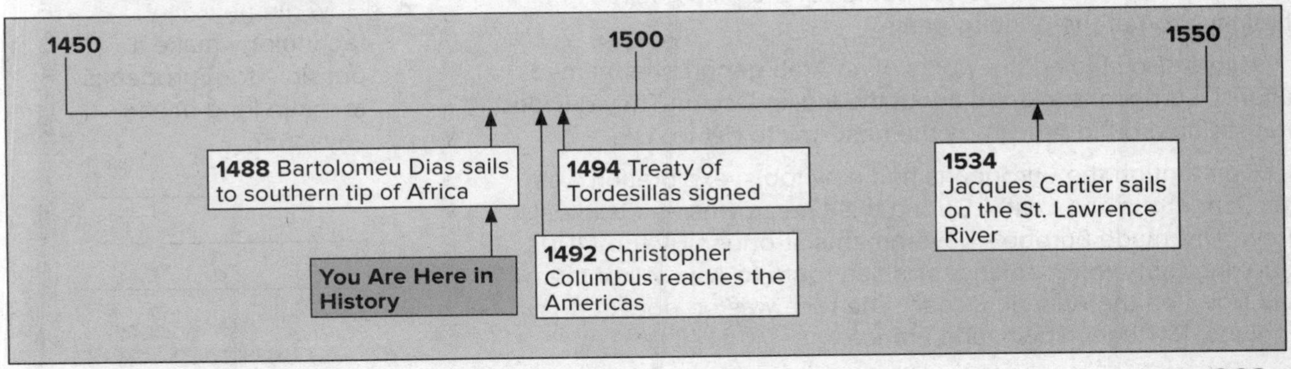

Europe Gets Ready to Explore

In the 1400s and 1500s, countries in Western Europe began exploring the world. They wanted spices, silk, and other goods from Asia.

Political change in the countries between Europe and Asia made it more difficult and expensive to trade goods by land. If European traders could not get there by land, maybe they could get there by sea. Their ships, however, were not equipped to travel the Atlantic Ocean.

By the 1400s, they had the tools they needed. From the Arabs, they learned about the astrolabe and the compass. The astrolabe was an ancient Greek tool used to find latitude. The compass was a tool that sailors used to figure out which direction they were going.

European shipbuilders made better ships. They used sails invented by the Arabs that were shaped like triangles. These sails let a ship go in any direction. No longer did they have to go just where the wind blew.

By the 1400s, many people in Europe knew the world was round. However, they had maps of only Europe and the Mediterranean region. Sailors began to study ancient maps and books.

What Europeans Needed to Find Asia

- astrolabe and compass for directions
- sails for ships
- maps from Ptolemy and al-Idrisi

A Greek geographer named Claudius Ptolemy had drawn maps of the world. He wrote down the latitude and longitude of over 8,000 places. Europeans began studying his maps. Sailors and explorers were able to get copies of the maps because of the invention of the printing press.

Sailors also studied the works of an Arab geographer named al-Idrisi. Europeans learned about the Indian Ocean. They decided that sailing around Africa was the best way to get to Asia.

Even though the Europeans had new tools, exploration was still dangerous and costly. During this time, towns and trade also grew. This made Europe's governments stronger. By the 1400s, four kingdoms were looking for a sea route to Asia. All of them had ports on the Atlantic Ocean. The race was on between England, Portugal, Spain, and France.

Marking the Text

1. Underline the reason Europeans decided to sail to Asia.

Describing

2. What improvements did Europeans make to their ships?

____

____

____

Identifying

3. Who were Ptolemy and al-Idrisi?

____

____

____

Reading Check

4. How did new technology make it possible for Europeans to make long ocean voyages?

____

____

____

FOLDABLES®

Describing

5. Place a two-tab Foldable along the dotted line to cover the text *Early Voyages of Discovery*. Cut the tabs in half to form four tabs. Title the anchor tab *Explorers*. Label the four tabs *Portugal*, *Spain*, *England*, and *France*.

Identify the explorers of each country and briefly describe their travels in the new world.

Drawing Conclusions

6. Why was Portugal able to begin exploring before other countries?

____

____

____

Marking the Text

7. Circle the names of explorers who came to the Americas.

Glue Foldable here

Early Voyages of Discovery

In the early 1400s, England and France were still fighting each other, and Spain was battling the Muslims. Portugal was free to lead the way to explore new trade routes to Asia. Prince Henry of Portugal paid for many voyages of exploration. About 1420, his sailors traveled along Africa's west coast. They made maps of what they found.

In 1488 Bartolomeu Dias reached the southern tip of Africa. Nine years later, Vasco da Gama rounded the tip of Africa. He raced across the Indian Ocean to the southwest coast of India. He had found a water route to East Asia.

An Italian navigator then came up with a different plan to get to Asia. His name was Christopher Columbus. He decided to sail west, not east, across the Atlantic Ocean.

Columbus had three ships: the *Santa María*, the *Niña*, and the *Pinta*. They left Spain in 1492 and headed west. After many weeks, they finally saw land. Columbus thought he was in Asia. He did not realize he was in the Americas.

He made several more trips. He brought **conquistadors,** or Spanish soldier-explorers, with him to conquer the people of the new lands. Europeans eventually realized they had found new continents.

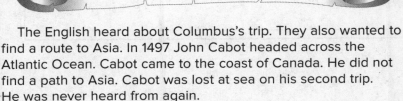

Major explorers:

- Bartolomeu Dias
- Vasco da Gama
- Christopher Columbus
- Ferdinand Magellan
- John Cabot
- Giovanni da Verrazano

The English heard about Columbus's trip. They also wanted to find a route to Asia. In 1497 John Cabot headed across the Atlantic Ocean. Cabot came to the coast of Canada. He did not find a path to Asia. Cabot was lost at sea on his second trip. He was never heard from again.

In 1520 Ferdinand Magellan sailed south along the coast of South America. He found a way around the continent. He then went west. His sailors almost starved. After four months at sea, they reached the present-day Philippines. There, Magellan died in a battle between local groups. His crew then went west across the Indian Ocean. They went around Africa and back to Spain. They were the first known people to **circumnavigate,** or sail around, the world.

In 1524 France sent Giovanni da Verrazano to find a northern route to Asia. He drew maps of the east coast of America, but he did not find a way to Asia. Ten years later, Jacques Cartier entered the St. Lawrence River. He claimed much of eastern Canada for France.

After these early trips, France stopped exploring for a time. By the mid-1500s, France and England were involved in religious conflicts and civil wars. It wasn't until the early 1600s that these countries begain exploring again. Spain and Portugal had territories in South America, Mexico, and the Caribbean. So France and England began to establish their colonies in North America.

Check for Understanding

List five things Europeans needed to find a new route to Asia.

1. ____________________

2. ____________________

3. ____________________

4. ____________________

5. ____________________

List two explorers who reached Asia from different directions.

6. ____________________

7. ____________________

Glue Foldable here

Defining

8. What does it mean to circumnavigate something?

____

____

Reading Check

9. Why was it important for the explorers of the Americas to use information they learned from earlier explorers?

____

____

____

FOLDABLES®

10. Place a two-tab Foldable along the dotted line. Title the anchor tab *Technology & Exploration.* Label the two tabs *Advances in Ships and Sailing* and *Explorers Try to Reach Asia.*

On both sides of the tabs, write five or more words that you remember about technology and exploration.

NAME ________________________________ DATE ____________ CLASS ________

networks

Age of Exploration and Trade

Lesson 2 Spain's Conquests in the Americas

ESSENTIAL QUESTION

Why do civilizations rise and fall?

GUIDING QUESTIONS

1. ***How did Spain conquer Mexico?***
2. ***How did Spanish conquistadors conquer the Inca?***

Terms to Know

allies those who support each other as helpers for a common purpose

smallpox a disease that causes a high fever and often death

ambush a surprise attack

hostage someone held against his or her will in exchange for something

When did it happen?

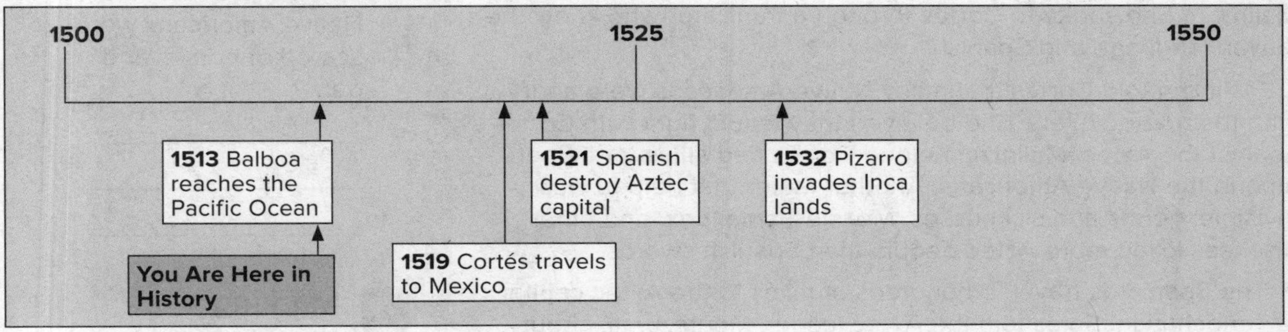

1500
1525
1550
1513 Balboa reaches the Pacific Ocean
You Are Here in History
1519 Cortés travels to Mexico
1521 Spanish destroy Aztec capital
1532 Pizarro invades Inca lands

What do you know?

Read each statement. Circle T if you think the statement is true. Circle F if you think the statement is false.

T F **1.** Native Americans had small, disorganized civilizations.

T F **2.** The Spanish used armies to fight a war against the Aztec.

T F **3.** The Native Americans were nearly wiped out by diseases.

T F **4.** The Inca conquered the Spanish.

T F **5.** Spain eventually controlled most of South America.

T F **6.** The Aztec were able to overthrow the Spanish.

The Spanish Conquer Mexico

Poor Spanish nobles such as 19-year-old Hernán Cortés were inspired by Christopher Columbus. They wanted to become conquistadors and travel to the Americas to search for riches. By 1519 Cortés was in Mexico and hoping to find gold.

He brought about 500 soldiers, 16 horses, 14 cannons, and a few dogs. How could such a small number of soldiers conquer the huge Aztec Empire that ruled most of Mexico? Cortés used his horses and guns to scare Native Americans. He forced thousands of them to surrender.

He also found another weapon. It was a Maya woman named Malintzin. She spoke to Cortés through a translator who knew the Mayan language and Spanish.

Malintzin told Cortés that many Native Americans were angry with their Aztec rulers. She believed they would fight with Cortés against the Aztec. Malintzin helped Cortés find **allies,** or helpers, among the Native Americans. Another factor that helped was invisible: germs and sicknesses. Measles, **smallpox,** and other diseases killed more Aztec people than Spanish swords.

The Spaniards traveled hundreds of miles to the Aztec capital of Tenochtitlán. Spies told the Aztec leader, Montezuma, about the Spaniards' every move. The Aztec believed in a god named Quetzalcoatl. According to legend, this god with light skin had sailed away long ago. He promised to come back someday to take back his land. Montezuma was afraid that Cortés was this god coming home. So Montezuma did not want to attack the Spanish right away.

As Cortés marched closer, Montezuma decided to attack the troops. Cortés heard about the planned **ambush.**

How Cortés Defeated the Aztec:

1. He had guns and horses.
2. He had other Native American allies.
3. He attacked first.
4. Disease weakened the Aztec.

Identifying

1. Who was the Maya who helped Cortés?

____

____

Making Connections

2. Why do you think the Native Americans were scared of horses and guns?

____

____

____

Marking the Text

3. Underline the cause of death for most of the Aztec people.

Drawing Conclusions

4. How was Cortés able to defeat the Aztec?

____

____

____

____

Lesson 2 Spain's Conquests in the Americas, *Continued*

Reading Check

5. Why did the Aztec allow Cortés to remain in their lands?

Marking the Text

6. Circle the names of the Spanish conquerors who tried to find gold in Peru.

Identifying

7. What empire did Pizarro want to find?

Analyzing

8. Why was Pizarro able to seize Atahualpa so easily?

In November 1519, the soldiers marched into the Aztec capital. They took control of the city. Cortés took Montezuma **hostage**, or prisoner. He then told the Aztec to stop sacrificing people.

Cortés made the Aztec people angry. They fought back. The Spanish killed thousands of Aztec. However, there were more Aztec than Spanish soldiers. The Spanish had to fight their way out of the city. They moved into the hills with their allies.

Cortés got ready for a second attack. Smallpox broke out in the city. Many Aztec died and the rest were weak. They were no match for Cortés. In June 1521, the Spanish destroyed the Aztec capital.

Spain Conquers Peru

In 1513 Vasco Núñez de Balboa led his soldiers across the mountains of present-day Panama. He was looking for a great empire filled with gold.

Balboa found a sea, known today as the Pacific Ocean, but he never found the golden empire. Francisco Pizarro was one of Balboa's soldiers.

The empire that Pizzaro wanted to find was the Inca Empire. By the 1530s, the Inca Empire had become weak. Even so, the Inca were not afraid of Pizarro. Pizarro had only 168 soldiers, one cannon, and 27 horses compared to the Inca's 30,000 warriors. Pizarro, too, was unafraid.

Spanish Explorer	Land Explored	People Conquered
Cortés	Mexico	Aztec
Balboa	Panama	None
Pizzaro	Peru	Inca

In late 1532, Pizarro made a bold plan. The Spanish invited the Inca ruler, Atahualpa, to a meeting. He agreed to come. However, he made the mistake of not bringing his army of 80,000 men. He thought his 4,000 guards would keep him safe. He also thought they would not need any weapons.

When they met, Pizarro demanded that the emperor give up his gods. When Atahualpa laughed at this, Pizarro ordered an attack. The Spanish fired into the unarmed Inca crowd. Pizarro then took Atahualpa captive.

Lesson 2 Spain's Conquests in the Americas, *Continued*

Atahualpa tried to buy his freedom. He said he would give Pizarro an entire room full of gold and silver. Pizarro accepted the offer but refused to release Atahualpa. He charged the emperor with many crimes. These crimes included planning a rebellion and worshiping false gods.

In 1533 a military court found the emperor guilty. Atahualpa was sentenced to death. As a reward, the Spanish king made Pizarro the governor of Peru. Pizarro chose a new emperor of the Inca. The new emperor had to obey Pizarro. Still, the Spanish could not completely control the Inca Empire.

Pizarro Conquers the Inca

Pizarro reaches the lands of the Inca Empire, but his small force is ignored.
↓
Pizarro meets with Inca emperor Atahualpa and takes him hostage.
↓
Pizarro puts Atahualpa on trial. Atahualpa is executed.
↓
Pizarro becomes governor of Peru and appoints a new Inca emperor who must obey him.

Even after Pizarro died, Inca rebels continued to fight the Spanish. However, the conquest of Peru allowed Spanish rule to move into much of South America.

Check for Understanding

List two actions of Cortés when he invaded Mexico.

1. ______________________

2. ______________________

List two ways Cortés and Pizarro were similar.

3. ______________________

4. ______________________

Glue Foldable here

Listing

9. Name two events that caused the Inca to fall from power.

____

____

Reading Check

10. How successful were the efforts of Atahualpa to free himself from Pizarro?

____

____

____

FOLDABLES®

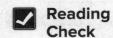

11. Place a two-tab Foldable along the dotted line to cover the Check for Understanding. Title the anchor tab *Spanish Conquests*. Label the top tab *Aztec* and the bottom tab *Inca*.

Use both sides to record what you remember about how Spanish conquests affected the Aztec and Inca.

NAME ______________________ DATE ____________ CLASS ________

networks

Age of Exploration and Trade

Lesson 3 Exploration and Worldwide Trade

ESSENTIAL QUESTION

Why do people make economic choices?

GUIDING QUESTIONS

1. ***How did European nations build empires in the Americas?***
2. ***How did Europe's merchants change the world trade system?***
3. ***How did trade change the world?***

Terms to Know

plantation a large estate or farm that used enslaved people or hired workers to grow and harvest crops

cash crops fruits and vegetables grown in large amounts to be sold for profit

mercantilism an economic system that depends on a greater amount of exports than imports

commerce exchange of goods; business

entrepreneur a person who organizes, pays for, and takes the risk of starting a new business

cottage industry a system for making goods in workers' homes

When did it happen?

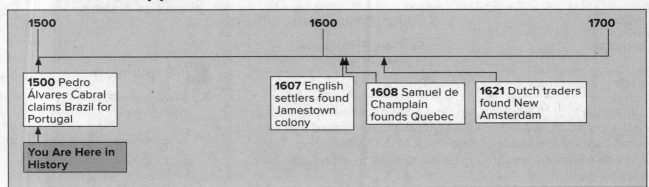

1500 | **1600** | **1700**

- **1500** Pedro Álvares Cabral claims Brazil for Portugal
  - **You Are Here in History**
- **1607** English settlers found Jamestown colony
- **1608** Samuel de Champlain founds Quebec
- **1621** Dutch traders found New Amsterdam

What do you know?

Read the list of foods and animals. Write *Europe* if you think it first came from Europe. Write *Americas* if you think it first came from the Americas.

Cows	________	Coffee	________
Peanuts	________	Wheat	________
Corn	________	Chocolate	________
Horses	________	Squash	________
Potatoes	________	Sheep	________

Lesson 3 Exploration and Worldwide Trade, *Continued*

Settling the Americas

By the 1600s, Spanish settlers were growing sugarcane on large farms called **plantations.** At first, Native Americans did all the work. Then disease and mistreatment caused most of them to die. Spain brought enslaved Africans to work on the plantations and in the gold and silver mines. The Portuguese also used enslaved Africans to do their hard work in Brazil.

The French came to North America to set up fur trading posts. French merchants hired explorer Samuel de Champlain in 1608 to help them get furs. He set up a trading post named Quebec. It became the capital of the colony of New France.

Crops/Goods/Services	Colony
fur	French
tobacco	English, Portuguese
sugarcane	Spanish, Portuguese, French
trade	Dutch

In 1682 a French explorer named La Salle followed the Mississippi all the way to the Gulf of Mexico. He named the region Louisiana in honor of King Louis XIV. The French in southern Louisiana brought enslaved Africans to grow sugarcane, rice, and tobacco.

During the 1600s, the English came to North America for many reasons. Some people wanted to make money. Others wanted religious freedom. Others came because they did not have a job and needed work. England's colonies grew quickly.

The Virginia Company established the first English settlement in North America in 1607. It was called Jamestown after King James I. Life in Virginia was very hard. There was not enough to eat. Some people died in the cold winters. Others were killed in fights with the Native Americans.

During those first years, the colony made no money. Settlers discovered that tobacco grew well in Virginia's soil. Tobacco became the first cash crop of the English colonies. A **cash crop** is grown in large amounts to sell and make money.

Defining

1. What is a *plantation*?

____

____

Marking the Text

2. Underline the name of the first English colony in North America. Circle the name of France's first territory in North America.

Explaining

3. Why was life hard in the Virginia colony?

____

____

____

Reading Check

4. Why did European colonists bring enslaved Africans to their plantations in the Americas?

____

____

____

Defining

5. What is *commerce*?

______

______

Explaining

6. Why do entrepreneurs need plenty of money to trade over long distances?

______

______

______

Reading Check

7. Why did Europeans in the 1600s create joint-stock companies?

______

______

______

Describing

8. How do people work in a cottage industry?

______

______

______

Another European country, the Netherlands, wanted to explore North America. Henry Hudson sailed up the Hudson River and claimed land for the Dutch. In 1621 Dutch traders established a settlement called New Amsterdam. Today it is part of New York City.

World Trade Changes

Europeans came up with the idea of **mercantilism.** This is a theory that a country's power depends on its wealth. Countries can increase their wealth by owning more gold and silver.

Rules of Mercantilism

Power comes from having gold and silver.

↓

Export more goods than you import.

↓

Keep more gold and silver in country.

↓

Set up colonies.

↓

Colonies provide raw materials that are not found in home country.

In addition to their colonies in North America, Europeans set up trading posts and colonies in Asia. In the 1600s, Europeans started doing business a new way, called the Commercial Revolution. **Commerce** is the buying and selling of goods in large amounts over long distances.

Merchants needed a lot of money to trade goods far away. They had to buy and store a large amount of goods and ship them over land and sea. This new business created **entrepreneurs.** Entrepreneurs invest, or put money, into a business. Their goal is to make money.

Many projects were so large that a group of entrepreneurs had to work together. They would form a joint-stock company. This is a business that many people can invest in by buying shares, or stocks, of the company. By owning stocks, investors share the expenses, the risks, and the profits.

Some merchants believed that artisans charged too much for their goods and took too long to make them. They created the **cottage industry.** This is when merchants hire people who work from their homes.

Lesson 3 Exploration and Worldwide Trade, *Continued*

A Global Exchange

Europe, Africa, Asia, and the Americas changed through trading. The world traded people, goods, tools, ideas, and even diseases. This is called the Columbian Exchange, after Christopher Columbus.

Corn and potatoes came to Europe from the Americas. Corn was fed to animals. The same amount of land could produce more potatoes than wheat. This fed more people. Tomatoes from America became popular in Italy. Chocolate came from Central America. European and Asian grains such as wheat, oats, barley, rye, and rice were planted in the Americas. Coffee and fruits were brought there, too.

The Americas	Europe
• corn, potatoes, squash, beans, tomatoes • chocolate, chili peppers, peanuts	• wheat, oats, barley, rye, rice • horses, cattle, pigs, sheep, chickens • coffee

Animals were brought from Europe. Chickens changed the diet of people in the Americas. Horses allowed Native Americans to hunt buffalo more efficiently.

Europeans took sugarcane from Asia and began growing it in the Caribbean. They moved millions of enslaved Africans to the Americas to plant and harvest the sugarcane. Not everything that passed between Europe and America was good. Europeans gave germs to the Native Americans. Some diseases were deadly and killed millions of people.

/ / / / / / / / / / / / / / Glue Foldable here / / / / / / / / / / / / / /

Check for Understanding

List two things that came from the Americas in the Columbian Exchange.

1. ______________

2. ______________

List two goods that came from Europe in the Columbian Exchange.

3. ______________

4. ______________

Identifying

9. List the continents that were involved in the Columbian Exchange.

1. ______________
2. ______________
3. ______________
4. ______________

Reading Check

10. Was the Columbian Exchange a benefit or a problem for the Americas?

____

____

FOLDABLES®

11. Place a one-tab Foldable along the dotted line. Title the anchor tab *World of Exchange*.

List key words and phrases to explain how the movement of people and goods changed the world.

NAME_______________________________ DATE _____________ CLASS ________

networks

The Scientific Revolution and the Enlightenment

Lesson 1 The Scientific Revolution

ESSENTIAL QUESTION

How do new ideas change the way people live?

GUIDING QUESTIONS

1. ***How were the scientific ideas of early thinkers passed on to later generations?***
2. ***Why did European ideas about the universe change during the 1500s and 1600s?***
3. ***Which discoveries did scientists make during the 1600s and 1700s?***
4. ***How did Europeans of the 1600s and 1700s develop new ways of gaining knowledge?***

Terms to Know

geocentric an earth-centered theory; having or relating to the earth as the center

Scientific Revolution a period from the 1500s to the 1700s in which many scientific advances changed people's traditional beliefs about science

heliocentric having or relating to the sun as the center

ellipses shapes like stretched circles; ovals

gravity the attraction that the Earth or another celestial body has on an object on or near its surface

elements substances that consist of atoms of only one kind

rationalism the belief that reason and experience must be present for the solution of problems

scientific method the steps for an orderly search for knowledge

Where in the world?

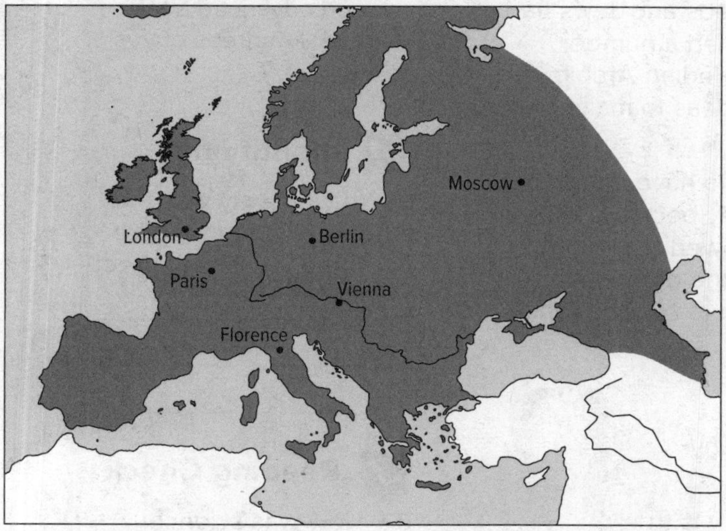

When did it happen?

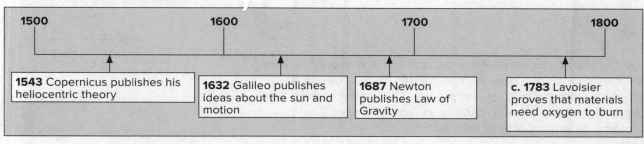

1500 — 1600 — 1700 — 1800

1543 Copernicus publishes his heliocentric theory

1632 Galileo publishes ideas about the sun and motion

1687 Newton publishes Law of Gravity

c. 1783 Lavoisier proves that materials need oxygen to burn

Lesson 1 The Scientific Revolution, *Continued*

Glue Foldable here

Early Science

Science is any organized study of the natural world. During ancient times, people used science to solve problems. For example, they used mathematics to keep records.

The ancient Greeks used reason to learn about nature. They also used common sense. As they studied the world, they developed theories, or ideas about how and why things worked. However, a theory is not always correct. It must be proven many times. The Greeks did not use experiments to test their theories. As a result, many of their theories were wrong. For example, Ptolemy said that the sun and the planets move around the Earth. People believed this **geocentric,** or Earth-centered, theory for 1,400 years.

During the Middle Ages, most Europeans were interested in religion. Not many people wanted to learn about nature. They did not think they needed to do research. They relied on copies of old writings that sometimes contained errors.

Outside of Europe, in the Islamic Empire, Arabs and Jews had saved much Greek knowledge. They also learned a number system used in India. This system is called the Indian-Arabic system. Also, Arabs and Jews built on Greek ideas to make their own advances in science.

During the 1100s, thinkers in Europe began to have more contact with the world of Islam. As a result, they became interested in science again. Some thinkers showed that Christianity and reason could work together. One of these thinkers was Thomas Aquinas. Students began to study science. They did this at schools called universities.

theory an explanation of how or why something happens

experiment a test to see if a theory is true

research the collection of information on a certain subject

In the 1400s, people started to explore the world. Because of this, Europeans were able to make better maps. These maps helped explorers reach far-away lands. They brought back new information about oceans, continents, animals, plants, and diseases. Scientists organized it all.

FOLDABLES®

Describing

1. Place a three-tab Foldable along the dotted line to cover the text titled *Early Science*. Label the three tabs *Advancements*, *Losses*, and *Advancements*.

Use both sides of the tabs to explain how the study of science advanced, lost ground, and advanced again over hundreds of years.

Identifying

2. In what way was the geocentric theory of the universe incorrect?

____

____

____

Reading Check

3. How was science practiced in ancient and medieval times?

____

____

____

Visualizing

4. Below, draw the sun and the elliptical path of a planet around it.

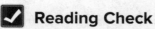

Reading Check

5. How did Galileo go about making scientific discoveries?

____

____

____

Identifying

6. What scientific contribution did Robert Hooke make?

____

____

____

New Ideas About the Universe

In the 1500s, scientists in Europe began to experiment and started the **Scientific Revolution.** The Scientific Revolution changed how Europeans understood science.

Astronomy is the study of planets, stars, and other bodies in space. Astronomer Nicolaus Copernicus disagreed with Ptolemy's theory. Copernicus believed that the Earth and other planets moved around the sun. This sun-centered view is called **heliocentric.**

Johannes Kepler corrected some of the findings of Copernicus. Kepler said that the planets move in oval paths. Such paths are called **ellipses.**

Galileo Galilei believed that conducting experiments was the correct way to achieve scientific knowledge. He developed a telescope that allowed him to find evidence that supported the heliocentric view. He also proved that all objects fall to the ground at the same speed.

Contributions in Astronomy	
Nicolaus Copernicus	• Stated that the Earth and other planets move around the sun
Johannes Kepler	• Stated that planets move in ellipses
Galileo Galilei	• Used telescope to support the heliocentric view of the universe

New Scientific Advances

Isaac Newton figured out some scientific laws. In science, laws are well-tested theories. Newton came up with the law of **gravity.** Gravity is the pull of the Earth and other bodies in space on objects that are on or near them.

Andreas Vesalius studied how the human body works by dissecting, or cutting open, dead bodies. His findings replaced many wrong ideas about the human body.

Robert Hooke began to use a microscope. A microscope makes large images of small objects. Hooke discovered cells, which are the smallest units of living matter.

Antonie van Leeuwenhoek improved the microscope by adding more powerful lenses. He became the first person to see bacteria. Bacteria are tiny living organisms.

Lesson 1 The Scientific Revolution, *Continued*

Robert Boyle proved that matter is made up of **elements.** An element is a basic material that cannot be broken down into simpler parts.

In the 1700s, scientists in Europe discovered gases, such as oxygen and hydrogen. French scientist Antoine Lavoisier showed that materials need oxygen to burn.

The Triumph of Reason

René Descartes studied the problem of knowing what is true. He used mathematics and reason to search for truth. In mathematics, the answers are always true. Descartes' ideas became known as **rationalism.** This is the belief that reason is the source of learning.

Blaise Pascal thought that reason and science could be used to solve problems in everyday life. Yet, he thought that Christianity must be used to find spiritual truth.

Francis Bacon came up with the **scientific method.** This method is an orderly way to collect and study facts.

Steps of the Scientific Method

- **Observation:** The scientist collects facts by studying an aspect of the world.
- **Hypothesis:** The scientist explains these facts with a theory.
- **Prediction:** The scientist makes a prediction.
- **Experiment:** The scientist does experiments to prove that the theory is true.
- **Theory:** If the theory seems true, the scientist develops it into scientific law.

Check for Understanding

Name two important astronomers during the Scientific Revolution.

1. ______________________

2. ______________________

List two advances made during the Scientific Revolution that are still taught today.

3. ______________________

4. ______________________

Glue Foldable here

Reading Check

7. According to Newton, how are the planets held in orbit?

____

Reading Check

8. Why did Descartes believe that mathematics is the source of scientific truth?

____

FOLDABLES®

9. Place a three-tab Foldable to cover the Check for Understanding. Write *Scientific Revolution* on the anchor tab. Label the three tabs *1500s*, *1600s*, and *1700s*.

Use both sides of the tabs to record information you remember about the Scientific Revolution during these centuries.

NAME ______________________________ DATE ____________ CLASS ________

networks

The Scientific Revolution and the Enlightenment

Lesson 2 The Enlightenment

ESSENTIAL QUESTION

How do governments change?

GUIDING QUESTIONS

1. ***How did European thinkers apply scientific ideas to government?***
2. ***How did French thinkers influence Europe during the Enlightenment?***
3. ***How did European monarchs model their countries on Enlightenment ideas?***

Terms to Know

Age of Enlightenment a period of time in which a European philosophical movement developed, based on reason and experience rather than on traditional thinking

absolutism a political system in which a ruler has total power

social contract an agreement between the people and their government

Glorious Revolution the overthrow of King James II of England

constitutional monarchy a political system in which a king or queen rules according to a constitution

separation of powers a government structure that has three distinct branches: legislative, executive, and judicial

When did it happen?

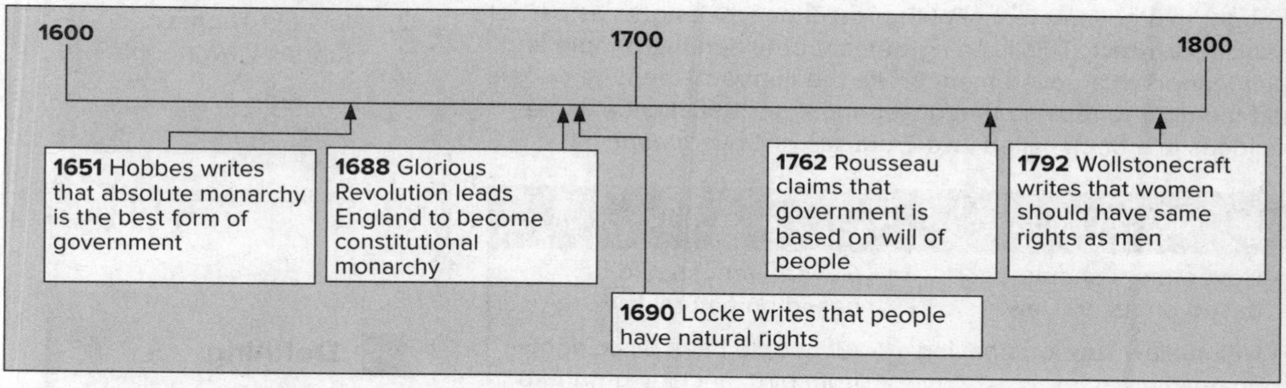

1600
1700
1800
1651 Hobbes writes that absolute monarchy is the best form of government
1688 Glorious Revolution leads England to become constitutional monarchy
1690 Locke writes that people have natural rights
1762 Rousseau claims that government is based on will of people
1792 Wollstonecraft writes that women should have same rights as men

What do you know?

In the K column, list what you already know about the Enlightenment. In the W column, list what you want to know. After reading the lesson, fill in the L column with the information that you learned.

K	W	L

Lesson 2 The Enlightenment, *Continued*

Reason and Politics

The Scientific Revolution used reason to solve problems. During the 1700s, educated Europeans saw reason as a "light" that could reveal truth. As a result, this time period became known as the **Age of Enlightenment.**

Some thinkers used reason to improve government. They claimed that government should be based on natural law. This is a body of law that applies to everyone.

The English thinker Thomas Hobbes wrote *Leviathan* in 1651. In this book, he argued that people were naturally violent and selfish. Hobbes believed that natural law meant people needed strong rulers to tell them what to do. His theory became known as **absolutism,** since it called for a ruler with absolute, or total, power.

John Locke was another English thinker. He believed that natural law gave all people basic rights from birth. These included the right to life, liberty, and to own property. Locke thought that government should protect people's rights as part of a **social contract.** This is an agreement between the people and their leaders. If a government broke the contract, then the people had the right to replace that government. In 1690, Locke wrote his ideas in a book called *Two Treatises of Government.*

Ideas of Hobbes	Ideas of Locke
• Government should be based on natural law. • Natural law supports having an absolute ruler. • People by themselves cannot make good decisions. • People need to obey a wise, powerful ruler.	• Government should be based on natural law. • All people have basic rights from birth, including right to life and liberty. • Government should protect people's rights. • If government fails to protect these rights, it can be replaced.

In the late 1600s, King James II of England wanted to be a total ruler. He left the country when civil war threatened. Parliament replaced him with a new king and queen. This event became known as the **Glorious Revolution.** The new rulers, William and Mary, agreed to a Bill of Rights. They made England a **constitutional monarchy,** a form of government in which laws limit the power of the ruler.

Determining Cause and Effect

1. What effect did the Scientific Revolution have on thinkers during the 1700s?

____

____

____

Explaining

2. How did Thomas Hobbes view people?

____

____

____

Defining

3. What is a *constitutional monarchy*?

____

____

____

Reading Check

4. How did Hobbes and Locke differ in their ideas about government and the people?

____

____

____

Summarizing

5. Who were the philosophes and what did they believe?

____

____

____

Identifying

6. Who wrote *A Vindication of the Rights of Woman*?

____

____

Reading Check

7. What was Diderot's *Encyclopedia*?

____

____

____

In France, Baron Montesquieu wrote a book called *The Spirit of the Laws*. Montesquieu said England had the best government because it had a **separation of powers.** Separation of powers means that the government's power should be divided into three equal branches.

- Legislative branch—makes laws
- Executive branch—puts the laws into effect
- Judicial branch—interprets the laws

Separating these powers stops any one part of government from getting too powerful.

The Philosophes of France

During the 1700s, France became the center of the Enlightenment. Thinkers in France and elsewhere were called philosophes. *Philosophe* is a French word that means "philosopher." A philosopher is a person who searches for wisdom. Philosophes wanted to use reason to improve society. They supported science and freedom of speech. Their ideas spread across Europe.

The Philosophes	
Voltaire	• Wrote plays, novels, and essays • Supported freedom of religion • Supported deism, a religious belief based on reason
Denis Diderot	• Wanted to spread Enlightenment ideas • Created a 28-volume encyclopedia, which covered religion, government, the sciences, history, and the arts
Mary Wollstonecraft	• Wrote *A Vindication of the Rights of Woman* • Believed that women should have the same rights as men • Started the modern effort for equal rights for women
Jean-Jacques Rousseau	• Wrote *The Social Contract* • Believed that government comes from what the people want

Absolute Monarchs

In the 1600s and 1700s, some kings and queens liked Enlightenment ideas. They used these ideas to improve their societies. Yet, they refused to give up any power.

In 1643 Louis XIV became the king of France. Known as the Sun King, he fought wars that gained land for France. However, the great cost of fighting weakened his country.

Other Enlightenment rulers supported a variety of reforms inspired by Enlightenment ideas.

Country	Absolute Monarch	Enlightenment Ideas
Prussia	Frederick the Great	• Dedicated himself to the good of his people • Allowed some freedom of speech and religion
Austria	Maria Theresa	• Set up schools • Tried to make the lives of serfs better
Austria	Joseph II	• Freed the serfs • Tried to reform taxes
Russia	Peter the Great	• Made reforms to government and military
Russia	Catherine the Great	• Supported some Enlightenment ideas • Considered freeing the serfs

Glue Foldable here

Check for Understanding

Name two ways the Enlightenment changed the government of England.

1. ______________________

2. ______________________

List two ways absolute monarchs responded to the Enlightenment.

3. ______________________

4. ______________________

? Comparing

8. How were the reforms of Maria Theresa similar to the reforms of Joseph II?

____

____

____

Reading Check

9. How was Frederick the Great influenced by the Enlightenment?

____

____

____

FOLDABLES®

10. Place a one-tab Foldable along the dotted line to cover the Check for Understanding. Write *The Enlightenment* on the anchor tab.

Use both sides of the tab to list words and phrases you remember about how governments changed during the Enlightenment.

NAME _______________ DATE _______________ CLASS _______________

networks

Political and Industrial Revolutions

Lesson 1 The American Revolution

ESSENTIAL QUESTION

Why does conflict develop?

GUIDING QUESTIONS

1. ***Why did England found colonies in North America?***
2. ***How did conflict develop between Britain and its American colonies?***
3. ***How did war between Britain and the American colonies lead to the rise of a new nation—the United States of America?***

Terms to Know

persecute to treat a group of people cruelly or unfairly

constitution a document that describes how a country will be governed and guarantees people certain rights

boycott to protest by refusing to do something

popular sovereignty the idea that government is created by the people and must do what the people request

limited government a government whose powers are limited by laws or a document such as a constitution

Where in the world?

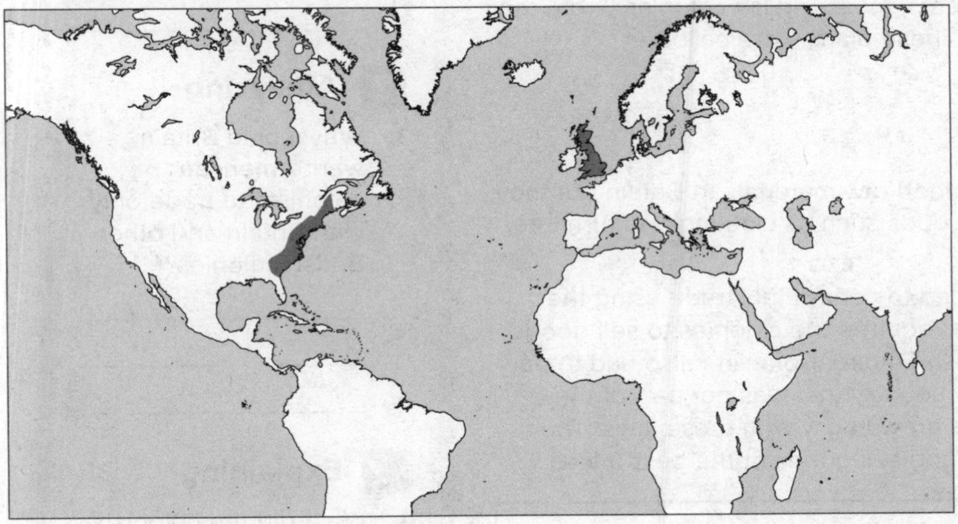

When did it happen?

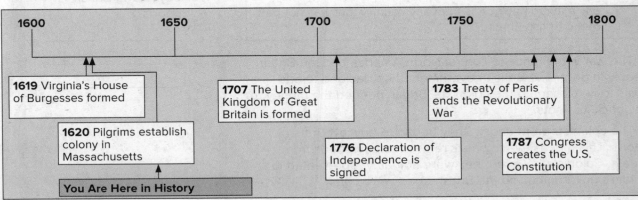

1600 | 1650 | 1700 | 1750 | 1800

1619 Virginia's House of Burgesses formed

1620 Pilgrims establish colony in Massachusetts

You Are Here in History

1707 The United Kingdom of Great Britain is formed

1776 Declaration of Independence is signed

1783 Treaty of Paris ends the Revolutionary War

1787 Congress creates the U.S. Constitution

Britain's American Colonies

Puritans set up English colonies in North America. In England, the Puritans were **persecuted,** or punished for practicing their religion. Puritans, known as Pilgrims, came to America and built the Plymouth settlement. Other Puritans, founded the Massachusetts Bay Colono. Non-Puritans looking for religious freedom, including the Quakers, came later.

The English settled thirteen colonies in North America. The southern colonies had large plantations. They used enslaved Africans to work the land. The northern colonies had smaller farms because of the cooler climate and rocky soil.

The early colonies set up rules to govern their people. The Pilgrims wrote the Mayflower Compact to govern Plymouth in Massachusetts. Settlers in Virginia elected a group of leaders to run their colony. Over the years, most English colonies wrote their own plans for government. These plans were called **constitutions.**

Road to Revolt

The American colonies provided raw materials to Britain but they also bought manufactured goods such as clothing and furniture from the country.

For many years, Britain tried to control this trade using the Navigation Acts. These laws required the colonies to sell goods only to members of the British Empire. Colonists also had to pay a tax to buy goods from any country that was not part of the British Empire. The colonists grew angry with these laws. They wanted the freedom to buy and sell goods at the best prices.

The Navigation Acts required colonists to:

- sell goods only to members of the British Empire
- pay a tax to buy goods from any country that was not part of the British Empire

The war with France to control North America had left Britain deeply in debt. The British government then decided to add taxes to items sent to the colonists. Britain needed the money to pay back its debts.

The colonists were angry. They began to **boycott** British goods. This means the colonists refused to buy goods from Britain. Colonists believed they were not fairly represented in Britain's government, so the British taxes were unfair.

Defining

1. What is a *constitution*?

____

____

Reading Check

2. What steps did the colonists take to govern themselves?

____

____

____

Analyzing

3. Why would Britain want American colonists to trade only with Britain and other British colonies?

____

____

____

Explaining

4. What did the colonists hope to achieve by boycotting British goods?

____

____

____

Reading Check

5. What were the Intolerable Acts?

____

____

How did the colonists respond to them?

____

____

Identifying

6. What was the First Continental Congress?

____

____

Comparing and Contrasting

7. What advantages did the American army have?

____

____

What advantages did the British army have?

____

____

____

In 1773 Parliament passed the Tea Act. This law said the British East India Company did not have to pay the same tax as the American tea merchants. In protest, some angry colonists dressed as Native Americans dumped a cargo of British tea into Boston Harbor. This event became known as the Boston Tea Party.

The British responded by passing the Intolerable Acts. These laws shut down Boston Harbor, put Massachusetts under military control, and forced colonists to house and feed British soldiers. Leaders from the colonies met in Philadelphia at the First Continental Congress. They discussed how the British laws could be reversed. Some leaders called for independence.

A War for Independence

Tension in the colonies led to a battle at Lexington, Massachusetts, between the British soldiers and the colonists. Congress tried to make peace with the British one last time. When that effort failed, the colonial leaders called for independence. On July 4, 1776, Congress issued the Declaration of Independence. The conflict became a war for independence.

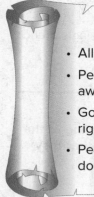

Declaration of Independence

- All men are created equal.
- People have rights that no one can take away.
- Governments must protect people's rights.
- People can overthrow governments that do not protect their rights.

The American army was smaller and less skilled than the British army, but it had a strong leader in General George Washington. The British had the disadvantage of fighting far from home. They did not know the land very well, and they had to conquer the whole country to win.

The colonists' victory at the Battle of Saratoga in 1777 changed the war. That is when the French became convinced the colonists could win and agreed to help the Americans. The British surrendered and two years later the Treaty of Paris ended the war. The United States was born.

Lesson 1 The American Revolution, *Continued*

U.S. leaders wrote a plan of government called the Articles of Confederation. The Articles created a national government, but the states held most power. Over time, the plan proved to be too weak to meet the needs of the new country. In 1787 leaders met to create a stronger plan. The Constitution they wrote is still the law today.

The Constitution included two important ideas. The first idea, **popular sovereignty,** says that government gets its power from the people. The second idea is **limited government.** This means that the government does not have total power. It has only those powers identified in plans such as the Constitution.

The Constitution made the United States a republic led by an elected president. The first president of the United States was the hero of the war, George Washington. Later, a Bill of Rights was added to the Constitution. It guaranteed certain rights to all citizens.

- The United States is a representative government led by a president.
- Some powers belong to state governments. Some powers belong to the national, or federal, government.
- The jobs of government are divided among the executive, legislative, and judicial branches.
- A system of checks and balances makes sure no single branch of government gets too much power.

/ / / / / / / / / / / / / / Glue Foldable here / / / / / / / / / / / / / /

Check for Understanding

Number the following sentences about the settling of the colonies and the forming of the United States so that they are in the correct order.

____ The Pilgrims settle Plymouth Colony.

____ The American colonies win their independence.

____ The U.S. Constitution is written.

____ The Battle of Saratoga is the turning point in the war.

____ Colonial leaders issue the Declaration of Independence.

____ The colonists boycott British goods.

Reading Check

8. What kind of government did the Americans set up after the American Revolution?

____

____

____

____

FOLDABLES®

9. Place a one-tab Foldable along the dotted line. Write *Rise of a New Nation* on the anchor tab. Write *War between Britain and Colonies* along the bottom of the tab and *The United States of America* at the top of the tab. Draw an arrow from the bottom title to the top title.

On the back, write what you remember about the war leading to the rise of a new nation.

NAME ______________________ DATE __________ CLASS ________

networks

Political and Industrial Revolutions

Lesson 2 The French Revolution and Napoleon

ESSENTIAL QUESTION

Why is history important?

GUIDING QUESTIONS

1. *Why did revolution break out in France?*
2. *How did supporters of France's revolution enforce their reforms?*
3. *How was Napoleon able to take over France's government?*
4. *How did Napoleon build and then lose an empire?*

Terms to Know

estate a social class in France before the French Revolution

bourgeoisie the French word for *middle class*

coup d'etat a change of government in which a new group of leaders seizes power by force

Where in the world?

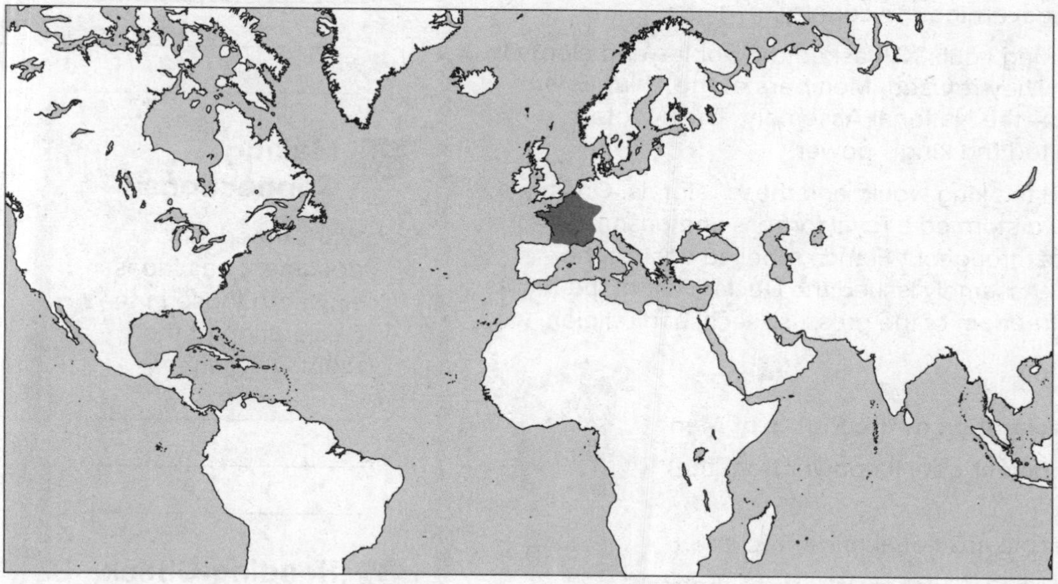

When did it happen?

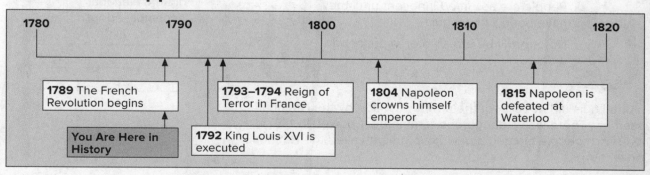

1780 — 1790 — 1800 — 1810 — 1820

1789 The French Revolution begins

You Are Here in History

1792 King Louis XVI is executed

1793–1794 Reign of Terror in France

1804 Napoleon crowns himself emperor

1815 Napoleon is defeated at Waterloo

Lesson 2 The French Revolution and Napoleon, *Continued*

The Revolution Begins

The American Revolution had a great influence on the world. Like the Americans, many French people wanted political changes, including more freedom and equality.

In the 1700s, France was one of the most powerful countries in Europe. Its people were divided into three **estates,** or social classes. The First Estate was clergy and church officials. They made money using church lands. The Second Estate was the nobles. They lived in luxury at the king's court or in country homes. Neither group paid taxes.

Everyone else in France belonged to the Third Estate. Merchants, doctors, and bankers were at the top of this group. They were called the **bourgeoisie,** or middle class. The Third Estate also included city workers and peasants. They paid taxes, but had no voice in governing the country.

During this time, King Louis XVI asked the nobles and clergy to begin paying taxes. They refused. Members of the Third Estate formed a new group—the National Assembly. They wrote a constitution that limited the king's power.

The people feared the king would end these reforms. On July 14, 1789, a large crowd stormed a royal fortress and prison called the Bastille. Peasants throughout France rebelled against the nobles. The National Assembly issued the Declaration of the Rights of Man. It promised freedom of the press, speech, and religion.

Declaration of the Rights of Man

- Government gets its power from the people.
- All people are equal under the law.
- People have freedom of press, speech, and religion.
- People are assumed innocent until they have been proven guilty.
- No one will be arrested or imprisoned unfairly.

King Louis did not accept the new laws made by the National Assembly. There was a dangerous scramble for power. In 1792 the French people elected a new government called the National Convention.

Defining

1. What was an estate? How many estates did France have?

____

____

Contrasting

2. Explain how the Third Estate was different from the other estates.

____

____

____

Making Connections

3. What American document has ideas similar to those in the Declaration of the Rights of Man?

____

____

____

Reading Check

4. What political reforms did the National Assembly adopt?

____

____

____

Explaining

5. How did life change for citizens in France under the Committee for Public Safety?

____

____

____

____

Reading Check

6. What was the Reign of Terror?

____

____

Defining

7. What is a *coup d'etat*?

____

____

____

Reading Check

8. How did Napoleon strengthen his control after becoming First Consul?

____

____

A Republic in France

The National Convention ended the monarchy and made France a republic. In December 1792, the National Convention found King Louis XVI guilty of helping France's enemies. A month later, he was beheaded on the guillotine. The king's death made the citizens of France feel powerful.

A group called the Committee of Public Safety put new reforms in place. It was led by Maximilien Robespierre. The committee opened new schools, taught peasants new farming skills, and worked to control prices.

The committee, however, also punished anyone it thought might be disloyal to the republic. Thousands of people were beheaded for doing or saying things against the government. Because of the fear this created, this time period is called the Reign of Terror. The people of France wanted to end the Reign of Terror. The National Convention removed Robespierre from power and had him executed.

A group of men called the Directory took over the government. The Directory tried to stop food shortages, rising prices, and attacks by other countries. They did not succeed. The French people began to look for a strong leader who could solve their problems.

Napoleon Leads France

Napoleon Bonaparte was a gifted military officer. He rose to the rank of general by the time he was 24 years old. While he was away serving in the French military, Napoleon heard of the weakening government in France. He returned to take part in a **coup d'etat.** This is when new leaders use force to take over the government.

Napoleon was called the First Consul and became a strong leader. He reorganized the government to strengthen his control. He created a new system of laws and made peace with the Catholic Church. However, not all of Napoleon's changes were good for citizens. For example, he put limits on freedom of speech. In 1804 he crowned himself emperor of France. This was the end of the republic governed by the people.

The Creation of an Empire

Napoleon wanted to build a great empire. He fought a series of battles. By 1807, he had nearly reached his goal. As emperor, Napoleon ruled France and parts of Germany and Italy. His relatives governed other lands.

Lesson 2 The French Revolution and Napoleon, *Continued*

The British stopped Napoleon's plans to invade their country at the Battle of Trafalgar. Napoleon next ordered his empire to stop trading with Britain. However, the boycott was hard to enforce and finally ended unsuccessfully.

Napoleon's Empire	
1805	French navy loses Battle of Trafalgar
1807	Napoleon has control of much of Europe
1812	Napoleon invades Russia and is defeated
1814	Borders of European countries redrawn
1815	Napoleon defeated at Waterloo

Napoleon then led 600,000 soldiers into Russia during the summer of 1812. The Russians refused to fight. They drew Napoleon deeper into their country and waited. When winter came, Napoleon's army did not have the clothing or the supplies they needed. Its retreat proved to be a disaster. The Russian winter caused more than 500,000 French soldiers to die.

Napoleon suffered his final loss at Waterloo, Belgium, in 1815. The French emperor was sent to an island in the southern Atlantic Ocean. He stayed there until his death in 1821.

European leaders met at a conference called the Congress of Vienna and brought back the powerful royal families who had ruled Europe before Napoleon. They tried to create a balance of power among the countries. They hoped this would keep all nations at peace.

Check for Understanding

Name two ways the French Revolution changed the lives of French citizens.

1. ______________________

2. ______________________

Who was Napoleon and what role did he play for France?

3. ______________________

____

Glue Foldable here

Explaining

9. How did the Russians defeat Napoleon's army?

____

____

____

____

Reading Check

10. Why did the Congress of Vienna support rule by powerful monarchs?

____

____

____

FOLDABLES®

11. Place a three-tab Foldable along the dotted line. Write the title *French Revolution* on the anchor tab. Label the three tabs *Before*, *During*, and *After*.

Use both sides of the tabs to list what you remember about France before, during, and after the revolution.

NAME_______________________________ DATE _______________ CLASS __________

networks

Lesson 3 Nationalism and Nation-States

ESSENTIAL QUESTION

How do governments change?

GUIDING QUESTIONS

1. *What political ideas shaped Europe during the 1800s and early 1900s?*
2. *Why did new nations arise in Europe during the mid-1800s?*
3. *How did the United States change during the 1800s?*
4. *How did the countries of Latin America win independence?*

Terms to Know

nationalism the desire of people with the same customs and beliefs for self-rule
guerrilla warfare a form of war in which soldiers make surprise attacks on their enemies
kaiser emperor of Germany
abolitionism movement to end slavery

Where in the world?

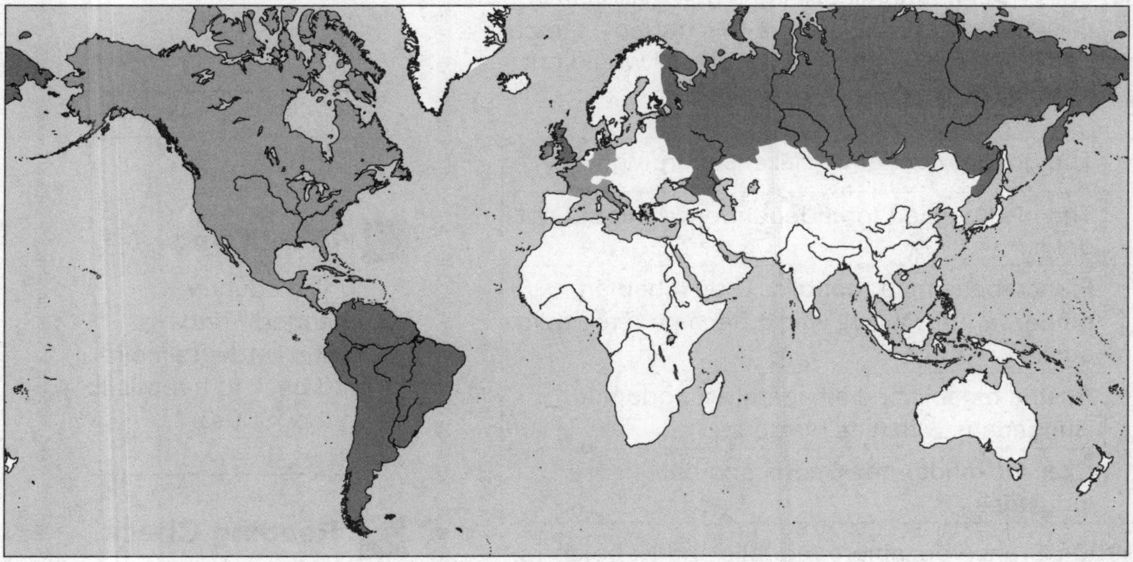

When did it happen?

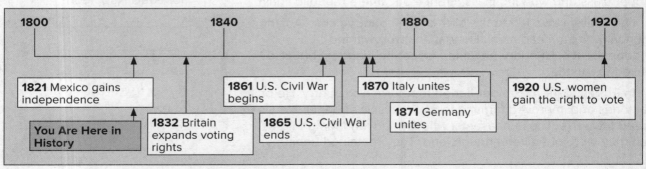

1800 — 1840 — 1880 — 1920

- **1821** Mexico gains independence
- You Are Here in History
- **1832** Britain expands voting rights
- **1861** U.S. Civil War begins
- **1865** U.S. Civil War ends
- **1870** Italy unites
- **1871** Germany unites
- **1920** U.S. women gain the right to vote

Lesson 3 Nationalism and Nation-States, *Continued*

Nationalism and Reform

Nationalism is the wish for self-rule among people who share the same culture. During the 1800s, nationalism and demands for political reform led to far-reaching changes in Europe and the Americas.

While the rest of Europe experienced war and revolution, Great Britain responded peacefully to the demands for political change. In 1832 the British government made a law that allowed most middle-class men to vote. Over time, more men in the country and in the cities gained the right to vote. Workers, however, were still not allowed to vote. British women first gained the right to vote in 1918.

The British government also faced the call for self-rule from Ireland. In the 1840s, Ireland suffered a famine. The British government did not send enough aid. At least one million Irish people died of starvation and disease. After this tragedy, the call for Irish independence increased, but the British still would not allow self-rule.

England	The government gave citizens more rights.
Ireland	The Irish pushed for independence but did not get it.
France	France became a republic. Then it had an emperor. After a civil war, it became a republic again.
Austria	Austria established a separate kingdom for Hungarians within its borders.
Russia	Czar Alexander freed serfs and built new industries.

In the mid-1800s, France became a republic and Napoleon's nephew, Louis Napoleon, was elected president. Louis Napoleon soon became Emperor Napoleon III. After a civil war between the upper class and working class, France became a republic again.

Nationalism also led to the birth of the country called Austria-Hungary. Austria had many Hungarians who wanted independence. Hungary became a separate kingdom but also linked to Austria.

In Russia, Czar Alexander II tried to reform his country. He built factories and improved farming to make Russia stronger. He also freed the serfs. These peasants, who farmed land for landlords, felt they were not given enough land. They remained unhappy.

Defining

1. What is *nationalism*?

____

____

____

Determining Cause and Effect

2. Why did the call for independence increase in Ireland?

____

____

____

Identifying

3. Which country changed from a republic to an empire and back to a republic in the 1800s?

____

Reading Check

4. Why might the people of France have voted for Louis Napoleon?

____

____

____

Identifying

5. Which country used guerrilla warfare to unite and gain independence?

____

Reading Check

6. What role did Bismarck play in uniting Germany?

____

Identifying

7. What is Manifest Destiny?

____

Reading Check

8. How were the economies of the North and South different before the American Civil War?

____

New Nations in Europe

In the mid-1800s, Austria controlled most of Italy. An independent kingdom called Piedmont forced Austria out of northern Italy. Nationalists in southern Italy used **guerrilla warfare** to fight for independence. Guerrilla warfare is a form of fighting that uses surprise attacks. By 1870, all of Italy was united.

Nationalism also grew stronger in the German states. The Prussian leader Otto von Bismarck strengthened the army and defeated Denmark, Austria, and France. Other German states decided to avoid war with Bismarck. In 1871, Germany united under an emperor called the **kaiser.**

Growth of the United States

During the 1800s, the United States pushed its borders westward. The idea that the United States should stretch from the Atlantic Ocean to the Pacific Ocean was called "Manifest Destiny."

Differences in the way of life between Americans in the North and South, however, caused tensions. The economy of the South relied on farming that used enslaved African Americans for labor. The North had an industrial and manufacturing economy. Some Northerners believed in **abolitionism.** This was a movement to end slavery.

Different Ways of Life	
North	**South**
• an industrial and manufacturing economy • used paid workers for labor	• economy relied on farming • used enslaved African Americans for labor

In 1860 Abraham Lincoln was elected president. He was against slavery. Southern states were afraid Lincoln would end slavery. Eleven states left the U.S. and formed their own nation. They called it the Confederate States of America. It was 1861 when the American Civil War began.

The North had more people and more factories than the South. Despite this, the South won most of the early battles. Finally, the North threw all of its resources against the South. After four years of fighting, the North won. More than 600,000 Americans had died in the Civil War.

After the war, African Americans were freed from slavery. New factories, railroads, and cities were built. Immigrants helped the population grow. Women fought hard for their rights. In 1920 they won the right to vote.

Independence in Latin America

Inspired by the American and French revolutions, a former slave named Toussaint L'Ouverture led enslaved Africans in a revolt in Haiti. In other Latin American countries, revolutions were led by priests and wealthy military leaders such as Simón Bolívar.

Latin America Independence in the 1800s

Year of Independence	Countries	Year of Independence	Countries
1804	Haiti	1825	Bolivia
1811	Paraguay	1828	Uruguay
1816	Argentina	1830	Ecuador, Venezuela
1818	Chile	1838	Costa Rica, Honduras, Nicaragua
1821	Mexico, Colombia, Peru	1840	El Salvador
1822	Brazil	1844	Dominican Republic
1823	Guatemala		

Glue Foldable here

Check for Understanding

Give one example of how nationalism affected each of these countries.

1. Ireland ______________________
2. Italy ______________________
3. Germany ______________________
4. The United States ______________________

Identifying

9. In what two years did the most Latin American countries gain independence?

____

____

Listing

10. Which Latin American countries gained independence in the 1820s?

____

____

Reading Check

11. How did Haiti's revolution differ from other Latin American countries?

____

____

FOLDABLES®

12. Place a one-tab Foldable along the dotted line. Write *Nationalism* in the middle of the tab. Draw four arrows pointing away from the title. Write words or phrases you remember about the rise of nationalism.

NAME_______________________________ DATE ____________ CLASS ________

networks

Lesson 4 The Industrial Revolution

ESSENTIAL QUESTION

How does technology change the way people live?

GUIDING QUESTIONS

1. *Why did the Industrial Revolution begin in Britain?*
2. *How did the new inventions help advance the growth of industry?*

Terms to Know

industrialism an economic system where machines do work that was once performed by animals or humans

corporation a type of company that sells shares of ownership of the company to investors

Where in the world?

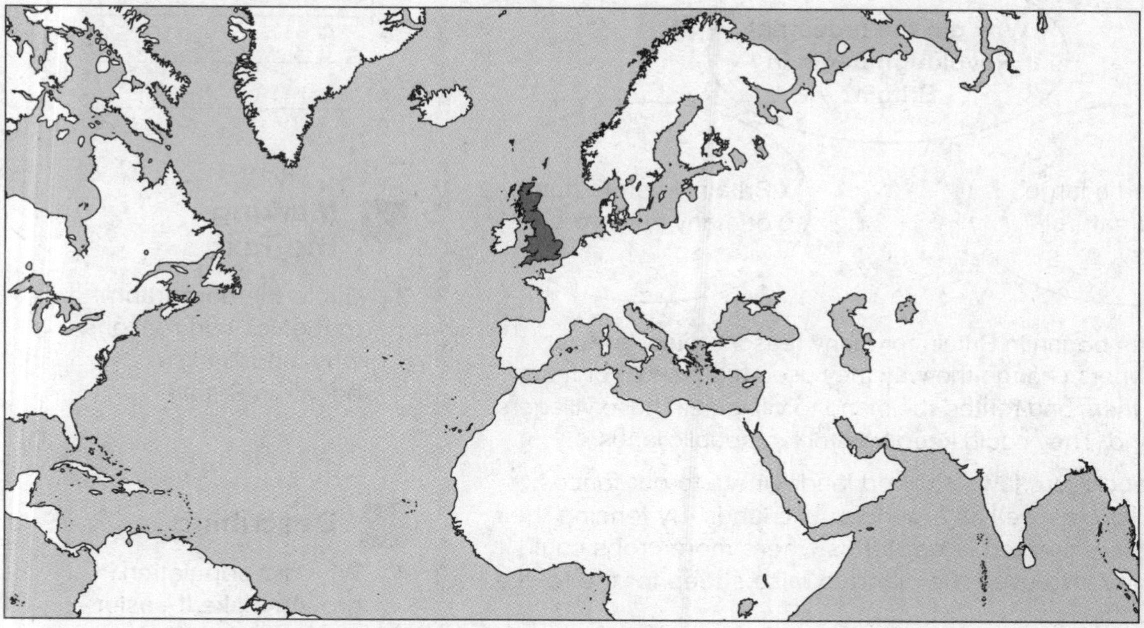

When did it happen?

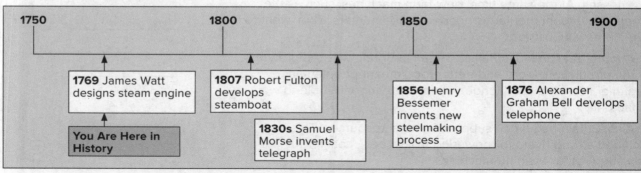

1750 — 1800 — 1850 — 1900

- **1769** James Watt designs steam engine
- **You Are Here in History**
- **1807** Robert Fulton develops steamboat
- **1830s** Samuel Morse invents telegraph
- **1856** Henry Bessemer invents new steelmaking process
- **1876** Alexander Graham Bell develops telephone

Lesson 4 The Industrial Revolution, *Continued*

Birth of Industry

Industrialism is the use of machines to do work that used to be done by people or animals. Industrialism started in Britain in the 1700s. Over the next 200 years, it spread to other parts of the world. It affected life so greatly that this period is known as the Industrial Revolution.

Why did the Industrial Revolution begin in Britain?

- British landowners had money to start new businesses.
- Britain had a large population.
- Britain had a large supply of natural resources.
- Britain was the home of many inventors.

Industrialism began in Britain for many reasons. New laws let British landowners change the way they used their land. For many years, landowners had rented their land to villagers. These villagers farmed the land. They could keep livestock on public lands.

The new enclosure laws allowed landowners to put fences around their land as well as around public lands. By fencing their land, landowners created larger farms where more crops could be grown. They also used their land to raise sheep for the textile, or cloth, industry.

These practices helped landowners earn more money than they had before. They spent their money investing in new businesses. At the same time, new farm machines, such as the steel plow, meant that farms needed fewer workers. They went to work in new industries.

Another reason industrialism began in Britain was the growth of the population. More and better food meant people had healthier lives and lived longer. There were more people to work in factories.

Also, Britain had a rich supply of natural resources. This included strong rivers for powering mill wheels, coal for fuel, and iron supplies for building machines.

Defining

1. What is *industrialism*?

____

____

Explaining

2. How did enclosure laws help landowners?

____

____

____

Marking the Text

3. Circle the paragraph that gives two reasons why industrialism began in Britain.

Describing

4. Why did population growth make it easier for industrialism to begin in Britain?

____

____

____

____

Explaining

5. Why did entrepreneurs form corporations?

Reading Check

6. How did successful farming and a growing population influence the Industrial Revolution in Britain?

Identifying

7. Where did the Industrial Revolution first take hold in the United States?

Finally, Britain was home to many inventors. The first inventions of this time period changed the textile industry. Before the Industrial Revolution, cloth was made by people who worked in their own homes. They worked alone using their own looms and sewing machines. However, machines became too big and too expensive to use at home.

Businesspeople called entrepreneurs built factories to hold the new inventions. In a factory, hundreds of workers use machines to make products. Factories provide a more organized and cheaper way to produce large amounts of goods.

Industrial Revolution

Inventor	Invention
James Hargreaves	spinning jenny (spun cotton into thread)
Richard Arkwright	water-powered spinning machine
Edmund Cartwright	powered loom (for weaving cloth)
James Watt	steam engine (to power machines)
Henry Bessemer	discovered how to make steel from iron

Over time, entrepreneurs looked for different ways to make money. They formed businesses called **corporations.** A corporation sells shares, or part ownership, of the company to investors. This gave the entrepreneurs the money to hire more workers and build new factories.

Growth of Industry

At first, the Industrial Revolution gave Britain an advantage over other countries. Britain became the richest country in the world. The British government tried to protect this advantage. They passed laws to keep ideas, inventions, and workers in Britain.

Despite these efforts, many inventors and entrepreneurs left anyway. They took their industrial knowledge with them. As a result, the Industrial Revolution spread.

Like Britain, the United States had many natural resources. This made it easy for the U.S. to industrialize. New England became the home of many factories. Pennsylvania was home to new coal mines and ironworks. Roads, railways, and canals helped move goods throughout the country.

Lesson 4 The Industrial Revolution, *Continued*

Science helped industry advance. During the 1800s, inventors found many ways to use electricity. Thomas Edison made the light bulb and used electricity to create light.

Electricity also made new forms of communication possible. In the 1830s, Samuel Morse invented the telegraph. It allowed coded messages to be sent across long distances. In 1876 Alexander Graham Bell invented the telephone. It used tiny electrical wires to carry sound. In 1895 Guglielmo Marconi made the first wireless telegraph, which later developed into the radio.

Other inventors changed transportation. Robert Fulton invented a steamboat. It changed the way people traveled on rivers. Rudolf Diesel and Gottlieb Daimler created a type of engine that burns oil-based fuel. It is called an internal combustion engine. At first, the new engines powered boats. Then they were used in two other inventions: the car and the airplane.

Marking the Text

8. Underline the three inventions that allowed new forms of communications.

Reading Check

9. How did electricity change communications?

____

____

____

Glue Foldable here

Check for Understanding

How were natural resources important to industrialization?

1. ______________________

____

Name two ways each item changed.

2. Land use ______________________

____

3. Manufacturing ______________________

____

4. Transportation ______________________

____

FOLDABLES®

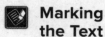

10. Place a two-tab Foldable along the dotted line to cover the Check for Understanding. Write *Industrial Revolution* on the anchor tab. Label the two tabs *Britain* and *America*.

Draw an arrow from Britain to America. Use both sides of the tabs to record information you remember about the spread of the Industrial Revolution.

NAME_______________________________________ DATE _____________ CLASS ________

Lesson 5 Society and Industry

ESSENTIAL QUESTION

How do new ideas change the way people live?

GUIDING QUESTIONS

1. ***How did industry change society in Europe and North America during the 1800s and early 1900s?***
2. ***What new political ideas arose as a result of industrial society?***
3. ***How did artists and writers describe the new industrial society?***
4. ***What advances made in science in the mid-1800s have transformed life today?***

Terms to Know

urbanization the increase in the number of people living in cities rather than in rural areas

liberalism a political philosophy based on the Enlightenment ideas of equality and individual rights

utilitarianism the idea that the goal of society should be to provide the greatest happiness for the largest number of people

socialism the idea that the means of production should be owned and controlled by the people, through their government

proletariat the working class

labor union an organized group of workers who try to improve wages and working conditions

When did it happen?

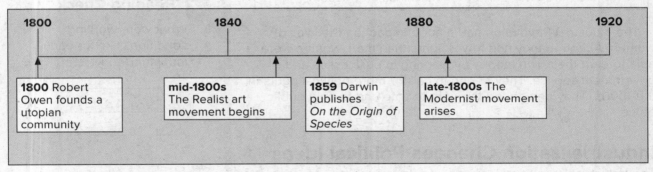

1800 — 1840 — 1880 — 1920

- **1800** Robert Owen founds a utopian community
- **mid-1800s** The Realist art movement begins
- **1859** Darwin publishes *On the Origin of Species*
- **late-1800s** The Modernist movement arises

What do you know?

For each inventor, write the name of his invention. If you do not know what the inventor created, leave the line blank.

Alexander Graham Bell	____________________
Thomas Edison	____________________
Samuel Morse	____________________
Guglielmo Marconi	____________________
the Wright Brothers	____________________

Lesson 5 Society and Industry, *Continued*

A New Society

The Industrial Revolution caused the growth of cities, or **urbanization.** Cities offered new jobs and a new way of life. Workers earned more money. The middle class began to grow.

Factory workers had a tougher life. Children and adults worked long hours for six days each week. Factories were hot, dirty, and unhealthy. Diseases spread quickly. Workers were often hurt by the machines they used. Reformers called for laws to make factories safer. New laws also improved pollution and water.

Working Conditions in Factories

- Children and adults worked long hours.
- Workers did the same tasks over and over.
- Factories were hot, dirty, and unhealthy.
- Diseases spread quickly.
- Workers were often hurt by the machines they used.

The Industrial Revolution had a huge impact on the lives of women. Although they had fewer rights than men, women were able to earn their own money by working in businesses and government service. They began to call for more political rights in the 1800s. They demanded the right to vote and to hold public office.

Industrialization Changes Political Ideas

The Industrial Revolution inspired people to find ways to improve society. **Liberalism** is the idea that all people have individual rights such as equality under the law and freedom of speech. Most Liberals, however, thought that the right to vote should belong only to men who owned property. Some, like British economist Adam Smith, thought government should not interfere with business.

Others believed that the government should help make society better. This was called **utilitarianism.** Other thinkers supported an idea called **socialism.**

Socialists believed that people should own and control the means of production, including factories, land, and raw materials. They wanted the government to manage these on behalf of the people. Some socialists, including Karl Marx, thought that this idea did not go far enough.

Defining

1. What is *urbanization*?

____

____

Marking the Text

2. Circle two demands women had in the 1800s.

Reading Check

3. What were working conditions like for early industrial workers?

____

____

____

Explaining

4. What did liberals believe about women and voting?

____

____

____

Lesson 5 Society and Industry, *Continued*

Explaining

5. What is a labor union?

____

____

Listing

6. Read the chart. Which schools of thought believed government should play a role in making society better?

____

____

Reading Check

7. What did Adam Smith believe about government and business?

____

____

____

Reading Check

8. What did the romantics emphasize in their works?

____

____

____

Marx believed that the working class, or **proletariat,** would revolt and create a society based on communism. Under communism, all people would be equal and share the wealth of the society.

Other efforts also improved the lives of workers. Workers formed labor unions to fight for their rights. A **labor union** is an organized group of workers who try to improve working conditions. Labor unions helped workers get higher pay and safer working conditions.

New Political Ideas	
Liberalism	• All people have individual rights. • Government should leave business alone.
Utilitarianism	• Government should work to make society better. • Utilitarians wanted full rights for women, better health care, and better education.
Socialism	• The people should own the means of production. • Government should manage the means of production for the people. • Wealth should be shared by all people.
Communism	• Social classes would not exist. • Workers would control government. • Workers would create a society in which people would share everything equally.

Revolution in the Arts

The growth of industry also sparked new movements in the arts. Artists and writers known as romantics wanted to use imagination to express their feelings and inspire strong feelings in others. The German composer Ludwig von Beethoven is among the most popular romantics.

In contrast, realists tried to show life as it really was. Britain's Charles Dickens became famous for describing the lives of everyday people. Modernists tried new subjects and new styles in their work. Some studied social issues such as crime, alcoholism, and women's rights. Others looked for meaning in dreams. Impressionist painters tried to show the color and light of the outdoor world.

Lesson 5 Society and Industry, *Continued*

The New Science

Scientific research increased in the 1800s. Charles Darwin developed a theory of evolution. In his book *On the Origin of Species*, he explained that plants and animals change very slowly over time. Darwin believed that humans developed from animal species. People argued about his ideas. Over time, many people came to accept his theory.

In 1796 Edward Jenner developed a vaccine, or type of medicine, that stopped people from getting a disease called smallpox. In the 1850s, Louis Pasteur discovered that bacteria can cause infectious diseases. Pasteur also showed that killing bacteria prevented many diseases.

Scientist	Discovery	Impact
Gregor Mendel	children receive their traits from their parents	became the father of genetics
Louis Pasteur	disease-causing bacteria	allowed doctors to fight disease more easily
Joseph Lister	ways to sterilize medical tools	saved lives of patients who would have died from infection
Albert Einstein	theory of relativity	led to the development of the atomic bomb

Check for Understanding

List five ideas that changed the way people lived.

1. ______________________

2. ______________________

3. ______________________

4. ______________________

5. ______________________

Reading Check

9. How did Louis Pasteur extend the work of Edward Jenner?

____

____

____

FOLDABLES®

10. Place a two-tab Foldable along the dotted line. Cut the tabs in half to form four tabs. On the anchor tab, write *Ideas Bring Change*. Label the four tabs *economics*, *politics*, *the arts*, and *science*.

Use both sides of the tabs to record one thing you remember about the changes that occurred in each area.

Glue Foldable here

NAME ______________________________ DATE ______________ CLASS ________

networks

Imperialism and World War I

Lesson 1 The New Imperialism

ESSENTIAL QUESTION

Why do people trade?

GUIDING QUESTIONS

1. ***Why did Europeans expand their empires at the end of the 1800s?***
2. ***What were the effects of British rule in India?***
3. ***Why did Europeans compete to take over Africa?***
4. ***How did the United States build an overseas empire?***

Terms to Know

imperialism the policy of one nation gaining power by directly or indirectly controlling the political or economic life of other areas

protectorate a relationship in which a nation has its own government, but the military is controlled by another government

sphere of influence a region where only one imperial power had the right to invest or trade

Where in the world?

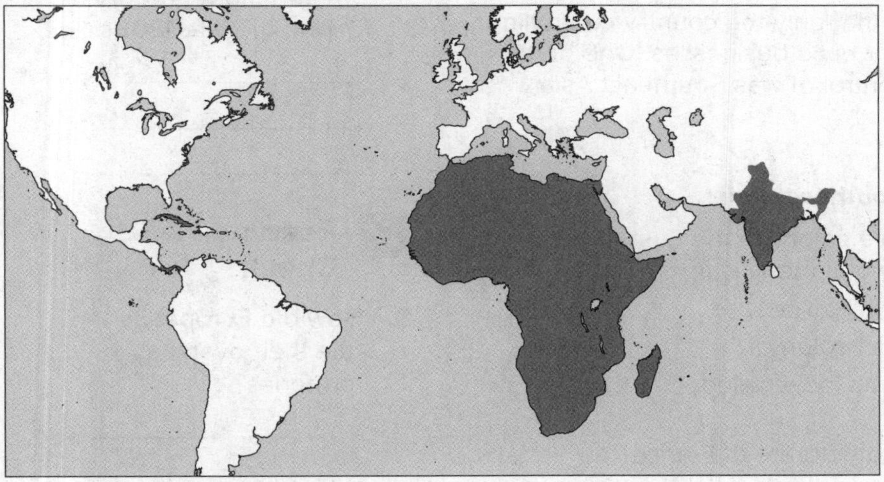

When did it happen?

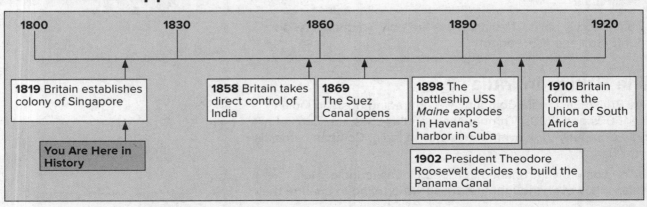

1800 — 1830 — 1860 — 1890 — 1920

- **1819** Britain establishes colony of Singapore
  - **You Are Here in History**
- **1858** Britain takes direct control of India
- **1869** The Suez Canal opens
- **1898** The battleship USS *Maine* explodes in Havana's harbor in Cuba
- **1902** President Theodore Roosevelt decides to build the Panama Canal
- **1910** Britain forms the Union of South Africa

The Rise of Imperialism

During the late 1800s, powerful countries in Europe raced to grab territory in Asia and Africa. One reason was to gain more power. Also, businesses and factories in Europe needed raw materials and new places to sell their goods.

A third reason was that Europeans believed their culture was better than other cultures. This move to take territory marked the rise of imperialism. **Imperialism** is a relationship in which one nation directly or indirectly controls another nation.

Europeans ruled their new territories in three ways. Colonies were ruled directly using appointed officials. In other cases, the Europeans set up a **protectorate**. In a protectorate, the local people had their own government, but Europeans ran the military.

Finally, European countries sometimes set up a **sphere of influence** in a region. This meant that only the country controlling the region had the right to trade or build businesses. One of the first areas that Europeans took control of was Southeast Asia.

European Control of Southeast Asia:

- The Dutch had set up a colony in the East Indies before the Age of Imperialism.
- Spain controlled the Philippines.
- Singapore was a British colony.
- Britain controlled Burma (now called Myanmar).
- Vietnam became a protectorate of France.

Siam (today called Thailand) was the only Southeast Asian country to keep its freedom.

The British in India

The British East India Company set up trading posts in India in the 1600s and 1700s. Through wars and treaties, the British East India Company took over more areas of India. Company officials grew rich.

The company introduced European ideas to India. Many Indians, however, thought the British were trying to change their

Identifying

1. On which continents did Europe rush to take territory during the late 1800s?

____

____

____

Listing

2. Name one reason the nations of Europe wanted more territory during the late 1800s.

____

____

____

Reading Check

3. How did Europeans rule their overseas territories?

____

____

____

____

Reading Check

4. How did British rule of India change in 1858?

Identifying Cause and Effect

5. How did the Suez Canal help trade between India and Europe?

Explaining

6. Who were the Boers? Who did they fight in the Boer War?

culture. In 1857 some of them revolted. The British crushed the revolt, but it convinced the British government to take direct control of India in 1858.

The new government was called the Raj. Under the Raj, the British united India. They brought railroads, the telegraph, and a postal service to India. The Raj also made some terrible changes. The British forced Indian farmers to grow cotton instead of wheat. This caused food shortages. In the 1800s, millions of Indians starved to death.

The Raj

Good Changes	Bad Changes
• Railroads • Telegraph • Postal Service	• Grow cotton instead of wheat • Food shortages • Millions of Indians starved to death

Many Indians were angry. Some of them formed a political group called the Indian National Congress. These leaders supported independence for India.

European Rule in Africa

During the late 1800s, European powers were scrambling to control as much of Africa as they could. In North Africa, the French took over Algeria, then Tunisia, and later they claimed Morocco.

In Egypt, European businesses developed. Europeans and the Egyptians built the Suez Canal, which opened in 1869. The canal shortened the trade route between India and Europe. Britain eventually made Egypt a protectorate.

By the mid-1800s, many European countries were ending slavery. They then wanted to control the trade of West Africa's resources, such as gold, timber, hides, and palm oil. The only West African country to stay independent during this time was Liberia. It had been founded by African Americans who had been freed from slavery.

In Central Africa, the king of Belgium claimed much of the Congo region. He enslaved the people and forced them to work on rubber plantations. In East Africa, Ethiopia remained independent after stopping the Italians' attempt to conquer it.

In South Africa, war broke out when Europeans competed for land. Dutch settlers were known as Boers. This is the Dutch word for "farmers." The British and the Boers went to war over control of gold and diamonds in Boer territory. This conflict, called the Boer War, lasted three years and ended with a British victory.

Europeans paid African workers low wages and forced them to pay taxes. European schools for Africans taught that European ways were best. In some places, African traditions declined as a result of European influences.

By the early 1900s, many European-educated Africans believed that colonial rule went against the European ideals of liberty and equality. They started to form groups to push for self-rule.

America's Quest for Empire

American government and business leaders believed the United States needed overseas markets and raw materials to keep the economy growing.

The United States gained territory in Latin America and the Pacific Islands in the late 1800s. After the Spanish-American War, Cuba became a republic under American protection. The United States also gained Puerto Rico and the Pacific islands of Guam and the Philippines.

The trip around South America took too long for fast military action. In 1902 U.S. president Theodore Roosevelt decided to build a canal across Panama to connect the Atlantic and Pacific Oceans. At that time, Panama was part of Colombia. The Colombians refused to give up their land.

In 1903 Americans helped the people of Panama revolt. Once Panama won its independence, it signed a treaty that allowed the United States to build the canal. After 10 years of work, the first ships steamed through the canal in 1914. The Panama Canal was hailed as one of the world's great engineering feats.

Check for Understanding

Identify two causes of imperialism.

1. ______________________

2. ______________________

Identify two effects of imperialism.

3. ______________________

4. ______________________

Glue Foldable here

Reading Check

7. Why were Europeans drawn to Africa in the 1800s?

____

____

____

____

Reading Check

8. How did the United States gain the rights to build the Panama Canal?

____

____

____

____

FOLDABLES®

9. Place a three-tab Foldable along the dotted line. Write *Age of Imperialism* on the anchor tab. Label the tabs *Colonies, Protectorate*, and *Sphere of Influence.*

Write what you learned about each on the reverse sides of the tabs.

NAME ______________________ DATE ____________ CLASS ________

networks

Imperialism and World War I

Lesson 2 Nationalism in China and Japan

ESSENTIAL QUESTION

Why does conflict develop?

GUIDING QUESTIONS

1. ***How did the arrival of Europeans change Chinese society?***
2. ***How did revolution in 1911 bring changes to China?***
3. ***How did the Japanese reorganize their society and economy as a result of Western influences?***

Terms to Know

extraterritoriality the legal practice of foreigners living in a country but not being subject to the laws of that country

Where in the world?

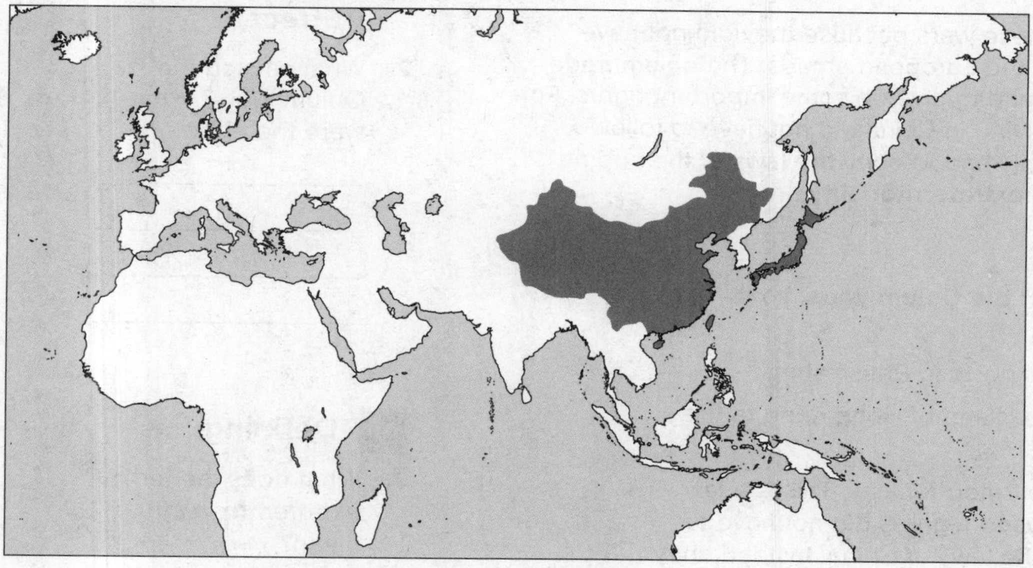

When did it happen?

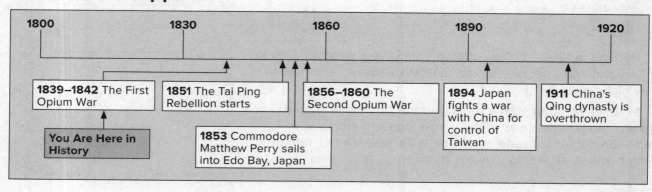

1800 — 1830 — 1860 — 1890 — 1920

1839–1842 The First Opium War

You Are Here in History

1851 The Tai Ping Rebellion starts

1853 Commodore Matthew Perry sails into Edo Bay, Japan

1856–1860 The Second Opium War

1894 Japan fights a war with China for control of Taiwan

1911 China's Qing dynasty is overthrown

China Faces the West

During the early 1800s, the Chinese were not very interested in goods from Europe or trade with the West. The British, however, had a great demand for Chinese tea, silk, and porcelain. To get these items, the British had to trade valuable goods like silver.

The British wanted to increase their trade with China. They began selling opium from India to the Chinese. Opium is an addictive drug. When Chinese people became addicted, the demand for opium grew. Demand was especially high in southern China.

China's emperor warned the British to stop the opium trade. The British refused and fought the Chinese in two wars—the First Opium War (1839 to 1842) and the Second Opium War (1856 to 1860).

The Chinese lost these wars because they did not have modern weapons like the European armies. The opium trade continued and China had to give up some important rights. For example, Europeans living in China did not have to follow Chinese laws. They only had to obey the laws of their home country. This is called **extraterritoriality.**

China lost the Opium Wars, so it had to ...

- open its ports to British ships.
- give the island of Hong Kong to the British.
- allow extraterritoriality. This is a law that says foreigners did not have to follow the laws of China. Instead, they would follow the laws of their own country even when they were in China.

During the 1850s, China suffered from severe weather. Crops failed, and many people starved to death. Peasants also had to pay high taxes.

In 1851 a religious leader organized the Tai Ping Rebellion. The goal of the rebellion was to overthrow the Qing emperor. The rebellion did not succeed, but it made Chinese leaders realize they needed reforms to save the dynasty.

Marking the Text

1. Underline the sentence that tells the goal of the British in China.

Determining Cause and Effect

2. What caused the Opium Wars? What were the effects?

____

____

____

____

Defining

3. What does the term *extraterritoriality* mean?

____

____

____

____

Reading Check

4. What was the goal of the Tai Ping rebellion?

____

____

____

Identifying

5. When did the Nationalists gain power?

____

Reading Check

6. What kind of government did Sun Yat-sen want to establish in China?

____

____

Examining Details

7. What forced Japan to end its isolationism?

____

____

____

Local Chinese leaders began to allow Europeans to trade, mine, and build in their regions. European nations were able to control large areas of China as spheres of influence.

The United States wanted to influence China as well. It proposed an Open Door Policy that would open China to trade with all countries. Hatred of foreigners began to rise in China. The Chinese organized secret societies to drive out foreigners. In 1900 the Boxers attacked foreigners and Chinese Christians. Foreign powers sent in troops and crushed the rebellion.

China's 1911 Revolution

The desire for reform in China continued. In 1905 Sun Yat-sen organized a movement that became known as the Nationalist Party. Its members wanted to remove the Qing dynasty. Sun had a three-step plan: (1) take over China's government, (2) prepare the people for self-rule, and (3) create a constitution and a democracy.

Sun Yat-sen's Goals
(1) take over China's government
(2) prepare the people for self-rule
(3) create a constitution and a democracy

In 1911 revolution swept China, and the Qing dynasty collapsed. The nationalists set up a new government. The head of the Chinese army, General Yuan Shikai, took power and ruled as a dictator.

Yuan died in 1916, and China slipped into chaos. The following year, Sun Yat-sen rebuilt his Nationalist Party. He worked with a young officer, Chiang Kai-shek. Sun died in 1925, but three years later Chiang set up a Nationalist government.

The Rise of Modern Japan

For many centuries, Japan had been isolated from the rest of the world. The period of isolation ended in 1853 when four American warships sailed into Edo Bay (now Tokyo Bay). Commodore Matthew Perry brought a letter from U.S. president Millard Fillmore. It asked Japan to trade with the United States. Perry returned six months later with a larger fleet of ships to pressure Japan for an answer.

Lesson 2 Nationalism in China and Japan, *Continued*

The Japanese feared an attack and agreed to open their ports to the United States and European nations. Many Japanese feared that the agreements would keep Japan weak. In 1868 a group of powerful samurai overthrew the government. This marked the beginning of a more modern Japan, called the Meiji Era.

The Meiji created a new government. They set up a modern army and navy. The Meiji also improved schools and required everyone to be educated. By 1914 Japan had become a leading industrial country. Japan's working class did not benefit from this growth. Factory workers earned low wages and worked long hours.

Meiji Accomplishments

- created a new government
- set up a modern army and navy
- improved schools and required everyone to be educated
- made Japan a leading industrial country

Japanese leaders believed that Japan could become a world power if it held an overseas empire. In 1894 Japan fought a war with China for control of Korea. After the Chinese were defeated, they agreed to give the island of Taiwan to Japan and independence to Korea. The victory in the war gave Japan some control over Korea's trade.

As it created its empire, Japan faced conflict with Russia. In 1904 Japan's modern navy defeated the Russians and sank most of their ships. The victory against powerful Russia made Japan into a world power.

Check for Understanding

List two effects of the Opium Wars in China.

1. ______________________________

2. ______________________________

List two changes in Japan that happened as a result of Commodore Matthew Perry's arrival.

3. ______________________________

4. ______________________________

Identifying

8. What countries did Japan come into conflict with as it created its empire?

____

____

Reading Check

9. What changes did the Meiji rulers bring to Japan?

____

____

____

FOLDABLES®

10. Place a two-tab Foldable along the dotted line. Write *Changes in China & Japan* on the anchor tab. Label the tabs *Opium Wars in China* and *Commodore Matthew Perry*.

Use both sides of the tabs to list words or phrases that explain how each helped create changes in China and Japan.

Glue Foldable here

NAME ______________________ DATE __________ CLASS ________

networks

Lesson 3 World War I Begins

ESSENTIAL QUESTION

Why is history important?

GUIDING QUESTIONS

1. ***What factors threatened the peace in Europe after 1900?***
2. ***Why did war break out in Europe in 1914?***
3. ***How did World War I affect the world outside of Europe?***

Terms to Know

militarism a strong attraction to war and military power

conscription the policy that requires the citizens in a country to serve in the military for a certain period of time

entente a formal agreement between two nations to cooperate for specific purposes

mobilization the process of assembling armed forces into readiness for a conflict

propaganda biased information used to influence public opinion

blockade the closing of a port or harbor to prevent entrance or exit

Where in the world?

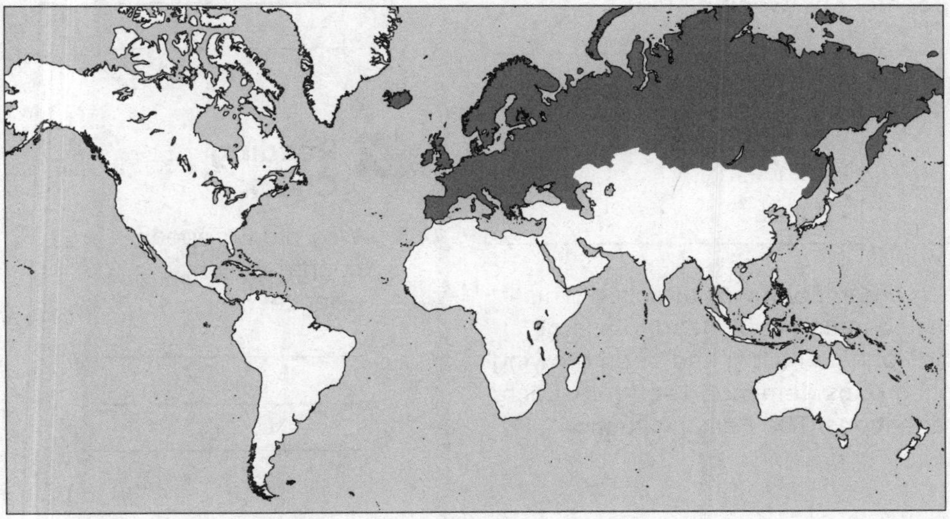

When did it happen?

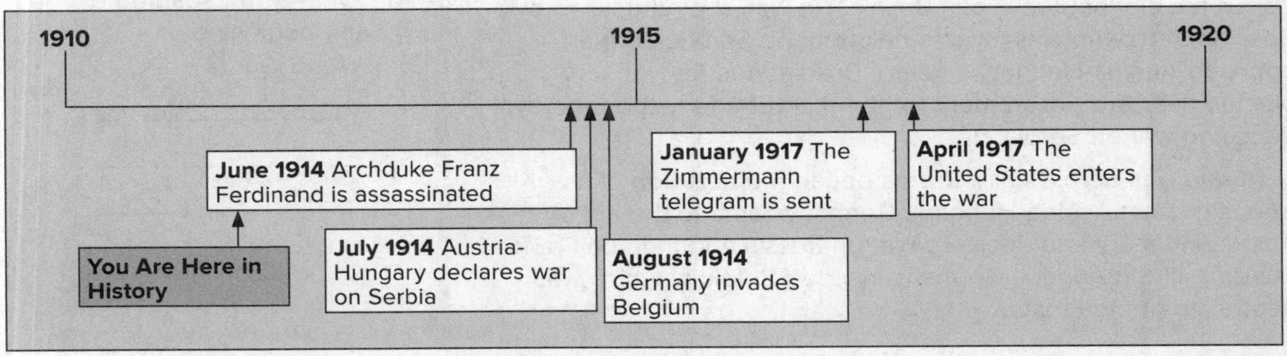
1910
1915
1920
June 1914 Archduke Franz Ferdinand is assassinated
You Are Here in History
July 1914 Austria-Hungary declares war on Serbia
August 1914 Germany invades Belgium
January 1917 The Zimmermann telegram is sent
April 1917 The United States enters the war

Causes of Conflict

Nationalism is a strong feeling of loyalty to one's country. In the early 1900s, nationalism made some countries strong, but weakened others.

By 1900 European powers controlled much of the world's land area. European nations often came into conflict with each other while trying to expand. As European nations grew, they increased the size of their military forces. This caused other nations to increase their own militaries. This type of competition between nations is called **militarism.** Powerful nations used **conscription,** or a draft, to require their citizens to serve in the military.

Another way that European countries increased their power was to form alliances with other nations. These were agreements to help one another in the event of war. Two powerful alliances were created. These were the Triple Alliance and the Triple Entente. An **entente** is an agreement between nations.

The Triple Alliance	The Triple Entente
• Germany	• Britain
• Austria-Hungary	• France
• Italy	• Russia

Allies promised to help each other if one was attacked. This meant that an attack on any allied nation could lead to a large war. In the early 1900s, feelings of nationalism had been growing in the Balkan Peninsula. Ethnic groups demanded self-rule. Each group had alliances with other nations. The Balkan situation increased tensions in Europe.

War Breaks Out in Europe

In June 1914, Archduke Franz Ferdinand of Austria-Hungary visited the city of Sarajevo in Bosnia. He was shot and killed by a Bosnian Serb who was loyal to neighboring Serbia. Serbia opposed Austria-Hungary's rule of Bosnia. Austria-Hungary blamed the Serb government for the murder and responded by declaring war on Serbia.

Russia was Serbia's ally. Russia began **mobilization** of its troops against Austria-Hungary. Germany came to the aid of Austria-Hungary and declared war on Russia and then on France, Russia's ally. In August, Germany invaded Belgium, which was neutral, to get to France.

Marking the Text

1. Underline the reason imperialism created tensions in Europe.

Explaining

2. Why did military alliances create danger in Europe?

____

____

____

Reading Check

3. Why did European countries form alliances?

____

____

____

Identifying

4. What event sparked the beginning of World War I?

____

____

____

Describing

5. What was a trench, and how was it important in the war?

____

____

____

____

Marking the Text

6. Circle the new weapons used during World War I.

Reading Check

7. What is a total war?

____

____

____

Explaining

8. How was Russia able to weaken Germany?

____

____

Alliances lined up quickly. On one side were the Allies. On the other side were the Central Powers.

The battle zone between France and Germany was called the Western Front. The war became a standoff. Neither side could gain any ground for three years. Each side dug deep trenches to protect their soldiers. To move forward, soldiers had to climb out of the trenches and cross open ground against the enemy guns.

Allies	Central Powers
• France	• Germany
• Russia	• Austria-Hungary
• Britain	• Ottoman Empire
• Italy (joined in 1915)	• Bulgaria

New weapons made this war deadlier than any other. Cannons and machine guns were more powerful. Tanks and poison gases were used for the first time. Submarines and airplanes were also used to fight the enemy.

The war required huge resources. Each nation needed to involve all of its citizens in the war effort. Governments took over industries and railroads. They rationed civilians' use of food and materials needed for the war. They used **propaganda** to convince the public to support the war. It was a time of "total war," when entire societies were involved in fighting.

Women began working in factories, taking the place of the men who had left to fight. They made weapons, supplies, and war goods. Their contributions helped women's rights. After the war, many countries were ready to give women the right to vote.

A Global War

Germany and Austria-Hungary continued to fight on the Western Front against France and Britain. They were also determined to conquer Russia on the Eastern Front. Russia did not have the modern weapons like France and Britain, and it suffered many losses. It was, however, able to weaken Germany by forcing Germany to split its forces between the two fronts.

When the war began, the United States declared itself neutral. Advisers to President Woodrow Wilson supported the Allies. They argued that if the Allies won, it would strengthen democracy and maintain a balance of power in the world.

The powerful British navy placed a **blockade** on Germany. This prevented ships from leaving or entering German ports. Germany tried to break the blockade with its submarines.

The event, however, that finally brought the United States into the war was the Zimmermann telegram. The telegram from Germany suggested to Mexico that the two should become allies. Germany would then help Mexico reclaim territory from the United States.

The Zimmermann Telegram

- Sent from Germany to Mexico
- Suggested Mexico become allies with Germany
- Germany would help Mexico reclaim Texas, New Mexico, and Arizona
- Outraged many Americans
- Brought the United States into the war

Americans were outraged. They demanded war with Germany. The anger grew even greater when German submarines sank four American merchant ships. On April 6, 1917, the United States declared war against Germany.

Check for Understanding

List two causes of World War I.

1. ______________________

2. ______________________

List two members of the Allies and two members of the Central Powers as of April 1917.

Allies	**Central Powers**
3. ____________	5. ____________
4. ____________	6. ____________

Glue Foldable here

Reading Check

9. Why did the U.S. favor the Allies in World War I?

____

____

____

FOLDABLES®

10. Place a two-tab Foldable along the dotted line to cover the Check for Understanding. Write *Assassination of an Archduke* on the anchor tab. Label the tabs *Cause* and *Effect*.

Use both sides of the tabs to write what you remember about the outbreak of war in Europe in 1914.

NAME ________________ DATE ________ CLASS ________

networks

Imperialism and World War I

Lesson 4 World War I Brings Change

ESSENTIAL QUESTION

How do governments change?

GUIDING QUESTIONS

1. ***What changes came to Europe and the Middle East after World War I?***
2. ***Why did revolution break out in Russia during World War I?***

Terms to Know

armistice a truce or agreed-upon temporary stop in fighting; a cease-fire

genocide the deliberate killing of an ethnic group

reparations payments for war damages made to winning countries from defeated ones

mandate a territory that is officially controlled by the League of Nations but is governed by a member nation

soviet a committee to represent the concerns of the Russian people

When did it happen?

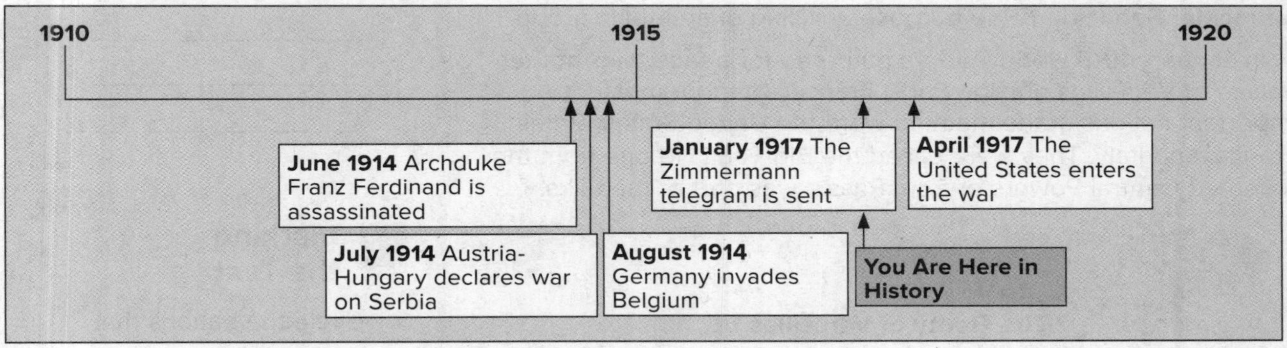

1910
1915
1920
June 1914 Archduke Franz Ferdinand is assassinated
July 1914 Austria-Hungary declares war on Serbia
August 1914 Germany invades Belgium
January 1917 The Zimmermann telegram is sent
April 1917 The United States enters the war
You Are Here in History

What do you know?

Write at least one detail about each of the following terms.

Allies ________________

Central Powers ________________

Western Front ________________

Eastern Front ________________

Treaty of Versailles ________________

Big Four ________________

League of Nations ________________

Peace at Last

After years of fighting the war, the Allies needed help badly. The arrival of American troops offered new hope. At about the same time, Russia pulled out of the war.

This let Germany focus on the Western Front. The French and American armies stopped the Germans' advance. When Americans invaded Germany, the German people revolted. On November 11, 1918, Germany signed an **armistice**, or cease-fire. The war had ended.

Europe suffered terribly from World War I. About 22 million people had died from fighting, starvation, or disease. Another 21 million had been wounded. Some civilians were killed deliberately. The Ottomans believed the Armenians supported the Allies. They killed hundreds of thousands of Armenians in a **genocide**. Genocide is the purposeful killing of an ethnic group.

In January 1919 world leaders gathered for peace talks at the Palace of Versailles outside Paris, France. The four most important nations at the meeting were the United States, Britain, France, and Italy. They were called the Big Four. No one from the defeated Central Powers or from Russia was part of the talks.

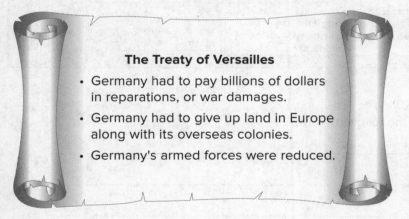

The Treaty of Versailles

- Germany had to pay billions of dollars in reparations, or war damages.
- Germany had to give up land in Europe along with its overseas colonies.
- Germany's armed forces were reduced.

At the meeting, U.S. president Woodrow Wilson presented a peace plan called the Fourteen Points. It said that all national groups in Europe should be able to decide how to run their own government.

It also called for a League of Nations. The League was designed to keep peace and prevent future wars. The League idea was included in the final peace agreement, called the Treaty of Versailles. Wilson, however, could not convince the United States Senate to approve the treaty.

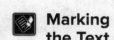

Defining

1. What is *genocide*?

____

____

Summarizing

2. What effect did World War I have on the people of Europe?

____

____

____

____

Marking the Text

3. Circle the nations that were called the Big Four.

Explaining

4. What was the goal of the League of Nations?

____

____

____

____

Reading Charts

5. What nations lost territory after World War I?

Predicting

6. What conflicts do you think grew in the Middle East?

Reading Check

7. What effects did the Treaty of Versailles have on Europe's population?

Senators were afraid the League of Nations might force the United States into more foreign wars. When the League formed, the United States did not join.

Germany was ordered to pay **reparations,** or money for damages caused by the war. Other treaties were written to make peace with the other members of the Central Powers. These treaties redrew the map of Europe so that members of a single ethnic group could be in one country.

Empire	After WWI
German	lost territory
Russian	lost territory
Austro-Hungarian	disappeared
Ottoman Empire	broken up and became present-day Turkey

As much as they tried, the peacemakers at Versailles could not make everyone happy with the new borders. The Middle East had been part of the Ottoman Empire. Instead of giving independence to the Arab areas, the treaty made them **mandates** of Britain and France. The Arab people did not want to be ruled by Europeans.

During the 1920s, the leader Ibn Saud united the Arabs and formed the kingdom of Saudi Arabia. At first the new nation was very poor. Then, American businesses struck oil there. The kingdom quickly became very wealthy.

Nationalism in Palestine caused conflict during the same time. During World War I, the British promised Jews a homeland where the ancient Jewish city of Jerusalem was located. The Arabs who lived in Palestine were angry that Britain would allow a Jewish homeland in an area where most of the people were Arab.

Revolution in Russia

During the early 1900s, many Russians were unhappy. Taxes were high, very few peasants owned the land that they worked, and people worked long hours for little pay.

In 1905 Russia lost a war with Japan. Workers staged an uprising to demand change. Russia's ruler, Czar Nicholas II, did not want to make large reforms. Instead, he agreed to small changes and formed a duma, or parliament. This was not enough change for many Russians.

Lesson 4 World War I Brings Change, *Continued*

World War I made conditions worse in Russia. There was not enough food or fuel. Angry Russians rebelled in March 1917. Finally, the czar was forced to give up his throne.

The fall of the czar did not solve Russia's problems. Many workers, soldiers, and peasants set up **soviets**, or committees, to take their concerns to the government. They wanted a classless society in which everyone shared wealth equally. The most radical of these socialist groups was called the Bolsheviks. Their leader was Vladimir Lenin.

Civil War in Russia

- Two groups called the Reds and the Whites fought each other.
- The Reds, once called the Bolsheviks, supported Lenin.
- The Whites opposed Lenin with support from the Allies.
- In 1921 the Whites gave up.
- After that, Lenin controlled all of Russia.

Lenin promised to get Russia out of the war, give land to peasants, and put the soviets in charge. In November 1917 the Bolsheviks took over the government. This change led to a civil war between the Reds and the Whites.

The Reds, now called Communists, supported Lenin. The Whites, who wanted to rejoin the war, opposed him with support from the Allies. The aid did little to help the Whites. In 1921 they gave up. Lenin and the Communists now controlled all of Russia.

/ / / / / / / / / / / / / Glue Foldable here / / / / / / / / / / / / /

Check for Understanding

List two ways that the Treaty of Versailles punished Germany after World War I.

1. _______________

2. _______________

List two hardships that Russia suffered as a result of World War I.

3. _______________

4. _______________

Analyzing

8. Why might the Allies have supported the Whites against the Reds?

____

____

____

Reading Check

9. What role did the soviets play in the Russian Revolution?

____

____

____

FOLDABLES®

10. Place a one-tab Foldable along the dotted line. Write *Treaty of Versailles* in the center of the Foldable tab.

Create a memory map by drawing arrows around the title. List five words or phrases that you remember about the peace agreement.

Use the reverse side to list additional information.

NAME ______________________ DATE __________ CLASS ________

networks

World War II and the Cold War

Lesson 1 The Rise of Dictators

ESSENTIAL QUESTION

What are the characteristics of a leader?

GUIDING QUESTIONS

1. ***How did the world's industrialized countries respond to economic troubles after World War I?***
2. ***Why did people in Italy and Germany support rule by dictators?***
3. ***How did Stalin's rule affect the peoples of the Soviet Union?***
4. ***Why did the Japanese turn to military rule and territorial expansion during the 1930s?***

Terms to Know

depression a period of low general economic activity marked especially by rising levels of unemployment

totalitarian state a form of government in which citizens are under strict control by the state

collectivization an economic system where a government controls production and distribution of all goods

Where in the world?

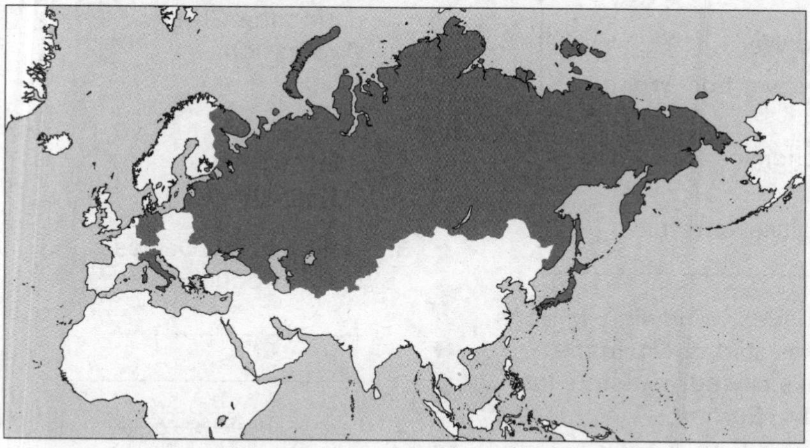

When did it happen?

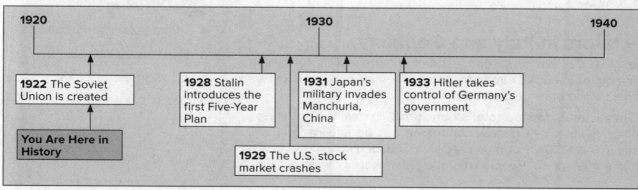

1920 — 1930 — 1940

- **1922** The Soviet Union is created
- You Are Here in History
- **1928** Stalin introduces the first Five-Year Plan
- **1929** The U.S. stock market crashes
- **1931** Japan's military invades Manchuria, China
- **1933** Hitler takes control of Germany's government

Economic Troubles

Peace after World War I did not bring political order or economic success to many countries. Germany, for one, was in great trouble.

The Germans were forced to pay for the damage of the war. Germany struggled to make its payments. The German government printed too much money. This led to inflation, which meant that the value of German money fell. The economy worsened. The United States and European nations created the Dawes Plan to make sure Germany recovered. The plan reduced the amount of money Germany owed. The economy improved but not for long.

During the 1930s, an economic depression struck many countries in the world. A **depression** is a time of low economic activity. This crisis was so bad it became known as the Great Depression.

Troubles After World War I

- Many countries struggled to recover from World War I.
- The Great Depression hurt economies around the world.
- Economic problems caused political unrest.

The Great Depression affected economies worldwide. Millions of people lost their jobs. Many businesses shut down. In the United States, stock prices fell, and banks closed. Investors lost their money. The problems soon spread to Europe.

In the United States, President Franklin Roosevelt introduced a program to boost the economy and provide jobs. It was called the New Deal.

Dictators in Italy and Germany

The Great Depression spread fear and uncertainty. Citizens in some nations wanted strong leaders to fix their problems. These leaders often became dictators.

The dictators formed **totalitarian states**. In totalitarian states, political leaders try to totally control the way people live and think. In the 1930s, dictators used print, radio, film, and the arts to enforce their views. People who disagreed were punished.

Identifying

1. Why did Germany's economy struggle after World War I?

____

____

____

Marking the Text

2. Underline the text that describes what happened to people during the Great Depression.

Reading Check

3. Why was the Dawes Plan introduced?

____

____

____

Defining

4. What is *totalitarianism*?

____

____

____

Lesson 1 The Rise of Dictators, *Continued*

Identifying

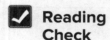

5. Who gave Hitler the legal power to be a dictator?

______

______

Reading Check

6. How were Mussolini and Hitler alike in their ruling methods?

______

______

______

FOLDABLES®

Comparing

7. Place a three-tab Venn diagram Foldable along the dotted line to cover the table. Write *Dictators* on the anchor tab. Label the tabs *Mussolini*, *Both*, and *Hitler*.

On the reverse sides, write facts about each to compare and contrast their roles as dictators.

Italy was the first European country to become a totalitarian state. It had a large debt to repay after World War I, because Italy was an ally to Germany. Many people were jobless, and there was political unrest. Benito Mussolini came to power in 1922.

Mussolini promised to restore order. He quickly ended democracy in Italy. He banned all political parties except his Fascist Party. People lost their personal freedoms.

	Mussolini	Hitler
Led ...	Fascist Party	National Socialist Party
Promised ...	To fix economy, restore order, make Italy great	To fix economy, make Germany great again
Once in Power ...	• Banned other political parties • Took away freedom of speech and press	• Took away freedom of speech, assembly, press, and religion • Sent Jews and others who disagreed with Nazi ideas to concentration camps

Glue Foldable here

The Great Depression also led to the rise of a totalitarian state in Germany. Germans were angry at how Germany had been punished by the Treaty of Versailles. Adolf Hitler was a powerful speaker who promised to provide jobs and restore German power in the world.

Hitler led the National Socialist (Nazi) Party. The Nazis said that Germans were a master race and better than other people. They blamed Jews for Germany's problems.

In 1933 the German Parliament named Hitler chancellor of Germany and passed a law that gave Hitler total power. This gave Hitler a legal way to become dictator.

Under Hitler, the government set up a secret police force. Other political parties and labor unions were banned. The Nazis set up prisons called concentration camps. They sent people who disagreed with Nazi ideas there. The government issued the Nuremberg Laws. It said that Jews were no longer citizens and took control of Jewish businesses and jobs.

The Soviet Union Under Stalin

The Soviet Union formed in 1922. It replaced the old Russian Empire. The Soviet Union was a communist state. Communist Party leader Joseph Stalin became dictator of the Soviet Union in the late 1920s.

Stalin wanted to turn the Soviet Union into an industrial power. He introduced Five-Year Plans that set economic goals. Under these plans, the state built and controlled all factories, power plants, and oil refineries.

Stalin also set up a system of **collectivization** in the countryside. Small farms of the peasants were combined into factory-like farms run by the government. The peasants fought back. They destroyed their property rather than join the system. However, their resistance did not last long. Those who refused to cooperate were killed or sent to prison.

Military Rule in Japan

Japan had an industrial economy and was hard hit by the Great Depression. Many workers lost their jobs and faced starvation. The workers and farmers turned to the military. Military leaders blamed Japan's problems on the spread of Western ideas. They wanted to return to old warrior traditions.

Military leaders wanted new territory and raw materials to make the Japanese economy stronger. In 1931 army leaders conquered Manchuria in China's northeastern region. When the Japanese prime minister tried to stop the war, the military killed him.

After that, the government began to do what the military wanted. Japan made plans to build an empire in Asia.

/ / / / / / / / / / / / / Glue Foldable here / / / / / / / / / / / / / /

Check for Understanding

List three countries that had totalitarian governments by 1939.

1. _______________

2. _______________

3. _______________

Reading Check

8. Why did Stalin force collective farms on Soviet peasants?

____

____

____

Reading Check

9. Why do you think Japanese military leaders blamed Japan's problems on the spread of Western ideas?

____

____

____

FOLDABLES®

10. Place a one-tab Foldable along the dotted line. Write *totalitarian state* in the center.
Create a memory map by drawing four arrows around the title. List words or phrases that help define the term and describe the lifestyle that it creates. Use both sides.

Lesson 2 World War II Begins

ESSENTIAL QUESTION

How does conflict develop?

GUIDING QUESTIONS

1. ***How did European leaders respond to the demands Hitler made for territory?***
2. ***How did war in Europe develop into another world war?***

Terms to Know

appeasement the act of trying to avoid war with an aggressive nation by giving in to its demands

Where in the world?

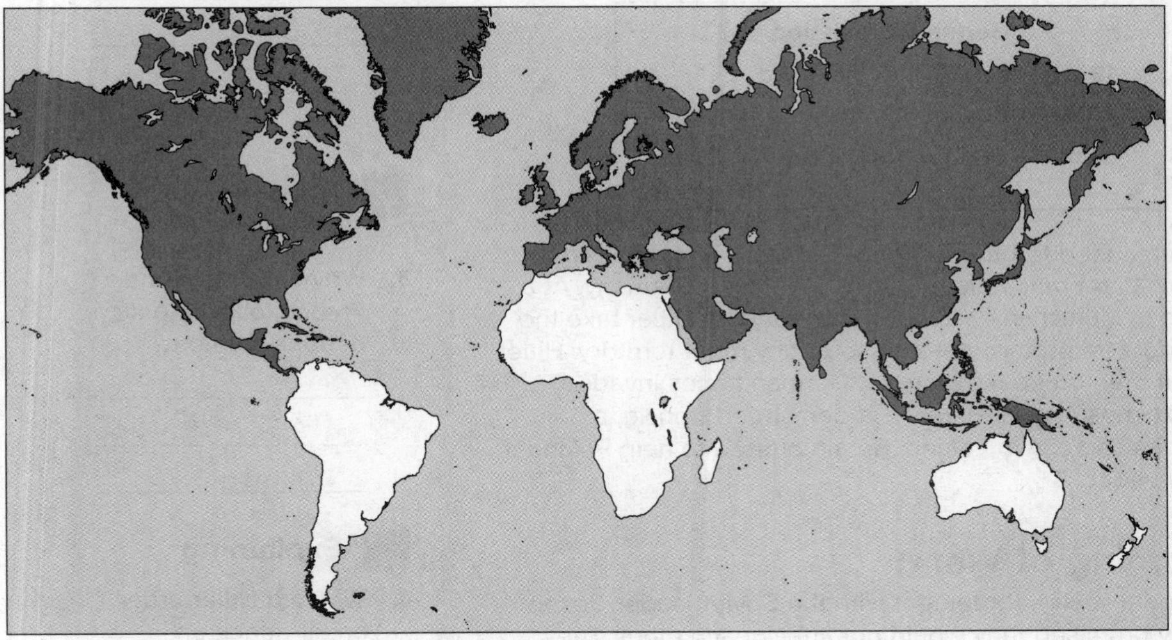

When did it happen?

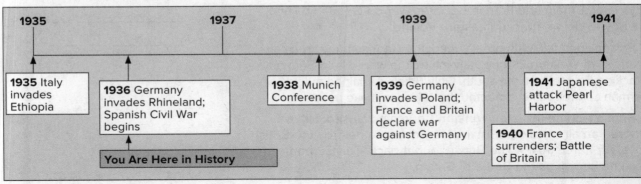

1935	1937	1939	1941

- **1935** Italy invades Ethiopia
- **1936** Germany invades Rhineland; Spanish Civil War begins
- You Are Here in History
- **1938** Munich Conference
- **1939** Germany invades Poland; France and Britain declare war against Germany
- **1940** France surrenders; Battle of Britain
- **1941** Japanese attack Pearl Harbor

The Path to War

The Treaty of Versailles ended World War I. Many Germans believed the treaty was unfair. It greatly limited the size of Germany's military. It also said no German troops could be in the Rhineland. This German area bordered France.

Hitler rejected the terms of the treaty. First he increased the size of Germany's armed forces. Then he sent German troops to occupy the Rhineland in 1936. Britain and France responded with a policy called **appeasement.** This meant they tried to avoid a fight by accepting Hitler's demands. Hitler continued taking territory in Europe.

German Expansion

1936: Occupied the Rhineland

1938: Took control of Austria

1938: Seized the Sudetenland in Czechoslovakia

Hitler demanded territories where German-speaking people lived. Britain and France did not want a war with Germany. At a conference in Munich in 1938, they agreed to let Hitler take the Sudetenland if he promised not to seize any more territory. Hitler agreed, but then broke his promise. German forces invaded western Czechoslovakia. Hitler next demanded Danzig, a German-speaking city in Poland. Britain offered to help Poland if Germany invaded.

The Coming of War

Hitler signed a secret agreement with the Soviet leader, Joseph Stalin. They promised they would not attack each other. They also agreed to divide Poland.

On September 1, 1939, Germany invaded western Poland. Two days later, Britain and France declared war on Germany. Then, the Soviet Union attacked eastern Poland.

Poland soon fell. With great speed, the German army then seized nearly all of Western Europe. Italy joined the war to help Germany, attacking France from the south. Only Britain remained outside of German control. Hitler expected the British to make peace.

Britain's prime minister, Winston Churchill, refused. Hitler ordered an air attack on Britain. He wanted to destroy the British Royal Air Force (RAF). The British fought back. This air battle became known as the Battle of Britain.

Defining

1. What is *appeasement*?

______

______

Identifying

2. What region did Hitler occupy in 1936?

______

______

______

Reading Check

3. Why did Britain and France follow a policy of appeasement?

______

______

______

Explaining

4. Why did Hitler order an air attack on Britain?

______

______

______

Lesson 2 World War II Begins, *Continued*

Marking the Text

5. Circle the name of the technology the British used in the air war against Germany.

Explaining

6. Why was the Battle of Britain important?

Analyzing

7. Why do you think Roosevelt believed Britain needed American help to stop Hitler?

Contrasting

8. How did the war change for the German military from the beginning of 1940 to the end of 1941?

The Germans bombed British airfields, aircraft factories, and cities. They destroyed large areas of London and killed many people. The RAF, however, used a new technology called radar, that used radio waves to track German planes. This helped British fighter pilots find the enemy. The Germans suffered heavy losses. Two months later, Hitler canceled his invasion plans.

Hitler turned his attention to invading the Soviet Union. He ignored the treaty with Stalin. In June 1941, German troops invaded the Soviet Union. They destroyed Soviet equipment and captured half a million soldiers.

Stalin ordered a scorched-earth policy. As the Soviets retreated, they burned their cities, destroyed their crops, and blew up dams. This made it difficult for the Germans to support their troops with food and other supplies.

When the rainy season began, the roads became muddy. German trucks and tanks got stuck. Soon after, the harsh winter set in. German invaders were unprepared for the cold. They reached Moscow in December 1941. The Soviets struck back, however, forcing the Germans to retreat.

The United States tried to stay out of the war in Europe. In the 1930s, Congress had passed laws making it illegal for the United States to help any country at war if the United States itself was not in the war.

President Roosevelt, however, saw Germany as a danger to the United States. In 1940 he convinced Congress to approve a law that would help Britain. The law let Britain buy food and weapons from Americans if they paid cash.

Congress Passes Wartime Laws

1930s: United States not allowed to help warring countries if U.S. itself was not in the war

1940: British allowed to buy U.S. goods under two conditions:

1) pay cash

2) use British ships to take goods to Britain

1941: U.S. lends weapons to Britain

British ships also had to carry the goods from the U.S. to Britain. Then in 1941, Congress passed the Lend-Lease Act. This law allowed the U.S. to lend weapons to Britain.

Just as Germany was expanding in Europe, Japan was also expanding in Asia. Japan had taken over Manchuria in northern China. Then they began moving south.

Lesson 2 World War II Begins, *Continued*

In 1937 the Japanese took over the Chinese capital of Nanjing. When France fell to the Germans in 1940, the Japanese invaded the French colony of Indochina. They had plans to seize the Dutch East Indies, British Malaya, and the American territory of the Philippines.

The United States tried to use economic pressure to stop Japanese expansion. President Roosevelt blocked the Japanese government from withdrawing money it had in American banks. Roosevelt also stopped selling oil, gasoline, and other resources to Japan.

Japan's reaction was to go to war. Japan bombed American ships and planes in Pearl Harbor, Hawaii, on December 7, 1941. Congress then declared war on Japan. Four days later, Germany and Italy declared war on the United States. The world was at war again.

The United States Enters World War II

Japan invades south China and Indochina.

↓

The United States freezes Japanese funds in U.S. banks and refuses to sell oil and other resources to Japan.

↓

Japan attacks Pearl Harbor on December 7, 1941.

↓

The United States declares war on Japan.

↓

Germany and Italy declare war on the United States.

/ / / / / / / / / / / / / Glue Foldable here / / / / / / / / / / / / /

Check for Understanding

List the countries Germany was fighting at the end of 1941.

1. ______________________

2. ______________________

3. ______________________

What event led to the U.S. entrance into World War II?

4. ______________________

Identifying

9. What is one economic action the United States took against Japan?

____

____

Reading Check

10. What was Stalin's scorched-earth policy?

____

____

____

FOLDABLES®

11. Place a one-tab Foldable along the dotted line. Write *Pearl Harbor* in the center of the tab. Create a memory map by drawing four arrows around the title.

List words or phrases that you remember about this event. Use the reverse side to add information.

NAME________________________ DATE ____________ CLASS ________

networks

World War II and the Cold War

Lesson 3 Allies Win the War

ESSENTIAL QUESTION

Why is history important?

GUIDING QUESTIONS

1. ***How did the Allies gradually push back Germany, Italy, and Japan in World War II?***
2. ***Why is the Holocaust considered a dark chapter in human history?***
3. ***What actions did the Allies take to win the war?***

Terms to Know

D-Day June 6, 1944, the day on which Allied forces began the invasion of France in World War II

When did it happen?

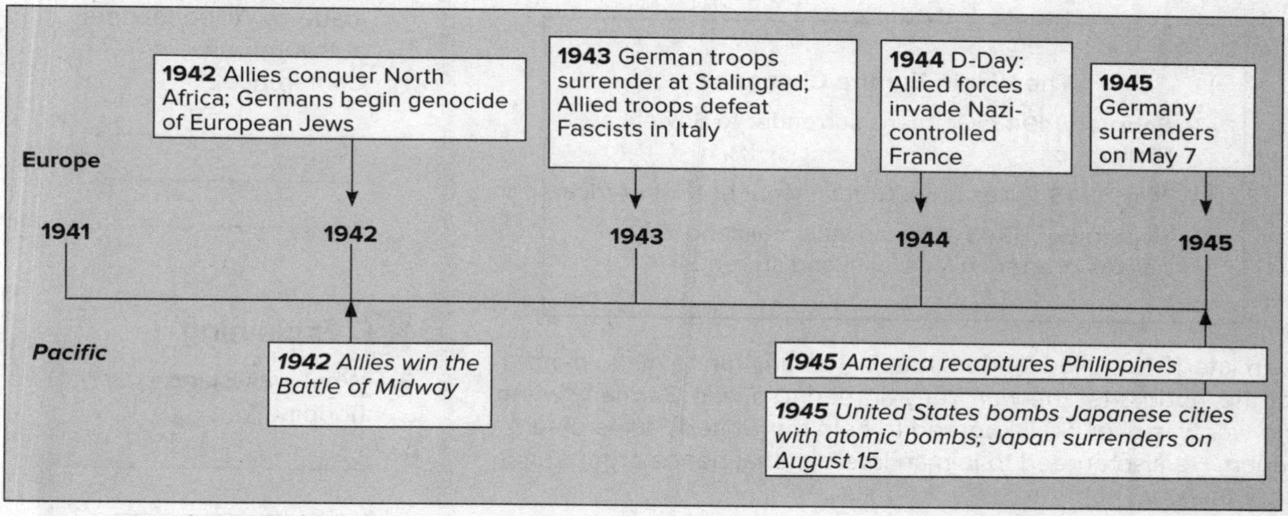
Europe
1942 Allies conquer North Africa; Germans begin genocide of European Jews
1943 German troops surrender at Stalingrad; Allied troops defeat Fascists in Italy
1944 D-Day: Allied forces invade Nazi-controlled France
1945 Germany surrenders on May 7
1941
1942
1943
1944
1945
Pacific
1942 Allies win the Battle of Midway
1945 America recaptures Philippines
1945 United States bombs Japanese cities with atomic bombs; Japan surrenders on August 15

What do you know?

In the K column, list what you already know about how the Allies won World War II. In the W column, list what you want to know. After reading the lesson, fill in the L column with the information that you learned.

K	W	L

The Global Struggle

World War II was a massive conflict. The war was fought mostly in two major areas, or theaters—Europe and the Pacific. The key nations on the Allied side were the United States, Britain, China, and the Soviet Union. They fought against the Axis powers of Germany, Italy, and Japan.

After defeating the Germans in North Africa, the Allies advanced on Italy. The Italians overthrew their dictator Mussolini and surrendered.

Meanwhile, the Soviets were fighting Germany in Eastern Europe. In the Soviet Union, the German army was surrounded in the city of Stalingrad. After a long fight, they surrendered. This marked a major turning point in the war.

The War in Europe Changes

- **February, 1943**: Germans surrender to Soviets at Stalingrad
- **May, 1943**: Allies drive Germany out of North Africa
- **September, 1943**: Allies invade mainland Italy; Italians overthrow Mussolini and surrender

In late 1943, Allied leaders met in Tehran, Iran to make plans for the world after the war. They agreed to divide Germany when the war was over. Stalin agreed to help the United States defeat Japan. He also agreed to join an international peace organization after the war.

In the Pacific, the United States won a major victory at Midway Island. Then the Americans began to push back Japan. They used a strategy called island-hopping. They attacked certain key Pacific islands. After taking an island, they used it as a base to help them reach other islands.

The War in the Pacific

- **June, 1942:** United States wins air and sea battle at Midway Island, ending Japanese advancements in the Pacific
- **1942–1945:** Americans island-hop to recapture key Pacific islands from Japanese
- **1945:** United States recaptures Philippines

Marking the Text

1. Underline the names of the main Allied countries. Circle the names of the Axis powers.

Listing

2. List three agreements made by Allied leaders at the Tehran Conference.

____

____

____

Explaining

3. What was island-hopping?

____

____

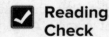

Reading Check

4. How was the war in Europe different from the war in the Pacific?

____

____

____

Defining

5. What is *genocide*?

____

____

Summarizing

6. What was the Holocaust?

____

____

____

____

Reading Check

7. Why do you think the Holocaust was a world human rights issue?

____

____

____

Identifying

8. What was D-Day?

____

____

The Holocaust

The Nazis believed the Germans were superior to other groups of people, such as the Jews, Gypsies, and Slavs.

The Nazis believed that the Jews were a threat to the "racial purity" of the German people. The Nazis began a program of genocide, the deliberate killing of an entire group of people. They called this the "final solution."

They rounded up Jews and sent them to death camps. There, the Jews were either poisoned in gas chambers or starved to death. As many as 6 million Jews, along with many Slavs and Gypsies, were killed in what is known as the Holocaust.

Nazi Persecution of the Jews

- **1930s:** German Jews lose their personal and political rights.
- **1938:** The "Night of Broken Glass"—Nazis burn synagogues, destroy Jewish businesses, and send thousands of Jewish men to prison camps.
- **1939–1945:** Jews are forced to live in ghettos and wear yellow stars to identify them as Jews.
- **1941:** Nazis begin mass killing of Jews in the Soviet Union.
- **1942:** Nazis send millions of Jews to death camps.

Ending the War

By 1944 Germany and Japan were retreating everywhere. On June 6, 1944, western Allied forces invaded Nazi-controlled France. That day is known as **D-Day**. Within a few weeks, a million Allied soldiers had landed in France. German forces retreated, and the western Allies moved into Paris.

Meanwhile, Soviet forces from the east pushed into Germany. After weeks of fighting, western Allied forces moved into Germany. Hitler committed suicide. On May 7, 1945, Germany surrendered. The war in Europe was over.

The war in the Pacific, however, continued. The Japanese would not surrender even though most of their navy and air force had been destroyed.

Lesson 3 Allies Win the War, *Continued*

In April 1945, Franklin Roosevelt died and Harry S. Truman became president. In the secret Manhattan Project, American scientists had developed the atomic bomb. Not everyone was sure that such a powerful weapon should be used. Truman had to make the decision.

The Manhattan Project

- Begun under President Roosevelt
- A secret project to build an atomic bomb
- Scientists worked at a laboratory in Los Alamos, New Mexico

Truman felt the atomic bomb could end the war while saving American lives. On August 6, 1945, the United States dropped an atomic bomb on the Japanese city of Hiroshima. Three days later, another bomb was dropped on the city of Nagasaki. Hundreds of thousands of Japanese people were killed. Japan surrendered on August 15, 1945. The war in the Pacific was over.

More than 70 million people fought in World War II. Millions of people died. The Allies put some German and Japanese leaders on trial for crimes against humanity. After the war, fifty countries formed the United Nations to keep world peace. In response to the Holocaust, the United Nations issued the Universal Declaration of Human Rights. It detailed the rights and freedoms of all people.

Check for Understanding

List two key changes that occurred as a result of World War II.

1. ______________________

2. ______________________

Name the cities, in order, on which the atomic bomb was dropped.

3. ______________________

4. ______________________

Glue Foldable here

Marking the Text

9. Circle the date that Japan surrendered.

Explaining

10. What caused Japan to surrender?

____

____

Reading Check

11. Why did President Truman decide to drop atomic bombs on Japan?

____

____

FOLDABLES®

12. Place a two-tab Foldable along the dotted line to cover the Check for Understanding. Write *Ending the War in ...* on the anchor tab. Label the tabs *Europe* and *Japan*.

List words or phrases that tell how the Allied Powers ended the war in Europe and in the Pacific.

NAME______________________________ DATE ______________ CLASS ________

Lesson 4 The Cold War

ESSENTIAL QUESTION

How do governments change?

GUIDING QUESTIONS

1. ***How did the United States try to stop the spread of communism without going to war?***
2. ***How did the Cold War affect countries in Asia?***
3. ***How did countries develop at home during the Cold War era?***

Terms to Know

containment preventing the spread of communism beyond its existing borders

Truman Doctrine the U.S. policy of granting aid to countries threatened by communist takeover

Marshall Plan U.S. program that gave aid to European countries to help them rebuild after the war to prevent the spread of communism

racial segregation the act of forcing a race to use separate facilities

Where in the world?

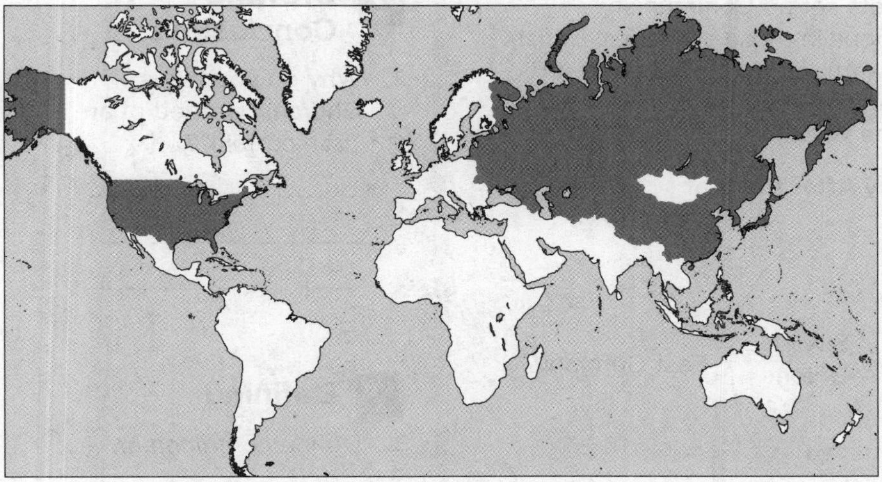

When did it happen?

1945 · 1950 · 1960 · 1970

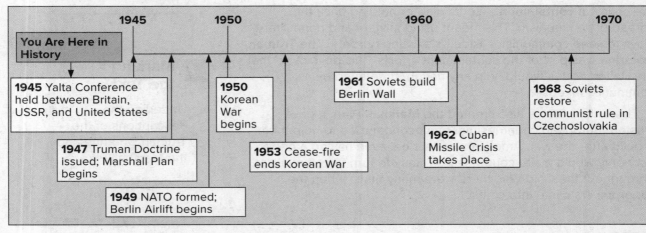

You Are Here in History

1945 Yalta Conference held between Britain, USSR, and United States

1947 Truman Doctrine issued; Marshall Plan begins

1949 NATO formed; Berlin Airlift begins

1950 Korean War begins

1953 Cease-fire ends Korean War

1961 Soviets build Berlin Wall

1962 Cuban Missile Crisis takes place

1968 Soviets restore communist rule in Czechoslovakia

Cold War Beginnings

The Soviet Union and the United States emerged from World War II as superpowers. They disagreed about how the world should be after the war. Their rivalry for world leadership was known as the Cold War.

The first problems began before the end of World War II, at the Yalta Conference. The Allied leaders agreed to split Germany into four parts. The eastern part was to be controlled by the Soviet Union. The western part was to be divided among the United States, Britain, and France. The capital, Berlin, was located deep inside the area controlled by the Soviet Union. It was also split into four parts, the same way the rest of Germany was.

The Allied Powers agreed to free elections in countries released from Nazi rule. The Soviets set up Communist governments instead and kept troops in those countries. British Prime Minister Winston Churchill warned that an "iron curtain" was descending on Europe. This meant that the Soviets were cutting off Eastern Europe from the West.

Dividing Germany After the War

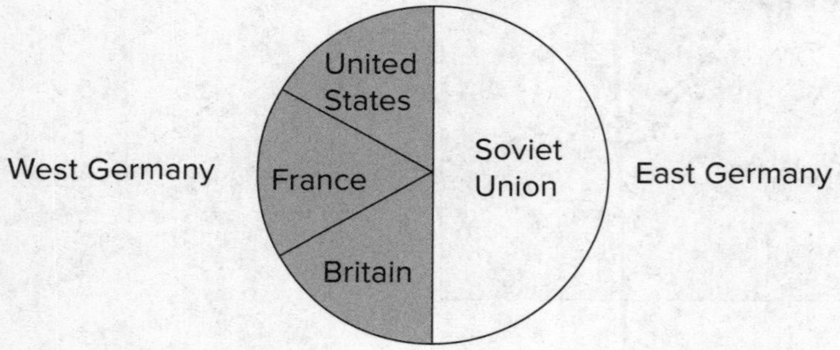

To stop the spread of communism, the United States adopted the policy of **containment**—containing or holding back the spread of communism. This meant using military and nonmilitary ways to keep communism inside its existing borders. The **Truman Doctrine** was part of the containment efforts. This policy said that the United States would help any nation threatened by a communist takeover.

The United States also created the **Marshall Plan**. It gave western European countries massive economic aid to help them rebuild after the war. American leaders believed having a better economy would make countries less likely to turn to communism. Throughout the Cold War, there were many times when the superpowers came into conflict.

Identifying

1. Identify the four nations that controlled a divided Germany after World War II.

____

____

____

____

Drawing Conclusions

2. Why do you think Churchill warned of an "iron curtain"?

____

____

____

Defining

3. Define *containment.*

____

____

____

Marking the Text

4. Underline the descriptions of the Truman Doctrine and the Marshall Plan.

Analyzing

5. Why did the Soviets place a blockade on West Berlin?

Reading Check

6. Why did the United States want Soviet missiles removed from Cuba?

Reading Check

7. Why did Chinese Nationalists create a government on the island of Taiwan?

In 1948 the western zones of Germany were united. They formed a new nation, West Germany. France, Britain, and the United States also united their sections of Berlin to create West Berlin. The Soviets responded by surrounding West Berlin and cutting off supplies. The West began bringing supplies into the city by airplane. The airlift forced the Soviets to end their blockade.

The Soviets built a concrete wall to keep East Germans from escaping to freedom in West Berlin. The Berlin Wall became a symbol of the divisions created by the Cold War.

During the Cold War, the United States and the Soviet Union competed in a nuclear arms race. Each side tried to build more nuclear weapons than the other. In 1962 the Soviets put missiles on the island of Cuba, which had a new Communist government. These missiles could easily reach the United States.

President Kennedy ordered the U.S. Navy to blockade Cuba. He also threatened to launch a nuclear attack on the Soviet Union if they fired the missiles at the United States. After five days, the Soviets agreed to remove the missiles.

The Cold War in Asia

After World War II, nationalists and communists fought each other for control of China. Communist leader Mao Zedong wanted to make China a great power. In the 1950s, the communist government took over all the businesses and industries in China. After Mao took over the mainland, Chinese Nationalists created a government on the island of Taiwan. They claimed to rule all of China from there.

Korea was divided into two nations after World War II. North Korea was communist. South Korea was backed by the United States.

North Korea	South Korea
• communist government • supported by China • invaded South Korea in 1950	• democratic government • supported by the United States • fought off North Korea for 3 years

In 1950 the North invaded the South. The United Nations and the United States sent troops to defend South Korea. Then China joined the fighting on North Korea's side. In 1953 a cease-fire agreement was signed that kept North and South Korea divided.

Lesson 4 The Cold War, *Continued*

Japan made a dramatic recovery after World War II. Under American occupation, Japan adopted a democratic constitution and a bill of rights. American aid helped Japan become a major economic power by the 1970s.

The Cold War Era

As the Cold War continued, the Soviet Union built up its manufacturing industries. In democratic Western Europe, economies prospered.

Life During the Cold War

Western Europe	The United States
• Marshall Plan helped countries rebuild • France became a center for manufacturing • Britain developed a service economy	• People fought to advance civil rights • Strong economic growth • Introduced Great Society programs to end poverty, improve education, and provide medical care

In 1954 the U.S. Supreme Court ruled against **racial segregation**, or separation of different races, in public schools. This was an important civil rights victory. Led by Dr. Martin Luther King, Jr., the civil rights movement used civil disobedience to change the laws. A new Civil Rights Act and Voting Rights Act were passed in the 1960s.

President Lyndon Johnson also introduced the Great Society programs. These were designed to end poverty, to improve education, and to provide medical care to the poor and elderly. Women also gained greater equality in the workplace with the passage of the Equal Pay Act in 1963. It outlawed paying women less than men for performing the same work.

Glue Foldable here

Check for Understanding

List three conflicts that occurred between the United States and the Soviet Union during the Cold War.

1. ______________________

2. ______________________

3. ______________________

Summarizing

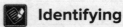

8. What helped Japan recover from World War II?

____

Identifying

9. Name two laws that expanded civil rights in the United States.

____

Reading Check

10. What was the Great Society?

____

FOLDABLES®

11. Place a three-tab Venn diagram Foldable along the dotted line. Write *The Cold War* on the anchor tab. Label the tabs *United States*, *Both*, and *Soviet Union*.

List facts about each to compare and contrast their roles after World War II.

NAME_________________________ DATE ____________ CLASS ________

networks

Lesson 5 The End of Empire

ESSENTIAL QUESTION

How do new ideas change the way people live?

GUIDING QUESTIONS

1. *How did Indians convince the British to give their country its freedom?*
2. *How did nations in Southeast Asia become independent?*
3. *How did Africans seek better treatment and independence from European rulers?*

Terms to Know

civil disobedience when people refuse to obey unjust laws by protesting peacefully

Pan-Africanism a movement for the political union of all the African nations

apartheid racial segregation system once enforced in South Africa

Where in the world?

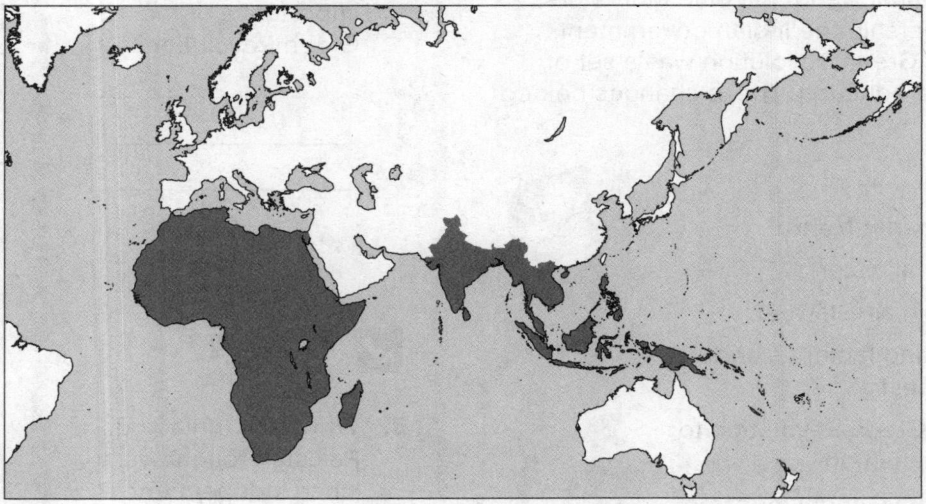

When did it happen?

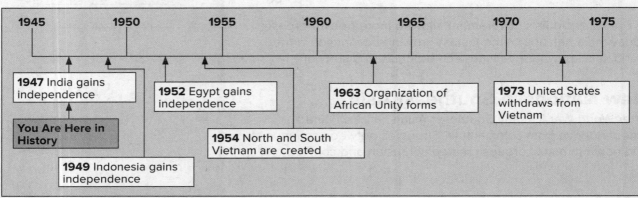

1945	1950	1955	1960	1965	1970	1975

- **1947** India gains independence
- **You Are Here in History**
- **1949** Indonesia gains independence
- **1952** Egypt gains independence
- **1954** North and South Vietnam are created
- **1963** Organization of African Unity forms
- **1973** United States withdraws from Vietnam

India Wins Independence

Indians formed the Indian National Congress in 1885 to work for independence from Britain. After World War I, Mohandas Gandhi became India's most popular leader. Gandhi protested British rule with nonviolent civil disobedience. Nonviolent **civil disobedience** means that people refuse to obey unjust laws by protesting peacefully.

Britain knew it could not keep control in India. In 1947 British India was split into two countries. One was India, which was mainly Hindu. The other was Pakistan, which was mainly Muslim. Pakistan was made up of two areas separated by India's territory. The two countries have fought several wars over the border region of Kashmir. In 1971 the eastern area of Pakistan became a new country, Bangladesh.

After independence, Jawaharlal Nehru became India's first prime minister. Under his leadership the Indian government focused on the economy. The Green Revolution was a set of changes that increased food production. These changes helped India feed its people.

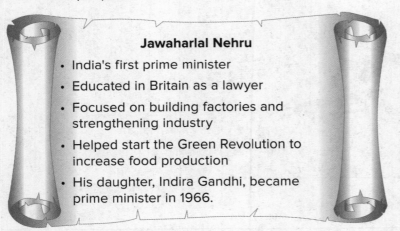

Jawaharlal Nehru

- India's first prime minister
- Educated in Britain as a lawyer
- Focused on building factories and strengthening industry
- Helped start the Green Revolution to increase food production
- His daughter, Indira Gandhi, became prime minister in 1966.

Eventually India's government allowed more free enterprise. Today India has one of the fastest-growing economies in the world. It is known for its high-tech products and software.

New Nations in Southeast Asia

After World War II, many Southeast Asian nations gained independence from colonial rule. Struggles between communist and noncommunist groups created confusion and conflict.

Defining

1. What is *civil disobedience*?

____

____

____

Analyzing

2. What was the importance of the Green Revolution?

____

____

____

Reading Check

3. Why have India and Pakistan fought wars since independence?

____

____

____

Marking the Text

4. Underline the British colonies in Southeast Asia that gained independence.

Identifying

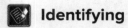

5. Which countries have fought for control of what is now Vietnam?

____
____
____
____

Reading Check

6. Why did the United States become involved in the Vietnam conflict?

____
____
____
____

In 1949 the East Indies gained independence from the Dutch. The country was led by Achmed Sukarno. It changed its name to Indonesia. Sukarno did much to unite the many islands of Indonesia, but he ruled as a dictator. In 1965 violence between communist rebels and the military led to General Suharto taking power. He was an anti-communist dictator. More than 20 years later, Suharto fell from power. By 2004, Indonesia was a democracy.

Burma, now called Myanmar, became independent from Britain in 1948. In the 1960s, Myanmar became a socialist country under military rule. Britain also granted independence to its colonies on the Malay Penninsula. These became known as Malaysia in 1963.

French Indochina was the site of major conflict after World War II. Japan had seized Indochina during World War II. After the war, France wanted the colony back. People in Indochina, however, wanted independence.

In Vietnam, the communist leader Ho Chi Minh formed a group called the Vietminh to drive out the Japanese. French troops then fought the Vietminh for control of Vietnam but lost. In 1954 an agreement called the Geneva Accords divided the country into North and South Vietnam.

North and South Vietnam were supposed to hold elections for a unified government. The elections never took place. North Vietnam then tried to unite the country by force. Ho Chi Minh formed an army called the Vietcong.

The United States in Vietnam

1954—President Dwight D. Eisenhower sends military advisers and aid to South Vietnam.

1964—Congress gives President Lyndon Johnson the power to fight a war in Vietnam.

1965—The United States begins bombing North Vietnam.

1965—Johnson sends the first American combat troops.

1973—President Richard Nixon withdraws American forces from Vietnam.

The United States feared the spread of communism in Southeast Asia. President Eisenhower sent military advisers to help South Vietnam. Then President Johnson sent American troops to Vietnam in the mid-1960s. The war dragged on and became unpopular in the United States. In 1973 President Nixon withdrew American troops. At least 2 million people died in the conflict.

Independence in Africa

After World War II, European countries held on tightly to their African colonies. Many Africans wanted independence. In North Africa, Egypt became fully independent from Britain in 1952. After a bloody civil war, Algeria finally won its independence from France in 1962.

In the late 1950s and 1960s, many colonies south of the Sahara also gained their independence. The new nation of Ghana was formed from the British colony called the Gold Coast. In Rhodesia, the black majority won their struggle and renamed the country Zimbabwe.

Ghana's Kwame Nkrumah was a leader in the movement for **Pan-Africanism**—the unity of all black Africans. Thirty-two African nations formed the Organization of African Unity (OAU). Today, the African Union (AU) is a closely united organization that has replaced the OAU.

South Africa had been independent since the early 1900s. Most people were black, but a small white European population ran the government. In 1912 black South Africans created the African National Congress (ANC) to gain political power. White South Africans, however, set up the system of **apartheid**. This system separated ethnic groups and limited the rights of blacks. Blacks could not vote. Their jobs and food were limited.

Black South Africans protested, but the government dealt harshly with them. Police jailed Nelson Mandela, the leader of the ANC. The UN condemned apartheid. Many countries cut off trade with South Africa. It took more than 30 years for the apartheid system to end.

Glue Foldable here

Check for Understanding

List one event that occurred in each of the following places as people there moved toward independence after World War II.

1. India _______________
2. Southeast Asia _______________
3. Ghana _______________
4. South Africa _______________

Analyzing

7. What African movement did Nkrumah and others work for?

____

____

____

____

Reading Check

8. Why might people have believed that Pan-Africanism would help African people?

____

____

____

FOLDABLES®

9. Place a two-tab Foldable along the dotted line to cover the Check for Understanding. Label the tabs *civil disobedience* and *freedom*.

Recall what you have learned about each in the chapter. Write one or two sentences using the terms. Use both sides of the tabs.

NAME _______________________ DATE ___________ CLASS ________

networks

Building Today's World

Lesson 1 Challenges in Latin America

ESSENTIAL QUESTIONS

How do governments change?

GUIDING QUESTIONS

1. ***What economic challenges have Latin America's people faced?***
2. ***Why has progress been difficult in the Caribbean and Central America?***
3. ***How have political leaders dealt with the challenges facing Mexico?***
4. ***How has the desire for prosperity and democracy affected the recent history of South America?***

Terms to Know

nationalize to place private property under the control of a government

embargo a ban on trading or doing business with another country

deforestation the cutting of forests without replanting

Where in the world?

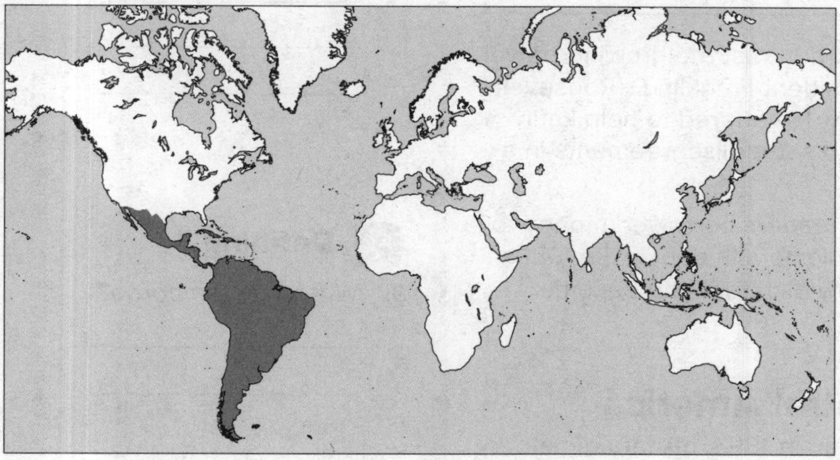

When did it happen?

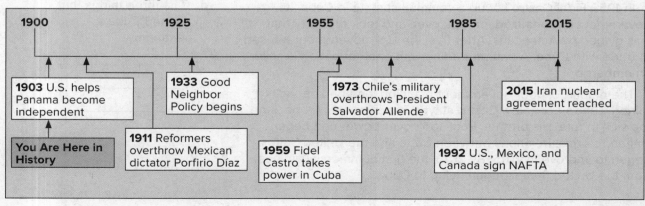

1900 | 1925 | 1955 | 1985 | 2015

1903 U.S. helps Panama become independent

You Are Here in History

1911 Reformers overthrow Mexican dictator Porfirio Díaz

1933 Good Neighbor Policy begins

1959 Fidel Castro takes power in Cuba

1973 Chile's military overthrows President Salvador Allende

1992 U.S., Mexico, and Canada sign NAFTA

2015 Iran nuclear agreement reached

Economic Developments

Countries in Latin America became free from European control in the 1800s. The rich controlled political life, however. The poor had little power.

Latin America's economy was based on farming and mining. Businesspeople from industrial nations set up companies there. Some Latin American countries depended on one or two exports, such as sugarcane or coffee. When demand for these goods was high, profits grew. When demand fell, businesses closed, and workers lost jobs. Foreign investors paid for new construction. Cities grew, and a middle class formed. Most people, however, had a hard time earning enough money to live.

Foreign investors built:

- shipping ports
- roads and railroads
- new factories

Many Latin American countries did not trust the growing power of the United States. In 1933 U.S. president Franklin D. Roosevelt announced the Good Neighbor Policy. He offered to help Latin American economies and promised to settle disagreements in a peaceful way.

After World War II, Latin American leaders borrowed money to boost their economies. This led to problems with debt in the 1980s. It caused some countries to overthrow dictators and become democracies.

The Caribbean and Central America

After Cuba won its freedom from Spain in 1898, military dictators ruled the island nation. U.S. companies controlled most of the wealth, which came from sugar and mining.

In 1959 Fidel Castro set up a communist state in Cuba. Its government **nationalized**, or took over, and took property that was owned by Americans. After this, the U.S. government refused to trade with Cuba. A ban on trading with another nation is called an **embargo**.

The embargo, poor government planning, and bad harvests ruined Cuba's economy. Castro stayed in power until he became too sick to rule. His brother, Raul, took over power and began limited reforms. Relations between Cuba and the United States began to improve in 2015. By 2016, the first commercial airlines from the United States began flying to Cuba.

Explaining

1. What was the Good Neighbor Policy?

____

____

____

Reading Check

2. How did dependence on exports affect Latin American economies?

____

____

____

Defining

3. What is an *embargo*?

____

____

Listing

4. List three things that ruined Cuba's economy.

____

____

____

Lesson 1 Challenges in Latin America, *Continued*

Explaining

5. What role did the military play in Haiti?

______

Reading Check

6. What nation was deeply affected by a U.S. embargo on trade?

______

Drawing Conclusions

7. What changes did President Cárdenas bring to Mexico?

______

Reading Check

8. Why did Mexico build new industries after it signed the NAFTA agreement?

______

In the Caribbean republic of Haiti, François Duvalier and his son Jean-Claude Duvalier ruled using terror. Jean-Claude was finally overthrown by the military in 1986. Life in Haiti remains very hard. In 2010 a strong earthquake killed tens of thousands of people.

In Central America, Panama became wealthy due to the trade and fees brought in by the Panama Canal. In 1999 the United States gave the canal to Panama. Many other countries in Central America suffered from civil wars.

Civil Wars in Central America

Nicaragua	Guatemala
• Sandinista rebels overthrow Nicaragua's dictator. • The United States supports rebels called contras who fight the Sandinistas. • Sandinistas lose power in 1990 but regain it in 2006.	• United States helps Guatemala's government fight rebels from 1960 to 1996. • The civil war kills about 200,000 people and weakens the economy.

Changes in Mexico

In 1911 Mexican reformers overthrew dictator Porfirio Díaz. Revolution swept Mexico and led to a new constitution.

Later, President Lázaro Cárdenas tried to free industries from foreign control. In 1938 he nationalized foreign-owned oil wells. This means he had the Mexican government take them over. Mexico's oil industry helped the country's economy grow.

Mexico also tried to improve ties with other countries. In 1992 it signed the North American Free Trade Agreement (NAFTA) with the United States and Canada. Under NAFTA, Mexico built new industries. Foreign companies have built *maquiladoras* in Mexico. *Maquiladoras* are factories where workers put together parts made in other countries.

Even with these factories, many Mexicans cannot find jobs. Many become migrant workers. These are people who travel to find work, such as planting or harvesting crops. The work does not pay well, but migrant workers can earn more in the United States than in Mexico.

Nations of South America

During the 1900s, many South American governments were officially republics, but were ruled by dictators. Juan Perón was a military leader who became president of Argentina in 1946. Argentina finally became a democracy again in 1982. The country elected its first woman president, Cristina Fernández, in 2007.

South American countries that became democracies:
- Argentina
- Chile

South American countries that elected female presidents:
- Argentina: Cristina Fernández
- Chile: Michelle Bachelet

The military ruled Brazil from 1964 to 1985. It then became a federal republic. Brazil is a world economic leader. Farming, logging, and mining, however, have led to the **deforestation** of the Amazon rain forest. Deforestation means that trees are cut down without replanting new ones. Brazil is now working to protect its forest.

In 1970 the people of Chile elected Salvador Allende. The military forced him out of power in 1973. General Augusto Pinochet became dictator of Chile, ruling harshly until he was forced to resign in 1990. In 2006 voters elected the country's first woman president, Michelle Bachelet.

In Venezuela, former military leader Hugo Chávez was elected president. Some people supported him, but others criticized his lack of concern for human rights. In Colombia, competing political groups and government forces began fighting each other in the 1970s. Even though peace talks started in 2012, the conflict still continues. Since the 1980s, drug dealers have been a powerful force in the region.

Check for Understanding

List four challenges faced by the countries of Latin America.

1. ______________________

2. ______________________

3. ______________________

4. ______________________

Glue Foldable here

Marking the Text

9. Underline the names of two dictators in South America.

Reading Check

10. What role did military forces play in South America's efforts to become democratic?

____

____

____

FOLDABLES®

11. Cut a two-tab Foldable into a four-tab Foldable. Place it over the Check for Understanding. Write *U.S. Presence in Latin America* on the anchor tab. Label the tabs *Spanish-American War, Good Neighbor Policy, Panama Canal*, and *North American Free Trade Agreement (NAFTA).*

Use both sides of the tabs to list what you remember about the effects and/or the outcomes of each.

NAME _______________ DATE _________ CLASS _______

networks

Building Today's World

Lesson 2 Africa and the Middle East

ESSENTIAL QUESTION

Why does conflict develop?

GUIDING QUESTIONS

1. ***How have Africans tried to build nations after winning independence?***
2. ***What issues have shaped the Arab-Israeli conflict?***
3. ***How have revolution and war changed the Middle East?***

Terms to Know

refugee person who flees to another country to escape war, violence, or natural disaster

terrorism the use of violence against civilians to achieve a political goal

intifada an uprising

Where in the world?

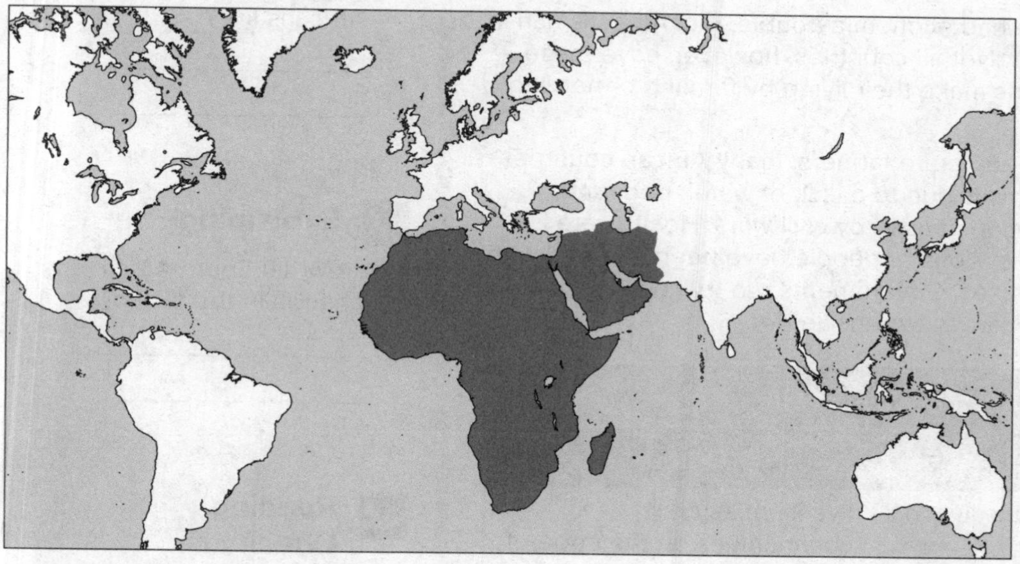

When did it happen?

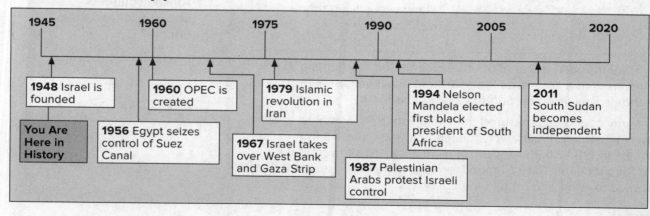

1945 | 1960 | 1975 | 1990 | 2005 | 2020

- **1948** Israel is founded
- **You Are Here in History**
- **1956** Egypt seizes control of Suez Canal
- **1960** OPEC is created
- **1967** Israel takes over West Bank and Gaza Strip
- **1979** Islamic revolution in Iran
- **1987** Palestinian Arabs protest Israeli control
- **1994** Nelson Mandela elected first black president of South Africa
- **2011** South Sudan becomes independent

Nation-Building in Africa

In the 1800s, Europeans divided Africa into colonies. They put together religious and ethnic groups that did not get along. After African nations gained their independence, many kept the colonial borders. Ethnic groups began to fight. Many people died. Others became **refugees**, people who flee to other countries to find safety from violence, mistreatment, or disaster.

In Sudan, a civil war killed nearly 2 million people. After a peace agreement was reached, an election was held. Most voters in southern Sudan voted for independence. In 2011 South Sudan became an independent country. In Nigeria, a violent Islamic group called Boko Haram has taken land and captured and imprisoned many people.

African nations have had economic trouble, too. Africa is rich in oil, gold, and diamonds. Not all countries, however, have these resources. Most Africans make their living by farming or herding livestock.

Even though most people are farmers, many African countries have to import food. This is due to a lack of water, poor crop production, and disruption caused by civil wars. Health care is also an issue in Africa. Millions of people have been infected with the Ebola and AIDS viruses. Governments are trying to help, but providing good health care is expensive.

African Ways of Life

Rural	Urban
• 70 percent of Africans live in villages • farm or herd animals • work on company-run farms	• live in cities or in communities on the edge of cities • city jobs provide a higher standard of living than rural jobs • better education

The European rulers of South Africa limited the rights of black Africans with a system called apartheid. Black leader Nelson Mandela was jailed for fighting to end apartheid.

Many countries pressured the white-run government to end apartheid in the 1990s. Nelson Mandela was released from prison. In 1994 South Africans of all races were allowed to vote for the first time. They elected Mandela to be their president. He worked to unite and rebuild the country.

Listing

1. List three challenges that Africa faces.

____

____

____

Identifying

2. Where do most Africans live?

____

____

Explaining

3. How did South Africa change in the 1990s?

____

____

Reading Check

4. Why do so many African countries struggle to feed their people?

____

____

____

Explaining

5. Why was a Jewish nation created after World War II?

____

____

____

____

Defining

6. What is *terrorism*?

____

____

____

Marking the Text

7. Underline the names of the leaders who helped reach the Camp David Accords.

The Arab-Israeli Conflict

After World War II, European empires in the Middle East ended and independent Arab nations were created. Oil was discovered. The world needed this oil. The Middle East became an important center of trade.

In 1948 the Jewish state of Israel was created. Israel gave Jews a home after the horrors of the Holocaust. Many Jews from Europe, Asia, and Africa came to live in Israel. Many Arabs did not want this.

The United Nations divides the Palestine Mandate into a Jewish state and an Arab state in 1947.

↓

Jewish settlers create the state of Israel in 1948.

↓

Arabs and Israelis fight over land. Israelis win.

↓

Palestinian Arabs flee to refugee camps.

In 1967 war broke out again between Israel and its Arab neighbors. In six days, Israel wiped out the Arab air forces. Israeli troops moved into the Gaza Strip, Egypt's Sinai Peninsula, and Syria's Golan Heights. They took over the city of Jerusalem and the West Bank of the Jordan River. The Six-Day War brought one million Palestinian Arabs under Israeli rule.

In the 1960s, Yasir Arafat became leader of the Palestinian Liberation Organization (PLO). The PLO wanted to destroy Israel and take its land for the Palestinians. The PLO carried out acts of **terrorism** against Israelis. Terrorism is the use of violence against civilians to achieve a political goal.

In 1960 many oil-producing nations, including Arab countries, formed the Organization of Petroleum Exporting Countries (OPEC). The countries control world oil prices and oil production. During a 1973 war between Egypt and Israel, the United States and other countries supported Israel. OPEC countries refused to sell oil to those countries. This created an energy crisis.

In 1978 Egyptian President Anwar Sadat met with Israeli leader Menachem Begin and U.S. president Jimmy Carter at Camp David in Maryland. The talks led to the Camp David Accords. In this treaty, Egypt agreed to recognize Israel, and Israel agreed to give up the Sinai Peninsula.

In the 1980s, Palestinian Arabs began an **intifada**, or uprising. Palestinian fighters were angry about a new peace plan. They set off bombs in Israel. To keep out attackers, Israel built a wall along its borders with Palestinian areas.

PLO leader Yasir Arafat died in 2004. The new Palestinian leader, Mahmoud Abbas, wanted to work with Israel. To begin the peace process, Israel left the Gaza Strip in 2005. Israel and Palestine continued to disagree about control of old Jerusalem and Jewish settlements in the West Bank.

Conflict in the Middle East

Oil makes some Middle Eastern countries rich. Others have few resources. These challenges have helped political and religious movements grow. Groups based on the religion of Islam are among these movements. These groups believe their societies should return to traditional Islamic values.

Iran was the first to experience an Islamic Revolution. After World War II, the United States supported Iran's shah, or king. However, many Iranians disliked his harsh rule. They turned to religious leaders who organized protests. The shah left the country and Iran became an Islamic republic.

In the 1990s, many Iranians demanded more freedom. The government blocked reforms. Iranian President Mahmoud Ahmadinejad supported Iran's strict religious policies. He won reelection in 2009, but protestors claimed there was voter fraud. In 2013, Hassan Rouhani was elected president. He promised more moderate policies.

In 2011, protests swept across the Arab world. Protestors were able to organize using social media. They demanded democratic reforms in their governments. Governments such as Egypt, Libya, and Syria became more unstable. The rise of the militant Islamic group, the Islamic State in Iraq and Syria (ISIS), further complicated issues in Southwest Asia.

/ / / / / / / / / / / / / Glue Foldable here / / / / / / / / / / / / / /

Check for Understanding

Tell how each of these people participated in events in Africa and the Middle East.

1. Nelson Mandela ______
2. Anwar Sadat ______
3. President Mahmoud Ahmadinejad ______

______

Reading Check

8. What were the effects of the Six-Day War?

______

______

______

Reading Check

9. What happened to Iran after the overthrow of the shah?

______

______

______

FOLDABLES®

10. Glue a one-tab Foldable along the dotted line. Draw a large circle on the tab. Label it *After World War II.* Next, draw two smaller circles inside the large circle. Label the small circles *Africa* and *Middle East.*

In the small circles, list important facts about the changes in each location following World War II.

networks

Building Today's World

Lesson 3 End of the Cold War

ESSENTIAL QUESTION

How do new ideas change the way people live?

GUIDING QUESTIONS

1. ***Why did the Soviet Union and Eastern European Communist governments collapse?***
2. ***How have the policies of China's government changed since the 1960s?***

Terms to Know

détente a relaxing or easing of tensions between rival nations

glasnost Soviet policy of openness that allowed freedom of speech

perestroika Soviet plan of reforming government and economic policies

ethnic cleansing removing or killing an entire ethnic group

Where in the world?

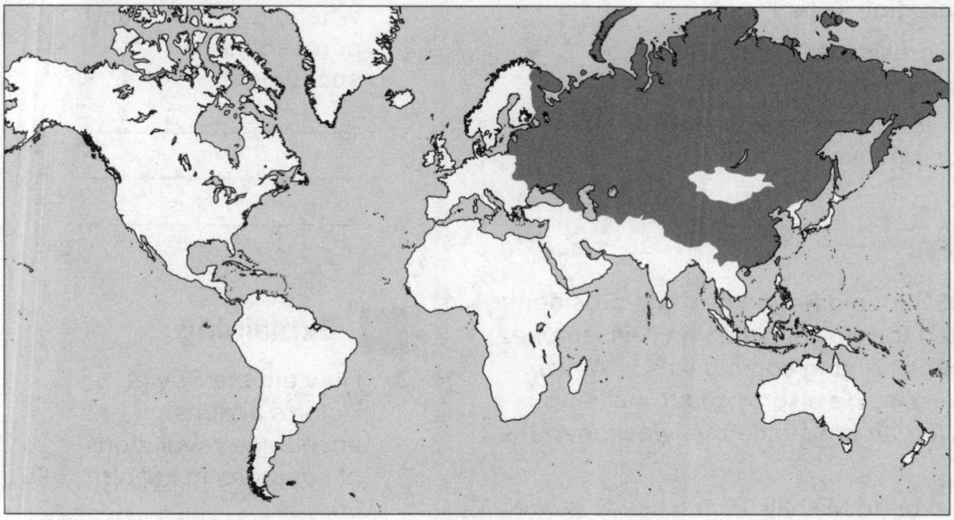

When did it happen?

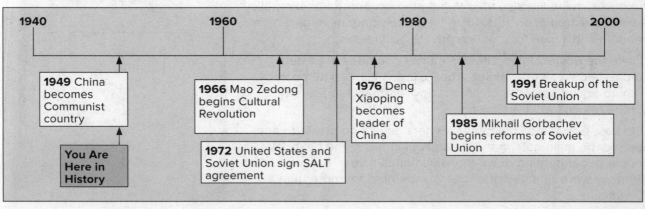

1940	1960	1980	2000

- **1949** China becomes Communist country
- You Are Here in History
- **1966** Mao Zedong begins Cultural Revolution
- **1972** United States and Soviet Union sign SALT agreement
- **1976** Deng Xiaoping becomes leader of China
- **1985** Mikhail Gorbachev begins reforms of Soviet Union
- **1991** Breakup of the Soviet Union

The Collapse of the Soviet Empire

After many years of Cold War tensions, relations began to improve among the United States and the Soviet Union and China. The Soviet Union felt more secure. The United States was recovering from the Vietnam War.

During the 1970s, the United States and the Soviet Union began a new policy of **détente.** Détente comes from a French word that means "a relaxing of tensions." As part of the détente, the U.S. and the Soviet Union signed the Strategic Arms Limitation Treaty or SALT. SALT limited the number of nuclear weapons that both countries could have.

SALT, the Strategic Arms Limitation Treaty

- Signed by U.S. president Richard Nixon and Soviet leader Leonid Brezhnev
- Limited the number of nuclear weapons of the two superpowers

Détente did not last. In 1981 Ronald Regan became president of the United States. He called the Soviet Union an "evil empire." Reagan gave support to groups fighting communists in Africa, Central America, and Afghanistan. He also began to build up U.S. military power. This started an arms race that weakened the Soviet economy.

The economic crisis helped bring Mikhail Gorbachev to power in 1985. He began a policy of **glasnost**, or "openness." The Soviet people could speak and write freely without fear of punishment by the government. He also tried to help the economy with the policy called **perestroika**, or "rebuilding." It gave factory managers more freedom and called for creating private businesses.

Like the Soviet Union, the communist countries of Eastern Europe had weak economies. Their citizens wanted democracy. With no Soviet help, the communist governments in Eastern Europe fell one after another.

In East Germany, Communist leaders gave in to pressure and opened the main gate in the Berlin Wall in 1989. The next day, people began tearing down the wall. Within a year, East and West Germany were reunited after being separated for more than 40 years.

Explaining

1. Why did relations improve between the United States and the Soviet Union?

____

____

____

Summarizing

2. What did glasnost and perestroika encourage?

____

____

____

Explaining

3. How did the Soviet Union's actions encourage revolutions of countries in Eastern Europe?

____

____

____

Defining

4. What is *ethnic cleansing*?

____

____

____

Reading Check

5. What were the two new policies that Gorbachev introduced?

____

____

____

Comparing

6. In what way are the policies of Deng Xiaoping like those of Mao Zedong?

____

____

____

At the same time, Gorbachev received criticism from both hard-liners and reformers. Hard-liners, who supported communism, wanted to stop changes. Reformers wanted Gorbachev to speed up the changes in the Soviet Union.

Boris Yeltsin led the reformers. He became president of Russia, the largest Soviet republic. In 1991 hard-line Communists tried to take over the government but failed. The Soviet Union collapsed. In recent years, Russia's president, Vladimir Putin, has tried to extend Russia's influence in the Crimea region and Southwest Asia.

National and ethnic groups began to fight in the country of Yugoslavia on the Balkan Peninsula. In the early 1990s, four republics declared independence. They were Slovenia, Croatia, Bosnia-Herzegovina, and Macedonia. The republic of Serbia wanted to keep the country united. Serbia's leaders used force to control other republics.

- The worst fighting took place in Bosnia-Herzegovina.
- Serbs fought Croats and Muslims there.
- The Serbs carried out **ethnic cleansing,** removing or killing an entire ethnic group, against non-Serbs.
- Many people died. Others fled the country.

In 2004 Serbia's government renamed the country Serbia and Montenegro. Other territories declared independence. The country once known as Yugoslavia is now as many as six different countries.

China Under Communism

Communist leader Mao Zedong feared China was losing its commitment to communism. In 1966 he began the Cultural Revolution. People who disagreed with communist ideas were jailed. Students called Red Guards accused leaders and ordinary people of not supporting communism.

The Cultural Revolution failed. It hurt China's economy and society. Finally the Chinese army was called out to end the revolution. Mao Zedong died in 1976.

China's new leader, Deng Xiaoping, wanted to build China's economy. He relaxed government control of factories and farms. He set up economic zones in China where people from other countries could run businesses.

By 2000 these reforms had made China a powerful economic force. Growth in China's manufacturing industry created problems, however. Some factories make unsafe products. China also suffers from some of the worst pollution in the world.

Lesson 3 End of the Cold War, *Continued*

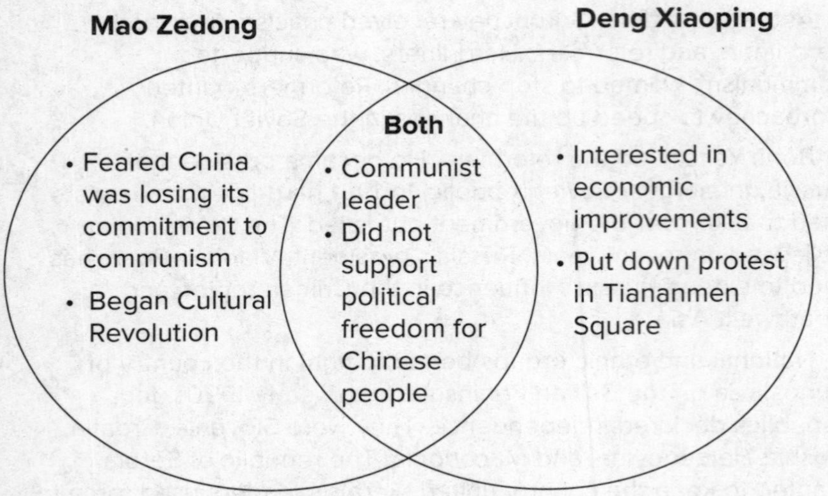
Mao Zedong
Deng Xiaoping
Both
• Feared China was losing its commitment to communism
• Began Cultural Revolution
• Communist leader
• Did not support political freedom for Chinese people
• Interested in economic improvements
• Put down protest in Tiananmen Square

China increased economic freedom for its people, but it has not allowed more political freedom. In 1989 thousands of people gathered in Tiananmen Square in Beijing calling for more democracy. The government sent soldiers into the square to break up the protest. Many people were killed or hurt.

China also has been criticized for taking over the Buddhist kingdom of Tibet in 1950. Tibet is an area in southwestern China. Tibet's Buddhist leader, the Dalai Lama, has asked world leaders to support Tibet's call for independence. China refuses to make changes.

China also regained Hong Kong and Macau, territories that were taken by Europeans in the 1800s. Now, they are centers of manufacturing, trade, and finance.

Check for Understanding

Name the events that caused Communist governments to fall in the following countries.

1. East Germany ______

2. Soviet Union ______

Describe what happened in Tiananmen Square.

3. ______

______

Examining

7. What are the positive and negative results of China's economic growth?

______

______

______

Reading Check

8. What was the Cultural Revolution in China?

______

______

______

FOLDABLES®

9. Place a two-tab Foldable to cover the Check for Understanding. On the anchor tab, write *Challenges to Communism*. Label the top tab *Bosnia* and the bottom tab *Tiananmen Square*.

Use both sides of the tabs to record what you remember about these events challenging communism.

Glue Foldable here

NAME________________________ DATE ____________ CLASS ________

networks

Building Today's World

Lesson 4 The World Enters a New Century

ESSENTIAL QUESTION

How does technology change the way people live?

GUIDING QUESTIONS

1. *How has the world changed politically during the past 20 years?*
2. *How has the world become more connected in the early twenty-first century?*
3. *What challenges face the global community in the early 2000s?*

Terms to Know

interdependent relying on one another for goods, information, and other resources

pandemic disease that occurs over a wide area and affects a large number of people

When did it happen?

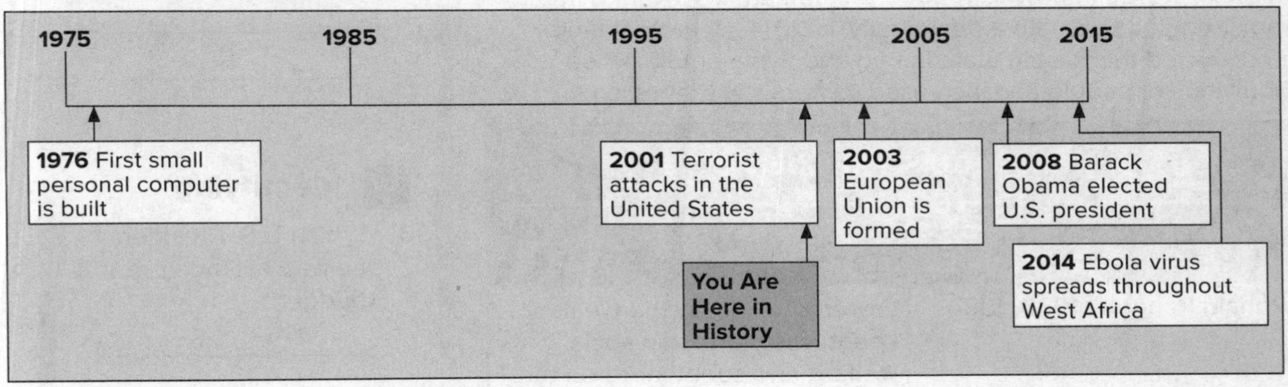

1975
1985
1995
2005
2015
1976 First small personal computer is built
2001 Terrorist attacks in the United States
You Are Here in History
2003 European Union is formed
2008 Barack Obama elected U.S. president
2014 Ebola virus spreads throughout West Africa

What do you know?

Read each statement. Circle T if you think the statement is true. Circle F if you think the statement is false.

1. The acts of terrorism on September 11 affected mostly soldiers.	T	F
2. Computers were invented in 1980.	T	F
3. About 85 percent of Americans say they use the Internet.	T	F
4. Interdependent countries rely on one another.	T	F
5. There is a small gap between developed and developing nations.	T	F
6. New technologies have improved health care.	T	F
7. Barack Obama reformed welfare and balanced the budget.	T	F

A Changing World

The world now has a global economy. Various cultures and governments around the world also influence each other.

On September 11, 2001, Islamic terrorists crashed four U.S. passenger planes into the Pentagon and the World Trade Center. These 9/11 attacks killed nearly 3,000 people.

The terrorists were part of al-Qaeda. Al-Qaeda was created to fight Soviet forces that invaded Afghanistan in 1979. Osama Bin Laden later turned al-Qaeda into an Islamic terrorist group. In Afghanistan, the Taliban government provided shelter to al-Qaeda. American and allied forces invaded Afghanistan in 2001. In 2011, U.S. forces killed bin Laden in Pakistan.

In 1990 Iraq seized the oil-rich country of Kuwait. U.S. and allied troops forced the Iraqis out. However, Iraq's leader, Saddam Hussein, stayed in power. In 2003 U.S.-led armies invaded Iraq. Iraq struggled to create a democracy. In 2014 a violent Islamic group called the Islamic State in Iraq and Syria, or ISIS, killed thousands of people and increased its forces in the region.

RECENT U.S. PRESIDENTS

President	Years Elected	Key Issues
Ronald Reagan	1980, 1984	Lowered taxes for the wealthy, spent less money on social welfare and spent more on the military
George H.W. Bush	1988	Dealt with weak economy and first war against Iraq
Bill Clinton	1992, 1996	Helped balance the budget, reformed welfare system
George W. Bush	2000, 2004	Dealt with the war on terrorism and the second war against Iraq
Barack Obama	2008, 2012	Dealt with effects of Great Recession, reformed health care system

Asian nations have developed strong economies. India has an educated, skilled labor force that is fluent in English. In 2011 a huge earthquake and tsunami, or tidal wave, in Japan caused destruction and economic setbacks. In Europe, many countries still face economic challenges. Conservative governments have been elected in Britain and France to deal with economic problems.

Explaining

1. How did al-Qaeda develop?

______

______

______

Making Connections

2. Why did U.S. troops invade Afghanistan in 2001?

______

______

Identifying

3. Which U.S. President helped balance the budget?

______

Reading Check

4. How did the downturn in the global economy affect governmental elections in Britain and France?

______

______

______

Defining

5. How are people around the world *interdependent*?

Explaining

6. How do computers contribute to the technology revolution?

Reading Check

7. Why have countries in some world regions formed trade groups?

The Global Community

The world has become **interdependent.** This means that we rely on one another for goods, information, and other resources.

The technology revolution has contributed to interdependence and the computer is at the center of it. In 1976 Stephen Wozniak and Steven Jobs built the first personal computer. In the 1980s, Bill Gates developed software that tells computers how to do specific tasks. Personal computers allow people to go on the Internet. The Internet has made global communications almost instant.

Today, few nations can fully meet all the needs of their people without global trade. Nations have set up organizations to encourage this trade. Nations also have formed regional trading groups. European nations formed the European Union (EU) in 2003. The EU unites Europe politically and economically. The North American Free Trade Agreement (NAFTA) set up a free-trade area for Canada, the United States, and Mexico.

Organization	Purpose
International Monetary Fund (IMF)	helps get businesses to invest in other countries
World Bank	helps get businesses to invest in other countries
General Agreement on Trade and Tariffs (GATT)	works to make global trade easier and cheaper
World Trade Organization (WTO)	helps with trade agreements and conflicts
European Union (EU)	unites Europe politically and economically
North American Free Trade Agreement (NAFTA)	sets up a free-trade area for Canada, the United States, and Mexico

In 2008 the United States and the rest of the world suffered the Great Recession. This was the worst economic crisis since the Great Depression of the 1930s. During the economic crisis, banks stopped lending money. The economy slowed. Companies went bankrupt and workers lost jobs. Nations around the world struggled to recover.

Global Challenges

One challenge facing the world is the gap between developed and developing nations. Developed nations include the United States, Germany, and Japan. Their economies are a mix of agriculture, manufacturing, and services. Many nations in Africa, Asia, and Latin America are developing nations. They often have little industry and depend on developed nations for economic aid.

Developed Nations	Developing Nations
• Long history of industrialization • Use technology to make many goods • Economies rely on a mix of goods and services • Help developing nations with economic aid	• Have very little industry • Depend on agriculture • Depend on developed nations for economic aid

Nuclear weapons pose a danger to the world. Many countries, however, use nuclear power. In 2011 an earthquake in Japan damaged nuclear reactors. This caused radiation to leak into the air and water. People are now more aware of dangers to the environment, such as oil drilling accidents. Most scientists think the Earth is getting warmer. They believe that pollution may be the cause.

Health care is another important issue in today's world. **Pandemics** are disease outbreaks that occur over a wide area. In 2014, the Ebola virus spread from Africa to other continents. Meanwhile, new technologies have improved health care. Doctors use lasers, devices that create a powerful beam of light, to perform surgery.

Check for Understanding

List four challenges that the world faces.

1. ______________________

2. ______________________

3. ______________________

4. ______________________

Identifying

8. What are two dangers facing the environment?

____

____

____

Reading Check

9. How are developing countries different from developed countries?

____

____

____

FOLDABLES®

10. Place a two-tab Foldable along the dotted line to cover the Check for Understanding. On the anchor tab, write *A Shrinking World.* Label the top tab *How* and the bottom tab *Why.*

Use both sides of the tabs to list what you remember about how technology led to a "shrinking" world.

Glue Foldable here

FOLDABLES®

Instruction and Templates

Table of Contents

For each kind of Foldable®, you will find an instruction page followed by several template pages.

Notebook Foldables®

Using Foldables® in the *Reading Essentials and Study Guide* will help you develop note-taking and critical-thinking skills.

One-Tab

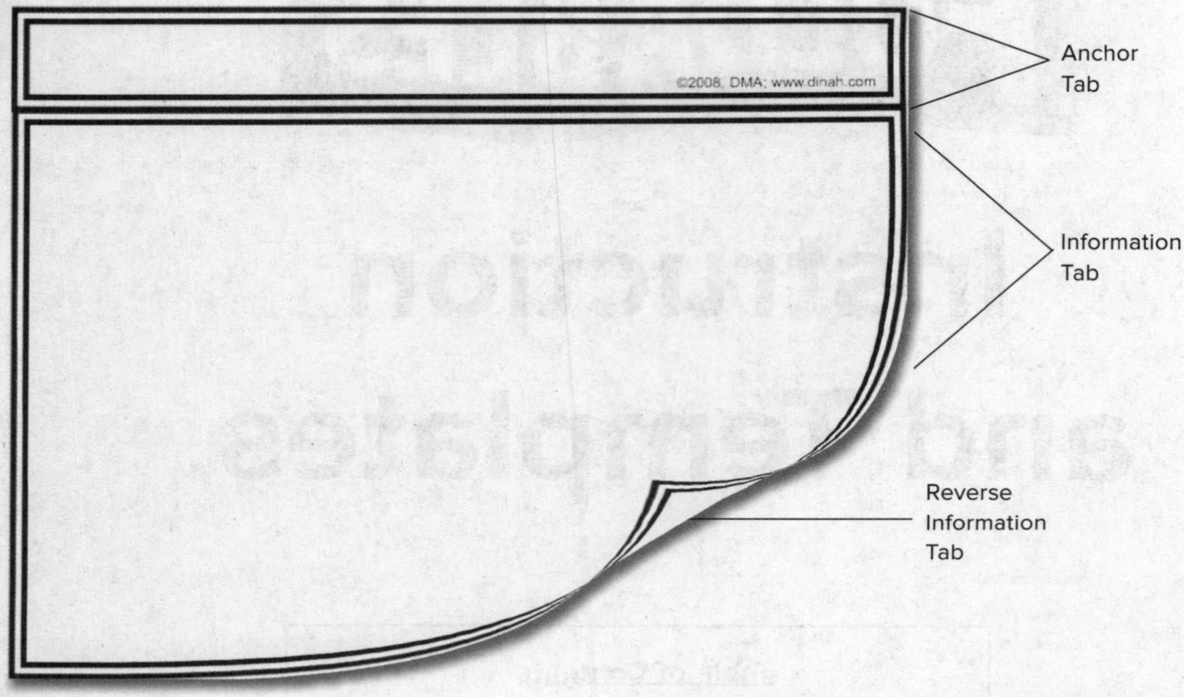

Folding Instructions

1. Cut out the One-Tab Foldable® template found on the following pages.
2. Fold the anchor tab over the information tab.
3. Glue the anchor tab to your workbook according to the instructions in the lesson.

Tip: Multiple Foldables® can be glued on top of each other by gluing anchor tabs on top of anchor tabs. This would make a small book on the page.

One-Tab Foldable® glued onto a Two-Tab Foldable® to make a study book.

One-Tab

Cut out your Foldable® along the dotted line.

You can position a Foldable® three ways.

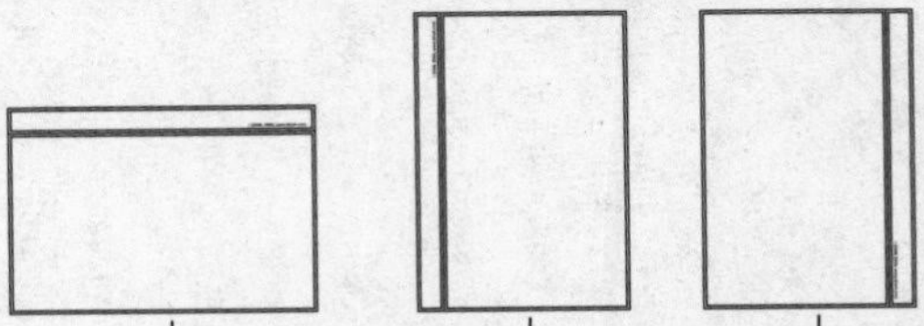

horizontally   vertically   vertically

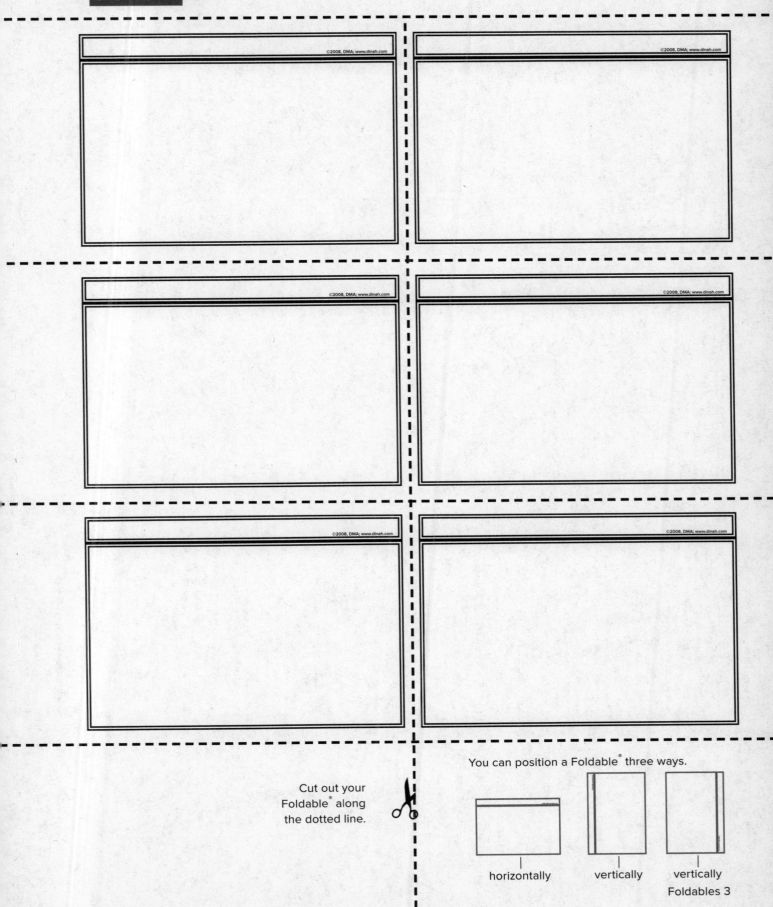

One-Tab

Cut out your Foldable® along the dotted line.

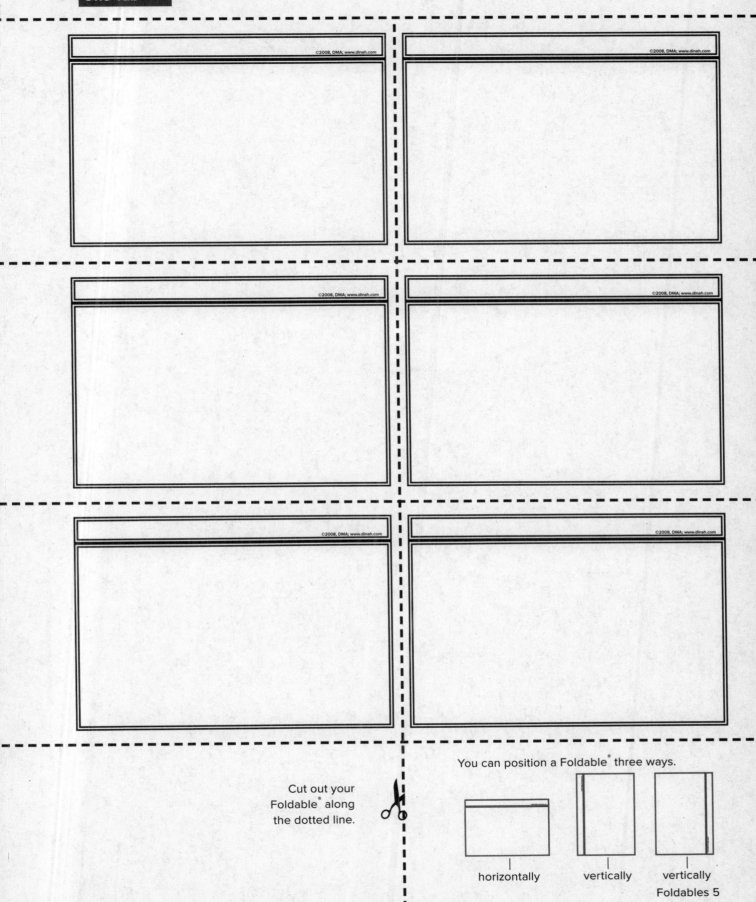

You can position a Foldable® three ways.

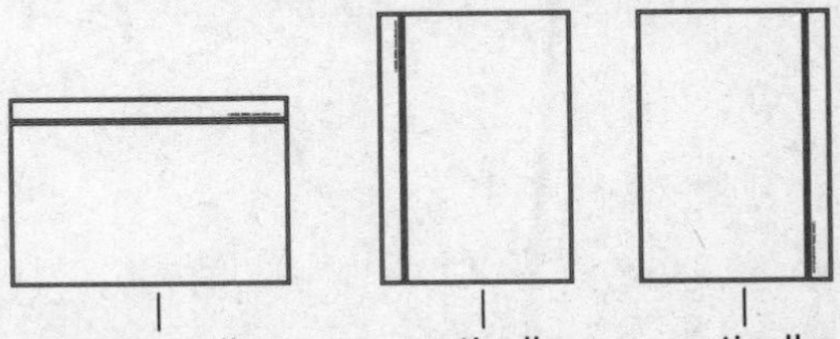

horizontally | vertically | vertically

One-Tab

©2008, DMA; www.dinah.com

©2008, DMA; www.dinah.com

©2008, DMA; www.dinah.com

©2008, DMA; www.dinah.com

©2008, DMA; www.dinah.com

Cut out your Foldable® along the dotted line.

You can position a Foldable® three ways.

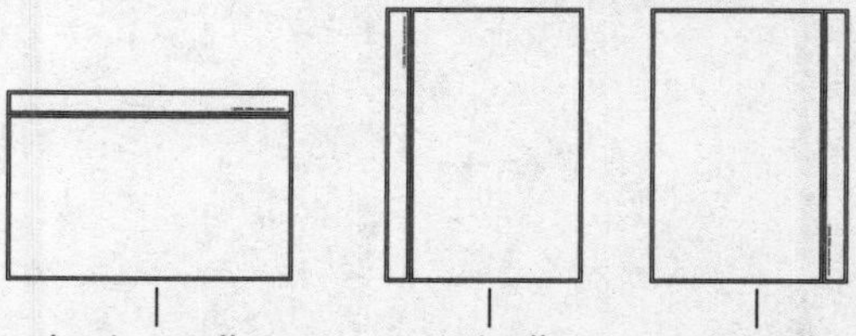

horizontally | vertically | vertically

One-Tab

©2008, DMA; www.dinah.com

©2008, DMA; www.dinah.com

©2008, DMA; www.dinah.com

©2008, DMA; www.dinah.com

©2008, DMA; www.dinah.com

Cut out your Foldable® along the dotted line.

You can position a Foldable® three ways.

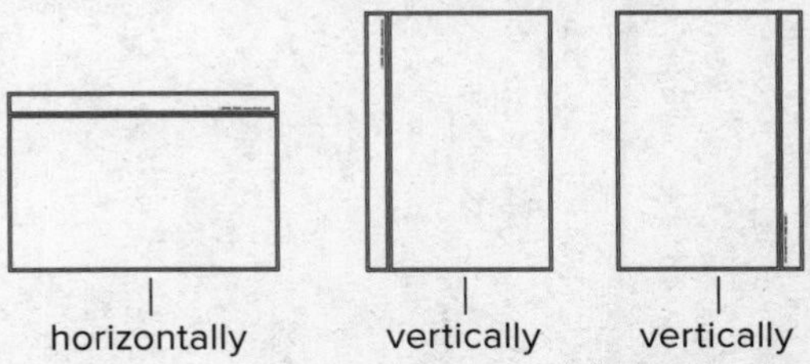

©2008, DMA; www.dinah.com
©2008, DMA; www.dinah.com
©2008, DMA; www.dinah.com
©2008, DMA; www.dinah.com
©2008, DMA; www.dinah.com

Cut out your Foldable® along the dotted line.

You can position a Foldable® three ways.

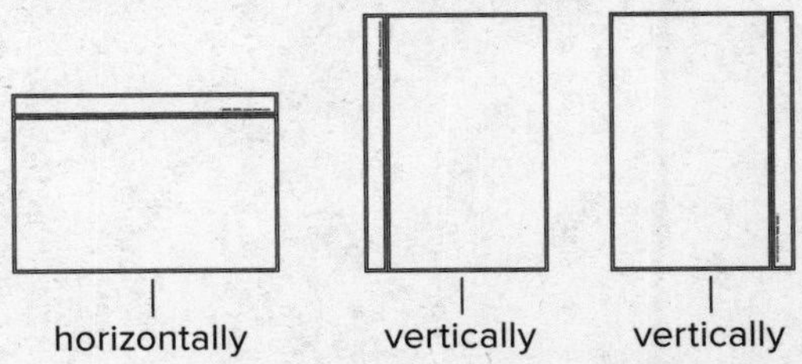

©2008, DMA; www.dinah.com

©2008, DMA; www.dinah.com

©2008, DMA; www.dinah.com

©2008, DMA; www.dinah.com

©2008, DMA; www.dinah.com

Cut out your Foldable® along the dotted line.

You can position a Foldable® three ways.

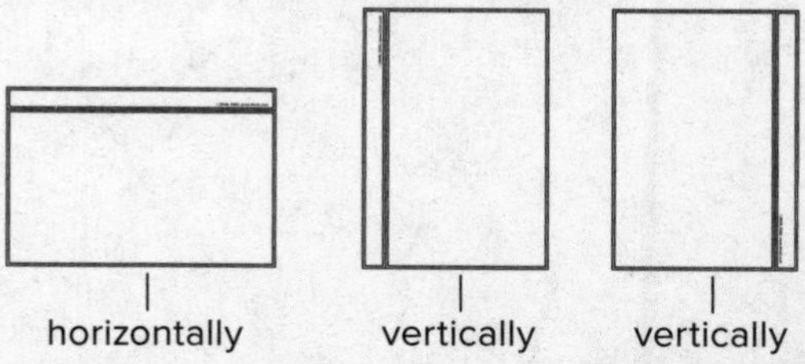

Notebook Foldables®

Using Foldables® in the *Reading Essentials and Study Guide* will help you develop note-taking and critical-thinking skills.

Two-Tab

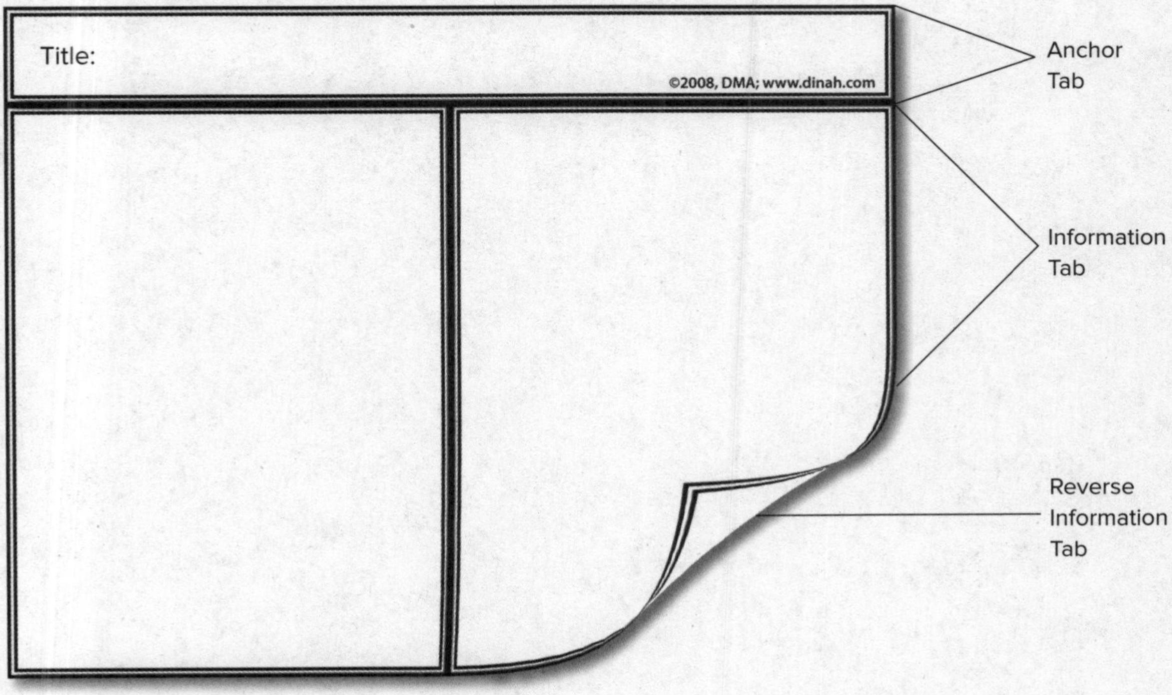

Folding Instructions

1. Cut out the Two-Tab Foldable® template found on the following pages.
2. Fold the anchor tab over the information tab.
3. Glue the anchor tab to your workbook according to the instructions in the lesson.
4. Cut the information tab up to the anchor tab to create two tabs.

Tip: Multiple Foldables® can be glued on top of each other by gluing anchor tabs on top of anchor tabs. This would make a small book on the page.

One-Tab Foldable® glued onto a Two-Tab Foldable® to make a study book.

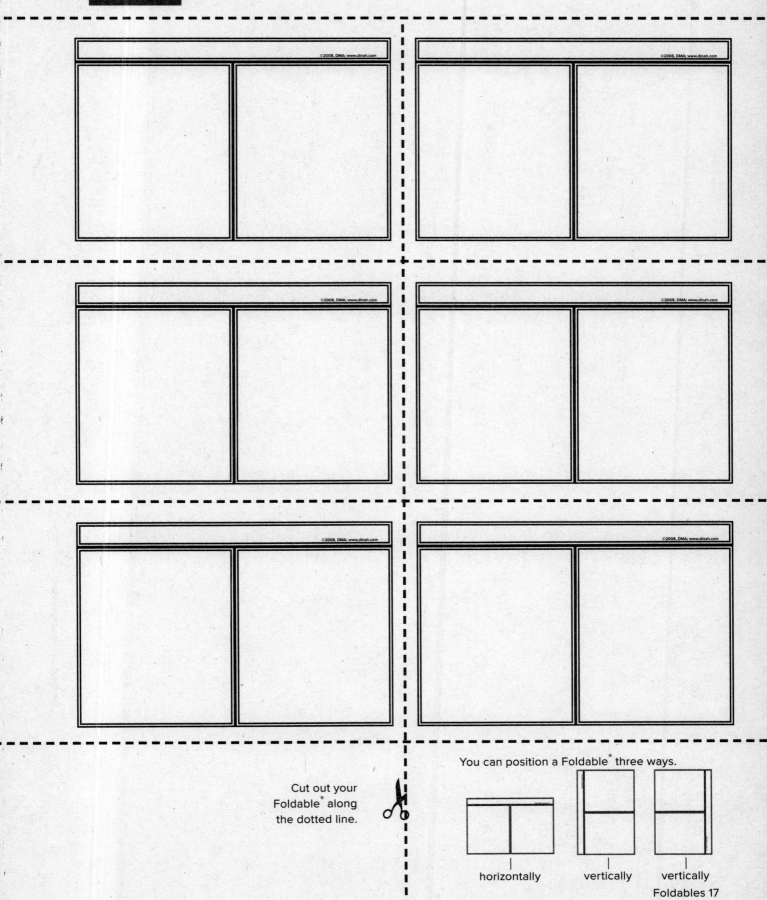

Cut out your Foldable® along the dotted line.

You can position a Foldable® three ways.

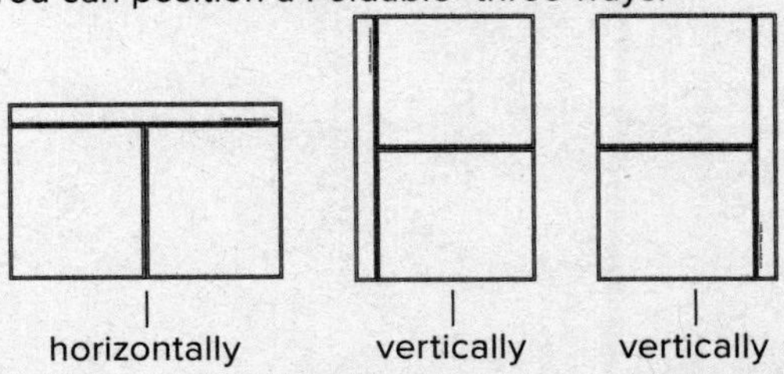

Two-Tab

©2008, DMA; www.dinah.com

©2008, DMA; www.dinah.com

©2008, DMA; www.dinah.com

©2008, DMA; www.dinah.com

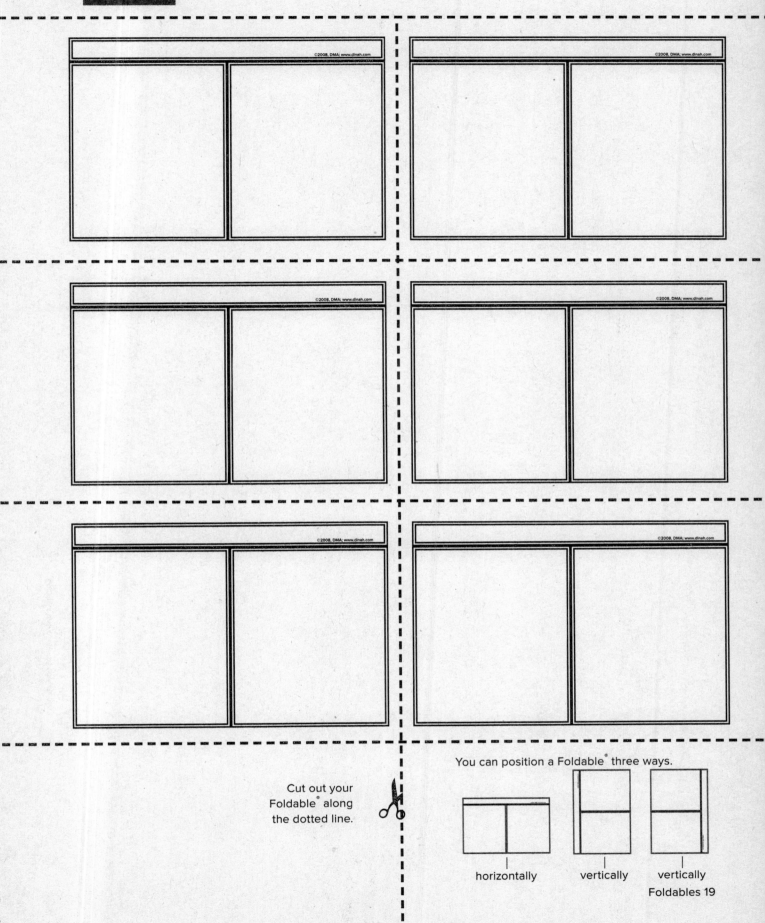

©2008, DMA; www.dinah.com

Cut out your Foldable® along the dotted line.

You can position a Foldable® three ways.

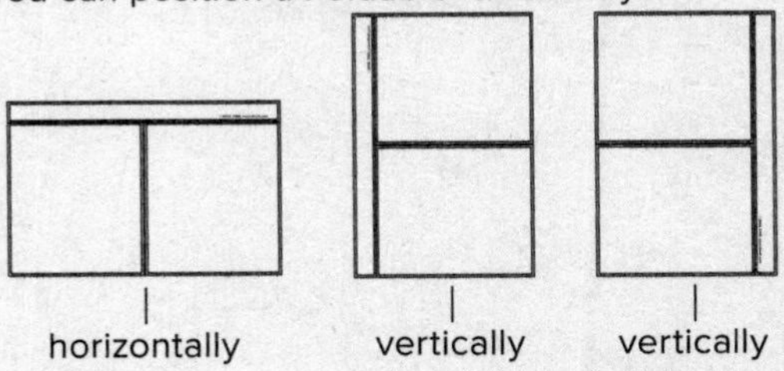

Two-Tab

©2008, DMA; www.dinah.com

©2008, DMA; www.dinah.com

©2008, DMA; www.dinah.com

©2008, DMA; www.dinah.com

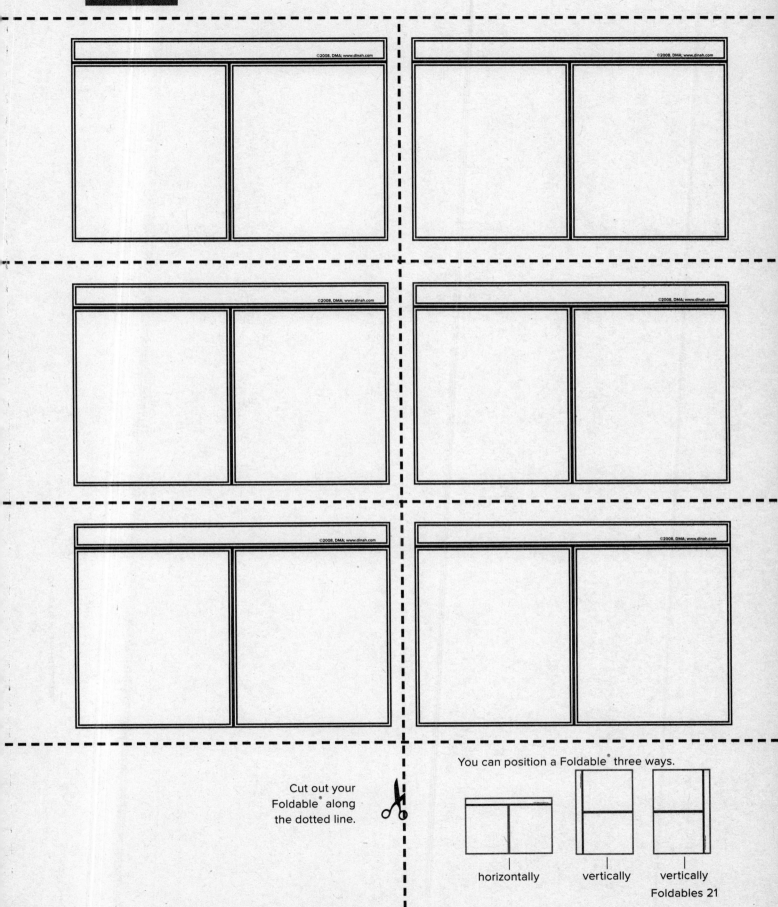

©2008, DMA; www.dinah.com

Cut out your Foldable® along the dotted line.

You can position a Foldable® three ways.

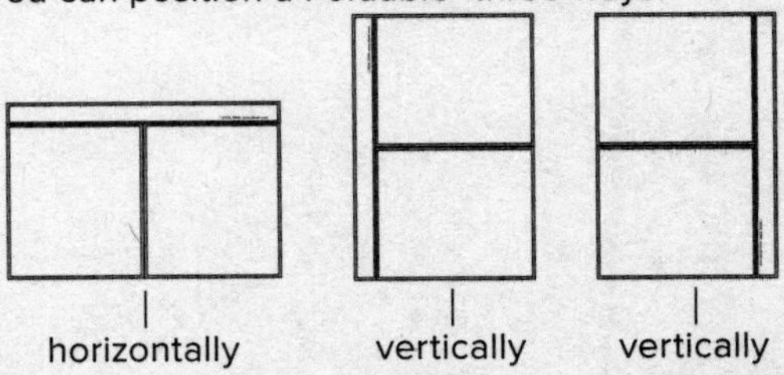

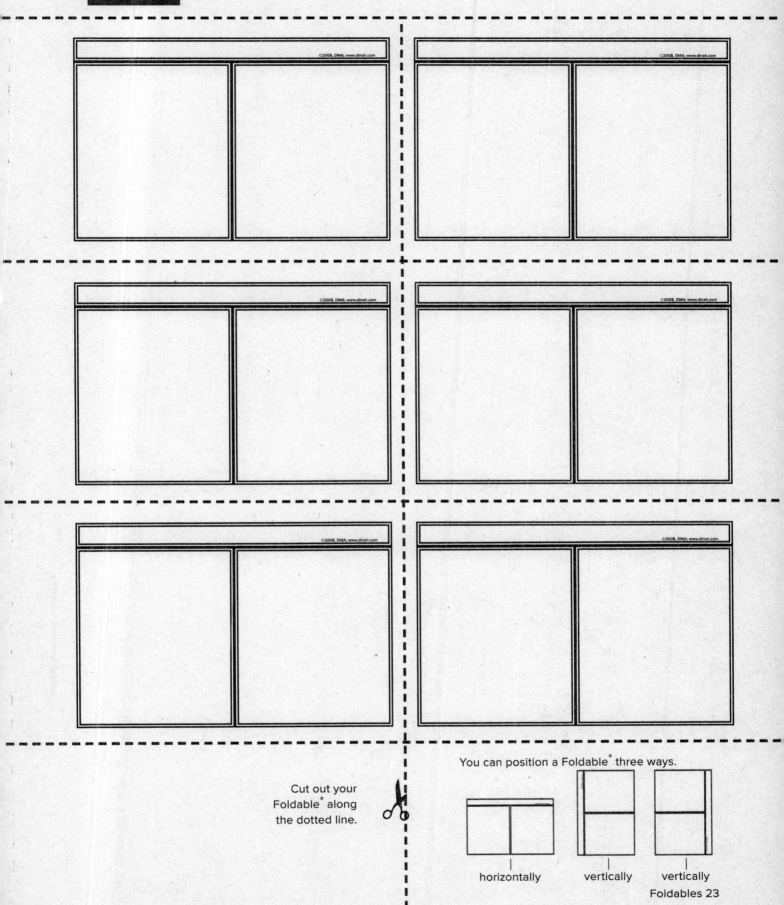

Two-Tab

©2008, DMA; www.dinah.com

©2008, DMA; www.dinah.com

©2008, DMA; www.dinah.com

©2008, DMA; www.dinah.com

©2008, DMA; www.dinah.com

Cut out your Foldable® along the dotted line.

You can position a Foldable® three ways.

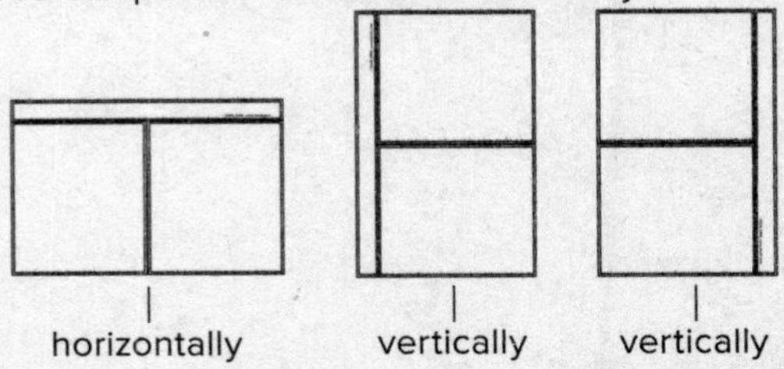

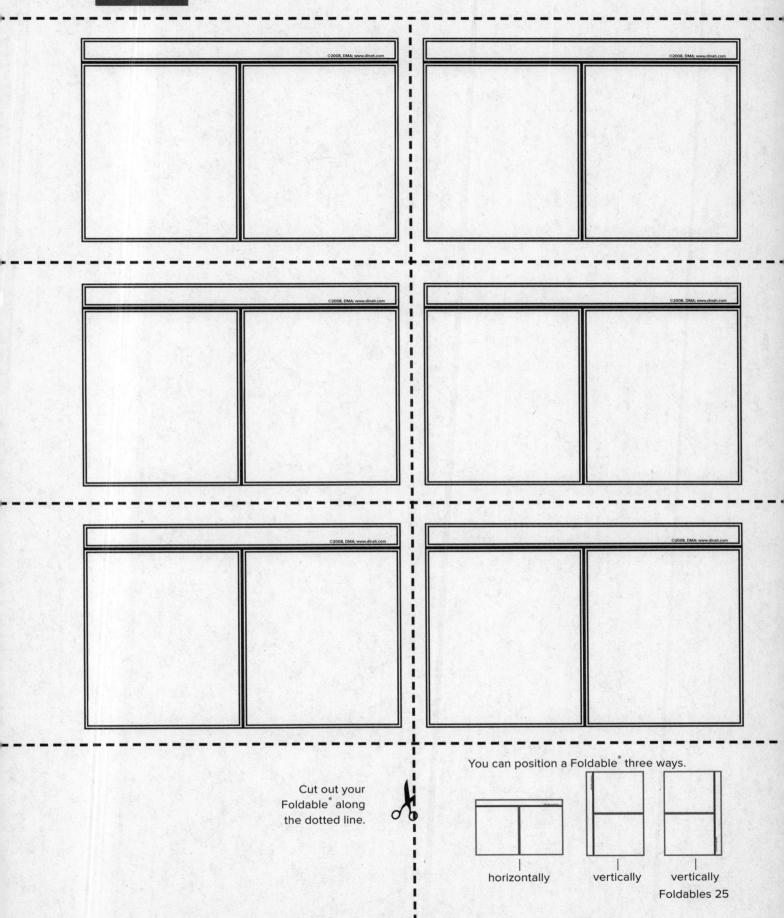

©2008, DMA; www.dinah.com
©2008, DMA; www.dinah.com
©2008, DMA; www.dinah.com
©2008, DMA; www.dinah.com
©2008, DMA; www.dinah.com

Cut out your Foldable® along the dotted line.

You can position a Foldable® three ways.

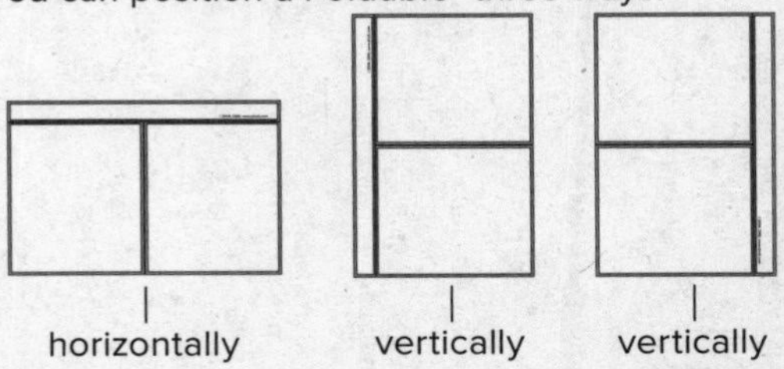

©2008, DMA; www.dinah.com

©2008, DMA; www.dinah.com

©2008, DMA; www.dinah.com

©2008, DMA; www.dinah.com

©2008, DMA; www.dinah.com

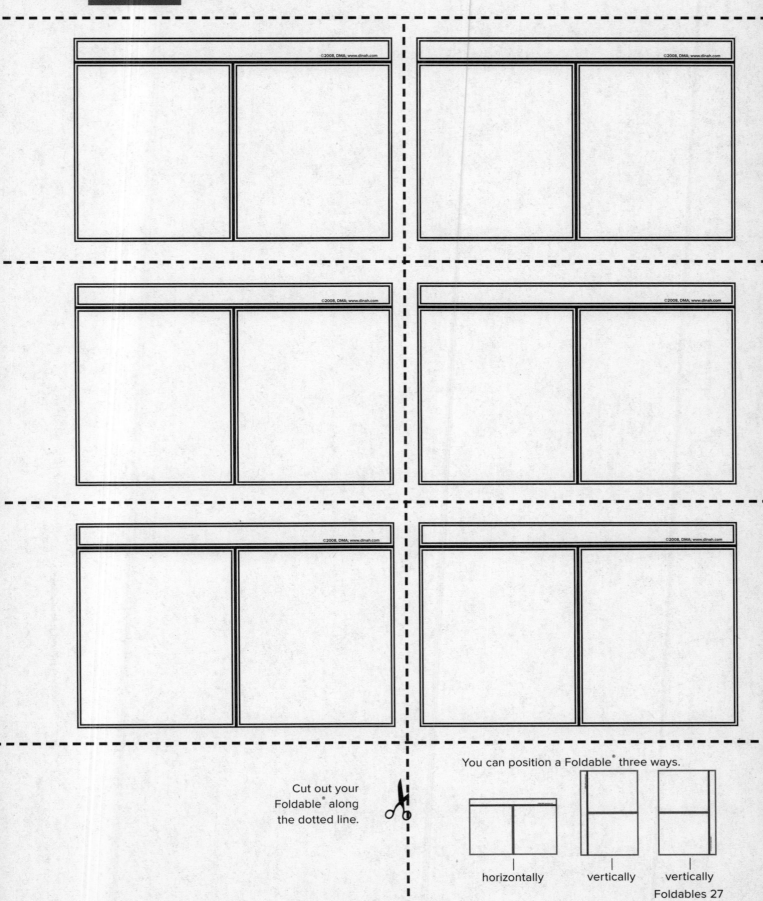

Cut out your Foldable® along the dotted line.

You can position a Foldable® three ways.

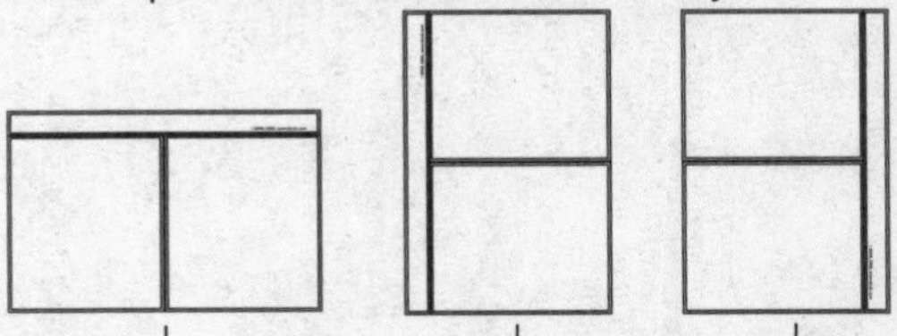

horizontally vertically vertically

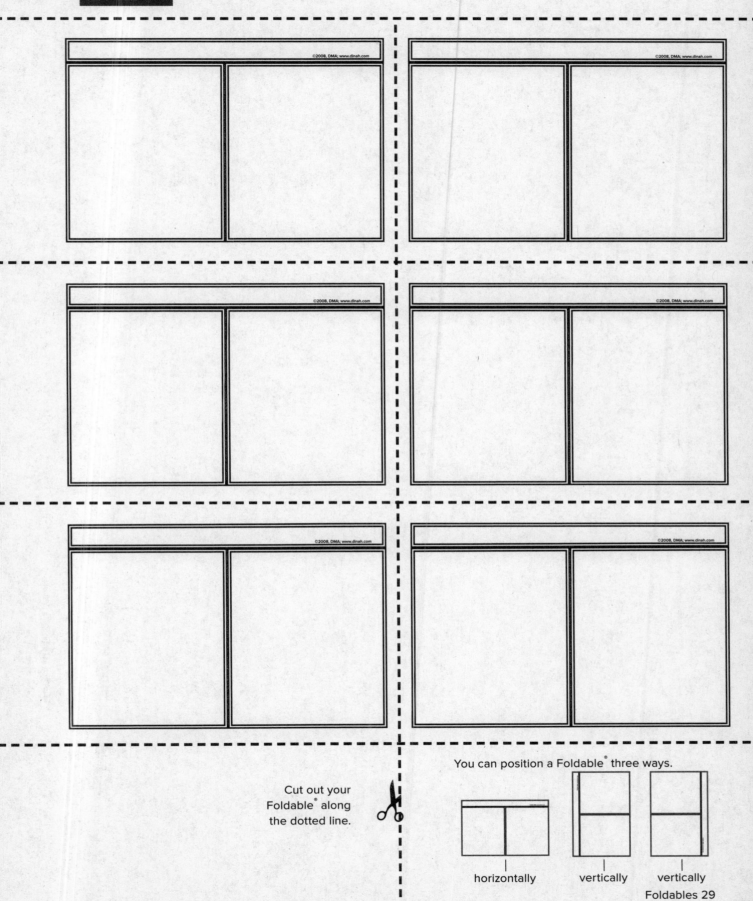

Cut out your Foldable® along the dotted line.

You can position a Foldable® three ways.

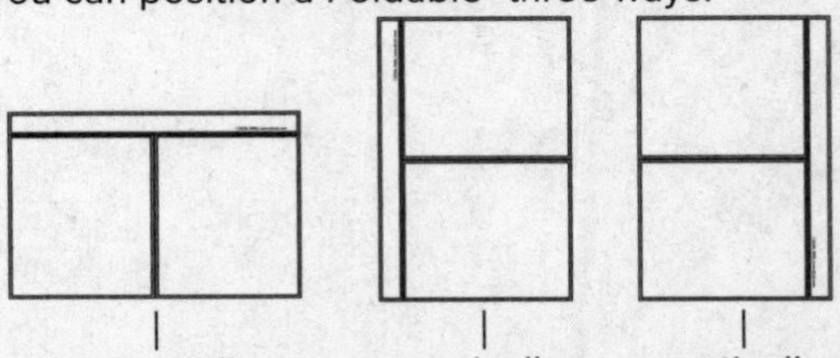

horizontally vertically vertically

©2008, DMA; www.dinah.com

©2008, DMA; www.dinah.com

©2008, DMA; www.dinah.com

©2008, DMA; www.dinah.com

©2008, DMA; www.dinah.com

Cut out your Foldable® along the dotted line.

You can position a Foldable® three ways.

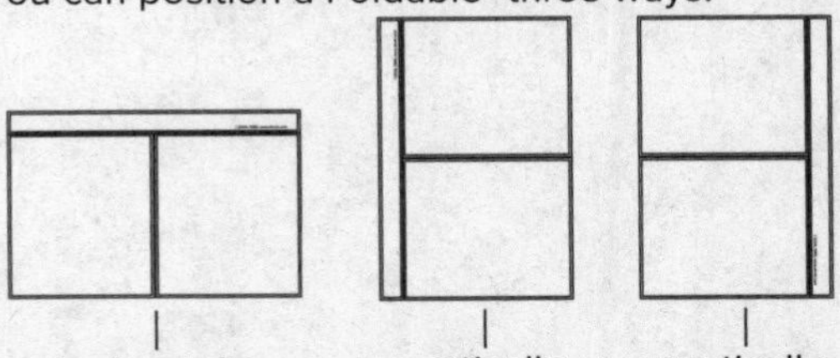

horizontally vertically vertically

©2008, DMA; www.dinah.com

©2008, DMA; www.dinah.com

©2008, DMA; www.dinah.com

©2008, DMA; www.dinah.com

©2008, DMA; www.dinah.com

Cut out your Foldable® along the dotted line.

You can position a Foldable® three ways.

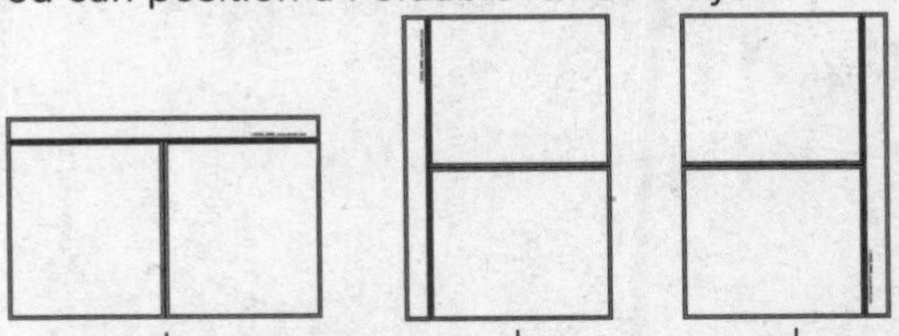

©2008, DMA; www.dinah.com
©2008, DMA; www.dinah.com
©2008, DMA; www.dinah.com
©2008, DMA; www.dinah.com
©2008, DMA; www.dinah.com

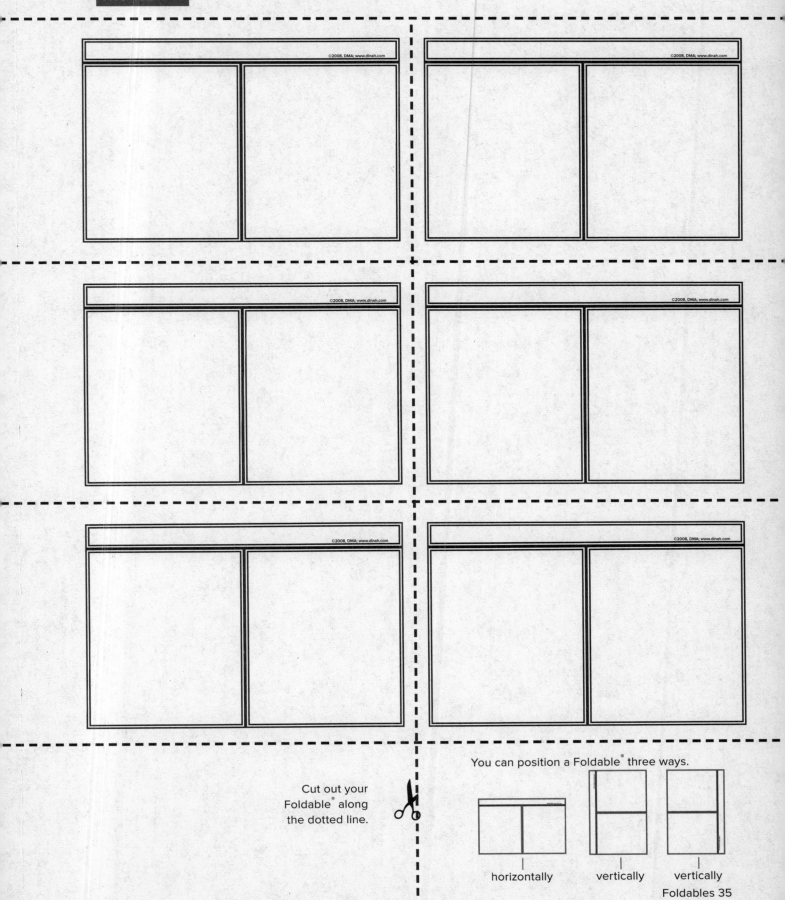

Cut out your Foldable® along the dotted line.

You can position a Foldable® three ways.

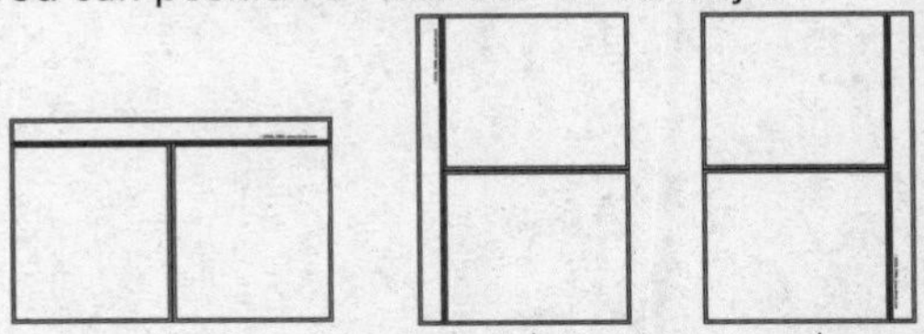

horizontally | vertically | vertically

Notebook Foldables®

Using Foldables® in the *Reading Essentials and Study Guide* will help you develop note-taking and critical-thinking skills.

Three-Tab

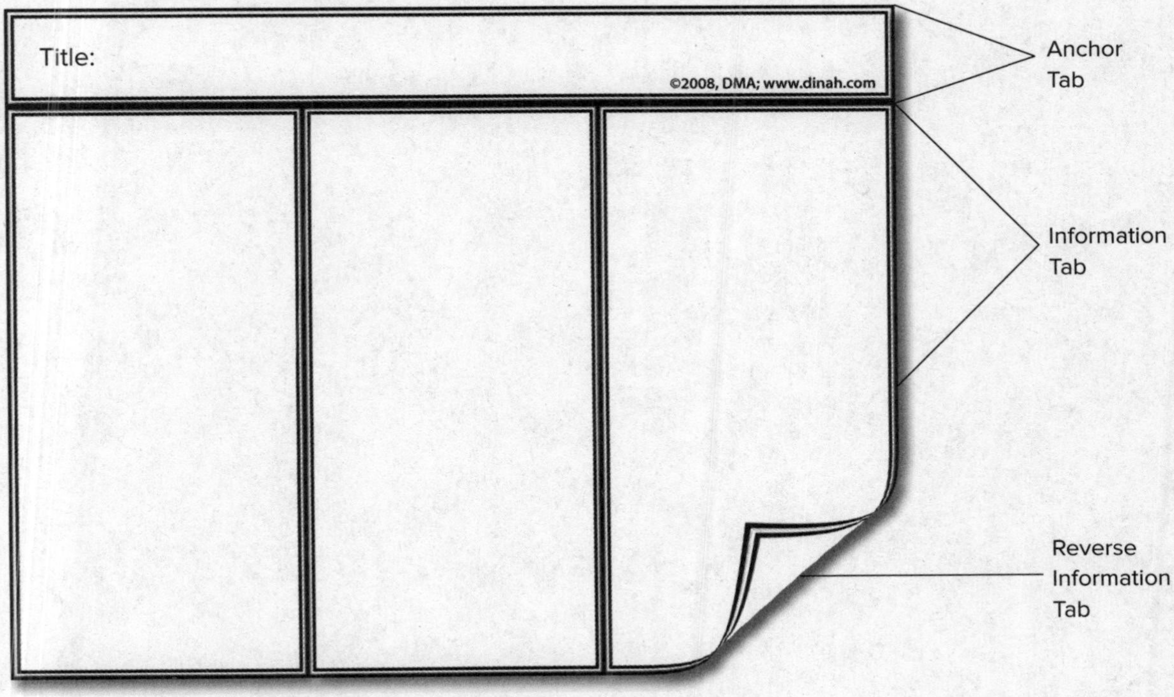

Folding Instructions

1. Cut out the Three-Tab Foldable® template found on the following pages.
2. Fold the anchor tab over the information tab.
3. Glue the anchor tab to your workbook according to the instructions in the lesson.
4. Cut the information tabs up to the anchor tab to create three tabs.

Tip: Multiple Foldables® can be glued on top of each other by gluing anchor tabs on top of anchor tabs. This would make a small book on the page.

One-Tab Foldable® glued onto a Two-Tab Foldable® to make a study book.

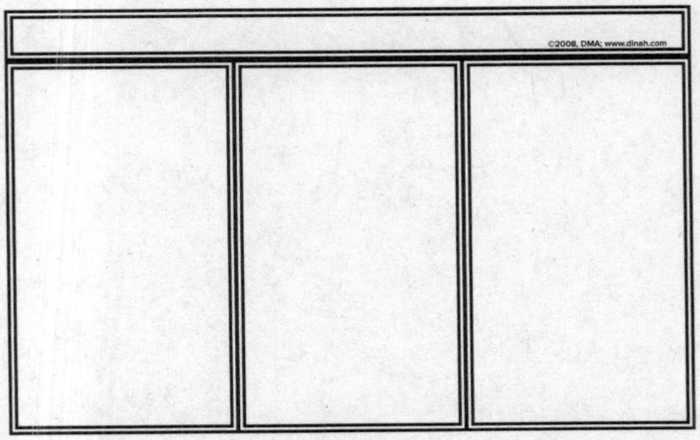

Cut out your Foldable® along the dotted line.

You can position a Foldable® three ways.

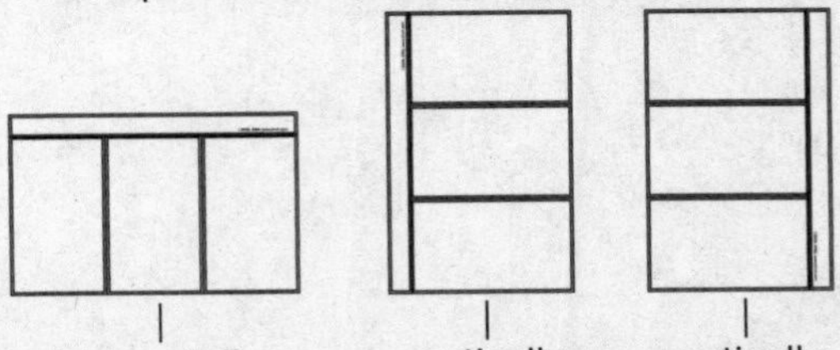

horizontally | vertically | vertically

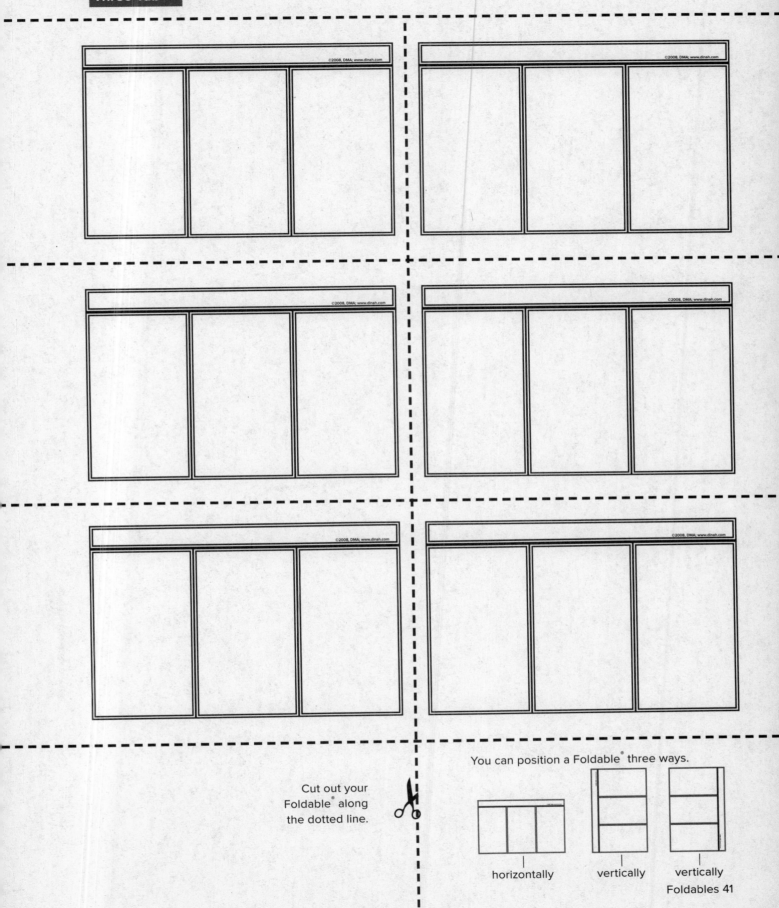

Cut out your Foldable® along the dotted line.

You can position a Foldable® three ways.

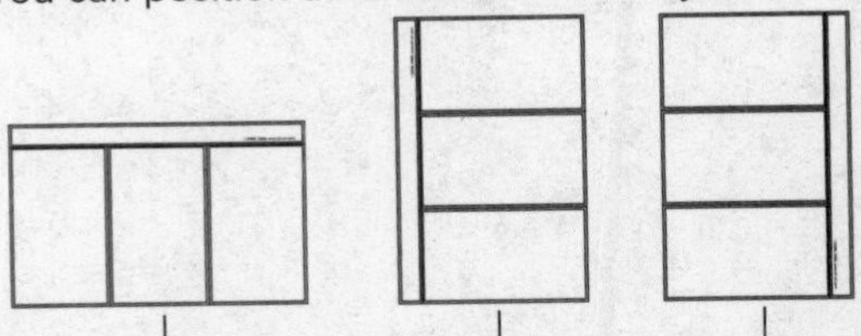

horizontally vertically vertically

Three-Tab

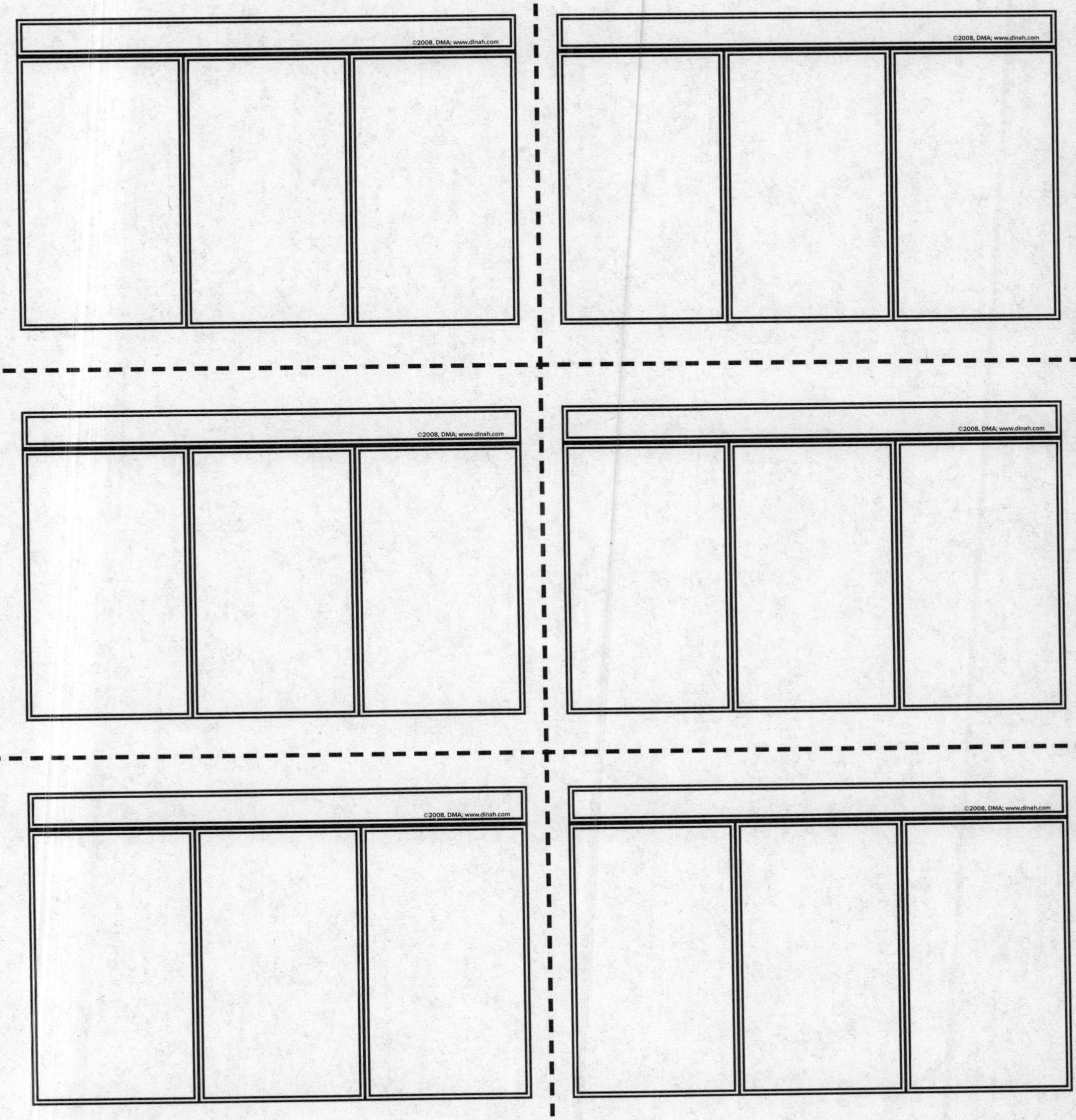

Cut out your Foldable® along the dotted line.

You can position a Foldable® three ways.

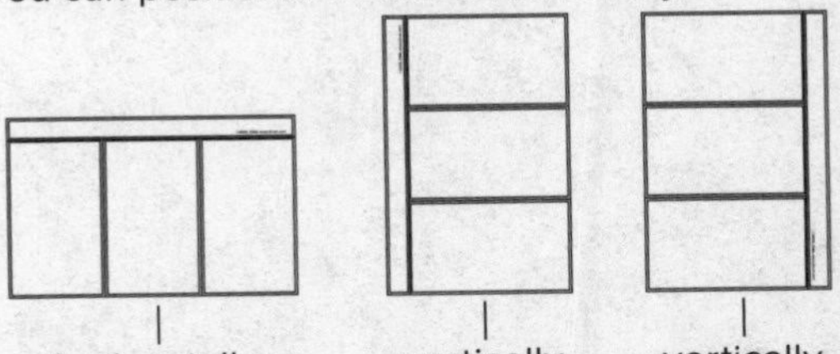

©2008, DMA; www.dinah.com
©2008, DMA; www.dinah.com
©2008, DMA; www.dinah.com
©2008, DMA; www.dinah.com
©2008, DMA; www.dinah.com

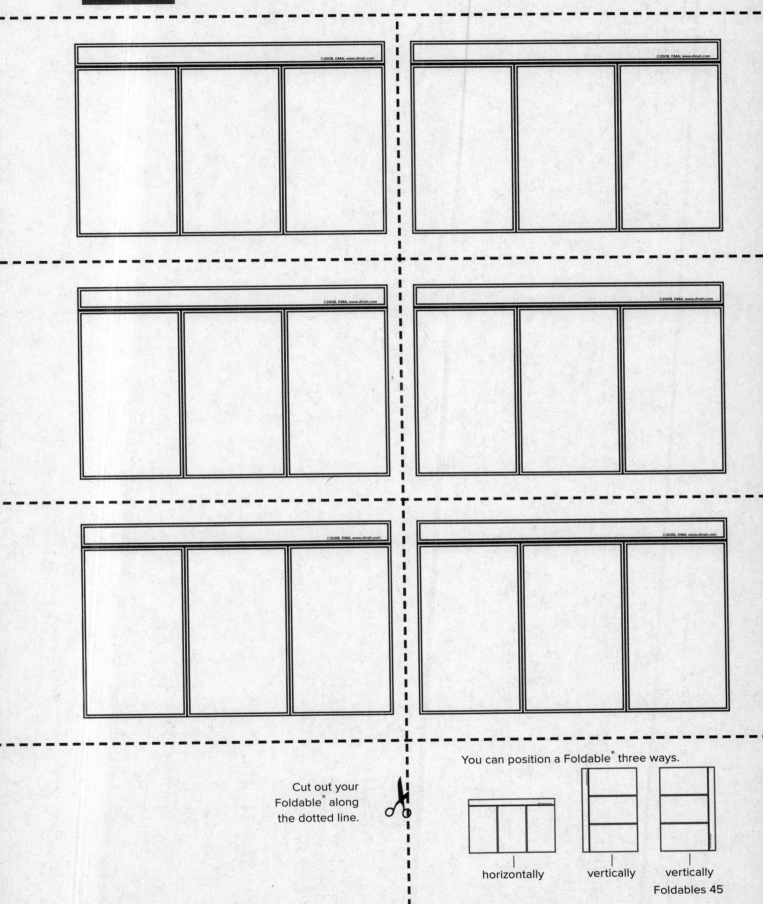

Cut out your Foldable® along the dotted line.

You can position a Foldable® three ways.

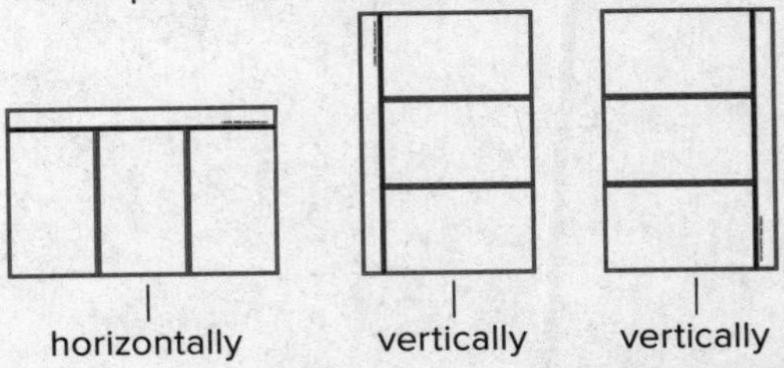

Notebook Foldables®

Using Foldables® in the *Reading Essentials and Study Guide* will help you develop note-taking and critical-thinking skills.

Venn Diagram

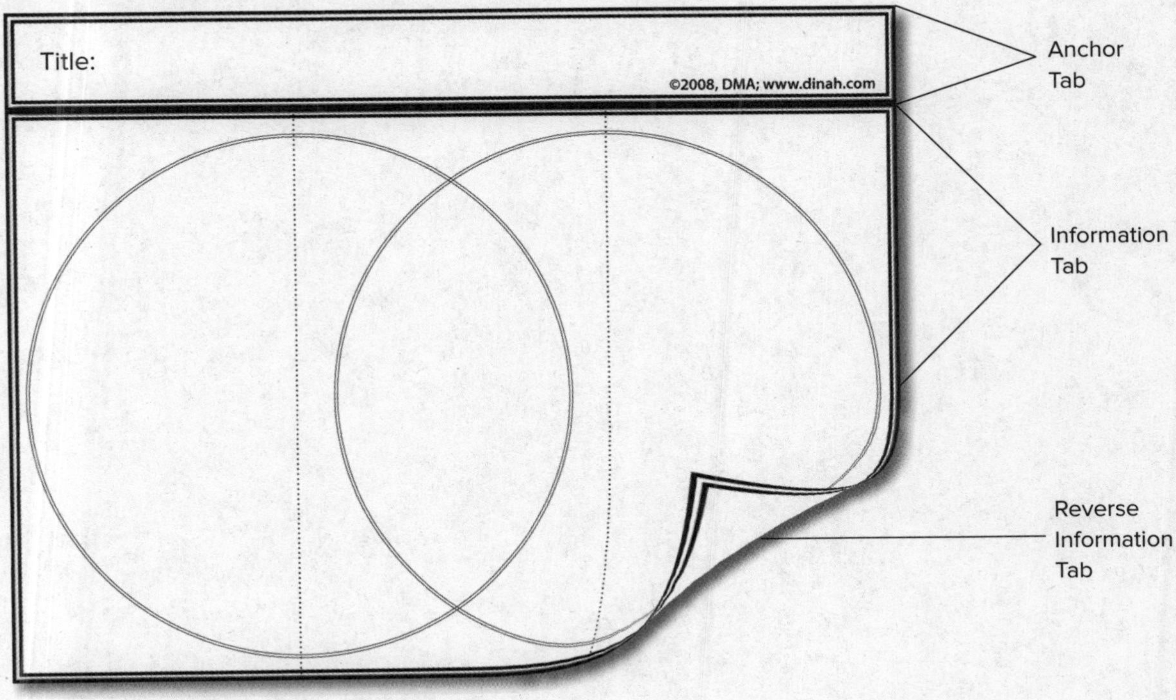

Folding Instructions

1. Cut out the Venn Diagram Foldable® template found on the following pages.
2. Fold the anchor tab over the information tab.
3. Glue the anchor tab to your workbook according to the instructions in the lesson.
4. If directed, cut the information tabs up to the anchor tab in the center of each circle to create three tabs.

Tip: Multiple Foldables® can be glued on top of each other by gluing anchor tabs on top of anchor tabs. This would make a small book on the page.

One-Tab Foldable® glued onto a Two-Tab Foldable® to make a study book.

Venn Diagram

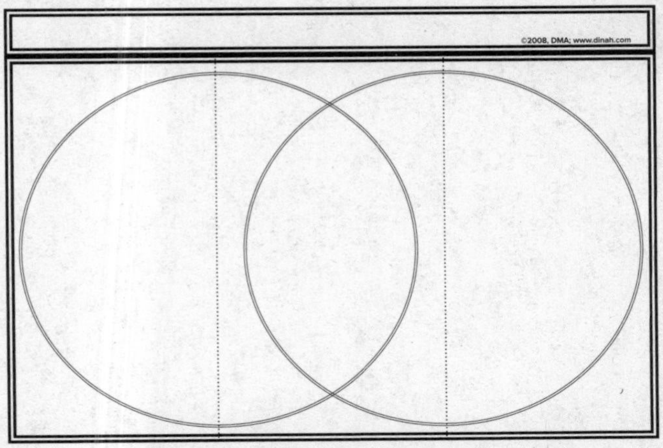

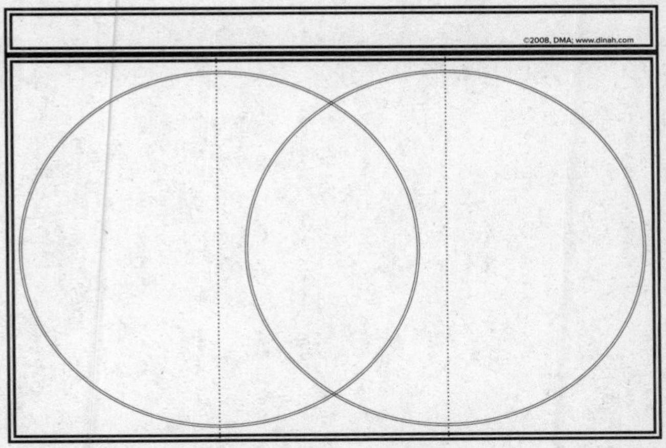

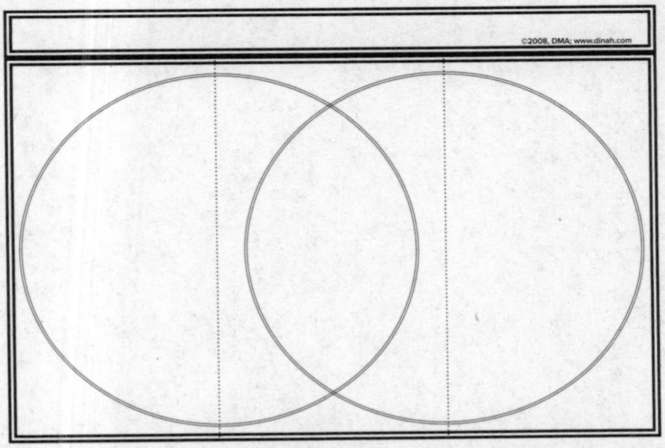

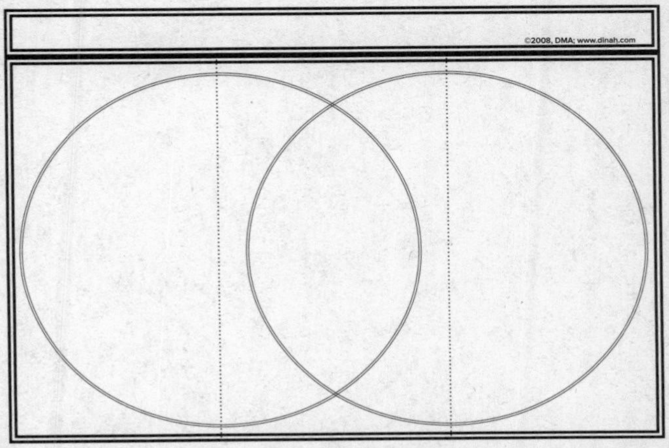

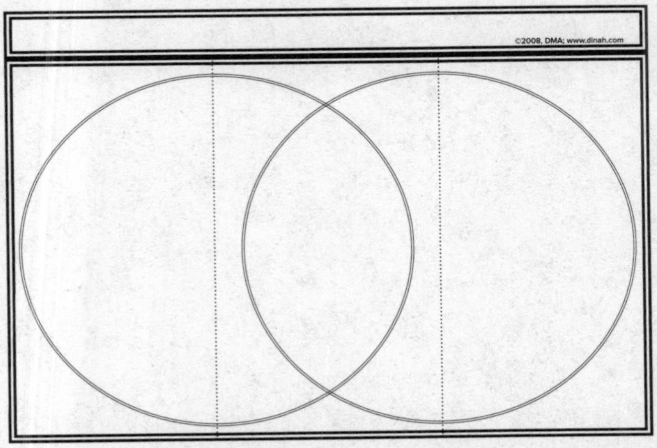

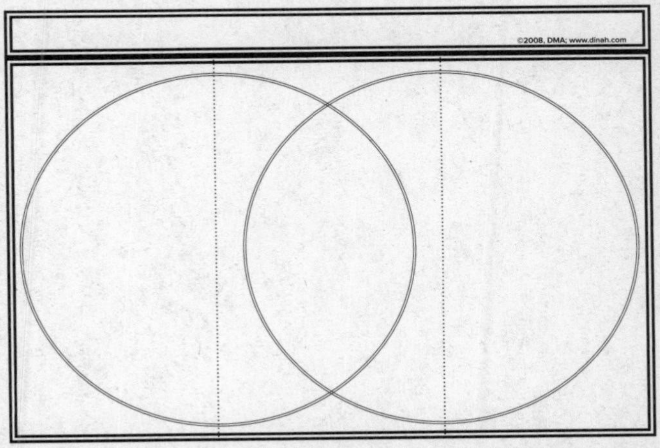

Cut out your Foldable® along the dotted line.

You can position a Foldable® three ways.

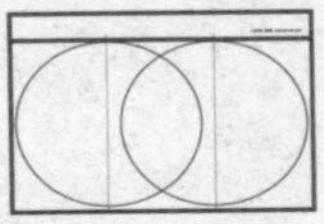

horizontally

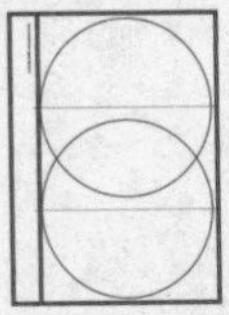

vertically

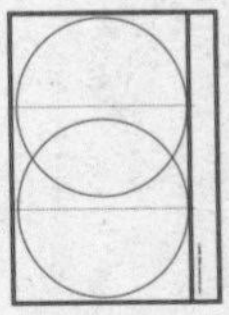

vertically

Venn Diagram

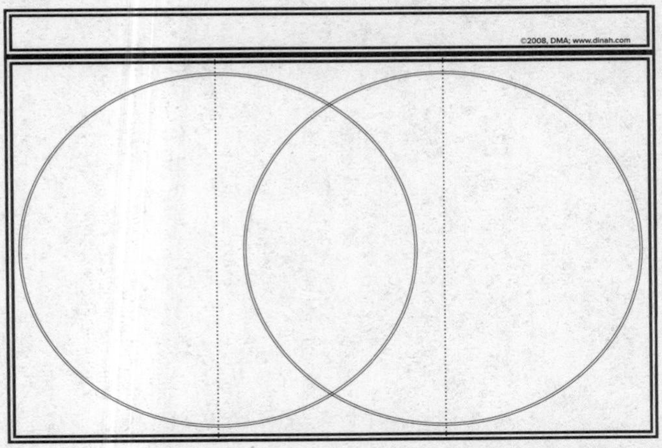

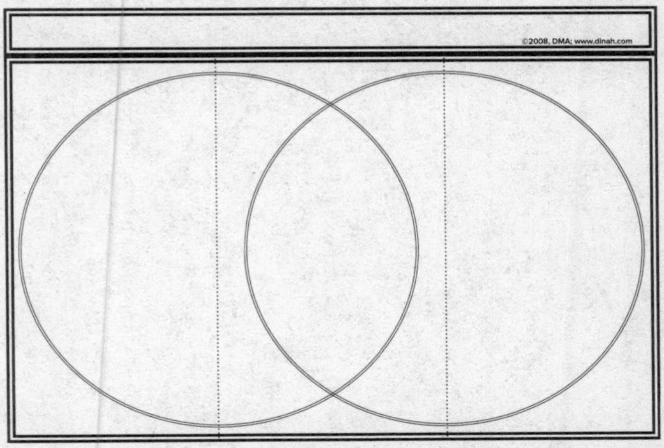

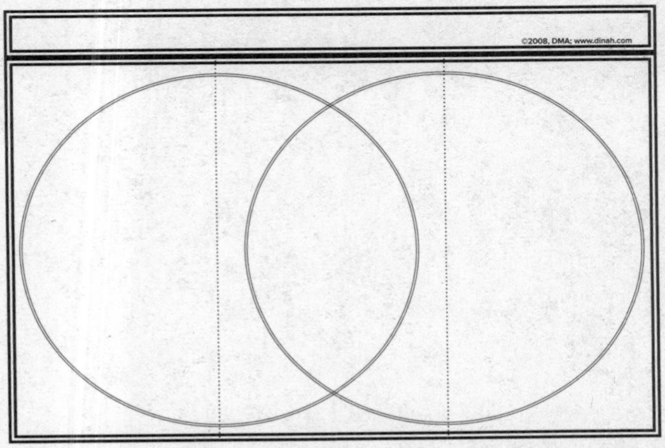

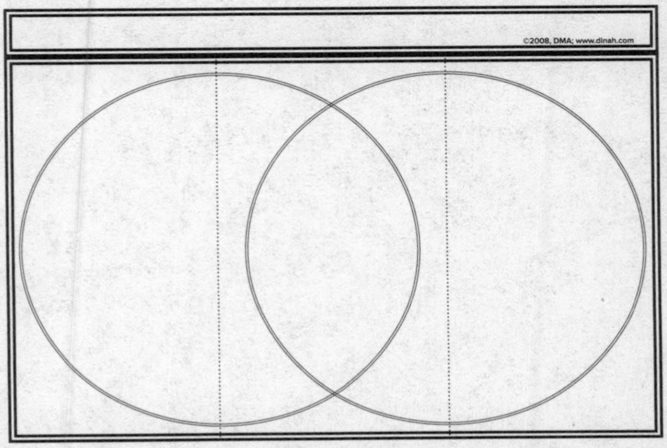

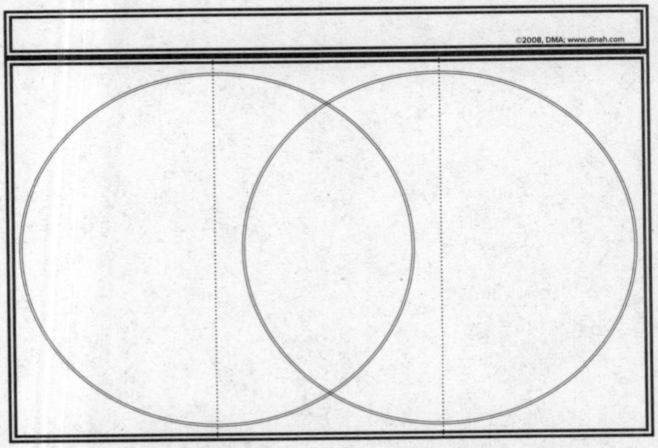

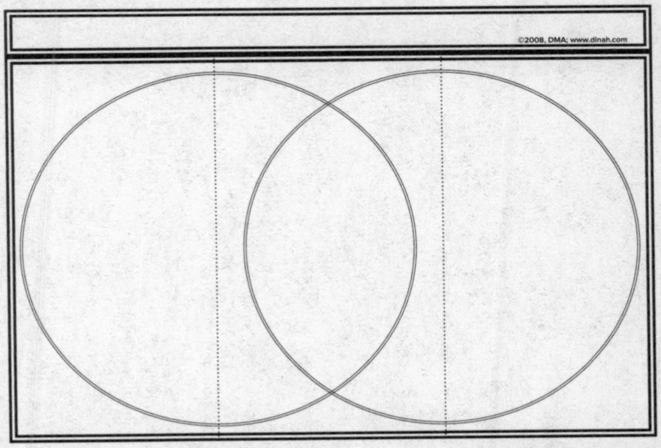

Cut out your Foldable® along the dotted line.

You can position a Foldable® three ways.

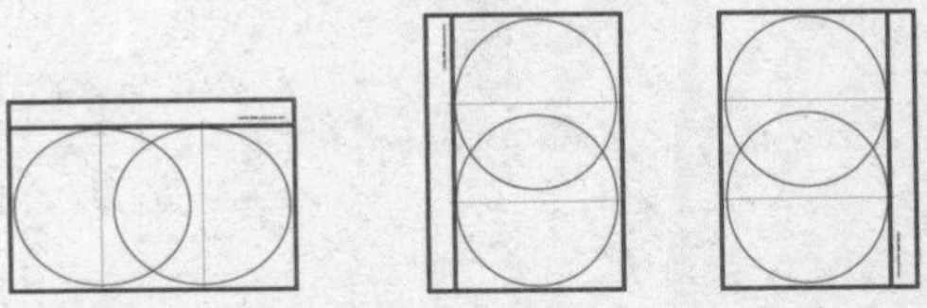